REGNUM EDINBURGH CENTENARY SERIES
Volume 27

Reflecting on and Equipping for Christian Mission

The centenary of the World Missionary Conference of 1910, held in Edinburgh, was a suggestive moment for many people seeking direction for Christian mission in the 21st century. Several different constituencies within world Christianity held significant events around 2010. From 2005, an international group worked collaboratively to develop an intercontinental and multi-denominational project, known as Edinburgh 2010, based at New College, University of Edinburgh. This initiative brought together representatives of twenty different global Christian bodies, representing all major Christian denominations and confessions, and many different strands of mission and church life, to mark the centenary.

Essential to the work of the Edinburgh 1910 Conference, and of abiding value, were the findings of the eight think-tanks or 'commissions'. These inspired the idea of a new round of collaborative reflection on Christian mission – but now focused on nine themes identified as being key to mission in the 21st century. The study process was polycentric, open-ended, and as inclusive as possible of the different genders, regions of the world, and theological and confessional perspectives in today's church. It was overseen by the Study Process Monitoring Group: Miss Maria Aranzazu Aguado (Spain, The Vatican), Dr Daryl Balia (South Africa, Edinburgh 2010), Mrs Rosemary Dowsett (UK, World Evangelical Alliance), Dr Knud Jørgensen (Norway, Areopagos), Rev John Kafwanka (Zambia, Anglican Communion), Rev Dr Jooseop Keum (Korea, World Council of Churches), Dr Wonsuk Ma (Korea, Oxford Centre for Mission Studies), Rev Dr Kenneth R. Ross (UK, Church of Scotland), Dr Petros Vassiliadis (Greece, Aristotle University of Thessalonikki), and co-ordinated by Dr Kirsteen Kim (UK, Edinburgh 2010).

These publications reflect the ethos of Edinburgh 2010 and will make a significant contribution to ongoing studies in mission. It should be clear that material published in this series will inevitably reflect a diverse range of views and positions. These will not necessarily represent those of the series' editors or of the Edinburgh 2010 General Council, but in publishing them the leadership of Edinburgh 2010 hopes to encourage conversation between Christians and collaboration in mission. All the series' volumes are commended for study and reflection in both church and academy.

Series Editors

Knud Jørgensen	MF Norwegian School of Theology. Former Chair of Edinburgh 2010 Study Process Monitoring Group
Kirsteen Kim	Leeds Trinity University and former Edinburgh 2010 Research Co-ordinator, UK
Wonsuk Ma	Oxford Centre for Mission Studies, Oxford, UK
Tony Gray	Words by Design, Bicester, UK

REGNUM EDINBURGH CENTENARY SERIES
Volume 27

Reflecting on and Equipping for Christian Mission

Edited by
Stephen Bevans, Teresa Chai,
J. Nelson Jennings, Knud Jørgensen
and Dietrich Werner

First published 2015 by Regnum Books International
Regnum is an imprint of the Oxford Centre for Mission Studies
St Philip and St James Church
Woodstock Road
Oxford OX2 6HR, UK
www.ocms.ac.uk/regnum

09 08 07 06 05 04 03 7 6 5 4 3 2 1

British Library Cataloguing in Publication Data
A catalogue record for this book is available from the British Library

ISBN: 978-1-908355-87-4

Typeset by Words by Design
Printed and bound in Great Britain for Regnum Books International
by TJ International Ltd, Padstow, Cornwall

Front cover image painted by César Ayala Torres,
photographed by Christian Tauchner, SVD

The publication of this volume is made possible through the
generous financial assistance of the the Lund Mission Society and
Bread for the World's Department for Theology and Development.

CONTENTS

PREFACE

The Edinburgh 2010 Common Call emerged from the Edinburgh 2010 study process and conference marking the centenary of the World Missionary Conference, Edinburgh 1910. The Common Call, cited below, was affirmed in the Church of Scotland Assembly Hall in Edinburgh on 6 June 2010, by representatives of world Christianity, including Catholic, Orthodox, Evangelical, Pentecostal, and other major Protestant churches.

As we gather for the centenary of the World Missionary Conference of Edinburgh 1910, we believe the church, as a sign and symbol of the reign of God, is called to witness to Christ today by sharing in God's mission of love through the transforming power of the Holy Spirit.

1. Trusting in the Triune God and with a renewed sense of urgency, we are called to incarnate and proclaim the good news of salvation, of forgiveness of sin, of life in abundance, and of liberation for all poor and oppressed. We are challenged to witness and evangelism in such a way that we are a living demonstration of the love, righteousness and justice that God intends for the whole world.

2. Remembering Christ's sacrifice on the Cross and his resurrection for the world's salvation, and empowered by the Holy Spirit, we are called to authentic dialogue, respectful engagement and humble witness among people of other faiths – and no faith – to the uniqueness of Christ. Our approach is marked with bold confidence in the gospel message; it builds friendship, seeks reconciliation and practises hospitality.

3. Knowing the Holy Spirit who blows over the world at will, reconnecting creation and bringing authentic life, we are called to become communities of compassion and healing, where young people are actively participating in mission, and women and men share power and responsibilities fairly, where there is a new zeal for justice, peace and the protection of the environment, and renewed liturgy reflecting the beauties of the Creator and creation.

4. Disturbed by the asymmetries and imbalances of power that divide and trouble us in church and world, we are called to repentance, to critical reflection on systems of power, and to accountable use of power structures. We are called to find practical ways to live as members of One Body in full awareness that God resists the proud, Christ welcomes and empowers the poor and afflicted, and the power of the Holy Spirit is manifested in our vulnerability.

5. Affirming the importance of the biblical foundations of our missional engagement and valuing the witness of the Apostles and martyrs, we are called to rejoice in the expressions of the gospel in many nations all over the world. We celebrate the renewal experienced through movements of migration and mission in all directions, the way all are equipped for mission by the gifts of the Holy Spirit, and God's continual calling of children and young people to further the gospel.

6. Recognising the need to shape a new generation of leaders with authenticity for mission in a world of diversities in the twenty-first century, we are called to work together in new forms of theological education. Because we are all made in the image of God, these will draw on one another's unique charisms, challenge each other to grow in faith and understanding, share resources equitably worldwide, involve the entire human being and the whole family of God, and respect the wisdom of our elders while also fostering the participation of children.

7. Hearing the call of Jesus to make disciples of all people – poor, wealthy, marginalised, ignored, powerful, living with disability, young, and old – we are called as communities of faith to mission from everywhere to everywhere. In joy we hear the call to receive from one another in our witness by word and action, in streets, fields, offices, homes, and schools, offering reconciliation, showing love, demonstrating grace and speaking out truth.

8. Recalling Christ, the host at the banquet, and committed to that unity for which he lived and prayed, we are called to ongoing co-operation, to deal with controversial issues and to work towards a common vision. We are challenged to welcome one another in our diversity, affirm our membership through baptism in the One Body of Christ, and recognise our need for mutuality, partnership, collaboration and networking in mission, so that the world might believe.

9. Remembering Jesus' way of witness and service, we believe we are called by God to follow this way joyfully, inspired, anointed, sent and empowered by the Holy Spirit, and nurtured by Christian disciplines in community. As we look to Christ's coming in glory and judgment, we experience his presence with us in the Holy Spirit, and we invite all to join with us as we participate in God's transforming and reconciling mission of love to the whole creation.

Themes Explored

The 2010 conference was shaped around the following nine study themes:

1. Foundations for mission
2. Christian mission among other faiths
3. Mission and post-modernities
4. Mission and power
5. Forms of missionary engagement
6. Theological education and formation
7. Christian communities in contemporary contexts
8. Mission and unity – ecclesiology and mission
9. Mission spirituality and authentic discipleship

The Regnum Edinburgh Centenary Series to Date

Against this background a series of books was commissioned, with the intention of making a significant contribution to ongoing studies of mission. This series currently includes: [1]

Edinburgh 2010: Mission Then and Now, David A. Kerr and Kenneth R. Ross (eds).

Edinburgh 2010 Volume II: Witnessing to Christ Today, Daryl Balia and Kirsteen Kim (eds).

Mission Continues: Global Impulses for the 21st Century, Claudia Wahrisch-Oblau and Fidon Mwombeki (eds).

Holistic Mission: God's Plan for God's People, Brian Woolnough and Wonsuk Ma (eds).

Mission Today and Tomorrow, Kirsteen Kim and Andrew Anderson (eds).

The Church Going Local: Mission and Globalization, Tormod Engelsviken, Erling Lundeby and Dagfinn Solheim (eds).

Evangelical and Frontier Mission: Perspectives on the Global Progress of the Gospel, A. Scott Moreau and Beth Snodderly (eds).

Interfaith Relations after One Hundred Years: Christian Mission among Other Faiths, Marina Ngursangzeli Behera (ed).

Witnessing to Christ in a Pluralistic Age: Christian Mission among Other Faiths, Lalsangkima Pachuau and Knud Jørgensen (eds).

Mission and Post Modernities, Rolv Olsen (ed).

A Learning Missional Church: Reflections from Young Missiologists, Beate Fagerli, Knud Jørgensen, Rolv Olsen, Kari Storstein Haug and Knut Tveitereid (eds).

Life-Widening Mission: Global Anglican Perspectives, Cathy Ross (ed).

Foundations for Mission, Emma Wild-Wood and Peniel Rajkumar (eds).

Mission Spirituality and Authentic Discipleship, Wonsuk Ma and Kenneth R. Ross (eds).

A Century of Catholic Missions, Stephen Bevans (ed).

Mission as Ministry of Reconciliation, Robert Schreiter and Knud Jørgensen (eds).

Orthodox Perspectives on Mission, Petros Vassiliadis (ed).

Bible in Mission, Pauline Hoggarth, Fergus Macdonald, Knud Jørgensen and Bill Mitchell (eds).

Pentecostal Mission and Global Christianity, Wonsuk Ma, Veli-Matti Karkkainen and J. Kwabena Asamoah-Gyadu (eds).

Engaging the World: Christian Communities in Contemporary Global Society, Afe Adogame, Janice McLean and Anderson Jeremiah (eds).

Mission At and From the Margins: Patterns, Protagonists and Perspectives, Peniel Rajkumar, Joseph Dayam, I.P. Asheervadham (eds).

The Lausanne Movement: A Range of Perspectives, Margunn Serigstad Dahle, Lars Dahle and Knud Jørgensen (eds).

---

[1] For an up-to-date list and full publication details, see www.ocms.ac.uk/regnum/

Global Diasporas and Mission, Chandler H Im & Amos Yong (eds).
Theology, Mission and Child: Global Perspectives, B Prevette, K White,
   CR Velloso Ewell & DJ Konz (eds).
Called to Unity for the Sake of Mission, *John Gibaut and Knud Jørgensen*
   (eds).

FOREWORD

The World Missionary Conference held at Edinburgh in 1910 proved in retrospect to have reshaped the contours of Christian thinking, not simply about mission, but also about the mutual relationships of Christian churches. It is too early to judge whether Edinburgh 2010 – the centennial commemoration of the World Missionary Conference – will turn out to be equally influential in re-drawing the ecclesiastical landscape. What is already clear, however, is that the 2010 conference and the study process that preceded it have provoked a veritable explosion of new collaborative publications seeking to promote deep reflection on the subject of Christian mission. This volume is the latest example of this encouraging trend, and I count it a privilege to have been invited to write the Foreword.

Christian mission over the last century or more has been plagued by a divorce between action and reflection. The most evangelistically active practitioners have too often been the shallowest theological thinkers, whilst the deep reflectors have frequently been so embarrassed about the demonstrable pitfalls of previous mission practice, and so hesitant about the likely pitfalls of future mission practice, that they have effectively withdrawn from active engagement in the task of spreading the good news of Jesus Christ. This volume calls for a bridging of this unhappy gulf between action and reflection. It calls for a rediscovery of the centrality of self-critical reflection in the mission of the churches, but equally urges theological educators to seek to reverse the marginalisation of mission from their curricula. At least in the western world, 'theological education' is assumed to mean, first and foremost, education for pastoral ministry. Pastoral theology is conventionally regarded as the *sine qua non* of all ministerial education, whereas missiological or missional education is treated as an optional extra for the enthusiastic minority of intending religious professionals who have a peculiar leaning in that direction. The resulting separation between ministry and mission has been equally disastrous for both partners. Christian ministry, which the New Testament consistently regards as an activity dedicated to equipping the whole people of God for the task of bringing the Gospel to the world, is instead conceived of primarily in terms of maintenance – how to keep the ecclesiastical ship afloat in the choppy waters of secular society. Christian mission, on the other hand, is by implication assumed to be a non-ministerial pursuit, that is, one that has rather little to do with the essential work of pastoral service in the name of Christ, but is instead associated with the controversial propagandist enterprise of proselytism – of trying to persuade others to think and be like us. By their tacit separation between ministry (which, after all, means 'service') and mission, the churches thereby unwittingly reinforce the critiques of post-colonial and radically pluralist scholars who insist that Christian mission is by definition about religious intolerance or domination, and is therefore an affront to contemporary ethical norms. This challenge is one that confronts with particular sharpness those who write and teach about Christian mission in universities or university-validated theological institutions. The 'mission' word that recurs repeatedly through this volume is one that arouses almost automatic hostility in such circles, and hence the study of Christian mission in much theological education therefore has to be wrapped in alternative packaging, disguised as 'inter-cultural education' or 'World Christianity' (as if there were any other kind). As a professor in a leading British university I do not in any way dismiss the value of the pursuit of high academic standards in theology, yet the awkward fact is that in the contemporary post-modern and pluralist context, theological education that continues to place a high priority on the wider secular recognition that is measured by the award of university degrees will inevitably struggle to be authentically missional. Conversely, the more informal or 'bottom-up' style of theological education that is represented throughout the globe by countless church-based Christian discipleship or Theological Education by Extension programmes will remain at the sharp end of equipping Christians for mission, but at the price of a radical disconnection from the first-order theological and ideological questions with which Christian mission has to grapple in university contexts. If this volume turns out to have played even a small role in bringing together these two separated spheres of discourse about Christian mission, it will have served its purpose, and played its part in showing that Edinburgh 2010 was more than just another global talking-shop for Christians.

Brian Stanley
Professor of World Christianity
School of Divinity, University of Edinburgh

EDITORIAL INTRODUCTION:
REFLECTING ON AND
EQUIPPING FOR CHRISTIAN MISSION

An important study theme of Edinburgh 2010 was *Theological Education and Formation.* The theme is highlighted in the *Edinburgh 2010 Common Call* in the following way:

> Recognising the need to shape a new generation of leaders with authenticity for mission in a world of diversities in the 21st century, we are called to work together in new forms of theological education. Because we are all made in the image of God, these will draw on one another's unique charisms, challenge each other to grow in faith and understanding, share resources equitably worldwide, involve the entire human being and the whole family of God, and respect the wisdom of our elders while also fostering the participation of children.[1]

The Listening Group at Edinburgh 2010 notes in their report 'a strong affirmation not only of Christian faith as committed to education, but that mission should be a key, integrating element, and that we need a new vision for theological education within a missional model'.[2]

This concern has been a guiding light in the work on this volume on *Reflecting on and Equipping for Christian Mission.* We believe that a mission-less church will see no need for missiology and missional training. Today the situation has changed: the rediscovery of the missionary nature of the church in the conciliar ecumenical movement in the 1960s, the evangelical renewal of the Lausanne movement in the 1970s, and the post-Vatican II encyclicals on the missionary nature of the church have had a profound impact on redefining the missionary task and perspectives of theological education.[3]

The key issues and questions for the study group on Theological Education and Formation before Edinburgh 2010 were:

1. How can every member of the people of God be motivated and empowered for mission?
2. How can formation of mission spirituality become integrated into theological training programmes?

---

[1] The Edinburgh 2010 Common Call is found in the Preface to this volume.
[2] Kirsteen Kim and Andrew Anderson (eds), *Edinburgh 2010. Mission Today and Tomorrow* (Oxford: Regnum, 2011), 316.
[3] Daryl Balia and Kirsteen Kim (eds), *Edinburgh 2010. Witnessing to Christ Today* (Oxford: Regnum, 2010), 153.

3. How can the study of missiology become an integral part of the theological curriculum? How can mission perspectives be integrated into every theological discipline?
4. The role of accreditation in relation to mission and ministry.
5. How can churches best develop relevant curricula for local contexts?
6. Specific training for cross-cultural ministries and for those involved in reconciliation ministry.
7. Catalysts for theological training and formation where theological institutions are lacking.

Answers to these issues and questions are found in:

Report on Theme 6: Theological education and formation, in Daryl Balia and Kirsteen Kim (eds), *Edinburgh 2010. Witnessing to Christ Today* (Oxford: Regnum 2010).

Parallel Session on Theme 6: Theological education and formation, in Kirsteen Kim and Andrew Anderson (eds), *Edinburgh 2010. Mission Today and Tomorrow* (Oxford: Regnum, 2011).

These two documents are major references for this volume. We have, however, also asked the contributors to this volume to keep the original seven issues and questions in mind as they worked on their individual chapters.

In the documents from Edinburgh 2010 we have noted several references to the widespread consensus that theological education is part of the holistic mission of the church. This was very well expressed by the global conference on theological education enabled by WCC/ETE (World Council of Churches Ecumenisal Theological Education) in Oslo in 1996:

There is consensus among us on the holistic character of theological education and ministerial formation, which is grounded in worship, and combines and interrelates spirituality, academic excellence, mission and evangelism, justice and peace, pastoral sensitivity and competence, and the formation of character. For it brings together the education of:

*   the ear to hear God's word and the cry of God's people;
*   the heart to heed and respond to suffering;
*   the tongue to speak to both weary and arrogant;
*   the hands to work with the lowly;
*   the mind to reflect on the good news of the Gospel;
*   the will to respond to God's call;
*   the spirit to wait upon God in prayer, to struggle, to be silent, to intercede for the church and the world;
*   the body to be the temple of the Holy Spirit.[4]

---

[4] Ecumenical Theological Education, 'Message of the Oslo Conference on Theological Education 1996', in John Pobee (ed), *Towards Viable Theological Education* (Geneva: WCC, 1997), 1-6.

As we affirm the holistic character of theological education, we also want to affirm the desire to *educate the whole people of God*; we see this as a key to mission, and Christian mission should be the organising focus and reference point of theological education. Here is one of the reasons why we have chosen as a title for this volume *Reflecting on and Equipping for Christian Mission.* Theological education in the broad sense participates in the task of equipping people for God's mission in today's world. At the same time, we affirm that all theological education is contextual and that no particular context should exercise dominant influence (as it has during the long era of Christendom).

We are acutely aware of some of the challenges facing theological education and missionary training:

- Disparity in the availability of resources between North and South;
- The urgent need in many contexts to create more space for women in theological education, theological leadership and in the ministries of the church;
- Denominational fragmentation of the international landscape of theological education institutions;
- The implications of global migration movements for mission and for theological education;
- The intense need for greater diversity in methods and programmes of theological training and learning, including non-formal and non-residential models. In both the North and the South we must continue to explore new and innovative forms of theological education – mission-minded models for both lay people and for ordained ministry;
- The call for integrating academic learning and spiritual growth and missionary spirituality, and for developing spiritual competence among both educators and students;
- A stronger focus on ecumenical learning in such a way that theological education is guided by an ecumenical vision of a church renewed in mission.

Our hope is that the present volume will deal with these challenges in a fresh and constructive manner. This volume will review and point to the future of theological education with a particular focus on mission. The volumes listed below,[5] produced together with the WCC in the Regnum Studies in Global Christianity, have sought to map where theological

---

[5] Regnum Studies in Global Christianity – www.ocms.ac.uk/regnum/list.php?cat=2
- Handbook of Theological Education in World Christianity –
www.ocms.ac.uk/regnum/detail.php?book_id=73
- Handbook of Theological Education in Africa –
www.ocms.ac.uk/regnum/detail.php?book_id=98
- Asian Handbook for Theological Education and Ecumenism –
www.ocms.ac.uk/regnum/detail.php?book_id=101

education is today, and to bring varied voices from the globe. The main difference in comparison with the Global Christianity series of volumes will be the specific lens of mission in this volume. With many new mission players rising today, it is essential to review how theological education has been (or failed to be) a key mover in shaping mission thinking and mission players.

Our main emphasis is on mission formation for all Christians and missionary formation for mission workers, agencies and churches in a changing situation of mission. This volume includes a sound critique of traditional theological education (from a global perspective), an overview on newly emerging models (especially from the global South, e.g. mission with less money), and their evaluation and future direction.

We have struggled to make it a readable and accessible book, using language and concepts that also can open this landscape to users without degrees in theology or missiology.

The understanding of 'mission' undergirding this book will reflect the Common Call from Edinburgh 2010 (see the Preface to this volume).

We have aimed at producing a volume with broad participation and broad perspectives. The book includes both scholarly and practical input on various aspects of the topic and from different parts of the world. There is, as far as we know, no other conceptual treatment of this issue from such a broad ecumenical perspective. Pulling in a broad and diverse team of contributors has served to strengthen the ecumenical and professional focus of the project.

The book is composed of three sections. Section I deals with historical and missiological perspectives. Dietrich Werner provides an overview of theological education in the changing context of world Christianity, while Kenneth Ross takes us back to Edinburgh 1910 and its reports on education and the preparation of missionaries. Nelson Jennings reflects on the topic in the perspective of *missio Dei*, while Vidar L. Haanes discusses the relationship between missiology and theology. The two last chapters in Section I focus on Theological Education by Extension (Graham Aylett, Tim Green and Kangwa Mabuluki).

Section II discusses a number of crucial issues such as a reorientation towards missionary formation (Stephen Bevans) and Orthodox perspectives on theological education (Eric Tosi). Marina Ngursangzeli Behera highlights the inequality between North and South, and Atola Longkumer focuses on women in mission and theology. Christopher Wright provides a Lausanne perspective, while Knud Jørgensen looks at spiritual formation and missionary training. In the last chapter, Jay Moon takes on the challenge of oral learners.

In Section III we have collected a number of case studies on integral mission training (Ruth Wall), GlobeTheolLib (Stephen Brown), and equipping for mission in the 21st century (Steve Cochrane). Emmanuel Chemengich highlights the importance of networking, Richard Hart looks at new models of online education and e-learning, while Jonny Baker tells the story of CMS Pioneer Mission Leadership Training. The section continues with a Korean (Hyunmo Lee) and an African perspective (Ben Quarshie), followed by a Catholic perspective from Australia (Therese D'Orsa). Edmund Chia deals with interfaith learning, and Dawit Olika Teferssa and Werner Kahl open doors to migration and theological education. Ian Shaw tells the story of the Langham programme, and Wen Ge and Yalin Xin provide two different reflections on equipping for mission in China. The section closes with the story of the City Seminary of New York (Mark Gornik and Maria Liu Wong) and the story of the Foundation for Theological Education in South East Asia (H.S. Wilson). Nelson Jennings provides the concluding chapter on 'Divine Superintendence'.

All this is the work of thirty-one people representing various church traditions and different views and positions. They come from five continents and bring with them both their context and experience. Here lies the strength of this volume. We want to thank our contributors and colleagues for over a year of challenging co-operation and sojourning.

Stephen Bevans, USA, Teresa Chai, Malaysia, J. Nelson Jennings, USA,
Knud Jørgensen, Norway, and Werner Dietrich, Germany.
June 2015

SECTION ONE

HISTORICAL AND MISSIOLOGICAL PERSPECTIVES

THEOLOGICAL EDUCATION IN THE CHANGING CONTEXT OF WORLD CHRISTIANITY: AN UNFINISHED AGENDA. GLOBAL AND ECUMENICAL PERSPECTIVES FROM THE EDINBURGH 2010 PROCESS AND BEYOND[1]

Dietrich Werner

The Early Beginnings in Edinburgh 1910 –
A Vision for Global Ecumenical Co-operation in Theological Education and Missionary Training.

In 2010 Christian leaders commemorated 100 years of Christian mission after the 1910 World Mission Conference in Edinburgh, commonly regarded as a key event in the history of world Christianity and the ecumenical movement in the 20th century.

Edinburgh 1910 referenced theological education and missionary training in five major ways:

1. As Bishop Gore, Chairman of Commission III on 'Education in Relation to the Christianisation of National Life' stated,[2] Edinburgh 1910 highlighted the *strategic importance of (theological) education* as an indispensable element of any Christian mission, both past and future.

2. Suggesting a need today for a similar project in regions of Asia and Africa, Edinburgh 1910 attempted an *empirical world study and survey on the state of Christian education and theological education* by collecting reports from all regions at that time, leading to the final 455-page report (including appendices) of Commission III.[3]

3. Edinburgh 1910 called for a *massive quality improvement in the training of missionaries.* According to the report of Commission V on 'The Preparations of the Missionaries', missionary preparation

---

[1] This is a shortened version of the first two parts of a public lecture delivered at Philadelphia Lutheran Theological Seminary, 5th October 2010 on the occasion of the meeting of the Board of the Foundation for Theological Education for South East Asia (FTESEA); complete version: www.oikoumene.org/en/news/newsmanagement/eng/a/article/1634/promoting-theological-edu.html

[2] Bishop Gore, Chairman of Commission III, in *World Missionary Conference, 1910, Education in Relation to the Christianisation of National Life, Report of Commission III* (Edinburgh and London, 1910), 6.

[3] David A. Kerr and Kenneth R. Ross (eds), *Edinburgh 2010, Mission Then and Now* (Oxford: Regnum, 2009), 87.

should be drastically upgraded and broadened – in language studies, the history of religions, the sociology of mission territories, and in general principles of missionary work – portending an early foretaste of the contextualisation-debate that arose half a century later.

4. In a visionary and revolutionary manner, Edinburgh 1910 promoted the *establishment of 'central mission colleges'*,[4] jointly supported by different denominations and mission agencies. Early foretastes of ecumenical theological education and learning that developed decades later thus began in such major cities as Shanghai, Madras, Calcutta, Beirut and Cairo.

5. Finally, Edinburgh 1910 advocated a deliberate move towards *theological and Christian education in vernacular languages.*

Born out of missionary situations that demanded ecumenical learning and interdenominational co-operation, Edinburgh 2010 thus promoted a paradigm shift in theological education long before the established churches were ready to adjust their own ministerial formation programmes.[5] Edinburgh 1910 left behind such a legacy for the international missionary movement as to make theological education a first priority in any serious mission strategy.

From Missionary Vision to Joint Action for Theological Education – the Theological Education Fund of IMC and Subsequent PTE/ETE Programmes of WCC

Though implementation of some of Edinburgh 1910 visions was severely delayed by two world wars and a new decolonised world order, the passion for joint action for mission and theological education, remarkably, stayed alive. The deep commitment to joint action in theological education was renewed and found visible expression in the eventual creation of the Theological Education Fund (TEF) during the Accra Assembly of the International Missionary Council in 1958.

The three decisive marks and main concerns of TEF's work were

- Quality – combining intellectual rigour, spiritual maturity and commitment;
- Authenticity – involving critical encounter with each cultural context in the design, purpose and shape of theological education;
- Creativity – understood as promoting new approaches of the churches' obedience in mission.

---

[4] *World Missionary Conference 1910, The Training of Teachers. Commission V Report* (Edinburgh and London, 1910), 300.
[5] See also the following article by Kenneth Ross in this volume: 'Perspectives on Education and Formation from the World Missionary Conference, Edinburgh 1910'.

TEF was a remarkable enterprise and an example of high-level international co-operation in the funding and promoting of indigenous institutions of theological education and textbook programmes for churches in the global South. Limited and particular interests of individual mission boards and churches were set aside to achieve the common goal of international co-operation in promoting joint action in theological education. In its three mandate periods (1958-1977) TEF achieved much, including:

1. support for local faculty development programmes in all major regions;
2. strategic support for a crucial number of interdenominational 'centers for advanced theological study in the third world';[6]
3. an advanced theological textbook programme in regional languages (many of which were translations of western theological books into Asian and African languages, an impressive collection of which are in the WCC archives);
4. the formation of regional associations of theological schools (for instance, Association for Theological Education in South East Asia (ATESEA) was formed in 1957 in Singapore with its first executive directors John R. Fleming and Kosuke Koyama who had close working relations with TEF);
5. the launching of the debate and programme on contextualisation of theology and theological education by Shoki Coe (from Tainan Theological College who spent 14 years as staff and Director of TEF), which led to the emergence of liberation theologies in many churches and colleges in the southern hemisphere;[7]
6. the encouragement of alternative models of theological education such as Theological Education by Extension;[8]

---

[6] See TEF staff paper on 'Centers for Advanced Theological Study in the Third World: A Survey and Evaluation of Developments', in *Learning in Context. The Search for Innovative Patterns in Theological Education* (London: TEF, 1973), 155ff.

[7] See Shoki Coe, 'Recollections and Reflections', introduced and edited by Boris Anderson (second edition, 1993), *Formosan Christians for Self-Determination.* See particularly 'Contextualization as the way towards Reform in Theological Education', 275; also J. Gordon Chamberlin, *Contextualization: Origins, Meaning and Implications: A Study of What the Theological Education Fund of the World Council of Churches Originally Understood by the Term 'Contextualization', with Special Reference to the Period 1970-1972.* William P. Russell (Rome: Tipografia Poliglotta della Pontificia Universita, Gregoriana, 1995), 515; also David J. Hesselgrave and Edward Rommen, *Contextualization: Meanings, Methods, and Models* (Grand Rapids, MI: Baker Book House, 2003).

[8] F. Ross Kinsler, 'Extension: An Alternative Model for Theological Education', in *Learning in Context*, 27-49; F. Ross Kinsler (ed), *Diversified Theological Education: Equipping all God's People* (Pasadena, CA: William Carey International University Press, 2008).

7. the stimulation of debate about appropriate West/North-South partnership models of theological education.[9] The robust and diverse history, both of TEF and the subsequent programme of the Programme on Theological Education (PTE), as it was called after the integration of the TEF into the WCC in 1977 under its first Director Aharon Sabsezian, prevents detailed description here.[10] The innumerable archive boxes of TEF and PTE's history which are located in the Ecumenical Center in Geneva still wait for several PhD research projects on the history of theological education in Asia, Africa and Latin America to find their rich material base. Shoki Coe emphasised that equipping and qualifying theological education in the churches of the South in many aspects remains 'an unfinished task'.[11] Coe also prophetically emphasised that 'regionalization is a missiological necessity... but its role, function, and its structures need careful mutual consultation and... the effectiveness of the new PTE will depend on its ability to evolve this healthy relation between the regions and the PTE'.[12]

Where are We with Theological Education at the Beginning of the 21st Century? – Signposts of Crisis and New Opportunities from the Edinburgh 2010 Process

Edinburgh 2010 provided an opportunity to reflect on the dramatic global changes in the landscape of world Christianity that were inconceivable one hundred years ago. The new *Atlas of Global Christianity* by Todd M. Johnson and Kenneth Ross[13] provides extensive details on the well-known shift of the centre of gravity in Christianity. Since this data is vital as general background for looking at theological education in today's world, here are some of the key trends and figures:

1. While 66% of all Christians lived in Europe in 1910, by 2010 only 25.6% Christians were located in Europe. By contrast, less than 2% of all Christians lived in Africa in 1910, but this figure sky-rocketed to almost 22% by 2010. The global North (defined as Europe and

---

[9] See the case studies on Missions Academy University of Hamburg, in *Learning in Context. The Search for Innovative Patterns in Theological Education* (Bromley, UK: TEF, 1973), 132ff.
[10] For the history, see Christine Lienemann-Perrin, *Training for a Relevant Ministry. A Study of the World of the Theological Education Fund* (Madras/Geneva, 1980); Dietrich Werner, 'ETE – Jubilee Issue on the history of PTE/ETE in the World Council of Churches', in *Ministerial Formation*, No 110, April 2008; also ETE Jubilee Issue of *International Review of Mission*, April 2009, 388, 1-214.
[11] Shoki Coe, Director's Report for the last *TEF Committee Meeting, Bromley*, July 1977, TEF Archives, Box 35 (1977), WCC, 15-16.
[12] Coe, Director's Report, July 1977, 16-17.
[13] Todd M. Johnson and Kenneth Ross (eds), in *Atlas of Global Christianity* (Edinburgh University Press: Center for the Study of Global Christianity, 2009).

North America) contained over 80% of all Christians in 1910, but fell to under 40% of all Christians by 2010. However, the overall percentage of Christians in the world population did not change much, causing Dana Robert in her opening speech in Edinburgh 2010 to remark: 'A century ago the participants at Edinburgh 1910 complained that only one third of the world was Christian. Today we rejoice that one third of the world are followers of Christ'.[14]

2. Seen as a Christian percentage of the population per region, the shift becomes even more obvious in Africa. While Africa's Christian population was less than 10% in 1910, it was nearly 50% in 2010, with sub-Saharan Africa well over 70% Christian.

3. While Christianity remains a minority religion in most Asian countries, there has still been an overall increase of Christian population in Asia between 1910 and today, from 2.4% to 8.5%. That pushes the Asian Christian population to over 292 million today, with a particular increase in South-East Asia of 10.8% to 21.8%, but also a sharp decrease in Western Asia (22.9% to 5.7%). Statistically, Christianity in Asia should grow in countries like China, India, Nepal and Cambodia.

4. The general projection until 2050 is that Christianity will still grow in the global South, particularly West Africa, Middle Africa and Eastern Asia (China) and South-East Asia, but will also sharply contract in the global North (particularly in Europe).

Yet even with the new *Atlas of Global Christianity* (and World Christian Database), there are not yet adequate data available on how the changes in world Christianity were reflected (or contradicted) by the availability and numbers of theological colleges, faculties of religious studies and Bible schools worldwide. We know some of the regional developments: for instance, since ATESEA was founded at the 1957 meeting in Singapore, the number of its member-schools has grown from 16 to 104,[15] and that theological colleges in the Senate of Serampore system have grown to 54 since 1910.[16] It is also known that theological schools in China have experienced a remarkable new development with the reopening of Nanjing Union Theological Seminary in 1981, while in the period 1981-2009, some 10,000 theological students graduated from the nineteen theological seminaries in China.[17] There are approximately 2,000 theological colleges

---

[14] Dana Robert, ' Mission in Long Perspective', in Kirsteen Kim and Andrew Anderson (eds), *Edinburgh 2010. Mission Today and Tomorrow* (Oxford: Regnum, 2011), 56-68.

[15] http://en.wikipedia.org/wiki/Association_for_Theological_Education_in_South_East_Asia#History

[16] www.senateoframporecollege.edu.in

[17] Yilu Chen, 'Major Developments and Challenges for Theological Education in China', in D. Werner et al, *Handbook for Theological Education in World Christianity* (Oxford: Regnum, 2010), 431.

and Bible schools in world Christianity today,[18] thus presenting a tremendous increase over the past hundred years. However, secular statistics on world developments in higher education on investment, library and internet access, and scholarly publications in various countries,[19] point to sharp contrasts and growing inequalities in tertiary education levels between the global North and global South, a fact that impacts and exhibits parallel phenomena in higher theological education. Many indicators suggest that accessibility and numbers of programmes and institutions of theological education vary considerably between regions, and the standards and stability of theological education are still vastly different between the global North and the global South, and are in several aspects more polarised than 100 years ago.

The Edinburgh 2010 process formed nine international study groups connected with the different sub-themes of the conference, one of which dealt with theological education. Despite the absence of a comprehensive database on global developments in theological education, the group came forward with some new surveys and empirical observations concerning the developments in theological education on a world level. It belonged to the contributions of ETE within the Edinburgh 2010 process and the newly-formed international study group on theological education[20] that – based on some earlier publications and papers from ETE[21] – some important new publications and research papers were made available, including the following:

- The 100-page global study report on theological education: 'Challenges and Opportunities in Theological Education in the 21st century. Pointers for a new International debate on theological education', published in November 2009 and introduced during the session on theological education in Edinburgh June 2010;[22]
- The 800-page 'Handbook on Theological Education in World Christianity' (edited by Dietrich Werner, David Esterline, Namsoon Kang and Joshva Raja), released during the Edinburgh 2010

---

[18] The International Directory of Theological Colleges which was published in the 1990s had listed over 2,000 theological colleges worldwide: Alec Gilmore, *An International Directory of Theological Colleges* 1997, PTE (Geneva: WCC, 1996).

[19] Data are available in special graphic presentation from worldmapper.org (see tertiary education expenditure trends in various countries and on a world level).

[20] The group was moderated by Dietrich Werner and Namsoon Kang, composed of representatives from both historical churches and their institutions of theological education, evangelical organisations and Pentecostal educators.

[21] See the theme issue: Theological Education in Mission, *IRM*, Vol. 388, April 2009; Jubilee issue of Ministerial Formation on 50 years of work of PTE/ETE in the WCC, MF No 110, April 2008.

[22] Paper available from: www.oikoumene.org/en/resources/documents/wcc-programmes/education-and-ecumenicalformation/ecumenical-theological-education-ete/edinburgh-2010-international-study-group-on-theological-education.html

centenary conference, plus subsequent key volumes on theological education in Asia, Africa and the Orthodox world;[23]

- A report on the two sessions and major issues raised during the Edinburgh 2010 centenary conference which is part of the final conference volume;

- A major publication on 'The future of African theological education' which was developed after the Stellenbosch conference on the future of theological education in Africa in November 2009 (published in *Missionalia*, SAMS, Vol. 38 (2), 2010);

- In addition, a major 'resource book on women and mission in world Christianity', which was initiated in 2009 with a project group[24] and published in 2011.

Some of the results of these publications are important for reviewing the changing situation of theological education in the 21st century, and therefore should be briefly referred to.[25]

Accessibility gap in theological education
(the challenge of unequal distribution)[26]

The absolute majority of teaching staff, scholarship funds, theological libraries and publications are still located in the north. The crisis of world economy in past years has deeply affected theological education systems, both in endowment-based theological colleges as well as in state-funded departments for theology or religious studies. There is a widening gap between state-funded or endowment-driven theological colleges in the north and the smaller, highly vulnerable church-based theological colleges in the south. There is a grave lack of scholarships and grants available for higher studies in theological education in almost all theological colleges of the south, and several churches in the south are facing increasing difficulties in funding their institutions of theological education.

Thus, the 'most important of all ends which missionary education ought to set itself to serve, that is, of training those who are to be the spiritual leaders and teachers of their own nation' (Edinburgh 1910, Commission III) seems not yet to be met in a satisfactory manner.

---

[23] See the series of Handbooks on Theological Education: www.ocms.ac.uk/regnum/list.php?cat=2
[24] Moderated by Christine Lienemann, Atola Longkumer and Afrie Songko Joyce.
[25] The following points are also referred to in 'Report of parallel session on theological education and formation' in Kirsteen Kim and Andrew Anderson (eds), *Mission Today and Tomorrow* (Oxford: Regnum, 2011), 158ff.
[26] See also on this issue the article in this volume by Marina Ngursangzeli Behera, 'Inequality in Theological Education between the North and the South'.

Contextualisation gap in theological education
(the challenge of cultural dominance)

While the plea of Edinburgh1910 to develop contextualised forms of theological education in the Asian churches was partly answered by some indigenous models of theological education and contextual theologies worked out in the 20th century, western patterns and concepts of theology continue to be exported throughout the global South, so that the task of Edinburgh 1910 was only gradually and very incompletely fulfilled. Theological research and publications from Europe are present in African theological libraries, while theological research from Africa to a great extent is absent from western theological libraries. Voices from Africa and Asia point to a decline in the commitment to contextualised theologies and declining numbers of books published on Asian or African theologies. Instead there is an increased trend to create affiliated programmes of American, Asian or other western theological colleges to operate as branches in countries of the South, so that some voices speak of ambivalent trends of Koreanisation or Americanisation of theological education in Asia or Africa. Models and curricula of theological education from the West have often been coined and formed within a Constantinian or post-Constantinian church setting. Once they are transferred into contexts in the South (which in most cases have a pre-Constantinian setting) without much adaptation, problems and unsolved challenges for contextualisation of theological education in the churches of the South are becoming obvious. Much of what is happening in and through the rapid spread of evangelical or Pentecostal theological education today also reflects the unresolved needs of pre-Constantinian church settings for contextualised teaching materials and curriculum plans.

The challenge for contextualisation also holds true for centralised theological colleges in Asia or Africa which operate in the English medium: do they really serve the contextualisation of the Gospel and of church ministries, or do they – unintentionally – also serve the de-contextualisation and westernisation of theology in Asian or African contexts? Do candidates who have benefitted from their programmes, often located in urbanised areas with different modes and chances of communication, feel motivated and equipped to go back to parishes in rural areas where different needs are at stake? Many urgent needs remain for culturally and linguistically appropriate programmes and resources of theological education. The plea of Edinburgh 1910 to establish theological literature and education programmes in vernacular languages was overshadowed by the historic development which has given pre-eminence to English as the new global colonial language, outside the realm of which it is still difficult to find international recognition and chances for communication for indigenous theological knowledge production and related publications.

*Diversification gap in theological education
(the challenge of migration and pluralisation)*

While contextualisation of theological education is at stake, trans-contextuality and diversification of theological education have also become issues in many contexts, both in the South as well as in the North. As the world is shrinking and global migration brings different cultures, religions and denominational identities from isolated pockets into close and vibrant neighbourhoods, the need of theological education to address different identities, cultural milieus and social spheres within one context has become imperative – such as Malaysia having to address thousands of Filipino and Chinese immigrants, African nations like DRC or South Africa having to cope with thousands of refugees or migrants from war-torn neighbouring states, and American colleges having to open up for Hispanic or African communities as a result of decades of immigration. According to the International Organization for Migration (IOM), the number of international migrants increased by 45 million – an annual growth rate of about 2.1%, adding some ten million migrants each year.[27]

The fundamental implications of global migration for programmes of theological education are not yet fully spelt out. There is a need not only for higher degree programmes of theological education, but more often for informal and extension programmes of theological education. In many churches there is a great need for informal theological education for catechists, Bible women and lay preachers, as they bear the greatest burden for mission and evangelism today. Diversification of theological education is needed in terms of providing affordable and accessible courses for theological education for those groups carrying out the key tasks of mission and evangelism today.

*Unity and credibility gap of theological education (the challenge of
disintegration and fragmentation of world Christianity)*

The single most remarkable trend however in world Christianity today is that the degree of denominational fragmentation in the international and regional landscape of theological education networks and institutions is higher than ever before in the history of Christianity. The number of different Christian denominations has climbed to astronomical numbers,[32] of which in 1910 nobody could possibly have dreamt – particularly owing to the rise of the so-called Independent churches from 1.5% in 1910 to 16.1% of all Christians in the world in 2010, which is only one of the indicators.[28]

---

[27] Henry S. Wilson and Werner Kahl, 'Global Migration and Challenges to Theological Education', in D. Werner et al (eds), *Handbook on Theological Education in World Christianity*, 76ff.

[28] *Atlas of Global Christianity*, 70.

The missionary enterprise in Africa, for example, led to the creation of predominantly ethnic churches in Africa – ethnic identities aligned with denominational identities. There are about 2,600 ethnic groups in Africa. In many countries – like Kenya, Nigeria or DRC – there are thousands of different Christian denominations and churches today (Kenya: 4,000 denominations, Angola: 800 denominations).[29] Every major denominational family nowadays tends to have its own theological college or Bible school, tends to build up its own Christian universities and undertakes great efforts to strengthen its own denominational identity (and fewer associations of schools of an interdenominational character). There are different denominational world families of associations of theological schools (World Conference of Associations of Theological Institutions [WOCATI]/ETE as the ecumenical family, The World Alliance for Pentecostal Theological Education [WAPTE] as the Pentecostal family, and International Council for Evangelical Theological Education [ICETE] as bringing together schools from an evangelical background). As a result, financial streams of support do not any more join together into one global or one regional programme as was the case with TEF in the 1960s and 70s of the 20th century. Rather, funding sources follow denominational and bilateral lines, thereby creating complex multi-parallel, and often rival, systems of theological education, accreditation and degree-giving.

The vision and hope of the fathers and mothers of Edinburgh 1910, that co-operation in Christian mission would also lead to more unity and solidarity in theological education, have obviously not been fulfilled in major segments of world Christianity one hundred years later.

Ownership gap of theological education
(the challenge of long-term viability of theological institutions
and associations of theological schools)

The financial viability of theological education after the world's financial meltdown in 2008 is an issue not only within the US, but even more in many theological colleges in the South. The support and financial commitment of churches to their institutions of theological education has not increased but in several regions has instead collapsed – a perennial problem particularly in Asia.[30] Thus, the sense of ownership and the interlinking of church, Christian mission and theological education, which was highlighted by many authors and studies in the 20th century, seem to have been endangered at the beginning of our century.

---

[29] Details come from André Karamaga, General Secretary of AACC, Nairobi, 2009.
[30] See Wati Longchar in *Partnership in Training God's Servants for Asia. Essays in Honor of Marvin D. Hoff,* Sientje Merentek-Abram and A. Wati Longchar (eds) (Jorhat: ATESEA, 2006), 54-55.

Several churches in the South have had to reduce or withdraw their support to interdenominational theological colleges. Others have put their hope in becoming part of Christian universities or transforming former church-related theological colleges into departments of humanities in larger Christian universities and getting them financed by state resources. The global study report on theological education has therefore called for improved support by churches and a sense of ownership for institutions of theological education.[31]

Preliminary Conclusion and Evaluation

Here is a conclusion and preliminary summary evaluation of the relevance of the centenary conference of Edinburgh 2010 for theological education.

- Edinburgh was successful in that, for the first time in this century, it brought together all major streams of world Christianity to again be in dialogue with each other on key questions of Christian mission, including the place of theological education. The 'Common Call' issued at the close of the conference also presented some common language to define a broad common basis for the understanding of mission.

- Edinburgh 2010 was also successful as a study conference due to the commitment of all nine international study groups under the inspiring leadership of Kirsteen Kim. There is some major work and material available for research by several generations of missiologists and experts in world Christianity from this conference.

- The concluding report of the session on theological education from Edinburgh 2010 rightly states: 'The concern for Christian education, theological education and ministerial formation which has been a key task throughout the history of Christian mission from its very beginning, needs to be reaffirmed and identified as a strategic task of common action for all Christian churches in the 21st century.'[32] The problem is that this remains more a passionate claim then an actual common practical commitment because, unlike Edinburgh 1910, the centenary conference in June 2010 was neither designed nor able to move towards common action and international new joint practical commitments for mission in the area of theological education. Edinburgh 2010 was thus weak in terms of strategising for new models of real international and interdenominational co-operation. The reason might be that, with only four main days of conference meetings and only two very short 90-minute sessions on

---

[31] *Global Study Report on Theological Education* (Section 26: Churches support and sense of ownership for institutions of theological education (Geneva: WCC, 2013), 84-85.

[32] 'Report of parallel session on theological education and formation', 2.

each of the nine study themes, Edinburgh 2010 did not have the structural and time-related preconditions to achieve a similar depth and sense of commitment that the world mission conference had achieved 100 years ago.

- At a deeper level, the view that Edinburgh 2010 fell short of expectations of those who would have liked to see a clearer follow-up strategy and real commitment for joint action on theological education worldwide was also reflected in the enormous fragmentation of world Christianity and the weakening of the ecumenical spirit and international solidarity for this key area of the missionary task of Christianity in the early 21st century.

The famous statement of the 1938 Tambaram world mission conference – 'The weakest element in the enterprise of Modern Missions is theological education'[33] – which two decades later led to the formation of the TEF programme, to some extent still holds true under the different historical conditions of our time. The historic strength of Protestant as well as a major part of Roman Catholic Christian mission was to a large extent based on the famous tri-polar concept of mission which holds together evangelism, education and healthcare, and with it a fraternal relationship between faith and critical reasoning, spiritual or ministerial formation, and sound intellectual and academic reflection of theology. The changing landscape of world Christianity, which includes a stagnation or slight decline of Protestant churches in the past hundred years and a sharp increase of Independent (Charismatic) churches will not automatically continue the mainline churches' tradition of higher theological education. It will not automatically give priority to a type of theological education which is based on this Reformation heritage, giving prominence to biblical and historical education. Deliberate efforts are needed for this tradition of commitment to theological education, based in Reformation tradition, not to become marginalised within the context of world Christianity in the coming centuries. Or, as the Edinburgh 2010 report on theological education has stated:

> The integrity and authenticity of all the diverse streams of World Christianity in the 21st century can be maintained and deepened only if we move beyond a situation in which Christianity seems to flourish where theological education does not flourish and vice versa, but where instead innovative forms of theological education are emerging which are life-giving, renewing, participatory and relevant for the growing charismatic renewal movements in the South and for the renewing churches in the North.

---

[33] Coe, Director's Report, July 1977, 15.

Pointers and Open Questions for Possible Priorities for Joint Action and Solidarity in Co-operation for Theological Education in the 21st Century

In this concluding section we shall tentatively formulate some pointers to new priorities and some key challenges for strengthening international co-operation for theological education in the changed contexts of world Christianity today.

Attention to the needs of newly emerging churches in the contexts of poverty – avoiding a new apartheid in theological education

Mission agencies and churches worldwide have to be more attentive to the needs of newly emerging churches and their needs for theological education, particularly in churches which are growing in contexts of poverty and in societies which see rapid changes, marginalisation and poverty. No one could have imagined one hundred or even fifty years ago the changes and political openings which have come about in countries like China, Nepal, Cambodia, Laos, and growing churches in several African countries. For those churches that have only recently been established, careful attention, support and accompaniment are needed to develop contextualised systems and materials for theological education, without which organic growth and holistic Christian mission in their context cannot take place. Churches that have 500 or 200 years of history need to listen to the authentic needs of churches which have only 80 or 50 years of history and are at quite a different stage of development. Churches in a context of affluence need to overcome their cultural captivity and develop a sensitivity for newly-emerging churches which come from completely different backgrounds. It cannot be right that churches from established and affluent backgrounds look down on indigenous churches (like African independent churches), due to different theological trends or features, while at the same time in practice denying their rights for more and sounder theological education. There are several emerging churches in Africa that have grown significantly in numerical terms during the past two decades, but appear not to have grown theologically. The unity and inner coherence of world Christianity in the 21st century is to a large extent dependent on joint international efforts to make theological education accessible, affordable and meaningful for all. Otherwise world Christianity will see increased inner fragmentation with growing internal conflicts tearing it apart and with an increasingly massive loss of relevance in glaring contrast with booming Muslim higher education systems in the world of the coming century.

International co-operation for strengthening regional associations of theological schools and regional funds for faculty development

Unprecedented denominational fragmentation and isolation between the different networks of theological education are not encouraging for the future and common witness of Christianity in interfaith contexts and in general societies. New mechanisms of international co-operation between agencies and churches of different denominational orientation are needed, both internationally and regionally, to respond to the needs of theological education, both structurally and theologically.[34] The most important tool and platform for transformation in theological schools are the regional associations of theological schools, but unlike American theological schools, these entities are still very fragile, dependent on external support or are even non-existent, particularly in Africa. As the ETE programme in WCC, which at present is supported only by three major funding partners and churches, is changing its role from becoming more relational in its global networking role and less directly involved in operational (grant-giving) work in the regions, it is certainly interested in exploring ways of bringing about a new global platform of co-operation within the area of theological education in order to mobilise more support for associations of theological schools in networking with regional organisations. Without dominating or intending to recreate something like TEF, some regular form of international exchange might be helpful with a number of key partners in order to identify development goals for theological education in different regions which are shared by several partners. The setting up of regional ecumenical funds for theological education has been proposed, and ETE has initiated processes around these goals as one of its strategies in Africa, in Asia and in Latin America, inviting other partners to join, though it is not yet clear how far this strategy can be sufficiently supported by the churches from the respective regions. Edinburgh 1910 produced a strategic global alliance of mission partners to build up theological education in the South. Perhaps Edinburgh 2010 should reinvent a strategic alliance of ecumenical partners and churches to support the creation and building of regional funds for theological education, particularly in Africa, Asia, Latin America and China, areas in which developments are fast taking place and improvement in theological education is urgently needed.

---

[34] The concluding report of the Edinburgh 2010 session on theological education recommended: 'An international working group for theological education should be considered – or explored to be established as a working group within IAMS – which would bring together representatives of all Christian confessions beyond all present divides, and which would serve as a continuation committee of this session of Edinburgh 2010 to explore common synergies and joint action in support of theological education for the mission of the Church', in 'Report of parallel session on theological education and formation', 164.

Stimulating proper empirical research in regional developments,
quality and financial viability in theological education

Another area for joint action and co-operation for theological education is research into changes and trends in theological education. More in-depth empirical data and historical and substantial theological research is needed on recent trends, financial viability and developments in theological education in Asia and Africa. Associations like ATESEA or the Senate of Serampore, not to mention associations in Africa, would be helped if somebody could do substantial research on what has been the impact on curriculum BD reform on church ministers or on the financial viability and church support for theological education in Asia throughout recent decades. Similar research would be needed on the impact of theological scholarship programmes of different providers in Asia and Africa.

Raising a common voice for the future of
theology within university settings

Reports from both Europe and some other countries in Africa have underlined that, in some countries, colleagues in theological education interpret the situation as a state of emergency in which time has or will come to stand up in order to fight for the legitimacy of theology as a discipline in public universities. Secularisation, de-Christianisation and also trends in research funding seem to move in a direction in which it is less likely to gain support for a theological faculty and for proper theological research than it is to gain it for projects in the area of religious studies. While religious studies do form an important part of theological education, warning signals have been sent out by some against a tendency to replace theology as a discipline by religious studies in general. Churches need theology as a confession-bound discipline of academia to claim its place and role in the public sphere and in the university context of post-modern society. The value decisions and the role, both of religions and spirituality which are at stake in society, still need serious theological reflection from a theological discipline which is bound and guided by position statements of faith rooted in the catholic heritage of the universal church.

Defining ecumenical standards for quality in theological education

Churches in dialogue with theological seminaries and faculties need to reach some common guidelines developing a common framework for understanding and defining the quality of theological education.[35] Because national and international accreditation agencies will continue to question

---

[35] See 'Towards International Standards of Quality in Theological Education – ETE Reference Document 2009', in: www.oikoumene.org/en/resources/documents/wcc-programmes/education-and-ecumenical-formation/ecumenical

theological institutions that cannot give sufficient answer with regard to their quality standards, it will be important for churches to come together in order to define some common standards for quality theological education and for minimum requirements for entering into the ministry (as Protestant churches in Europe and also a network of theological educators in Latin America have worked on already[45]).

Strengthening the disciplines of missiology, world Christianity and ecumenics

In the context of world Christianity in the 21st century, which is full of unexpected and decentralised examples of 'mission from everywhere to everywhere', theological education cannot fulfil its task without disciplines or fields like missiology and world Christianity playing their vital and indispensable part in the whole of the theological enterprise. The tendency to cut teaching staff positions in the field of missiology, ecumenics and interreligious dialogue should be countered by deliberate attempts to secure the interrelatedness of theological education and missiology/mission concerns and issues of world Christianity and interreligious dialogue. Carrying on the ecumenical memory within the ecumenical movement cannot be taken for granted any more. It needs to be seriously considered whether the WCC, as the primary catalyst and agent of the ecumenical movement, should not create and support a specialised theological scholarship programme focused on PhD programmes and MTH programmes on ecumenism, ecumenical missiology and ecumenical interfaith dialogue, in order to safeguard and enhance new ecumenical theological leadership in these key areas without which the ecumenical movement can easily die out from amnesia or gradual oblivion.

Building bridges of synergy and exchange between diaspora and homeland communities of theological educators

The implications of global migration for theological education have not yet been fully realised and explored for the international networking of theological education. It is very promising that FTESEA has put plans for more interaction between diaspora communities of Asian theological educators and theological education systems in their Asian home countries as one of its top priorities, and that the newly-formed Association of Asian Theological Educators in North America (AATENA) will play its role in enhancing theological teaching in Asian colleges.[46] Similar models are also to be worked on with regard to African networks between African diaspora churches and institutions of theological education on the African continent.

Overcoming mutual isolation and polarisation in theological education
– encouraging interdenominational schools and joint projects with
Pentecostal theological education.

The growing interest and self-confidence of Pentecostal churches in theological education programmes should be taken up and listened to carefully by theological colleges from mainline churches instead of following the path of separate development and reinforced denominationalism. There is a growing international community of highly qualified academic Pentecostal theological educators who have recently formed their own international network (WAPTE), demanding a more visible role for Pentecostal schools of theology in the international landscape of theological education, with better prominence being given to theological education within Pentecostal churches themselves, and with greater emphasis being put on Pentecostal denominational identity over against other networks (to some extent also linked with an openness to relate to other networks and institutions of theological education).[36]

Joining forces in creating one global portal for a
multi-lingual digital theological library

Theological knowledge transfer had taken the shape of theological textbook programmes within the TEF period some forty years ago. While the need for proper and contextualised theological textbooks continues today, the means of communication have changed in the 21st century. An immediate priority for today is about working out new systems for a more just model of theological knowledge transfer between North and North, East and West which makes use of internet facilities. A project group in Geneva has worked on a 'Global Digital Theological Library'[37] – a project which does have a proper software and tools for harvesting machines already by being linked to the existing Globethics.Net Library system,[38] but needs more support in terms of theological libraries and agencies co-operating and funds to allow for a quantum leap in making available proper theological information in all kinds of directions, particularly South to South and South to North. New developments in communication technologies open up better chances for programmes of theological e-learning and a global digital

---

[36] See their website: http://wapte.org and the scholarly papers of the World Alliance for Pentecostal Theological Education (WAPTE) consultation 2010 in Stockholm, 23rd-26th August 2010 (in co-operation with European Pentecostal Theological Association (EPTA)).
[37] See the article by Stephen Brown in this volume: 'Information Technology for Mission in the 21st Century: The Global Digital Library on Theology and Ecumenism'.
[38] See: www.globethics.net

theological library networking system which can be promising for the future.

Developing common guidelines or standards for international
ecumenical partnerships between institutions of theological education

A final point: WCC and its programme in Theological Education since Mexico City 1963 stood for a six-continent approach in theological education which implies that all regions of the inhabited earth should be in vital contact and proper partnership relationships with all other regions with regard to enabling each other for the task for theological education. We do think that we could benefit from a new understanding and new models of authentic and participatory cross-cultural partnership in theological education worldwide.[39] What are our standards, our expectations and our criteria for proper and authentic ecumenical partnership in theological education with institutions and networks from other regions of this world? Are there specific experiences or guidelines on standards for ecumenical partnerships in theological education which can be shared with others? It would be beneficial for many associations of theological schools like ATS or those from other continents if some guidelines based on recent expectations and experiences could be worked out which would pave the way for a more participatory, broad and future-oriented approach to partnership in theological education in a global perspective. This is vital for theological education in the changing context of world Christianity today. It is an unfinished agenda.

---

[39] The Concluding Report of the Edinburgh 2010 session on theological education had some provocative phrases on this issue: 'We also need new and authentic models of international partnerships between institutions of theological education in the North and the South, East and West. As it is a known fact that most of the Christians are in the South and most of the educational resources are in the North, it is not acceptable that those who are in control of the inequity should attempt to solve this crisis with "tokenism" by making unilateral decisions about who comes and who does not, rather than giving up some of their privileges and developing models of mutual sharing and decision-making. The richest seminaries of this world, rather than becoming the "experts" on the communities of the South and importing select southern students to kneel at the altar of accredited education, should contribute to credible and authentic models of authentic partnership with theological colleges and faculties in the South.' in 'Report of parallel session on theological education and formation', 164.

PERSPECTIVES ON EDUCATION AND FORMATION FROM THE WORLD MISSIONARY CONFERENCE, EDINBURGH 1910

Kenneth R. Ross

Introduction: Mission and Education

A cursory glance at the proceedings of the 'Edinburgh 1910' World Missionary Conference would be enough to show that education and formation were among its central concerns. As stated in one of its most influential reports: 'The subject of education in missionary work is of special and far-reaching importance. No one, who knows the history of mission, can doubt that missionaries were pioneers of education wherever they went, and it is hardly possible to exaggerate the debt of gratitude which is due to them for their labours in education, nor can it be doubted how important a part education has played in the process of evangelisation.'[1] It was axiomatic to the Conference delegates that mission and education were so closely intertwined as to be aspects of one and the same reality. In terms of programme, almost all the mission boards and missionary societies represented at the Conference were investing massively in education. This did not mean, however, that they were disposed to be uncritical in their analysis or naïve in their planning. They exhibited what Ogbu Kalu has described as an '... astonishing level of self-criticism...'[2] The starting point of the Conference was that, '... education, as pursued under missionary auspices, has exhibited certain weaknesses in its methods, and is exposed to certain perils, which make it necessary to review its principles and its processes.'[3]

An important part of the innovative genius of Edinburgh 1910 was the appointment of eight Commissions, each with a remit to carry out an exhaustive study of an aspect of the missionary movement thought to require urgent review. The Reports of the Commissions gave structure and substance to the Conference and their subsequent publication in book form

---

[1] World Missionary Conference, 1910, *Report of Commission III: Education in Relation to the Christianisation of National Life* (Edinburgh and London: Oliphant, Anderson & Ferrier; New York, Chicago and Toronto: Fleming H. Revell), 6.

[2] Ogbu U. Kalu, 'To Hang a Ladder in the Air: An African Assessment', in David A. Kerr and Kenneth R. Ross (eds), *Edinburgh 2010: Mission Then and Now* (Oxford: Regnum, 2009), 91-104, at 96.

[3] *Education in Relation to the Christianisation of National Life*, 6.

represents an important part of the ongoing legacy of Edinburgh 1910. Two of the eight Commissions were concerned with education and formation. Commission III addressed the question of mission and education in broad terms under the title: 'Education in Relation to the Christianisation of National Life'. Commission V was concerned with the more specific question of education and formation for missionary service under the title: 'The Preparation of Missionaries'.

Commission III was chaired by Charles Gore, the Anglican Bishop of Birmingham, and it is notable that eleven of the twenty members of the Commission were members of the Anglican Communion. The Vice Chairman was a Presbyterian theologian, Edward Caldwell Moore of Harvard University. Framed by an Introduction and Conclusion, the Report consists of nine chapters: the initial five are regional surveys, summarising the responses of missionaries in India, China, Japan, Africa and 'Muhammedan lands in the Near East' to the Commission's questionnaire; the final three chapters deal with thematic issues centred on training – both industrial and educational – and literature.

Between the two parts of the Report, Chapter Seven, entitled 'The Relating of Christian Truth to Indigenous Thought and Feeling', formed the heart of the enquiry. The Report is inspired by a vision of indigenous Christianity, coming to expression under the guidance of national leaders, educated and trained in their own vernacular. The catholicity of the church could come to full expression, argued the Report, only when the faith was appropriated by each nation in terms that were true to its own particular character.

Commission V was chaired by Professor Douglas Mackenzie – born of Scottish missionary parents in South Africa, Edinburgh-educated, Professor of Systematic Theology in Chicago, and from 1904 the President of Hartford Seminary Foundation which was already pioneering the professional training of missionaries in the United States, combining theological and regional studies with character formation. The Commission gathered evidence from the United States, Britain, Germany and Scandinavia, and from a wide cross-section of missionaries. The Commissioners were mainly theological educators from European and North American universities/colleges and theological colleges/seminaries.

The Report is divided into five parts: (1) a review of world conditions affecting Christian mission; (2) a review of the current theory and practice of missionary training; (3) an elaboration of principles for missionary training, and their application to various categories of missionary; (4) a consideration of what 'special missionary preparation' requires, and how it could be provided; and (5) a review of principles and practices of committees responsible for the selection and preparation of candidates. The rapidly changing world situation was seen as challenging the churches to produce a higher standard of missionary. Urgently needed were increased numbers of men and women who would combine genuine vocation with the highest possible level of professional and theological training.

This chapter aims to identify the principal concerns which Commissions III and V brought to the Conference and to evaluate these in terms of their influence on the understanding of mission and education in the subsequent century.

The Purpose of Missionary Education

The particular line of enquiry assigned to Commission III was based on a broad view of the purpose of missionary education which saw it as leavening, like yeast, the entire life of each nation with Christian beliefs and values. In tension with such a view was a more church-centred approach that put the priority on the formation of leadership for the emerging indigenous churches. The Report also acknowledged the directly evangelistic role of education which was emphasised by many of the missionary correspondents. There were therefore three purposes to the educational programmes run by Christian missions. These could be seen as mutually complementary but presented a dilemma when it came to the question of where priorities should lie.

The Commission was given a strong steer by the Conference organising committee when their remit was termed: 'Education in Relation to the Christianisation of National Life'. This might suggest a primary orientation to the leavening purpose of education: '... through it the life of the nation is gradually permeated with the principles of truth.'[4] The Commission, however, took a quite different line when it came to the question of priorities:

> It seems to us necessary, as a matter of general principle, to give a quite distinct priority to the first two functions, and, in countries in which a Christian community has already been brought into existence, to give the first place to the building up of the native Church. We wish to lay it down that we believe that the primary purpose to be served by the educational work of missionaries is that of training the native Church to bear its own proper witness. And inasmuch as the only way in which the native Church can bear its own proper witness, and move forward towards the position of independence and self-government in which it ought to stand, is through native leaders, teachers and officers, we believe that the most important of all ends which missionary education ought to set itself to serve, is that of training those who are to be the spiritual leaders and teachers of their own nation.[5]

As Brian Stanley observes: '... the report which the Commission produced on the basis of [over two hundred questionnaire] replies ultimately placed its most pronounced emphasis on a definition of the

---

[4] *Education in Relation to the Christianisation of National Life*, 369-70.
[5] *Education in Relation to the Christianisation of National Life*, 371-72.

function of Christian education which was noticeably more church-centric than the title of the Commission implied.'[6] In ultimately placing priority on the formation of leadership for the emerging indigenous churches of Asia and Africa, the Commission's conclusions were not uncontested. The veteran Scottish educational missionary William Miller, Principal of Madras Christian College from 1877 to 1907, was unable to attend the Conference on account of old age and infirmity but he circulated a paper which robustly defended the diffusionist strategy which had marked the contribution of Scottish colleges of higher education in India since their beginnings under the influence of Alexander Duff from the 1830s.[7] Miller had been one of the respondents to the Commission's questionnaire and had taken the opportunity to affirm that, '... the great central purpose of mission education is to influence the general life and thought of the community, and thereby to lay a greatly needed foundation for all forms of Christian work.'[8] Now, against the conclusions of the Commission III Report, he offered a robust defence of the diffusionist ideal of education as a Christian leaven in society at large. While Commission Chairman Charles Gore accorded great respect to the argument advanced by Miller, he made it clear that it was not one which the Commission could accept. The education and formation of leaders for the emerging indigenous churches took priority, in the estimation of the Commission, over the diffusion of Christian values and principles throughout wider society.

Indigenising the Faith

In introducing the subject of the Report, the Commission indicated a number of concerns that reveal how important the question of the indigenisation of the Christian faith was. First, it expressed concern that, 'There has been a tendency, especially in certain lands and districts, to denationalise converts, that is, to alienate them from the life and sympathies of their fellow-countrymen, so as to make it possible to suggest that Christianity is a foreign influence, tending to alienate its converts from the national life.' [9] Secondly, it observed that, 'There has been an astonishing awakening of national consciousness among the peoples of all the regions we are specially considering.'[10] Thirdly, it offered the conviction that, 'If

---

[6] Brian Stanley, *The World Missionary Conference, Edinburgh 1910* (Grand Rapids, MI: Eerdmans, 2009), 167.
[7]"Extracts from Pamphlet by Dr Miller of Madras, circulated among delegates attending the Conference", *Education in Relation to the Christianisation of National Life*, 441-46.
[8] Commission III Replies, Vol. 2, 20, cit. Stanley, *The World Missionary Conference*, 190.
[9] *Education in Relation to the Christianisation of National Life*, 6-8.
[10] *Education in Relation to the Christianisation of National Life*, 6-8.

the native Churches are to become independent, self-governing Churches, it is a matter of chief importance that leaders should be provided and trained.'[11] These introductory remarks provided a clue as to where the main burden of the Report would lie.

The vision of the Commission finds its most compressed and eloquent expression in the conclusion of its Report:

> A universal religion, a catholic religion, needs a common message such as is contained in the Apostles' Creed, and as is recorded in the Bible, but a common message comprehended by very different and various peoples and individuals, each with very different gifts, so that each in receiving the one message, brings out some different or special aspect of the universal truth or character which lies in the common religion. So it is, and only so, that the glory and honour of all nations are brought within the light and circle of the Holy City; so it is alone that the real breadth and catholicity of life is brought out.
>
> We look around, we see the profound and wonderful qualities of the Indian, and the Chinese, and the Japanese and the Africans, and we are sure that when the whole witness of Christianity is borne, when Christ is fulfilled in all men, each of these races and nations must have brought out into the world a Christianity with its own indigenous colour and character, and that the rising up of any really national Church will be to us, who remain, who were there before, life from the dead. We regard this question as central. We start from this. Are we by means of education, training truly national Churches to stand each on its own basis, and bring out that aspect of Christian truth and grace which it is the special province of each separate race to bring out?[12]

In this way, the Commission anticipated the concerns about indigenisation, inculturation and contextualisation which would preoccupy Christian communities, theologians and educators in the century to come. Though the thinking of Edinburgh 1910 was informed by essentialist and hierarchical theories of race which are discredited today,[13] nonetheless it was a significant advance to recognise that mission was *not* simply a matter of disseminating in new cultural contexts the form of Christian faith which had found expression in the western world. It was rather a matter of the common core of the faith being received and professed in the terms of many different cultures and contexts worldwide.

This involved, in the first instance, a critique of the western missionary movement:

> Though the original home of Christianity is, as it were, the half-way house between East and West, the modern missionaries have represented strongly defined or intensely western forms of Christianity. There has thus been a gulf, very difficult to bridge, between the whole mental equipment of the modern – especially the Anglo-Saxon – missionary and the people of the East. And on the whole it must be said that, though there have been among the missionaries

---

[11] *Education in Relation to the Christianisation of National Life*, 6-8.
[12] *Education in Relation to the Christianisation of National Life*, 406-407.
[13] See Stanley, *The World Missionary Conference*, 248-73.

men of great genius, as well as great zeal, yet singularly little attention was paid by the pioneers, and even until today, on the whole, singularly little attention has been paid to presenting Christianity in the form best suited to the Oriental spirit.[14]

The reference to the Orient reveals how much the thinking of the Conference was shaped by the experience of the missionary enterprise in Asia. It was here that the greatest potential for the advance of Christian faith was thought to lie. Though missions in Africa were also well represented at the Conference, there was little expectation that African churches would have much contribution to make in the foreseeable future. Nonetheless, the philosophy of mission advocated by Commission III called for application in every context: 'The aim of Christian missionaries should be not to transplant to the country in which they labour that form or type of Christianity which is prevalent in the lands from which they have come, but to lodge in the hearts of the people the fundamental truths of Christianity, in the confidence that these are fitted for all nations and classes, and will bear their own appropriate and beneficent fruits in a type of Christian life and institution consonant with the genius of each of the several nations.'[15]

It was principally the Commission Chairman Charles Gore who brought this powerful vision to its work, and it was he who took the opportunity to express it at the Conference itself. As a leading exponent of Anglo-Catholicism, Gore had become convinced that catholicity was not a matter of uniformity in every aspect of life and conduct. The universality of Christian faith was to be found, rather, in a shared adherence to the substance of the faith, as expressed in a statement such as the Apostles' Creed, which allowed for the faith to be appropriated and expressed in a great variety of ways according to the distinctive genius of each people and nation. Gore's address to the Conference '… makes it plain that his commitment to the encouragement of autonomous non-western churches was unambiguous: genuine catholicity required both clear agreement on essentials and a diversity of forms of appropriation of the gospel.'[16]

This comprehensive vision of the catholicity of the faith finding expression in manifold diversity of forms guided the thinking of the Commission in regard to its understanding of education. On the crucial question of prioritisation within the educational effort of Christian missions, the Commission was guided by its understanding of the indigenisation of the faith:

> We are convinced that, though foreign evangelists should study to present Christianity in the form best suited to its appropriation by orientals, yet the work of 'acclimatising' will be done in the main by native teachers; and from

---

[14] *Education in Relation to the Christianisation of National Life*, 245.
[15] *Education in Relation to the Christianisation of National Life*, 264.
[16] Stanley, *The World Missionary Conference*, 196, citing G.L. Prestige, *The Life of Charles Gore: A Great Englishman* (London: Heinemann, 1935), 312.

this point of view we desire to urge not only, as we have already done in other connections, that the training of native pastors and teachers is the pre-eminently important work of Christian missions, but also that profound study and attention should be given to the point of how they are to be trained, so that their training may not tend to denationalise them or to occupy their minds with distinctively western elements and controversies of religion.[17]

Such a pedagogical principle remains challenging one hundred years later as churches in many contexts worldwide struggle to overcome the sense that Christianity, even when it is highly valued, appears to be a faith that is foreign to the local culture and context.

One point at which the principle required to be put into practical effect was in regard to the question of language. A perennial dilemma in missionary education had been the relative merits of vernacular language and an international language such as English as medium of instruction. On this question the Commission took a bold stance:

> In particular, we desire to lay the greatest emphasis on the importance of giving religious teaching, not only of the elementary kind, but as far as possible throughout, in the vernacular. We feel certain that those of our witnesses are right who believe that religion can only really be acclimatised in the heart of the natives of any country if it finds expression in their native language – the language of their homes. And we feel sure that a theology, which is really indigenous as well as properly Christian and Biblical, must develop a native terminology, an end which is only likely to be attained where the vernacular is used for the expression of religious ideas. Again, we are sure that the greatest pains must be taken as far as possible to use all that is available in the literature of the nation to provide preparation for a distinctively Christian learning and literature, and it must never be left out of sight that an indigenous Christian Church means a native Christian literature by competent native writers. We cannot conceal from ourselves that a quite fresh effort seems to be required in this, the primary task of the evangelist, namely, the raising up of properly equipped and instructed native Churches and of native leaders who shall have no temptation to feel that they are alienated from the life and aspiration of their nation in becoming Christians.[18]

Here the Commission anticipated the work of theologians such as Lamin Sanneh and Kwame Bediako who many years later demonstrated the importance of the vernacular in the inculturation of the faith.[19] Their work exemplifies the fulfilment of the dream of Commission III and is perhaps a vindication of its insistence on the priority of training indigenous leaders, teachers and writers.

---

[17] *Education in Relation to the Christianisation of National Life*, 265-66.
[18] *Education in Relation to the Christianisation of National Life*, 373.
[19] Lamin Sanneh, *Translating the Message: The Missionary Impact on Culture* (Maryknoll, NY: Orbis Books, 1989); Kwame Bediako, *Christianity in Africa: The Renewal of a Non-Western Religion* (Edinburgh: Edinburgh University Press, and Maryknoll, NY: Orbis Books, 1995).

Lest the Commission might be thought to be concentrating exclusively on the ordained ministry, they were at pains to emphasise equally the importance of education for the laity: 'But while thus emphasising the importance of the education of those who are to be leaders of the Christian community, especially as preachers and teachers, we would lay great stress also upon the necessity of providing for the laity an education which shall at the same time equip them for positions of usefulness and influence in the community, and secure the development of strong Christian manhood and womanhood. Only as the Christian community contains a goodly proportion of men and women, trained to support themselves and serve the public good, can it exert its due influence on the life of the community at large.'[20] This illustrates what Brian Stanley has described as the '... close relationship in the mind of the Commission between the twin goals of raising up Christian leaders who were not exotic to their own cultures and the diffusion of Christian moral principles throughout society.'[21] The stand-off between Charles Gore and William Miller might suggest that these goals were contradictory or mutually exclusive. In fact, the Commission was eager to accommodate both and saw them as interlocking objectives, though it was through a primary emphasis on the formation of leaders for the emerging indigenous churches that the diffusion of Christianity throughout society was thought most likely to be achieved.

The Commission also placed important emphasis on the education of women: 'There can be no question at all that the education of women is, in every grade, quite as important as the education of men, and that educational training is quite as important in the case of women teachers as in the case of men.'[22] Though the Commission was by no means immune to the sexist stereotyping which prevailed in 1910, nonetheless their determination to promote the education of women would represent a radical move in many contexts. Of this they were aware but still determined to press their point: 'Indeed, in view of the fact that character is largely determined in the early years and by the influence of the mother in the home, the education of women acquires a place of first importance. While higher education may be less necessary in the case of women than of men, and while care should be taken not to offend unnecessarily traditional feeling respecting the place of women in society, yet in all plans for Christian education, women ought to receive equal consideration with men, and equal care should be exercised that the education provided for them is adapted to their needs.'[23] Despite the elements of caution and conservatism evident in the Commission's thinking, as M.P. Joseph points out: 'Missionary efforts to educate Dalits, women, tribal people and other

---

[20] *Education in Relation to the Christianisation of National Life*, 374-75.
[21] Stanley, The World Missionary Conference, 187.
[22] *Education in Relation to the Christianisation of National Life*, 377.
[23] *Education in Relation to the Christianisation of National Life*, 377.

marginalised communities demonstrated its potential to initiate a social revolution.'[24]

The Preparation of Missionaries

Whereas Commission III considered missionary education in broad perspective, Commission V had the more specific remit to examine the formation of the missionaries themselves. It brought to the Conference the conviction that the quality of the missionary was the decisive factor in the achievement of world evangelisation. As Douglas Mackenzie expressed it in his address to the Conference: 'The whole matter on the human side of it hinges on the quality of the missionary... The quality of the missionary will triumph over the absence of money. The quality of the missionary therefore becomes a supreme question for this Conference.'[25]

Like the other Commissions, they based their work on an extensive survey of the training and preparation which missionary societies offered to their candidates. This revealed that high ideals were rarely realised in practice:

> It is clear that the Mission Boards of America, the continent of Europe, and Great Britain, are, as a whole, aiming at a high standard of all-round missionary qualification in their candidates, and are, in some respects and to a considerable degree, attaining it. But in view of the admitted inability of the Societies to satisfy their own requirements, and the widespread opinion among missionaries that because of the modern situation abroad higher qualifications are needed, it is urgent that the richer resources of the Church should be more largely drawn upon for the best of her men and women, and that available material should be dealt with by methods related to the best thought of the Church at home, and the current needs of the Church abroad.[26]

In an attempt to determine from first principles the requirements of missionary training, the Commission sought to identify the primary functions of a missionary:

> (1) The Presentation of the Christian Message. Direct evangelisation is of course the most obvious form of missionary work. It is the first necessity. Whatever the means, whether by open preaching or by personal intercourse, the making of converts is its immediate and simple aim.

> (2) The Manifestation of the Christian Life. Christ, however, was more than a Teacher, and His messengers must do their best to manifest the power hidden in the Christian life. This comes out both in the personality and life of the evangelist, and in every variety of medical, educational and industrial work.

---

[24] M.P. Joseph, 'Missionary Education: An Ambiguous Legacy', in Kerr and Ross (eds), *Edinburgh 2010*, 105-18, at 106.

[25] World Missionary Conference, 1910, *Report of Commission V: The Preparation of Missionaries* (Edinburgh and London: Oliphant, Anderson & Ferrier; New York, Chicago and Toronto: Fleming H. Revell, 1910), 300.

[26] *The Preparation of Missionaries*, 25.

(3) The Organisation of a Christian Church and Nation. A living and effective Church in a Christian nation is the end of missionary work. To prepare the way for this on the ecclesiastical side requires theological colleges for native clergy; supervision and organisation of the native ministry; provision of a theological literature.[27]

These three primary functions suggested the main component parts of a missionary formation:

(1) The efficient preaching of the Gospel rests upon: (a) a real grasp of the message to be delivered, and a personal experience of its power; (b) an understanding of the needs and perplexities of human life in general, and in particular of the modes of thought of those to whom the message is to be delivered; (c) the ability to show how the message meets these needs.

(2) The manifestation of the Christian life by teachers, doctors, nurses, and industrial workers, requires ability in some profession not in itself 'theological' or missionary, but it cannot dispense with a fair measure of acquaintance with theology and with the fundamental implications of that Faith which as Christian missionaries they are sent out to propagate.

(3) The work of leading and organising will for the most part be done by men who have revealed or developed these powers in the mission field. Occasionally men may offer whose gifts seem from the first to mark them out for such work, but there are dangers in a too-confident anticipation. Men of exceptional ability and learning often fail curiously in a field where everything is new to them. The very fullness of a man's attainment may make docility and humility more difficult, and yet it is upon these childlike qualities more than on outstanding ability that true success in leadership depends.[28]

Missionary training, for all types of missionaries, should integrate spiritual, moral and intellectual elements. As regards the spiritual dimension, the Commission Report acknowledges that formal training has its limitations. At the heart of missionary service are the 'ways in which God rather than self becomes the actual centre of life. For that very reason they are purely the gift of God. No act of the self can win them, and it follows that no training can give them, though it may remove some obstacles in the way of their development.'[29] There are, however, 'special considerations which have to be taken into account in the spiritual training of a missionary. He has to be ready in case of necessity to face the tremendous spiritual dangers of isolation among heathen surroundings. He must know how to face great strain and heavy responsibility without the support of visible Christian fellowship, and to maintain a high level of spiritual life without the continual renewing which is supplied under normal conditions by the ordinances of common worship.'[30]

---

[27] *The Preparation of Missionaries*, 97-98.
[28] *The Preparation of Missionaries*, 99.
[29] *The Preparation of Missionaries*, 100.
[30] *The Preparation of Missionaries*, 100.

Moral training should cultivate four qualities: 'docility' in the sense of always being open and willing to learn; 'gentleness' or the 'spirit of courtesy' that enables missionaries to understand the customs of the people among whom they are called to live; and 'sympathy' that empowers missionaries to love the people they serve. These combine to produce a fourth quality that all missionaries should seek to attain: 'leadership' in respect of 'the special duties and responsibilities of a missionary's position.'[31] These qualities were considered in a self-critical perspective: 'The question of manner presents peculiar difficulties. The white man so instinctively feels that he is the lord of creation, that it is hard for him, no matter how Christian he may be, to get over the idea that men of a different colour are his inferiors. He is apt to be brusque and peremptory. He is always in a hurry and impatient of delays. His very kindness is apt to have an element of condescension, of which he may not be conscious but which the native is quick to detect.'[32] The Commission made the simple point that: 'A missionary is powerless to help a people whom he cannot love. All preparation, therefore, which has for its aim the development of a power of mutual understanding between ourselves and all with whom we come in contact, the quickening of our perception of the good points in our neighbours and associates which comes from the determination to look always for the Christ in every man, is directly missionary preparation.'[33]

The Commission also aimed high when it came to the question of intellectual training: 'The missionary must have the best education which his own country and Church can give him, whatever is to be his department of labour. If he is to be a preacher, theological teacher, or an educationalist, he must go through the task of technical equipment for these offices. If he is to be a medical man, he must have the full training and professional qualifications which are necessary to his standing as a physician in his own country.' [34] The Commission also advocated that missionaries should undergo such intellectual formation as would render them people of wide culture: 'It is becoming clear that this thoroughness of intellectual discipline is necessary, not merely on professional grounds, but because the mind which has been profoundly trained in any one direction, especially for a great profession involving varied culture, is most capable of self-adaptation to changing circumstances and to new calls upon its energy.'[35] With this in view, the Commission argued that, as a rule, missionaries should first complete undergraduate studies in the arts or sciences before going on to postgraduate theological studies alongside those preparing for ministry in the church at home.

---

[31] *The Preparation of Missionaries,* 101-105.
[32] *The Preparation of Missionaries,* 103.
[33] *The Preparation of Missionaries,* 104.
[34] *The Preparation of Missionaries,* 107-108.
[35] *The Preparation of Missionaries,* 107-108.

Like the Conference as a whole, the Commission was deeply impressed by the fact that the financial and human resources urgently needed on the mission field were available within 'the home church'. It sought to make the case that these resources needed to be mobilised for world mission as never before. Another recurrent theme was the observation that the level of co-operation which was being achieved on the mission field was often eluding missionary societies in their home countries. Missionary training was seen as an area which cried out for a higher degree of co-operation. The ideal was a Central College, or Colleges, where missionary societies could co-operate in providing a curriculum including the sciences, history and methods of mission, comparative religion, social sciences, pedagogy and linguistics. Yale School of Divinity and Hartford Seminary in the USA were already moving in this direction, as were German and Scandinavian colleges. To address the situation in Britain, the Commission recommended the creation of a Board of Missionary Studies, 'the general purpose of which will be to supply guidance and to render assistance to Missionary Societies in the preparation of missionaries for their work.'[36]

The Commission is notable for the attention it paid to the training of women missionaries. Their role was understood to extend far beyond 'women's work for women' towards the fulfilment of a vision of women building up the entire fabric of national life. In terms of training inspired by this wide-ranging vision, the example cited was the Women's Missionary College in Edinburgh whose Principal, Annie Small, was one of the four women Commissioners. An Appendix to the Report describes the philosophy of the College.[37]

Conclusion

Like the Conference as a whole, the educational vision of Edinburgh 1910 was a child of its time. Its hopes of great institutions being developed at home and abroad to further the education and formation dimensions of Christian mission reflected the prevailing imperial age. As it turned out, it would be at the margins rather than at the centre, among the poor rather than among the rich, that Christian education and formation would take wing in the century that followed. From the distance of 100 years, the flaws of Edinburgh 1910 are all too apparent. Yet its prescience and prophetic qualities also come into view. Its passion for forms of education which would serve the emergence of truly indigenous forms of Christianity proved to have great resonance throughout the 20th century. Theologically, the Conference anticipated the concentration on such themes as inculturation and contextualisation that would be key to maturity for the 'younger churches'. Its insistence that such a process of indigenisation

---

[36] *The Preparation of Missionaries*, 189.
[37] *The Preparation of Missionaries*, 250-52.

would necessarily be led by indigenous leaders and its consequent prioritisation of the formation of such leaders proved to be of far-reaching significance. At the start of the 21st century, the urgent need for high-quality leadership is as great as ever and Edinburgh 1910 still offers important clues as to what it takes to form it.

BROADER IMPLICATIONS OF THE MISSIO DEI

J. Nelson Jennings

Preparing missionaries for service assumes God's involvement, beginning with leading Christians into mission service. To be sure, instructors and trainers prepare potential missionaries using institutions, resources and methods. Even so, if God is not somehow involved in shaping mission servants, the most polished and carefully refined methods of preparation ultimately will prove inadequate.

Building on the assumption of God's involvement in missionary preparation, the *missio Dei* compels adding that God's initiative, oversight and involvement in missionary preparation are not confined to those specific individuals commonly called 'missionaries' (or similar designations). In addition, the twentieth-century worldwide demographic shift of sizeable Christian presence from Europe and North America to Africa and elsewhere should check an instinctive notion that the preparation of Christians for mission is restricted to Caucasians. In fact, God's mission includes all of God's people worldwide, that is, the entirety of the Christian church. Hence all people everywhere identified with Jesus Christ are called to participate in God's mission, and divine superintendence of that mission includes equipping all Christians for service – as laity or clergy, as missionaries or otherwise, and regardless of ethnic or national identity.

Related to this is that all theological education, whether for laity or clergy, is to be 'missional' or somehow focused on participation in the *missio Dei*. An approach born in Christian Europe that understands theology as a static and privileged 'Queen of the Sciences' must be revamped into a method that is more dynamic and plays a servant role towards equipping Jesus' followers for participating in God's mission in all of life and wherever life is lived. Stated comprehensively, God calls all Christians into the *missio Dei*, and all training, education and equipping for divine service is to focus inherently on *mission* service.

Having thus broadened categories from training 'missionaries' per se to equipping all Christians around the world for mission service, the *missio Dei* compels even yet more broadening of the scope of divine initiative, oversight and involvement in mission preparation. As increasing numbers of mid-twentieth-century church leaders came to realise that the Trinitarian *missio Dei*, even China and North Korea turning Communist and the resulting cessation there of foreign missionary activity, painful as those realities were, could somehow be seen to be part of God's activity throughout the world.[1] If that were the case, then certainly God was also involved – somehow – with all people throughout the earth, quite apart from any encounter they may have had with Christians or the church. The extent and type of such divine involvement with human beings has led to all sorts of discussions about the nature, salvifically and otherwise, of extra-ecclesiastical divine-human relations.[2] With specific reference to evil exhibited and suffering experienced in wars and genocides, as well as in natural disasters, theodicy seeks to vindicate God's ultimate governance over such a universe while human beings' existential trauma cries out for relief.[3] Whatever the precise characterisation might be about how God relates to people apart from explicitly Christian connections, the *missio Dei* compels a broad reach of understanding divine initiative, oversight and involvement in people's preparation for Christian mission, including (as will be explored further below) for people who have not yet embraced or even heard the Christian message.

Christian Heritage

Speaking from an instructor's point of view, divine involvement in the life or lives of the Christian(s) that one is seeking to equip for mission service did not commence when the trainee entered one's own field of instructional influence. God did not begin to shape a student when she took her first

---

[1] Several papers prepared for the July 1952 International Missionary Council meeting at Willingen particularly addressed the situation in China. The British Baptist missionary Victor E.W. Hayward, in his 'The End of a Missionary Era in China: Reflections on Lessons to Be Learned', analysed that 'In Communism we can indeed see God's judgment upon our Western civilisation' (Yale Divinity School Library Special Collections, 'I.M.C. Committees: Willingen, July 5-21, 1952', 264.009, Fiche 10), 21. US-American missionary to China, Charles C. West, in his 'China and the World Mission of the Church: The Lessons of a Failure', asserted that 'God did not fail in China... He is in Christ reconciling *the world* unto Himself... In Christ He has overcome the world, including all the powers therein' (YDS Special Collections, 264.011, Fiche 5), 7 (emphasis original).

[2] As R.K. Orchard noted in an August 1952, 'personal impression' written for his London Missionary Society colleagues about the July I.M.C. meeting, 'Willingen reflected our bafflements as well as our certainties' (YDS Special Collections, 264.011, Fiche 5), 5. Years later, one analyst pointed to 'the old Anglo-Saxon versus Continental disagreement concerning the doctrine of the Church, eschatology and "Heilsgeschichte" [that] continued at Willingen', in Tomas Shivute, *The Theology of Mission and Evangelism in the International Missionary Council from Edinburgh to New Delhi* (Helsinki: Missiologian ja Ekumeniikan Seura R.Y.; Suomen Lähetysseura, 1980), 131.

[3] J. Nelson Jennings, 'Hostility against Mission' (editorial in *International Bulletin of Missionary Research* 39, No. 2 (2015), 57-58: www.internationalbulletin.org/issues/2015-02/2015-02-057-jennings.html).

class session in a particular course offering. Nor did divine involvement begin with her matriculation into the school where one is teaching. Nor was the beginning of missionary training simultaneous with that individual's initial encounter with the Christian Gospel – whether through an individual Christian's witness or via an upbringing in a Christian family and congregation. The *missio Dei* pushes God's initiative, oversight and involvement in an individual's missionary preparation much further back in time – across generations, in fact – and in a much more multidimensional direction as well, including all aspects of a person's heritage.

The same is true about the backgrounds of individual Christians in settings other than theological institutions, be they local parishes, Christian villages, missionary orders or agencies into which new candidates have been accepted. In all these cases and others, a Christian's mission training has been divinely orchestrated for years and even generations earlier, as well as through all aspects of a person's background including ethnicity, language, socio-economic circumstances, learning preference (e.g. oral or textual), religion, etc. No Christian enters a teacher's field of instructional influence with a *tabula rasa*: a trainee's life and multifaceted heritage has always developed under divine superintendence. To state the matter in a more robust fashion, the life and heritage on display before one who is equipping that Christian for mission service have for generations been shaped, trained and equipped within the scope of the *missio Dei*. The instructor is now privileged to join in that ongoing training process.

An urgent segue is needed here with respect to both the mission equipper and the equipper's setting, be it a theological institution, local parish, mission agency or something else. Just as God's shaping of a missionary-in-training started much earlier than that Christian's appearance within one's particular sphere of influence, so did God's missional initiative in the instructor's life and setting begin long before the present training moment. Also, at least as complex as previous divine preparation of a missionary-in-training will have been the previous shaping of a mentor and training context. All sorts of factors have been divinely orchestrated to make the pastor/priest, professor, mission agency personnel trainer, or other category of equipper the particular individual that person is at the moment of instruction. Similarly, a plethora of factors will have been divinely orchestrated to shape the instructional setting into its present character. On top of that complexity, arriving at an adequate self-understanding of one's own heritage, as well as of the background of one's own training context, is never self-evident and is often an extremely difficult process. Indeed, particularly when there has been a lack of significant exposure to other contexts, learning to engage people of other cultures needs to be 'as much about discovering ourselves and understanding the cultures of which we're a part as it is about understanding others'.[4]

According to the *missio Dei*, the locus of God's people being equipped for mission service is not confined to the immediate setting. Noting that breadth of mission training should not diminish the importance of intentional equipping programmes, neither should it lessen the responsibility for giving proper care as to how training takes place. Rather, there is an additional challenge, both for trainers and trainees, to appreciate – as well as to understand through careful study – the wide scope of how God has prepared the present educational moment. Individualised research projects, institutional studies (including those designed for churches, mission agencies and other organisations), historical studies and other means, are vital for coming to understand how God has been at work through the avenues leading into the present training situation.

Divine initiative, oversight and involvement in Christians' preparation for mission include the complex heritages – including even the oppressive suffering and injustice caused by sinful rebellion and satanic initiatives – that have shaped the total settings within which the present mission training processes take place.

Non-Christian Heritage

In a fashion similar to how Christian heritage falls within the scope of the *missio Dei* in preparation for mission service, all people's mission preparations, whether individually or collectively, begin far earlier than their first encounter with Christianity. All people's mission training has been divinely orchestrated for years and even generations prior to their initial encounter with the Christian Gospel, through all aspects of their background. The Christian mission servant is now privileged to join in that ongoing training process, whether by initial announcement of God's good news of Jesus Christ or continued Christian instruction and modelling about following and serving the Crucified and Risen Christ.

Pointing out this reality of God's involvement with people prior to any Christian contact they have had is important for mission servants being able to focus on the full scope of the *missio Dei*. If training for mission has been restricted to what might be called Christian arenas (e.g. prayer and other practices, ministry strategies), then how God has been at work shaping and training people outside those arenas might be missed. Put more specifically, mission equipping – particularly the type of equipping that has neglected the heritages of trainees, trainers and training settings, as discussed earlier – can focus only on mission spirituality, biblical and theological content,

---

[4] David A. Livermore, *Cultural Intelligence: Improving your CQ to Engage our Multicultural World* (Youth, Family, and Cultures Series), Chap Clark (ed) (Grand Rapids, MI: Baker Academic, 2009), 13.

Christian organisational development, and communication processes in such a way that restricts mission servants' fields of attention to intra-Christian arenas. Such restrictions can blind mission servants from seeing both how the wider Kingdom of God is growing as well as the needs, hopes and growth processes of the very people whom Christians are seeking to serve.

It helps to remind ourselves at this point that the point of departure of this chapter is the *missio Dei*, the triune God's commitment to make the world right again. God is the initiator, manager and sustaining power of that macro project. As such, God deals with all the people involved, and all people fundamentally respond to God's dealings in a more basic way than we human beings respond to anyone else or any other created being, object or circumstance.

To expand on certain emphases articulated earlier, one instinctive and common approach to describing how Christians are equipped for mission would be to focus on how schools and mission organisations train missionaries. An ecumenically informed version of that approach would present and analyse missionary-training programmes of various Christian traditions, including Orthodox, Catholic, Protestant, Pentecostal and Independent. An up-to-date version would include schools and organisations based all over the world, not just where western modernity arose and facilitated the worldwide migration of European peoples.

That approach of focusing on Christian initiatives taken to educate and otherwise train missionaries would be fine, as far as it goes. However, such an approach could easily miss, or at least under-emphasise, crucial theological and missiological aspects of essential elements of theological education and Christian mission – at least, in the broad senses of those phrases demanded by the full scope of the *missio Dei*. In particular, the central roles within the drama of Christian mission played by the triune God and by the recipients of Christian mission could be overlooked if inordinate attention were paid to the supporting, servant roles played by Christian schools and mission organisations. If Christian mission is concerned with God's reconciliation of the world – and it is – then the *missio Dei* and the world's reception of the good news of Jesus Christ are central to any consideration of mission, including the relevant interface of theological education.

Thus, a *missio Dei* approach to the intricate and nuanced topic of 'Reflecting on and Equipping for Christian Mission' will self-consciously seek to keep the brightest spotlight on the divine initiative – even when the *missio Dei* per se is not the explicit, on-stage focus of one's attention. Moreover, spotlights will shine on how the Christian Gospel is received by people who do not yet believe in Jesus Christ. Human beings' contexts in all their complexities will thus necessarily receive significant attention. Indeed, the notion of 'theological education' will have enough elasticity to incorporate God's instruction or education of people who do not self-identify as 'Christian'. Such a wider notion of theological education both rings true with how God interacts with all people as well as keeps Christians attuned to the wider stage of God's mission drama. How mission servants are formed by Christian schools, local parishes and mission organisations thus needs to pay significant attention to those among whom mission is to be carried out.

Knowing the People Served

It is thus requisite for mission servants to know the people to be served. That is, trainers of mission servants, as well as those being shaped for service, must consciously focus on learning about those individuals and groups on whose behalf Gospel ministry will be conducted. To state the matter differently, equipping for mission is best focused not just on the servants being equipped but on the people among whom God will be shaping and using mission servants.

There are caution points, however, associated with such mission preparation that focuses on the recipients of mission and not just on the missionary. Perhaps the most potentially damaging caution is that of objectifying 'the other' people among whom mission service is to be carried out. This is especially true when those among whom mission service is to take place are not immediately accessible during training due to distance, language difference or other barriers. Knowing any individual or groups must involve personal relationship; merely 'studying' others, e.g. through reading printed or increasingly available electronic material, is inadequate and potentially harmful.

Even so, efforts must be made during equipping for mission service to focus attention on those among whom service is to be rendered. Within a theological institution, for example, instructors are to direct students to information about the particular people among whom the students are anticipated to be ministering. Hence a seminary in Seoul where students are being trained to serve in a part of Mindanao, southern Philippines, should direct those students to publications or other reports that inform the servants-in-training about the history, languages and other characteristics of those people in that part of Mindanao. Guatemalans training to serve among Algerians should similarly be directed to information about those Algerians where mission service will take place.

Accompanying that attention on information about the mission recipients should be a theological-missiological stress on developing a capacity and even inclination to see divine initiatives, as well as the effects of destructive forces that have been at work, among those to be served. On a personal-existential level, trainees need cultivation in contemplative practices and spiritual discernment. As asserted earlier, the human beings on display before a mission servant are divinely created, divinely superintended, divinely loved and divinely pursued people who have also been harassed and harmed by the evil one. How God has been caring for 'the other' must be discerned, appreciated and humbly joined by anyone seeking to communicate and cultivate the good news of Jesus Christ among people. Without a bent – combined with a contemplative spiritual discernment – towards learning how God has already been at work among others, information about people that has been previously acquired, and is then carried into actually coming to know them, runs the risk of buttressing preconceived notions and frameworks that can actually prevent genuine understanding of divine activity among the others. Acquired information about others should facilitate further understanding of them and how God has been at work in redeeming them from the ravages of sin and evil, and not creating encrusted stereotypes that have been formed more in connection with the missionary's background and context than in relationship with the actual people being served.

Equipping mission servants thus anticipates and prepares for actually coming to know people and divine work among them. Again, such preparation both provides information about those people and shapes missionaries to discern divine presence and activity. The former aspect of informing servants is more easily managed, measured and provided. Accessing books, websites and instructors familiar with people to be served takes time, effort and knowledge of accessibility channels for trainer and student alike – but those processes can be managed. More difficult to direct is the existential shaping of mission servants to discern and understand God's work and presence among other people.

Understanding the *missio Dei*

The mid-twentieth-century realisation among many Christian leaders of God's wider, extra-ecclesiastical work among people involved both theological articulation of the *missio Dei* and existential awakening to how God was at work in the world. In particular, the military and political ascendancy of Communist rule in China, accompanied by the expulsion of foreign (European and Caucasian-American) missionaries, was both intellectually inexplicable – How could the crown jewel of generations of mission efforts be stolen away? – and an unprecedented, offensive defeat of western Christianity's assumed, inexorable mission sweep over the earth. A half-century earlier, Japan's 1905 victory in its war of attrition with Russia had signalled that western advances were not in fact unstoppable. Even so, that wake-up call did not shatter the dream of a world soon full of westernised, enlightened Christian nations. However, China's turn towards Communism in the wake of Mao's 1949 takeover came both on the heels of two bloodbaths among European Christian nations and as those nations' empires were beginning to unravel. The Christianised world that western churchmen and mission leaders had assumed would unfold was instead, drastically and shockingly, turning in different directions.

As oft-analysed elsewhere,[5] the theological framework that emerged was the now-familiar *missio Dei*, namely that God was accomplishing his mission throughout the world, including through extra-ecclesiastical socio-economic-political events. God was no longer subconsciously assumed to be just the religious Creator and Redeemer who dwelt within the western, Christian church, distantly orchestrating the cosmos according to divine providence. God was now understood by many church and mission leaders to be engaged actively with the entire world, reigning 'in every moment and every situation'.[6]

That expanded framework broke through the intellectual and emotional conundrum created in the mid-twentieth century by the unrealised, and clearly unachievable, vision of a Christian earth. Subsequently it has opened up avenues for seeing divine action among people among whom mission servants intend to serve. Developing such vision is central to equipping mission servants.

One basic mindset to be instilled in servants entering a new setting is that God has not just *sent* them to people there, but that God has also – and in a sense more fundamentally – *brought* them there.[7] This mindset is vital whether or not geography is traversed. On the one hand, entering people's lives with the belief, assurance and even the conviction that divine calling has thrust one *out* from home into another setting locates God's residence back home; and, it keeps divine presence among the missionised tethered to the mission servant's presence: God arrives when the mission servant arrives. It is as though an authority has dispatched an emissary to people and territory living under an unknown and foreign ruler, alien to the emissary's home context and governing authority. The foreigners simply need to hear and believe the emissary's message from the dispatching authority, which in a Christian mission sense means obediently believing the alien good news about a previously unfamiliar God having done something special in an unfamiliar place and time that is nevertheless relevant to the hearers.

By contrast, a mission servant needs to be equipped with the understanding that God has not been brought to people by the emissary, but instead that God has long been present and active among the people among whom service is to take place, and has brought the mission servant there to participate in his ongoing divine work. Such an understanding will require

---

[5] For example, Shivute, 1980, 111-51, and Wilhelm Anderson, *Towards a Theology of Mission. A Study of the Encounter between the Missionary Enterprise and the Church and Its Theology*, IMC research Pamphlet No. 2 (London: SCM, 1955).

[6] Norman Goodall (ed), *Missions Under the Cross: Addresses Delivered at the Enlarged Meeting of the Committee of the International Missionary Council at Willingen, in Germany, 1952; with Statements Issued by the Meeting* (London: Edinburgh House Press, 1953), 190.

[7] Kwame Bediako, *Christianity in Africa: The Renewal of a Non-Western Religion* (Maryknoll, NY: Orbis Books, 1995), 118, 226.

the mission servant to have developed the sensitivity to discern that divine work. Training servants to that end will include instruction of content, for example, about God's cosmic intention for redeeming all of creation and peoples therein. Another area of content will be about peoples and societies, including their histories and contemporary developments. Such content will help to train mission servants instinctively to direct their attention to people outside of and different from themselves, as well as spiritually to make connections with God's work among them.

Along with content, instruction is the personal exposure to people who are different in language, history, nationality and in any number of other traits. Clearly, different trainees will have come into training periods with different types and amounts of interpersonal experiences. Those with little exposure to different sorts of people may need extra guidance for proactively interacting with 'strangers'. Such exposure can take the form of bringing people to the trainees, whether into a classroom, congregational gathering, home setting or otherwise. Exposure should also involve taking or otherwise enabling trainees to step into other people's settings through field trips, supervised internships, home visits or any number of other possibilities. For servants moving into different language settings, language learning methods can be introduced.[8]

Along with being equipped for the arduous and sometimes painfully slow process of language learning, personal trust in God will also need to be deepened to undergird the inherent challenge of being changed upon entering a new and different situation. Basic to participating in the *missio Dei* is relying on divine governance, prior presence and previous work among those where service is to be rendered. Being brought into that ongoing process of divine work among a different people and their setting inherently leads to being changed into a new person, whose character and traits are both unknown and uncontrolled by the mission servant. If outsiders are not able or willing to trust the God who has brought them into a new setting and who will faithfully guide and shape them, constructive change and growth will be halting and more difficult than should it be. Surprises and uncertainties will be inherent in the growth process connected with serving among those who are different – and into whose likeness the mission servant will inevitably need to change. Hence it is no surprise that an extensive survey of mission agencies in a recent study of missionary retention indicates that 'spiritual life was rated highest of all groups of questions'. [9]

---

[8] One time-proven method is associated with the book by Tom and Elizabeth S. Brewster, *Language Acquisition Made Practical (LAMP): Field methods for language learners* (Colorado Springs, CO: Lingua House, 1976).
[9] Rob Hay et al, *Worth Keeping: Global Perspectives on Best Practice in Missionary Retention* (Globalization of Mission Series, Pasadena, CA: William Carey Library, 2007), 131.

'Unorganised Missions'

Yet another vitally important area of mission training focus that emerges from an appreciation of the *missio Dei* is what might be called 'unorganised missions'.[10] While understanding divine guidance over, use of, and working through socio-economic-political events is a central feature of the impetus for emphasising the mission of God, inordinate attention can still be paid to the labours of missionaries, mission organisations, and churches in comparison to the roles of Christians not organisationally or even self-consciously recognised as mission servants. That is, the *missio Dei* is concerned about much more than the world's structures in addition to Christian structures. God's mission in the world includes divine guidance over, use of, and working through all of Jesus' followers as they go through their daily lives. The recognition of ordinary Christians' central roles in the *missio Dei* should be instilled in those being consciously trained for mission service.

There are several implications related to the extent to which missionaries and those who equip them – people who comprise the efforts, structures, and personnel of 'organised missions' – consciously recognise the mission roles of other Christians. Stated negatively, a lack of acknowledgement of those roles in, for example, missioners' update newsletters will draw attention, prayer support and attitudinal adulation primarily and perhaps even exclusively to those involved with 'organised missions', most especially the missionaries themselves. Even while there will also be focus, within a *missio Dei* framework, on God's extra-ecclesiastical work in the world, the Christian people understood to be participating most especially in God's mission will be missionaries and, secondarily, their financial, prayer and organisational supporters. The casualties of such emphases in terms of lack of attention, prayer support and encouragement from fellow Christians will be ordinary Christians who are not mission servants in an 'organised' sense.

Stated positively, 'organised' mission servants equipped to understand the central roles of 'unorganised' mission servants, i.e. ordinary Christians, will more steadily be able to avoid drawing attention, prayer support and attitudinal adulation to themselves, and will instead direct others' attention to the whole people of God serving the *missio Dei* throughout the world. In their mission practice, 'organised' missioners, equipped to see the vital importance of 'unorganised' missionaries, will be free to understand and serve those Christians for who they actually are, what they actually do in life, what their needs genuinely are, and what the Gospel benefits are of their lives and service. The goal of mission service will not be fixated on pulling Christians into involvement with one's own mission service per se. Rather, mission servants will understand and be free to serve, support and

---

[10] J. Nelson Jennings, *God the Real Superpower: Rethinking Our Role in Missions* (Phillipsburg, NJ: P&R Publishing, 2007), 117-22, 139-42.

facilitate ordinary Christians' 'unorganised' mission service and witness rendered through their ongoing lives and responsibilities.

With specific respect to cross-cultural mission service, the instruction and training given to 'organised' missionaries should give a clearer understanding and vision of how the *missio Dei* orchestrates, uses and works through Christians moving as immigrants and refugees, labourers, students, business people, government workers and otherwise, i.e. about 'unorganised' missionaries. While it would be impossible, unnecessary and foolhardy to compare the relative impact of 'organised' and 'unorganised' mission activities, yet within a *missio Dei* framework it would seem that 'unorganised' missions have a far greater effect, especially given the very much greater number of people involved. That is, stepping back and considering the world's immigrants, refugees, labourers, students, business people, government workers and other migrating peoples, then understanding the sizeable portions of those moving peoples who are Christian, then further understanding the settings into which such people migrate, live and serve that are often untouched by 'organised' mission efforts – for example, Christian Filipina house workers in Islamic settings inaccessible to 'organised' missionaries – leads at a minimum to an understanding of God's guidance over, use of, and working through people categorised here as 'unorganised' missionaries.

What is particularly relevant to the overall discussion here is that 'organised', cross-cultural missionaries need to be equipped and trained to embrace the vital roles that God gives in the *missio Dei* to Christians who migrate across cultural settings. The primary effect of mission servants being trained as such is that God is given proper due for orchestrating the total process of mission among the peoples of the earth. Related to this is the capacity and inclination towards co-operating with, supporting and otherwise enhancing the mission witness of fellow Christians whom God is guiding and using. Mission agencies and missionaries can all too easily, without at all intending to do so, focus on their own efforts – at the expense of God's mission and the service of others – due to a strong sense of calling and the importance of the mission work that they are carrying out. More in line with participating in the full *missio Dei* is a vision of those friends and colleagues in mission among whom God has placed one as a servant. Equipping mission servants to operate according to that posture is all too uncommon, yet such an approach is feasible if the trainers themselves appreciate God's 'unorganised' mission people.

Conclusion

Collectively, the broader implications of the *missio Dei* are that attention be given fundamentally to God's mission acts to make the world right again. God has never abandoned the creation that went astray and fell under the threatened curse of rebellion and death. Ever since that curse was enacted, the divine commitment has always been, 'Behold, I am making all things new' (Rev. 21:5) in Jesus Christ. Stated elsewhere, 'Of the increase of his government and of peace there will be no end... The zeal of the Lord of hosts will do this' (Is. 9:7). God is the one who ultimately will complete the *missio Dei* of re-creating all things in Christ.

So that they can most faithfully and effectively participate in the *missio Dei*, servants of that mission are to be equipped and trained to understand, appreciate and co-operate with the full scope of God's work in this beautifully created but sin-ravaged world. Mission work is not primarily (or even secondarily) about me, my agency or my church. God's work among the fascinating and bruised peoples of the world, including throughout history, currently and in the promised future, is to be the focus of mission involvement. Training for participating in the *missio Dei* thus needs to direct the inclinations and vision of servants towards seeing, understanding, facilitating and otherwise co-operating with God's ongoing saving work from the attacks of wicked powers and principalities among others, as well as among those who have preceded and shaped the servants' own particular ethnic, ecclesiastical and total heritages. What mission servants are trained to be and to do is to be predicated on the God who cares for all peoples of this glorious yet ruined world, and who has been at work among all of us throughout history – with a full re-creation of all things in Christ as the final vision in view.

MISSIOLOGY AND THEOLOGY IN DIALOGUE: HOW MAY A MISSIOLOGICAL UNDERSTANDING PERMEATE ALL THEOLOGICAL DISCIPLINES AND BE A PREMISE FOR THEOLOGICAL THINKING?[1]

Vidar L. Haanes

Introduction

Which came first, theology or mission? This is like the other question of what came first: the chicken or the egg? With a quotation of Martin Kähler, David J. Bosch stated that 'mission is the mother of theology'.[2] Martin Kähler (1835-1912) was a devote Lutheran, and Professor of Systematic Theology and New Testament Studies in Halle, Germany. What Kähler wrote (in German), was more like: 'Mission in the old church became the mother of theology' (Die älteste Mission wurde zur Mutter der Theologie).[3] The New Testament is mostly written within a missionary context. Theology, according to Kähler, began as an accompanying manifestation of Christian mission, and not as 'ein Luxus der weltbeherrschenden Kirche'.

When we are discussing the relation between theology and missiology, we often discuss at two different levels. At the first level we are concerned with missiology as an academic discipline. This level belongs primarily to the period before the last paradigm shift in theology of mission, as explained by David J. Bosch.[4] In a modern, enlightenment setting, it was vital to place missiology among the academic disciplines, to gain it a position in the academic world. But after the transformation of theology and mission, as a result of the emerging, ecumenical missionary paradigm (Bosch), we discuss the place and role of missiology at another level. We are more concerned with missiological approaches to theology as such, and for theological education this has implications for the entire curriculum. We

---

[1] Cf. my article 'Theological Education and Mission', in Tormod Engelsviken, Ernst Harbakk, Rolv Olsen and Thor Strandenæs (eds), *Mission to the World: Communicating the Gospel in the 21st Century. Essays in Honour of Knud Jørgensen* (Oxford: Regnum, 2008), 391-404.
[2] David J. Bosch, *Transforming Mission: Paradigm Shifts in Theology of Mission* (Maryknoll, NY: Orbis Books, 1991), 16.
[3] Martin Kähler, 'Die Mission – ist sie ein unentbehrlicher Zug am Christentum?' in *Schriften zu Christologie und Mission*, Herausgegeben von Heinzgünter Frohnes, Theologische Bücherei Bd. 42 (München: Chr. Kaiser Verlag 1971), 190.
[4] Bosch, *Transforming Mission*, 349-62.

are further concerned with the formation of theological students, encouraging spiritual life and congregational engagement. Several theological institutions have taken these criticisms seriously. New courses in practical theology, pastoral psychology, cross-cultural studies, missiology, studies in leadership and spirituality, and so on, have been added to an already over-stretched syllabus. The problem is that the timetable cannot take the strain, for hardly anything already existing is allowed to drop out. We may ask which elements are necessary for theological education to serve properly the church's obligation to respond in obedience to the *missio Dei*.

Missiology as an Academic, Theological Discipline

In the 1950s, Professor Olav G. Myklebust (1905-2001) at MF Norwegian School of Theology wrote his thesis on *The Study of Missions in Theological Education* in two volumes, still an international standard reference work.[5] Myklebust, a graduate from MF Norwegian School of Theology, started his work as a missionary at Umpumulo in Natal, Kwa-Zulu, and in 1933 he became the principal of the training institution there. Umpumulo is the first permanent Norwegian mission station in South Africa, founded by the Norwegian pioneer (and devout academician) Hans Paludan Smith Schreuder (1817-1882). Myklebust was an admirer of Schreuder, who had passed his theological examinations at the university with highest distinction, and later wrote readers, a grammar and a hymnbook in Zulu.[6]

In 1939 Myklebust was called to Oslo, to a chair in Church History at MF with a special obligation to lecture in Mission Studies. Myklebust stressed the importance of scholarly study of the missionary enterprise, and he became the founder of Missiology as an academic discipline in Norway, required in theological education. He was instrumental in founding the Egede Institute of Missionary Research (1946), and later in establishing the Nordic Institute for Missionary and Ecumenical Research (NIME). But Myklebust had a wide vision. In 1951 he published a proposal for 'An International Institute of Scientific Missionary Research', but it took twenty years for the first part of that dream to materialise in the International Association of Mission Studies (IAMS). He had important positions in national and international organisations such as the International Missionary Council and the Commission of World Mission and

---

[5] Olav Guttorm Myklebust, *The study of missions in theological education: an historical inquiry into the place of world evangelisation in western protestant ministerial training with particular reference to Alexander Duff's chair of evangelistic theology. Vol 1, until 1910* (Oslo: Land og Kirke, 1955), *Vol 2, 1910-1950* (Oslo: Land og Kirke, 1957).

[6] O.G. Myklebust, 'The Legacy of H.P.S. Schreuder', in *International Bulletin of Missionary Research*, Vol. 8, Issue 2 (1984), 70-75.

Evangelism in the World Council of Churches. Myklebust encouraged others to do research and to write, choosing dissertation topics of missionary interest.[7]

Myklebust credits Schleiermacher for appending missiology to one of the four main disciplines, namely practical theology.[8] But Schleiermacher did not really see mission as a task to be encouraged, but rather as an activity to be permitted: Mission as the propagation of the Christian faith is a task entrusted to believers as church (*gemeinschäftlich*) in those countries which have connection with non-Christian countries and areas, especially through colonialism.[9] Missiology, or the study of Mission, including Ecumenics, was nevertheless for the first time permitted a place in the theological curriculum. Theological study came to mean the study of a number of discrete disciplines pertinent to the ministry, a theory of practice about those tasks. In Edward Farley's words: 'Theology as personal quality continues as practical know-how, necessary to ministerial work. Theology as discipline continues as one specialised scholarly undertaking among others, as systematic theology.'[10] The very definition of theology as a set of disciplines or knowledge resulting therefrom is tightly correlated with education needed by the professional leadership of the religious community.

In the 1980s Schleiermacher's heritage was heavily debated among scholars and educators in theology, especially the problems created by the conventional fourfold model of the theological curriculum. Edward Farley wrote that Schleiermacher's legacy had contributed to these problems: 'The fourfold pattern is not now a genuine theologically based pattern, but a school-catalogue phenomenon, a way of organizing courses. Accordingly, it is more accurate to label the fourfold pattern catalogue-fields rather than disciplines.'[11]

The first struggle for missiology was to earn a place among the theological disciplines, and in the 1980s it was recognised as such at most theological schools and seminaries, as a subject in the theological curriculum in its own right. But after David J. Bosch wrote in his comprehensive work that a new paradigm for theology of mission was emerging, the discussion started again. Bosch was advocating 'a pluriverse

---

[7] Vidar L. Haanes, 'The first Professor of Missiology in Norway: Professor O.G. Myklebust (1905-2001)', in *Norwegian Journal of Missiology* 59:4 (2005), 239-46. Cf. 'Tormod Engelsviken, Olav Guttorm Myklebust: 1905-2001', in *Mission studies* 19:2 (2002), 12-13.
[8] Myklebust, *The study of missions in theological education*, 1955:85.
[9] Myklebust, *The study of missions in theological education*, 1955:87.
[10] Edward Farley, *Theologia: The Fragmentation and Unity of Theological Education* (Philadelphia, PA: Fortress Press, 1983), 39.
[11] Farley, *Theologia*, 141.

of missiology in a universe of mission'.[12] The questions raised by mission studies about the contextual nature of theology mean that missiology is party to the post-modern critique of theology, as Bosch tried to demonstrate. The modern era is not the last epoch of world history to exercise an influence on the thought and practice of mission. Modernity has now become the past, and is followed by the post-modern paradigm, Bosch stated 25 years ago.[13] Though whether Bosch's paradigm is post-modern is questionable.[14] What about theology and missiology in dialogue? Does missiology represent the old pattern of diverse theological disciplines belonging to the past? If we look into the curriculum of theological schools and faculties in Europe, one gets the impression that the terms mission/missiology are replaced by terms like dialogue, ecumenism, cross-cultural communication and so on. The same goes for the name of the chairs in Missiology, now seldom found in European universities.

Missiology and Church

Mission may be the mother of theology, but not the mother of the theologian. Mission puts the theologian into close contact with his/her mother: the church. Missiology is a discipline that studies the expansion of the church, and missiology addresses the crossing of barriers with the Gospel of Jesus Christ. Its concern about crossing boundaries is now becoming a central concern in theology as a whole. Theological education is about the facilitation of learning and obedience to this missiological concern. 'A theology of theological education must be grounded in *missio Dei* and in a proper understanding of the church (this faith community), her purpose and mission in the world.' This is a statement from an 'Issue Group' within the Lausanne Movement, working with 'Effective Theological Education for World Evangelization'.[15] The statement is probably representative for evangelical seminaries and colleges today. As we often use the words 'missionary' and 'mission' to express the sending of the church, we are in danger of understanding this only as an activity. Mission has been understood as an activity for missionaries and for especially 'mission-minded' people in the congregations, and not as an indispensable part of being church. Again we can turn to Martin Kähler: 'If

---

[12] Bosch, *Transforming Mission*, 8. Cf. G.M. Soares-Prabhu, 'Missiology or Missiologies?' in *Mission Studies*, No. 6 (1986), 85-87.

[13] Bosch, *Transforming Mission*, 349ff.

[14] Kirsteen Kim, 'Postmodern Mission: A Paradigm Shift in David Bosch's Theology of Mission?' in *International Review of Mission* LXXXIX/353 (2000), 172-79.

[15] Lausanne Occasional Paper No. 57, *Effective Theological Education for World Evangelization*. Produced by the Issue Group on this topic at the 2004 Forum for World Evangelization hosted by the Lausanne Committee for World Evangelization in Pattaya, Thailand, 29th September-5th October 2004, 17.

you first recognize the insoluble connection between church and mission,' Kähler wrote a hundred years ago, 'the relation between mission and theology follows.'[16] Kähler was addressing equally the matter of theologians being sceptical about mission as *Missionsfreunde* being sceptical about theology. A theology of mission is an important factor in overcoming the limitations of a local, culture-bounded ecclesiology. As Knud Jørgensen has stated, we have to develop a missional ecclesiology, as the church is inherently a missionary church, as the people of God in the world.[17] What are the issues at stake in order for theological education to recover a focus on the church? It is to participate fully in the Son's redemptive work as the Spirit creates, leads and teaches the church to live as the distinctive people of God.[18] Moltmann's connection of *ekklesia* and mission becomes another aspect of locating theological education in mission: 'Today one of the strongest impulses towards the renewal of the theological concept of the church comes from the theology of mission.'[19] We may ask whether contemporary theological education is properly focused on the real needs of local churches and mission agencies as leaders are being trained for church and mission work. There is no doubt that praxis-based theological education is conducive to ministry and mission.

Mission and Educational Practice

Andrew J. Kirk, the former Head of the School of Mission and World Christianity at Selly Oaks Colleges, wrote a paper in 2005, showing an alternative way of looking at theological education, trying to provoke serious critical reflection and hoping to encourage 'a rethinking of the content and methods of educational practice, in the light of God's missionary activity and purposes for his people'.[20] Kirk tries to re-envisage a process of theological education, which deliberately attempts to respond to the claim that proper theology, and therefore theological education, is through and through missionary in character.[21] According to Kirk, there is an apparently wide gap between his own, missiologically informed, programme and the more traditional, university-based style of education.

---

[16] Kähler, *Die Mission*, 184, 189.

[17] Knud Jørgensen, 'Trenger kirken omvendelse? På vei mot en missional ekklesiologi?' (Is the Church in need of repentance? Towards a missional ecclesiology): http://intercultural.dk/icms/filer/kj-omvendelse-art.pdf

[18] Craig Van Gelder, *Confident Witness – Changing World. Rediscovering the Gospel in North America* (Eerdmans: Grand Rapids, MI, 1999), 31.

[19] J. Moltmann, *The Experiment Hope* (London: SCM, 1975), 7.

[20] J. Andrew Kirk, 'Re-envisioning the Theological Curriculum as if the Missio Dei Mattered', in *Common Ground Journal*, Vol. 3, No. 1 (Fall 2005), 23: www.commongroundjournal.org. Cf. J. Andrew Kirk, *The Mission of Theology and Theology as Mission* (Valley Forge, PA: Trinity Press International, 1997).

[21] Kirk, 'Re-envisioning the Theological Curriculum', 40.

He then admits that the real distinction is between a genuinely theological programme of education and one which has as its presupposition the study of religion. Whether it is called theology or not, what happens in most universities is the latter rather than the former. Many theological education programmes fail, precisely because they are trying to combine two quite distinct aims and methodologies, Kirk concludes.

I understand Andrew Kirk to be saying that the main problem is the aim and methodology of religious studies not being able to focus on the uniqueness of Christ and Christian theology, and not necessarily the academic tradition of theology as such. In their desire to be relevant to the needs of the secular culture around them, some theological colleges are in danger of making the Gospel irrelevant. On the other hand, that may also happen if we are neglecting the culture we are rooted in. One has to run the risk of being put to question, to test one's own inherited set of values and ideas. Even for theological students, and maybe especially for them, this is a necessary part of their formation. In the paper by the Lausanne Issue Group already mentioned, we find the same critique against theological institutions as in the essay of Andrew Kirk.[22] Theological colleges and schools are said to imbibe secular values on the one hand, while on the other, there is a tendency for them to be isolated from the realities of the world around them. It is true that theological faculties in many European universities have suffered from a fear of not being relevant for their academic audience, which has resulted in a liberal theology, usually not relevant for the church. But the opposite is also possible, that theological schools and colleges, when leaving the university sphere or academic level, are in danger of being irrelevant for both society and church. Isabelle Stengers, a 'non-Christian' philosopher belonging to a tradition marked by relations between philosophy and theology, regrets that theology no longer features as an argumentative or creative force opposing the exclusive authority of the sciences, or assisting them in guarding against the arrogance and stupidity to which their present-day lack of fearless, imaginative interlocutors make them prone.[23]

An important part of European cultural heritage is to recognise various kinds of knowledge. Scientific reason alone cannot provide life with values or directions. We need wisdom and insight as well, as Karl Jaspers said: 'There is a form of thought which requires our personal commitment in order to achieve the status of truth.'[24] Education and research must aim for the formation of the whole person, education in the broad sense of the term, and not only the transmission of facts and skills. The aim of theological education is not only to transmit Christian beliefs, but also to foster the

---

[22] Lausanne Occasional Paper No. 57, 10.

[23] I. Stengers, 'Science and Religion. Beyond complementarity', in Nils H. Gregersen and U. Görman, *Design and Disorder: Perspectives from Science and Theology* (London: T & T Clark, 2002), 120.

[24] Karl Jaspers, *The Idea of the University* (Boston, MA: Beacon Press 1959), 12.

characteristic values, attitudes and dispositions of the Christian life. As such, it is also concerned with spiritual formation. Growing in the knowledge of God and in his purposes for his world is the ultimate purpose of all theological education. Consequently, a missional approach to theological education is vital.[25]

Mission and Theological Education

In the following I will use my own institution, MF Norwegian School of Theology in Oslo, as a lens for examining the connection between theological education and mission.[26] MF has a special place in the history of theological education in Europe, as a private, evangelical university institution having defended its position as the leading theological school in Norway since the 1930s. A majority of ministers and all the present bishops in the Church of Norway are graduates of MF, as well as a majority of Norwegian mission leaders, along with many missionaries and Free Church pastors.

While the Catholic Church after the Council of Trent renewed the seminary, and placed the education and formation of priests within the control of the church, the Lutheran churches in Germany and Scandinavia placed the education of the clergy in the universities. When MF Norwegian School of Theology (Det teologiske Menighetsfakultet) was established in 1907 as an alternative (congregational) to the Faculty of Theology at the University of Oslo, one had no choice but to follow the same curriculum as at the university. This continued more or less until the 1950s. Until recently, the difference in curriculum between the two institutions has been marginal. The difference between the two was more a matter of theological and spiritual formation. At MF students learned theology from teachers who in a special way focused on vocation, congregational work and mission. MF did not receive any financial support from the state until the 1970s, so students and faculty members were travelling all around Norway to preach, sing and collect financial and spiritual support. The late history of the Student Volunteer Movement and the early history of International Fellowship of Evangelical Students are in many ways connected with MF. The Norwegian IVF-movement (NKSS) was started by Professor Ole Hallesby in 1924 as an evangelical alternative to the Student Christian Movement of Norway. The Norwegian Student Volunteer Movement (AFMF) joined the new evangelical group in 1926. Robert Wilder and John R. Mott had started the Student Volunteer Movement in 1888, with the watchword: 'The Evangelization of the World in this Generation'. Wilder resigned in 1927 as general secretary of his own organisation, as the watchword faded. In 1934 he wrote to the British Inter-Varsity Fellowship

---

[25] Lausanne Occasional Paper No. 57, 46.
[26] www.mf.no

(IVF), urging them to adhere to the basic essentials of the evangelical faith, and the missionary obligations of the Christian. IVF then formed their own missionary fellowship for intending missionaries. Robert Wilder arranged a meeting between the British students and two Norwegian graduates, Carl Fredrik Wisløff and his fiancée Ingrid – who happened to be the niece of Wilder's wife. Since 1932 Wisløff had been secretary of the Norwegian IVF. The result of this British-Norwegian meeting was an international conference for evangelical student leaders, held in Oslo 1934. MF Professor Ole Hallesby was giving an address on 'The Hour of God', talking about the evangelical student movements suddenly and spontaneously springing up in so many countries at the same time:

> For many years a rationalistic theology has held most of our churches. On Christian work amongst students this theology has also laid its clammy hand... Today we are here, representatives of many nations... we can each tell of a Christian student work based on the Bible as the Word of God.[27]

After World War II, in August 1947, the International Fellowship of Evangelical Students (IFES) came into being.[28] The founder-members were Australia, Britain, Canada, China, France, Holland, New Zealand, Norway, Switzerland and the USA. Martyn Lloyd-Jones was the new chairman, Stacey Woods became general secretary, and Professor Ole Hallesby was appointed its president (1947-1954). The same year Carl Fr Wisløff became principal of the Practical Theological Seminary at MF, a position he held until 1962, when he was appointed Professor of Church History (until 1975). Wisløff was IFES chairman 1959-1967 and then president 1967-1977. The MF Professors Ole Hallesby, Olav G. Myklebust and Carl Fr Wisløff had substantial influence on theological students at MF. But you would not find traces of this in the curriculum, except for some small courses in mission studies. The formation of students belonged to what we today call 'the hidden curriculum'. Even in an evangelical school of theology like MF, theology as such was hardly in dialogue with missiology. Mission was a special interest for those engaged in foreign mission, and for teachers with special relationships with missionary agencies or international student work.

Is Missiology a Problem when Theology Seeks Accreditation?

Many evangelicals working with theological education are ambivalent about academic accreditation. Accreditation is seen as a problem for the missiological perspective in theological education, and a hindrance to change in the areas of contextual and inductive learning. Several examples can be found in Bernhard Ott's monograph on mission studies in evangelical theological education in Germany and German-speaking

---

[27] Pete Lowman, *The Day of His Power* (Leicester, UK: IVP 1983), 66-68.
[28] Lowman, *The Day of His Power,* 79.

Switzerland, especially schools in membership with the *Konferenz Bibeltreuer Ausbildungsstätten* (KBA).[29] He gives a detailed examination of the paradigm shifts which have taken place in recent years in both the theology of mission and the understanding of theological education. According to Ott, their requirements for certification or accreditation do not match the educational aspirations and aims of the institution. They are in conflict because the accrediting agency is working with a different set of parameters and a different definition of what makes an educating institution effective. These schools are theologically conservative, and resist the challenge of Bosch's mission paradigm shift in the areas of contextual and inductive learning, mostly because of disagreement in hermeneutics. Ott's thesis was that the evangelical Bible school movement, which historically has embodied many of the features of this new paradigm, nevertheless has jeopardised these by their pursuit of academic accreditation. The result, says Ott, is a continuation of the same downward spiral towards mediocrity and irrelevance.

I have no need to argue with Ott's thesis, but I wonder why the accreditation agencies would turn their thumbs down for the reason of adjusting to a contextual and inductive learning process. Today MF has full accreditation as a specialised university, with two PhD programmes, and several master's and bachelor's programmes. National, and therefore international (because of the Bologna process), accreditation has been very important, as MF is now treated as an equal member of the *Norwegian Association of Higher Education Institutions* and *Nordic University Association* (NUS). This gives MF the freedom to establish degrees, programmes and courses, and therefore an opportunity to meet demands for a renewal of theological education in the light of the paradigm shift.

Because of the Bologna process, working towards a European Higher Education Area, Norway – like most European countries – adopted the 3+2+3 year degree structure (bachelor, master, PhD). But at the same time the reform put much emphasis on 'Professional studies', with the result that in Norway the education of ministers, medical doctors and psychologists were allowed a six-year degree course, including one year of integrated praxis. We keep the structure from the Schleiermacher model, with emphasis on the four main disciplines, including Biblical studies built on obligatory courses in Greek and Hebrew. But applied and practical theology, including periods of praxis, takes the form of several integrated courses in the curriculum, the first rather early.

It is necessary for theological education to be characterised by praxis rather than by persisting polarities such as theory and practice. Theological education has to prepare the student for the realities of Christian ministry,

---

[29] Bernhard Ott, *Beyond Fragmentation: Integrating Mission and Theological Education. A Critical Assessment of some Recent Developments in Evangelical Theological Education* (Oxford: Regnum, 2002).

and thus be in communication with local churches. According to Robert Banks, for theological education to be missional, means that it is wholly or partly field-based, and that involves some measure of doing what is being studied (life-engaging). It requires observant participation and not merely participant observation. Only by maintaining its close links with mission will it remain relevant to changing circumstances, and hold true to the missionary impulse that gave rise to the church and theology.[30]

Theological students at MF Norwegian School of Theology will have several periods working in a congregation, in a hospital, prison or another institution, to put their skills, attitudes and understandings to work in real-life settings. During this praxis, they will have the opportunity for theological reflection upon these experiences, guided by a supervisor. The most effective experiential learning takes place when an appropriate level of oversight and support is offered and the experience is reasonably similar to the context in which the student is expected to eventually put their new learning into practice. A teaching approach that has become important in many professional studies is Problem-Based Learning (PBL). It is an approach designed to connect theory with real-life experiences, to encourage dialogue between reality and theory. PBL is a helpful way to overcome the fragmentation of disciplines in the curriculum. Often the specialisation of teachers in narrow subject areas creates obstacles to learning which could be overcome by a closer connection with the church and society, and by finding and verbalising central problems for PBL exercises. In the course of the development of this fresh way of doing theology, a number of traditional truisms have been challenged. Missiology is still a distinct discipline at MF, but also more than one section of the theological curriculum. During the annual 'mission week', lecturers in all the disciplines are encouraged to focus especially on mission perspectives. In addition, there is a variety of programmes for the students, with seminars and discussion panels. Mission agencies are invited to MF for exhibition and information, inspiration and focus on their special mission field.

European universities have been a model for unity in diversity and diversity in unity.[31] There is not *one* uniform culture in Europe, but different cultures and different religious traditions, be they Christian, Islamic or Jewish. In Oslo, having once a homogeneous, Lutheran population, there is now a strong Roman Catholic minority as well as a substantial Muslim population. In addition, we find as much as 100 migrant churches of all denominations. Only one generation back, mission studies were about foreign mission, especially western mission in other continents. Today, missiology's concern about crossing boundaries is becoming an

---

[30] Robert Banks, *Re-envisioning Theological Education: Exploring a Missional Alternative to Current Models* (Grand Rapids, MI: Eerdmans, 1999), 131-32.
[31] Vidar L. Haanes, 'Unity in Diversity and Diversity in Unity: The Role and Legitimacy of the European Universities', in *Higher Education in Europe* 31:4 (2006), 443-48.

ever more central concern in theological education for those going to serve as pastors in Norwegian congregations.

MF started as a strict, exclusively confessional Lutheran institution, but is today an ecumenical institution on a Lutheran platform. The Church of Norway is still the most important stakeholder. But today MF also educates pastors for the Methodist Church, Pentecostal churches and other free churches, as well as priests for the Roman Catholic Church. We have faculty members belonging to different churches and denominations. Some of our Lutheran students now follow courses in spiritual leadership designed for Pentecostal ministry, and Pentecostal students may follow courses in Catholic pneumatology and initiation. Many of these 'cross-denominational' courses are fitting the concept of ecumenical Missiology, or 'Mission as Theology' described by Bosch.[32] Hopefully the students now preparing for ministry will be able to co-operate and communicate when they one day become leaders of various churches and religious institutions.

Missiology as the Future of Theology

Stephen Neill used to say that 'if everything is mission then nothing is mission'.[33] Even if not everything is mission, we may widen the understanding of mission to more than the act of sending missionaries to proclaim the Gospel. At least it is clear that the study of mission interfaces with a wide range of disciplines in theology, history, cultural studies and social sciences. In the words of Kirsteen Kim: 'Theology of mission is therefore concerned with the relationship of truth and proclamation, gospel and society, salvation and history, Christian witness and other faiths, scripture and culture, church and kingdom, Word and world, revelation and theologies.'[34]

When it comes to theological education, we may ask whether we should take the next step, and let a missiological understanding permeate all theological disciplines and be a premise for all theological thinking. 'Missiology contends against all theological provincialism, advocating an intercultural perspective in theology,' said the Puerto Rican missiologist and contextual theologian Orlando Enrique Costas (1942-1987).[35] And he goes on:

> Missiology questions all theological discourse that does not seriously consider the missionary streams of the Christian faith; all biblical interpretation that ignores the missionary motives that shape biblical faith; all history of Christianity that omits the expansion of Christianity across cultural,

---

[32] Bosch, *Transforming Mission*, 489-98.
[33] Stephen Neill, *Creative Tension* (London: Edinburgh House Press, 1959), 81.
[34] Kirsteen Kim, 'Mission Studies in Britain and Ireland: Introduction to a World-Wide Web', in *British Journal of Theological Education* Vol. 11.1 (2000), 76.
[35] Orlando E. Costas, 'Theological Education and Mission', in C. René Padilla (ed), *New Alternatives in Theological Education* (Oxford: Regnum, 1988), 15.

social, and religious frontiers; and all pastoral theology that does not take seriously the mandate to communicate the Gospel fully and to the heart of the concrete situations of daily life. By fulfilling such a critical task, missiology also enriches theology because it puts theology in contact with the worldwide Church with all its cultural and theological diversity.

In a keynote address at the Faith and Learning Institute on the Internationalization of Curriculum in Christian Higher Education, Costas critiqued the provincialism of the Christian worldview of the schools and called for a willingness to 'cross intercultural, interethnic and interracial boundaries'. [36] In the same address, he set forth three goals for theological education. The first was to equip the student for reaching out to persons who have no appreciation or knowledge of the Christian faith. Next was the spiritual formation of women and men in ministry for the praxis of mission in the world. Lastly, in response to the fragmentation of the Christian church along racial, class and denominational lines, seminaries should prepare persons to promote Christian unity and human solidarity. This is to begin by becoming sensitive to the people who live among us from different ethnic and cultural groups. For this crossing of boundaries to take place, students, faculties and trustees are to be involved in learning experiences that expose them to perspectives other than their own. According to Costas, theological education is about discipleship, and theological and spiritual formation. In addition, Costas helped especially Hispanic evangelicals to open up to a new understanding and doing of theology from the perspective of marginalised people.[37] Education was political for him. It was about the work of evangelisation as well as social justice. He mobilised different denominations to respond to the needs of the theological education of minority groups. The world view of much of the emerging younger churches is much closer to that of the New Testament than that of western culture. These Christians read the Bible as a book that connects with amazing and revolutionary relevance with their own world view and experience. These churches are vigorously missionary; they have not been intimidated by the critique of missions that permeates much of western culture today. This was formulated in the Manila Manifesto (Lausanne II) in 1989: 'For the great new fact of our era is the internationalization of missions. Not only is a large majority of evangelical Christians now non-western, but the number of Two-Thirds World missionaries will soon exceed those from the West.'[38] On this background Kirsteen Kim is concluding her article on Mission Studies in Britain and

---

[36] Orlando E. Costas, 'Internationalizing the curriculum in Christian higher education', in Robert A. Hess (ed), *Internationalizing the curriculum* (St Paul, MN: The Christian College Consortium, 1986), 11.
[37] Cf. Samuel Escobar, 'The legacy of Orlando Costas', in *International Bulletin of Missionary Research*, 25 (2001), 50-56.
[38] J.D. Douglas (ed), *Proclaim Christ Until He Comes* (Minneapolis, MN: World Wide Publications, 1989), 34.

Ireland: 'The study of mission is an introduction to a world-wide web. It is a subject which crosses theological and academic boundaries in its reflection on the mission of God to the world expressed in the living Word and the life-giving Spirit.'[39] With the words of James A. Scherer, mission theology should assist with the task of creating a fresh vocabulary for missionary function in the new missionary era, taking into account that mission is the task of the church in all six continents.[40]

Theology started in a mission context. Thus mission became the mother of theology, and not the illegitimate daughter. But we must add that to be the mother of theology does not mean that the time for mission is over, but that true theology grows out of mission. Thus mission is not primarily the precedent, but the future of theology. Mission is the future of theology because we are entering a future with many cultural similarities to the first centuries, which was primarily an epoch of mission.

---

[39] Kim, 'Mission Studies in Britain and Ireland', 81.
[40] James A. Scherer, *Gospel, Church, Kingdom. Comparative Studies in World Mission Theology* (Minneapolis, MN: Augsburg Publishing House, 1987), 245.

THEOLOGICAL EDUCATION BY EXTENSION (TEE) AS A TOOL FOR TWENTY-FIRST CENTURY MISSION

Graham Aylett and Tim Green

We live in a rapidly changing world: a world of fragmentation, inequality, environmental challenges, continuing disease and poverty, populations on the move. All this change and dislocation has created much human need to be met in the name of Christ. It also fuels new trends in church growth. This chapter discusses the contribution that TEE (Theological Education by Extension) can make, and is making, as a tool for twenty-first century mission in its different dimensions.

God calls the global Church to equip all her members for mission in this contemporary context. This call is above all *theological*, because it issues from the mission of God Himself. Then comes the *strategic* question, of how training institutions and local churches can best work in partnership to provide accessible training to all church members. There is also an *educational* dimension, so that busy working Christians can be trained in ways that fit their capacity, interests and learning styles.

In this chapter we show how these considerations helped to shape TEE's philosophy and methodology when it began in Central America fifty years ago and then became a worldwide movement. The story is continued up to the present with examples of remarkable fresh growth in contemporary TEE, especially in Asia. However, no movement can afford to be complacent, and the chapter concludes with proposed areas for renewal and development of TEE in the 21st century.

A Vision for Equipping the Whole Church

Jesus taught his followers to pray, 'Hallowed be your name, your Kingdom come, your will be done on earth as it is in heaven'. Throughout Scripture, there is a close connection between the people of God and the hallowing of his Name.[1] A watching world sees the practices and character of God's people and either gives honour and praise to his Name, or feels free to mock, or ignore their God. The prayer that Jesus taught encapsulates the mission of God, in which God's people are intimately involved.

The Common Call issued at the Edinburgh 2010 conference recognizes the call of the church to share in God's mission:

---

[1] See especially Ezek. 36.16-32.

..we believe the church, as a sign and symbol of the reign of God, is called to witness to Christ today by sharing in God's mission of love through the transforming power of the Holy Spirit.[2]

For the church to play this central role then all church members, in all their relationships both inside and outside the church, are important.[3] Full-time church leaders are rarely on the front-line of missional opportunity because their main ministry is pastoral. Rather, it is the other members of the church who rub shoulders daily with friends, colleagues and family members of other faiths and no particular faith in the workplace, the market place and the community. These are 'non-professional missionaries', to recall Roland Allen's prophetic phrase.[4]

Therefore, as the Cape Town Commitment puts it:

We need intensive efforts to train all God's people in whole-life discipleship, which means to live, think, work, and speak from a biblical worldview and with missional effectiveness in every place or circumstance of daily life and work.[5]

The report from the Parallel Session on Theological Education and Formation at Edinburgh 2010 agrees:

We can say together: Educating the whole people of God is a key to mission and Christian mission should be the organising focus and reference point of theological education.[6]

So any understanding of the church as comprising a passive membership supporting professional leadership, as in Figure 1, urgently needs revision. A better model is Figure 2's inverted pyramid, with an active membership of front-line ministers, and a leadership committed to train and support them.

Accordingly the Cape Town Commitment affirms: 'We challenge pastors and church leaders to support people in such ministry – in the community and in the workplace – "to equip the saints for works of service [ministry]"- in every part of their lives.'[7] The question logically follows, as

---

[2] Kirsteen Kim and Andrew Anderson (eds), *Mission Today and Tomorrow* (Regnum Books International, 2011), 1

[3] Especially Eph. 4.11-16 and 1 Cor. 12

[4] R. Allen, 'The Need for Non-Professional Missionaries', *World Dominion*, 6.2 (April, 1928), 195-201; R. Allen, 'The Work of Non-Professional Missionaries', *World Dominion*, 6.3 (July, 1928), 298-304. Allen usually used this term for expatriate 'non-professionals', but equally had a vision for national churches mobilised for every-member witness.

[5] *The Cape Town Commitment* http://www.lausanne.org/content/ctc/ctcommitment, Part IIA, 3. C)

[6] Dietrich Werner and Namsoon Kang, 'Theme 6 Theological Education and Formation' in Kirsteen Kim and Andrew Anderson (eds), *Mission Today and Tomorrow* (Regnum Books International, 2011), 160

[7] *The Cape Town Commitment* http://www.lausanne.org/content/ctc/ctcommitment, Part IIA, 3. B)

the Edinburgh 2010 Study Group on Theological Education and Formation put it, 'How can every member of the people of God be motivated and empowered for mission?'. This question remains right at the heart of the challenge of Christian mission in the 21st century.

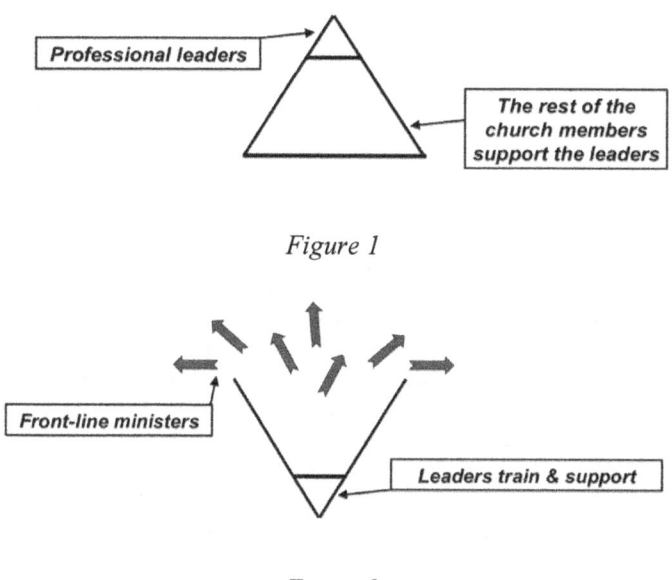

Figure 1

Figure 2

Approaches to Equipping the Whole Church

The above-stated vision and mandate answer the question '*Why* equip all church members for mission?' But this immediately raises another question '*How* can this happen?' This is a strategic consideration with educational aspects also. Clearly, to equip the whole church requires training strategies that are *affordable* financially, *accessible* geographically and educationally, *adaptable* to varied local contexts and *applicable* to ordinary working adults seeking to live and witness for Christ. Moreover, to hold these adults' interest and commitment, the training should fulfil best practice in adult learning.

Traditionally, three main models of training have been favoured: residential training, distance learning and church-based training. To what extent does each model meet the criteria of being affordable, accessible, adaptable and applicable?

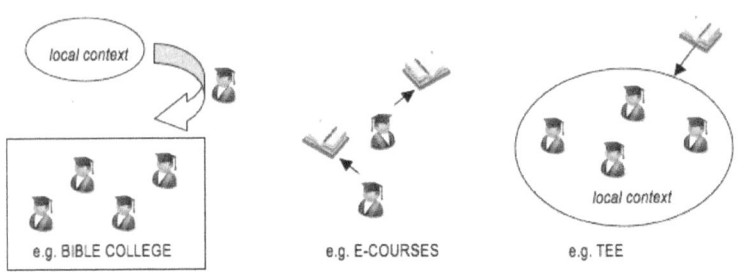

Figure 3. Different models of training

Residential training is designed for equipping pastors and scholars, but is not well placed to equip everyday Christians for everyday mission. Can all Christians leave their homes and jobs to attend full-time seminary? What about the daily wage-earner or the busy mother, or the person with insufficient formal education to meet seminary entry requirements? *Distance learning* courses overcome these challenges of affordability and accessibility, and in the internet age they offer a limitless choice of material. However they are not always adaptable to local contexts, especially when an e-curriculum is created in the West and is pumped out through cyberspace. Nor can the applicability of distance courses be best explored by an isolated student without learning partners. E-learning does an excellent job of transmitting information but this does not itself lead to application and transformation.

Church-based training potentially meets all four criteria. It is geographically accessible because local churches exist in nearly all countries, though this does not ensure that the curriculum itself is educationally accessible. Church-based training is relatively affordable because costs of infrastructure and faculty are already met. It is adaptable to local contexts and applicable to daily life, especially whenever the learning method includes group discussion. Well-designed church-based training, if it meets these four criteria, can multiply in a nation to offer the opportunity for every-member ministry and every-member mission. It also provides a community context for spiritual formation and character development.

In fact in the 21st century these three traditional training categories are starting to be reshaped. New options emerge for blended learning and part-time learning. Many theological institutions which once functioned purely in residential mode now run evening classes (which may or may not use dialogical methods and reflective learning). Flexible blends of short residential courses, in conjunction with learning-on-location, offer more options for working people who don't want to leave their employment. Purely online learning is supplemented by virtual learning communities.

Nevertheless, while recognising these trends, we believe that the local church should be the natural place to equip *most* of its members *most* of the time. This is for both theological and strategic reasons. Educational considerations are also important. How do adults learn best, and how can training for whole-life discipleship and ministry avoid an over-emphasis on the merely cognitive? Few local churches have the capacity to create an excellent curriculum and methodologies from zero. Therefore many of them work in partnership with training providers, as shown in Figure 4:

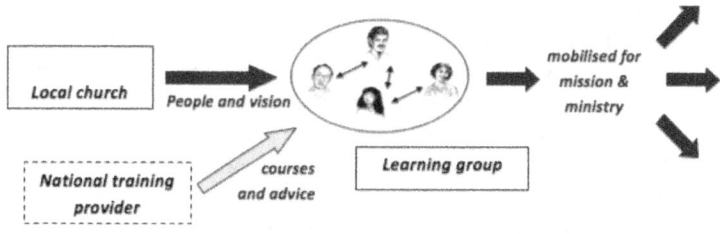

Figure 4. Training providers and local churches in partnership

Many providers help local churches to deliver church-based training in this way. TEE is one model among many of church-based training. It is not distance learning, since TEE students learn together in small groups,[8] not at a distance. Other ways to position TEE include 'in-context training', 'learning on location', or 'community learning',[9] though the methodology may be used in institutional settings also. TEE does not claim to be unique or perfect. But it is widely used, has stood the test of time and is still evolving. It is therefore helpful to review the TEE movement yesterday, today and tomorrow.

TEE as a Tool for Mission – Yesterday

TEE's philosophy and methodology

TEE was born as an experiment in response to failure. It is a wonderful example both of the grace of God in taking failure and making it fruitful,

---

[8] TEE practitioners do not regard TEE as a form of distance education. The engine driving the continuing learning process is the weekly, local, face-to-face group meeting, not a relationship with some distant provider. TEE learning groups are usually church-based but can be inter-church or linked to an institution.
[9] Stephen Cho's doctoral research on 'TEE community learning' was carried out in Korean and will be published in English.

and of the power of prayerful evaluation. A residential college in Guatemala City discovered that the great majority of their graduates did not return to the rural, pastoral ministries for which they had supposedly been trained. Those who were in fact leading those rural congregations had received no training. What should be done? TEE was born from an experiment in bringing training to those rural church leaders who needed it, where they were, in their context.

In this chapter, we use the term 'TEE' to refer to the different streams that see themselves as descendents of that Guatemalan experiment of the early 1960s.[10]

These streams are united by a commitment to local learning groups - training in context, without extraction. They are also united by a methodology.[11] These are programmes based around a threefold pattern of:

• regular personal study using carefully prepared texts;
• discussion of learning and reflection on practice led by a facilitator in a local learning
• group with regular face to face meetings;
• and then intentional practical application.[12]

Ted Ward used the picture of a split-rail fence to show the necessity for each one of these elements and their interconnection.[13]

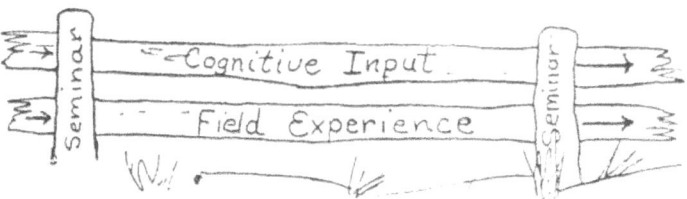

Figure 5a. Elements of TEE learning: the split-rail fence

---

[10] See Kenneth. B. Mulholland, 'A Guatemalan Experiment becomes a model for change', *International Review of Mission*, 71 (1982), 153-160 and references in Patricia J. Harrison, 'Forty Years On: The Evolution of Theological Education by Extension', *Evangelical Review of Theology*, 28.4 (2004), 315 - 328.
[11] Some training providers use the term 'TEE' for other methodologies. This paper works with the narrower definition given here.
[12] Therefore, 'TEE is not a correspondence course, it is not a part-time night school and it is not a series of short seminars.' (Harrison, Forty Years On, 319)
[13] Ted W. Ward and Samuel F. Rowen, 'The *Rail-Fence Analogy* for the Education of Leaders', *Common Ground Journal*, 11.1 (Fall, 2013), 47-51. Originally published in a working document of Michigan State University in 1969 with a later version in *Evangelical Missions Quarterly*, 9.1 (Fall, 1972) 17-27.

Subsequently, other TEE programmes have developed the same point using a variety of illustrations, depending on their contexts and emphases. TEE in Ethiopia uses the three-legged stool, the Bethany Fellowship in the Philippines a cooking pot balanced on three stones, ITEEN in Nepal a bamboo ladder, Mongolia TEE the railway track proposed by Fred Holland,[14] and the Christian Leaders' Training College Distance Theological Education department in Papua New Guinea a rope-bridge.

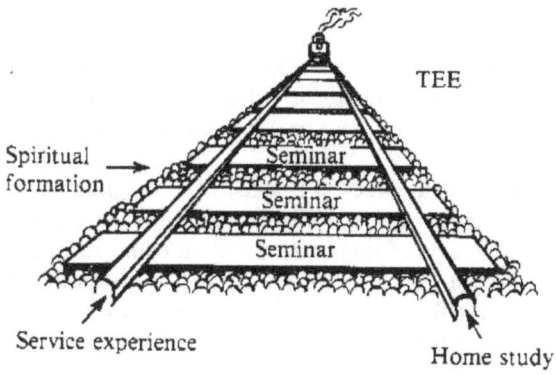

Figure 5b. Railway track (Fred Holland)

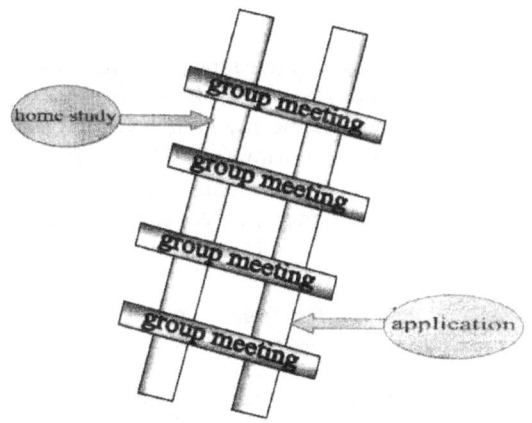

Figure 5c. Bamboo ladder (Nepal)

---

[14] Fred Holland, 'TEXT Africa: Programming for ministry through theological education by extension' in F. Ross Kinsler (ed) *Ministry by the People, Theological Education by Extension (1983)* 103-115. He proposed the model as early as 1978 in his doctoral dissertation.

The three elements reinforce each other educationally. The 'personal study' phase uses an active learning method to help learners grasp key concepts and to internalise them by reflecting on life experience in light of these concepts. In the 'group discussion' phase, learners externalise their own viewpoints, compare these with the viewpoints of others, and find their attitudes changed in ways which transcend mere head knowledge. The phase of 'intentional practice' then enables them to integrate learning and develop skills. These three elements in combination create a learning cycle which, repeated over many weeks, brings progress in each domain of learning. Volker Glissmann confirms the value of TEE's repeated opportunities for reflection and application. TEE is a 'system with a centrally in-built multi-directional reflection and application approach/ cycle' and it has 'an inbuilt and ongoing conversation based on reflection followed by application.'[15]

There is much that unites different TEE programmes. But there is diversity of purposes among TEE programmes, with different target groups, different levels of study, and different educational objectives. TEE is a methodology, a tool to serve a vision. The vision of the programme drives the course offerings in terms of subject matter, academic level, length, presentation and administration.

Different streams of TEE

The ongoing story of TEE over the past five decades has been documented at different points.[16] Theological Education by Extension, as the name suggests, was first seen as an extension of the seminary, sharing the same purpose as the seminary and the same academic level, but using a different methodology in a different location. However, TEE programmes need have no necessary connections with a residential seminary.[17] They do not need classrooms and teaching faculty, may well develop different curricula, and can be governed by their own independent boards. So the word 'Extension'

---

[15] Volker Glissmann, 'What is Theological Education by Extension?', *The Theological Educator*, (2014) http://thetheologicaleducator.net/2014/11/28/what-is-theological-education-by-extension/

[16] See especially: F. Ross Kinsler, 'Theological Education by Extension Comes of Age: a Regional Survey', *International Review of Mission*, 71 (1982), 145-152; Kenneth B. Mulholland, 'TEE Come of Age: A Candid Assessment after Two Decades' in Robert L. Youngblood (ed), *Cyprus: TEE Come of Age* (Exeter: Paternoster House, 1986) 9-25; Harrison, *Forty Years On*; and with an African focus, Kangwa Mabuluki, 'Diversified Theological Education: Genesis, Development and Ecumenical Potential of Theological Education by Extension' in Dietrich Werner, David Esterline, Namsoon Kang and Joshva Raja (eds), *Handbook of Theological Education in World Christianity: Theological Perspectives, Regional Surveys, Ecumenical Trends* (Eugene, Oregon: Wipf & Stock, 2010), 251-262.

[17] Most in Asia today do not, perhaps because there can be tensions in serving different target groups using different methodologies.

in Theological Education by 'Extension', is no longer relevant for many TEE programmes.

In addition, 'Theological Education' is understood in different ways. As the Edinburgh 2010 International study group on Theological Education noted in its Report some, especially in North America, will understand 'Theological Education' to describe programmes designed to prepare people for church-centred, 'professional' ministry of one form or another.[18] TEE has been understood in just this way. TEE has been viewed as an alternative to residential systems for training pastors and church leaders, both where there is, and where there is not, access to seminary education. Many TEE programmes still have this as part of their vision, and their graduates are recognised as having fulfilled churches' requirements for denominational recognition.

However, others, as the Report also notes, have a different understanding of Theological Education, as helping believers understand who they are in Christ, where they are coming from, and what in the world God is calling them to be and to do. Specifically, this understanding of Theological Education is to 'empower people for participating in the mission of God in this world'.

Many TEE programmes today would give a resounding, 'Amen!' to that description. Some explain 'TEE' as 'Tools to Equip and Empower' all believers for mission and ministry in their context. One vivid example of this comes from Pakistan in 2014. The question was put to a group of TEE students, 'How have these courses helped you?' At that very moment the Muslim call to prayer was sounding out loudly from the mosque next door. One woman explained, 'As we are living in a Muslim context, people ask us many questions about our faith. These courses help us to respond. They're very helpful.' Truly, here was a non-professional missionary![19]

TEE as a Tool for Mission – Today

TEE may be used at different academic levels including leadership training for both church and society, at Bachelors and Masters levels. But this section will focus on TEE as a tool for grassroots mission. Most examples are drawn from Asia because of its missional context.[20] More people live in Asia than in all the other continents combined,[21] most of the world's poor are in Asia, Asia is the heartland of the great non-Christian religions, and statistically Asia is the world's least-Christian continent. To be relevant to

---

[18] The 2009 World Study Report. http://www.edinburgh2010.org/en/resources/papersdocumentsf1e3.pdf, p.18

[19] See ATA News, Jan - Mar 2014, 5-6 available from www.ataasia.com

[20] Also, we are more familiar with Asia than elsewhere, having been involved with TEE in Asia for more than forty between us.

[21] Around 60% of the world's population is in Asia. There are three Asians for every two non-Asians in the world.

this context TEE must help Asia's churches equip their people with tools for mission as well as ministry.

Asian examples

TEE in Asia began in the 1970s and 1980s in the countries with established Christian populations (such as India, Pakistan, Bangladesh, Philippines, the Middle East and Papua New Guinea) and it served those populations with church leadership training. From the 1990s, and accelerating in the present century, the focus has shifted more to the grass-roots level and also to first generation contexts where believers are surrounded by non-Christians even in their own families (Nepal, China, Mongolia, Central Asia etc). This is not a total shift, since TEE continues to be used as a tool for ministry training. But it is an important shift since TEE as a tool for mission can equip, on a vast scale, ordinary Christians in their non-Christian environments in Asia.

In 2010, seventy-five TEE leaders, including sixty from more than twenty countries around Asia, met for a conference with the title, '21st Century TEE in Asia: Opportunities and Challenges'.[22] Their estimates indicate a total of around 100,000 active TEE students in Asia. Typically, these Christians are adults, without tertiary education, not engaged in full-time church work and having limited time for study. The great majority interact with friends, neighbours and workmates of other faiths or none and are on the front line of mission. Of the 19 TEE programmes represented, 13 had been established since 1990, (Fig. 6) and several more national programmes have been launched since 2010. So TEE in Asia has new growth, accompanying growing first-generation churches in nations with non-Christian majority populations.

The conference statement expressed participants' strong belief that TEE is indeed a tool for mission today:

> Above all, we believe TEE has the potential to equip all Church members as agents of transformation, moving them from being passive receivers to active servants, salt and light where they are. That's why we are excited about TEE![23]

For example, the Institute for Theological Education by Extension in Nepal, ITEEN, serves rapidly growing churches among Hindu-background believers.[24] Every year, over 6,000 believers are being equipped for the

---

[22] http://www.increasenetwork.org/about-increase/kathmandu-2010-press-release

[23] http://www.increasenetwork.org/about-increase/kathmandu-2010; the Conference Statement was prepared in a participative way as a digest of responses to the question, 'What excites you about TEE?'

[24] www.iteen.org.np and see Peter Bisset, 'The Institute of TEE in Nepal', in F. Ross Kinsler (ed), *Diversified Theological Education: Equipping All God's People* (Pasadena, California: William Carey International University Press, 2008), 107-132.

mission of God through the local church, in a country where two generations ago the church did not even exist. In Mongolia the church is even younger. Before 1990 there was just a handful of Mongolian Christians. In the 1990s, as this tiny seed began to grow, Mongolia TEE[25] grew with it. Up till December 2014, more than 4,300 believers had studied at least one course; the great majority of them had found Christ in the previous ten years. TEE courses gave them not only roots in their new faith but shoots in pioneer mission. One blind believer mastered TEE texts so thoroughly that he was able to leave the city and lead groups of herders; and a single lady, after training with TEE in a city church, took her hairdressing skills to a distant countryside location, set up shop, gossiped the gospel while snipping the hair, and planted a small church.

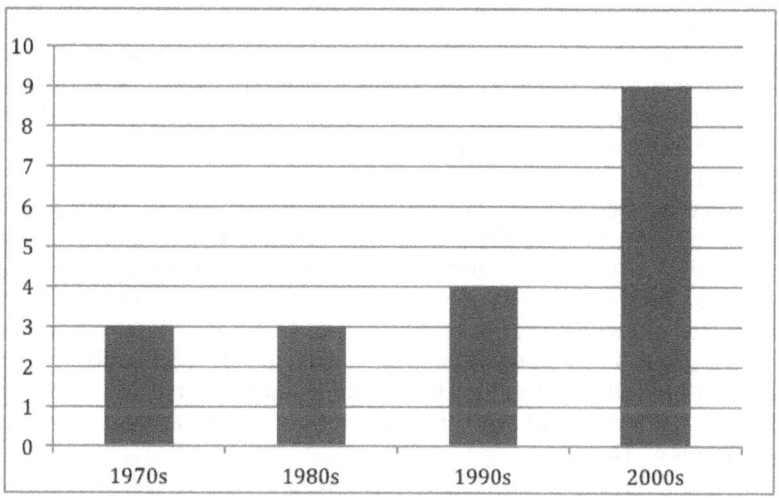

Figure 6. Founding dates of national TEE movements attending the 2010 pan-Asia conference

Estimates vary of the numbers of Christian believers in mainland China, but this is the largest church growth movement in history. TEE materials have helped new believers to grow. Chinese Church Support Ministries distributed over one and a half million copies of the SEAN[26] foundation TEE texts *Abundant Life* and *Abundant Light* to church networks. Another programme trained over 1,300 Group Leaders during the period 2007 -

---

[25] www.teemongolia.mn

[26] SEAN stands for Study by Extension for All Nations. SEAN's TEE courses are widely used worldwide, and as of May 2014, at least one SEAN course was available in 99 languages. Translations take place through the demand of users, and not through any centrally-driven programme. See www.seaninternational.org

2014 by taking them through SEAN's six-part TEE pastoral leadership training programme. Most of these Group Leaders were pastors, many of whom are now training their church members using the same programme. In 2014, these courses began to be published for official use in the Three Self churches.

The Open Russian Theological Academy[27] began in 1994, with TEE church groups in the far east of Russia. Within the next ten years groups had been planted in many corners of Russia's vast territory across a span of 10,000 kilometres! The volunteer Group Leaders and their trainers show remarkable dedication. The countries of Central Asia offer other challenges. Anneta Vyssotskaia[28] characterizes the context as one of continuous persecution and chronic economic hardship. Yet TEE can function in this context, being based around small groups which do not attract hostile attention and can frequently change location, and because study materials are affordable. In very recent years national TEE programmes have begun in all countries of Central Asia, three of these resulting from a remarkable training week in 2012. Vyssotskaia herself has a key ministry of connecting, encouraging and training these emerging TEE programmes.

In recent years Korean Christians have taken a strong lead using TEE as a tool both for making disciples and for mission. Korean church culture emphasises accountable, disciplined study programmes and this has favoured the spread of TEE. Several national programmes[29] equip between them tens of thousands of Korean Christians each year. Moreover, Korean church-planters in many countries have found TEE effective for discipleship and Christian growth, leading to a profusion of new initiatives in Asia and other continents. Koreans remain among the most vigorous exponents of TEE today.

TEE is long established in the Indian subcontinent. Chronologically its first wave has served to train church leaders, its second wave to equip lay people for active ministries and its emerging third wave to disciple new believers from non-Christian backgrounds. Actually each wave, while reaching more people than the one before, has not replaced it. Thus in India, while some study courses of TAFTEE (The Association For Theological Education by Extension) at Bachelor's level, around 8,000 students use courses at Certificate level in fourteen Indian languages.[30] Yet the greatest number of all could result from the discipleship level course

---

[27] See Michael Huggins, 'The Open Russian Theological Academy' in *Diversified Theological Education*, Kinsler, 269-295.

[28] Anneta Vyssotskaia, 'Theological Education in the context of persecution and economic hardship', *International Journal for Religious Freedom*, 5.2 (2012) 111-122.

[29] Including, for example, TEE Korea (www.teekorea.org), KTEE Ministries (www.ktee.org), BEE Korea (www.beekorea.org) and Train and Multiply.

[30] http://taftee.thecross.in/about-taftee/

Abundant Life. TAFTEE has a vision for 50,000 believers to have completed this course by 2020, and many of these will be new disciples of Christ.

Similarly the Open Theological Seminary (OTS) programme in Pakistan has trained church leaders since 1971 and continues to do so. However with the greatest needs at grass roots level, OTS responded with courses to equip everyday believers for everyday mission and ministry. The environment is quite hostile, including terrorist attacks which have directly impacted OTS personnel, yet the work continues to grow with around 4,000 students annually. A carefully designed curriculum at four levels enables even those with minimal background education to progress from foundation to certificate to diploma to degree. As the biggest developer of new TEE courses in Asia, OTS it has written many new courses specifically for the Pakistani context, including a whole curriculum for Christian youth.[31] In Bangladesh, believers from different backgrounds are served by two TEE programmes: the Shikkha Kalyan Trust (SKT) and the College of Christian Theology Bangladesh (CCTB).

Only some of the national TEE programmes in Asia have been described. The Program for Theological Education by Extension[32] has developed many new courses for the Arab world; so has the programme in Papua New Guinea for its context; the TEE Association of Cambodia[33] has a thousand active students. Actually, most countries of Asia have a TEE programme run by nationals for nationals. TEE is alive and well in the continent.

Brief examples from other continents

CIPEP, (Corporación Instituto para la Educación Pastoral)[34] in Colombia is an outstanding example of TEE as a tool for mission. CIPEP began in 1982 with about forty students. By 2010 over 18,000 pastors and leaders had been trained. About half of these were with the AIEC denomination, raised up as leaders for local churches whose number has quadrupled in the last thirty years! Recently CIPEP has started TEE among the Wayuu, an indigenous people whose pastors and leaders had very little training.

CIPEP made such an impact on the Columbian prison system that they were invited to minister in 23 of the 25 major prisons of the country. A guerrilla leader had been serving a sentence of 190 years for brutal and

---

[31] This ten-course curriculum was written from scratch based on issues faced by Pakistani teenagers. It includes such titles as *Me and My God*, *Me and My Identity*, *Me and My Family*, *Me and My Environment* and is a good example of a course which is not merely contextualised but created in a context and for a context.
[32] http://ptee.org/. Courses are created for Arab contexts but some are more widely applicable, including *The Art of Teaching* and *Christian Peacemaking*.
[33] https://www.facebook.com/pages/TEEac/335787733225556
[34] www.cipep.com

sadistic murder. But after turning to Christ his life dramatically changed. He enrolled in the TEE programme in prison, eventually completed it in 2005 and is now an active leader in the Prison Church. For his witness and continued good behaviour his sentence has recently been reduced to only 19 more years.

In Argentina, FIET (Facultad Internacional de Educación Teológica [International Faculty of Theological Education]) has provided TEE training for more than 35 years. In 2012 it had 7800 students in 40 active centres throughout Argentina and among Spanish speakers further afield. Its director Norberto Saracco wrote 'We do not conceive theological education as a rigid model to which the church must adapt, but as something dynamic at the service of the church and the mission'.[35] This serving heart is exemplified in the new Masters level curriculum developed by FIET to meet needs perceived by the local churches, especially relating to contemporary issues.

Terry Barratt, director of SEAN International, reckons that 90% of Latin American countries have functional TEE programmes making a significant impact for Christ in their nations. Also, from many countries, Latin Americans of European origin have returned to their ancestral homelands as missionaries, many taking TEE with them as their tool of mission.

In Africa, TEE has continued for more than forty years. Some TEE programmes have failed, and it is instructive to ask why.[36] Yet others continue to flourish, using the TEXT Africa curriculum, or their own courses, or those from SEAN.[37] TEE Malawi (TEEM) offers a recent example of TEE as tool for 21st century mission. Finding that stakeholder churches were passionate to learn more about evangelism and mission outreach, including outreach to their Muslim neighbours, they are writing an introduction to Islam to meet this need. TEEM has also partnered with African Initiated Churches (AICs) in Malawi, which because of cost are often excluded from more expensive forms of Theological Education.[38]

---

[35] Norberto Saracco, 'International Faculty of Theological Education', in Kinsler (ed), *Diversified Theological Education*, 173-189
[36] See Stewart Snook's useful study, *Developing Leaders through Theological Education by Extension: Case Studies from Africa*, (Wheaton, Billy Graham Center, 1992).
[37] Much more about TEE in Africa and further references can be found in Mabuluki, Diversified Theological Education. See also http://www.eecmymys.edu.et/TEE/index.html for the TEE programmes of Mekane Yesus Seminary with over 1500 students; http://www.tee.co.za and Michael Taylor and Craig Dunsmuir, 'Theological Education by Extension - a Case Study on TEE College Johannesburg' in Isabel Apawo Phiri and Dietrich Werner (eds), *Handbook of Theological Education in Africa* (Oxford: Regnum Books International, 2013), 958-965 for TEE College of South Africa with around 3,200 students; http://teezambia.org for TEE Zambia with more than 10,000 students all over the country.
[38] TEEM Director, personal communication, March 2015.

TEE has not become mainstream in western countries, though in some places there is more interest from diaspora Christians settled in those countries, including many Hispanic and Asian users in the USA.

TEE as a Continuing Tool for Mission in the 21st Century

Our vision is that in the 21st Century, the Lord would use the TEE movement in Asia powerfully to strengthen churches, helping them to multiply, equipping all believers to bring transformation in all areas of society for the growth of His kingdom and the glory of His Name.[39]

This was the vision articulated at the 2010 pan-Asia TEE conference. Only the Lord of the Church can bring such a vision to reality, and the first need is for TEE leaders to be humble, reflective and responsive to Him. In this spirit, TEE educators in Asia are increasingly working together to critique their past, collaborate in the present and plan for the future. Their recent discussions, along with written materials from past decades, suggest that at least the following areas remain priorities for the renewal and future of the TEE movement.

The quality of relations between TEE programmes and the churches they seek to serve

Some TEE programmes help churches provide new believers with strong foundations for discipleship and other programmes for leadership training. Still others offer a pathway of training from the first steps of faith through to active ministry, whether in church or society. In each case, strong partnerships with denominations and their local churches will surely be vital for 21st century TEE. As needs change and new challenges come, yesterday's relationships will not be sufficient.

21st century TEE programmes will work to stay in living relationship with the churches they seek to serve. This will include at least:

* developing and maintaining better processes for listening to the churches: collecting, processing and responding to comments churches make about their courses, and working together with churches to identify curricular areas not yet covered adequately.
* working together with churches to agree on appropriate criteria for choosing local learning Group Leaders, and to develop appropriate ways of recognising, encouraging and providing continuing training for Group Leaders
* helping to create 'a church culture' that gives great value to the ongoing growth, discipleship, and richly varied ministries of each and every church member.

---

[39] http://www.increasenetwork.org/about-increase/kathmandu-2010

The training and support of TEE Group Leaders

Regular group discussion is the beating heart of the TEE method. The Group Leader has the potential both to be TEE's greatest strength, and most serious weakness. A skilful, prayerful, servant Group Leader with vision and passion can bring even mediocre course materials to life, so that Group members cannot wait for next week's group meeting. By contrast, Group Leaders without understanding of their role can ruin the weekly group meeting, even when students have prepared for it using the most thoughtfully and effectively crafted of TEE self-study texts. So the choice, training, monitoring, support and continued upskilling of Group Leaders remain a priority for 21st century TEE.

Considerable energy has been devoted to developing effective Group Leader training packages in many programmes in Asia, including TEE Korea, ITEEN, TAFTEE, and ORTA. Since Group Leaders have a tendency to revert to a lecture style of leadership during group meetings, it will be important for TEE programmes to train Group Leaders using an interactive, group discussion-based approach. One major curriculum provider is preparing a document on basic requirements for Group Leader training.

Innovation and contextual relevance of TEE course materials

The early creative burst of TEE course-writing began in the 1960s and ran strongly for two decades. Courses were initially written for specific national or cultural contexts and were not intended for wider use. Over time, however, 'survival of the fittest' meant that the interesting, understandable and applicable courses spread widely because TEE students enjoyed them. Conversely, boring courses died a natural death. The outcome was educationally positive, but it led to some courses being used widely outside the contexts for which they were originally designed.

While recognising this homogenising trend, it remains true that TEE training is more easily contextualised than are distance-learning curriculum, because of its strong local dimension. Contextualisation takes place naturally when local Group Leaders and learners together apply the material to their local context. It is further strengthened when Group Leader guides are adapted or written for local contexts, recognising that there may be several 'contexts' in one country.[40] Many national TEE programmes already do this, as well as contextualising the learners' course books with local artwork, examples and sometimes deeper-level changes.

TEE national programmes have also created new courses to address particular contextual issues including community health, poverty and development, conflict resolution, folk religion, witness to other faiths and

---

[40] For instance Bangladesh has both Hindu-background and Muslim-background Christians, Kazakhstan has Russians and Kazakh and Uighur.

discipleship of new believers from other faith backgrounds.[41] Others would be helpful on such topics as alcohol addiction, creation care and cross-cultural outreach. Such courses demonstrate TEE's aim to be a tool for outward-looking mission in society. First-generation churches frequently express concern for Christian marriages to be established and the next generation to be nurtured, so national TEE programmes serve them by creating courses on these topics.[42] Not all national TEE programmes have the experience and capacity to develop new courses. The Increase Association (see f. below) helps them to connect with each other to share course materials, course-writing skills and collaboration on new writing projects.

The educational methodology underlying TEE self-study courses

TEE's classic methodology, combining personal study, group discussion, and intentional practice, has proved effective and transformative in many thousands of lives. However, does it stand up to the scrutiny of educational theory? A recent paper[43] identifies six strands of educational theory that influenced the origins of TEE fifty years ago. Five of these six are still strongly affirmed by modern theorists: open access education, principles of andragogy, domains of learning, critical reflection leading to transformative learning, and the importance of small group dialogue. Moreover, new theories including 'blended learning' and the 'flipped classroom' affirm what was already embedded in TEE methodology five decades ago!

However, in the one area of 'mastery learning using programmed texts', educationalists today diverge sharply from the behaviourist theories fashionable at the time of TEE's origins. Programmed instruction is often seen as indoctrinating and paternalistic, stifling critical thought. This is a serious point because many (not all) TEE courses do use programmed textbooks. However, programmed texts are not necessarily shackled to a rigid behaviourist philosophical foundation. Also when reflective questions are used alongside didactic ones in a well-designed TEE lesson, it leads to an appropriate combination of formative and critical education and hence to

---

[41] Just a few examples include *Poverty and Development* (TAFTEE India), *Folk Religion* (OTS Pakistan), *Deep Sea Canoe* (CLTC Papua New Guinea), *Taking the Good News to Muslims* (TEXT Africa).

[42] Courses on Christian marriage and family life have been written by several providers (TEXT Africa, TAFTEE India, Mongolia TEE, SKT Bangladesh, CLTC Papua New Guinea). A comparative review of existing materials would be beneficial.

[43] Tim Green, 'Should TEE in contemporary Asia be rejected, renewed or merely repackaged?', an unpublished paper available from tmwgreen@gmail.com.

the possibility of transformative learning.[44] Moreover, for learners whose previous education was limited or based on rote-learning, programmed texts provide the secure bottom rungs of a ladder which takes them toward the higher cognitive levels of analysis, synthesis and evaluation. These higher cognitive skills may be honed gradually by moving away from strictly programmed texts as learners progress through the curriculum.

Appropriate use of digital technology

Rapid advances in digital technology are changing the ways that many people approach learning and education. 21st Century TEE programmes will make use of the opportunities that digital technology is opening up, while being careful that technological innovations should serve to enhance learning. Technology does not need to replace what is already fruitful – but it can make it even better. Possible ways include delivery of interactive personal study materials on mobile phone or online; supplementary capacity-building and training materials for Group Leaders available online; connecting Group Leaders in remote situations with other Group Leaders for mutual learning and encouragement; and making available resources to support new Group Leader training in remote situations.[45] TEE programmes may also expand ways to serve 'oral preference learners' including courses where the teaching input is video-based rather than text-based.

Fruitful collaboration with other TEE programmes

21st Century TEE programmes will value networking for peer evaluation, sharing of resources and mutual learning and encouragement. In Asia, the Increase Association has these aims. Within the last five years Increase has:

- co-hosted the 2010 pan-Asia TEE conference;
- trained a cohort of twelve reflective practitioners, known as the TEE Equippers, who can
- act as consultants to national TEE programmes across Asia;
- supported the initiatives in Central Asia where four additional countries have started
- national TEE programmes since 2012;
- in 2013 organised a Curriculum Consultation, and supported a Translation and

---

[44] Tim Green makes this case from philosophical, educational and biblical perspectives. See his TEE in contemporary Asia and other unpublished essays. tmwgreen@gmail.com.
[45] Increase, 'Technology & TEE', *Go*, (July, 2014), 8-11 accessible from: http://www.interserve.org.nz/RESOURCES/PUBLICATIONS/GO+MAGAZINE.ht ml#Mission

- Contextualisation workshop;
- run a conference in 2015 'Exploring New Horizons: working together for church-based training in Asia' to address cutting-edge issues.

The relationships nourished through these various events have led to many joint initiatives and much blessing. Increase seeks to foster in the TEE movement a spirit of peer-learning, constructive self-criticism, openness to renewal, cooperation with other church based training programmes and exploration of new horizons. Increase's website[46] may serve as a platform for these initiatives.

Increase connects with similar networks in other continents. In Africa the All Africa TEE Association serves as a forum for TEE programmes in Africa, and has been effective in helping TEE programmes work together in response to common challenges.[47] In Latin America a 2012 conference brought together TEE leaders from across the continent.

Partnership in the mission of God with other forms of theological education

Twenty-first-century TEE programmes recognize the potential benefits to the Church and to the mission of God when they work with others to respond to contemporary challenges in Theological Education. Theological associations such as the Asia Theological Association (of which Increase is an affiliate member) can play an important role in connecting residential theological institutions with church-based training programmes.

Serving the needs of diaspora Christians

The peoples of the world are scattered abroad as never before, including Christian populations. This creates a need and opportunity wherever diaspora churches seek a way to disciple their own people and grow their own leaders using mother tongue materials. Such materials often already exist in their countries of origin, wherever national TEE programmes have created them. Challenges remain for sharing of information, supply of course books and training of Group Leaders. But these can be overcome, and the use of TEE by Christians 'from everywhere to everywhere' is likely to grow in the 21st century. It is also a tool for mission, supporting the outreach of diaspora believers to non-believers in their own ethnic groups.

---

[46] www.increasenetwork.org
[47] Mabuluki, Diversified Theological Education

Conclusion: TEE Tomorrow

Jesus command is to make disciples of all nations. Now that there are indigenous churches in most of them, the question remains, 'How can every member of the people of God be motivated and empowered for mission?'

As we described in this chapter TEE is proving to be one answer to that question. TEE serves churches with a 'Tool to Equip and Empower' and hundreds of thousands are being equipped for mission.

We long to see many more, and more relevant, courses available through a range of delivery mechanisms, so that many more can prepare for local learning groups effectively.

We long to see more national TEE programs providing the vital framework of training, encouragement and accountability.

We long to see to see TEE programmes networking effectively, strengthened and empowered, so that many millions are discipled and equipped for mission and ministry.

Where are those who will invest their lives in the strategic and fruitful ministry of TEE?

May the Lord of the harvest call many more!

THE RELEVANCE OF TEE IN AFRICAN TRAINING FOR MISSION

Kangwa Mabuluki

Theological Education by Extension has been a important form of theological training in Africa. It grew significantly since the introduction of the first two TEE programmes in the 1970s, and has since undergone its ups and downs. Since 2001 there have been efforts to restructure TEE and revive programmes which had collapsed.

This article explores the relevance of TEE in the quest for training for mission in Africa. The article starts with a brief look at the beginnings and the distinctives of this method of theological training and how it came to, and spread in, Africa, before we raise some points of its suitability for theological training needs in the continent, especially with regard to missiological work.

TEE – Its Beginnings

The TEE method of theological education was started in response to a challenge faced by the Presbyterian Church of Guatemala where the traditional residential method was incapable of producing enough leaders, swiftly enough, to cope with the rapid growth that was taking place in the church. A survey of its highly regarded seminary, Seminario Evangelico Presbiteriano de Guatemala, 'revealed that in the previous twenty five years of the institution, a mere ten men were trained and actively serving in the denomination and this all in the context of two hundred growing churches'.[1]

> This was a compound problem which required a radical response, and the seminary found the solution in decentralizing the seminary. Tutors from the seminary began to prepare courses and go out to where the people were. They established centers where students would come together once a week and have a session with a tutor from the seminary. The tutor would help them review the lesson of the previous week. Using the same textbooks as those used at the seminary, the tutor would then introduce and give input on the next lesson and give the students work to do at home for the following week. This new approach meant that the seminary could reach more students within their setting, reduce on costs, and also deal with the problems of uprooting the students from their context which brought about the problem of changing

---

[1] Justice C. Anderson, 'Theological Education by Extension', in A. Scott Moreau (ed), *Evangelical Dictionary of World Mission* (Grand Rapids, MI: Baker, 2000).

their theological approach. While in 1962 the seminary could only enroll 6 students, with the new approach the enrollment increased to about 200 students.[2]

This marked the birth of TEE.

Distinctives of the TEE Method

While the TEE method shares some aspects with general distance-learning or correspondence programmes, the summary description given above shows that this method was designed differently from most distance-learning or correspondence programmes which mostly engage individual students receiving study material (either by physically collecting the material from the school, or by mail, or through electronic means) and studying it on their own in preparation for an exam. The TEE method has this individual or personal study as only one component. There are three interrelated   components   or   pillars,   namely: *Self-study,   Group meetings/discussions, and Practical work.*

Ross Kinsler illustrates the three components by sharing from his experience in Guatemala:

> In Guatemala, since our students were local church leaders, heads of families, mostly employed in secular jobs or subsistence farming, scattered over large areas, we could only plan to meet with them once a week or twice a month at locations accessible for them, though some travel for them and more for our faculty was often necessary. Since those meetings could only last for two or three hours, we had to use that time for discussion and debate, not for lectures or monologue. This in turn meant that the students had to be able to get the basic course content (cognitive, affective, practical) on their own in preparation for each group meeting. So we devised basic self-study materials for the relevant 'academic' levels and cultural contexts. The third component, in addition to daily individualized study and weekly or bi-monthly group discussion, was ongoing, practical testing or application of the substance and issues of the course material in the students' local ecclesial and social contexts.[3]

TEE practitioners have various symbolic illustrations of TEE; the most popular one is the railway analogy developed by Ted Ward. The other one is the one used by the Ethiopia TEE, the African three-legged stool.

The three components, as illustrated by the African stool analogy or Ward's railway analogy, are of critical importance; the absence of any one will lead to the collapse of functionality. However, it is important to note

---

[2] Kangwa Mabuluki, 'Diversified Theological Education: Genesis, Development and Ecumenical Potential of Theological Education by Extension', in Werner, Dietrich, David Esterline, Namsoon Kang and Joshva Raja (eds), *Handbook of Theological Education in World Christianity: Theological Perspectives, Regional Survey, Ecumenical Trends* (Oxford: Regnum, 2010).
[3] Kinsler, *Diversified Theological Education.*

and stress that the three are also supported by other aspects. For example, self-study would be a firm leg of the stool only if the study material is appropriate. The study material has to be in a distance-study format and must conform to the objective of TEE of offering cognitive knowledge, but it should also point to practical application and lead the student to have effective personal reflection and application appropriate to his or her own context. The material ought to be professionally written. As Kinsler rightly observes, 'If the materials are confusing or abstract or simplistic, or if group meetings are too widely separated or irrelevant or boring, students will be discouraged, and many will drop out. When the three basic educational components are ideally combined and balanced, participants are constantly challenged to work effectively towards their mission, the church's mission, God's mission.'[4]

Sam Burton compares elements of the TEE method with those which Jesus used to teach his disciples:

> i) Teaching by example – that is, practising what he preached. ii) Teaching in real life situations – that is, using the circumstances they found themselves in as tools for educating. iii) Teaching from the known about the unknown – that is, understanding at what level the disciples were already at and building upon that foundation. iv) Teaching in a highly personalized way – that is, teaching lessons which were specific to the needs of the people. v) Teaching by constant assessment – that is, always ensuring that the disciples had understood what was being taught. vi) Teaching by delegating important tasks – that is, allowing a degree of responsibility.[5]

TEE in Africa – Growth and Challenges

TEE has been a significant part of the African theological landscape since 1970 when the first two TEE programmes were established in Ethiopia and Zambia, after a workshop (to look into expanding TEE in Africa) organised by the World Council of Churches in Nairobi, Kenya. Because of its appropriateness to the African church situation, the programme spread so rapidly that by 1977 a survey revealed that 'there were already fifty-seven programmes in Africa and Madagascar with a total of 6,869 extension students.'[6]

But despite its rapid spread and growth, the TEE movement slowed down and in some countries totally collapsed. This downward trend was, however, not because the method was inappropriate for Africa, but was due to other factors; we raise here three critical reasons:

---

[4] Kinsler, *Diversified Theological Education*.

[5] Sam Westman Burton, *Disciple Mentoring: Theological Education by Extension* (Pasadena, CA: William Carey Library, 2000).

[6] F. Ross Kinsler, *The Extension Movement in Theological Education: A call to the Renewal of Ministry*. Pasadena, CA: William Carey Library (revised edition, 1981).

Dominance of missionaries and mission personnel in establishing TEE

Most TEEs were established at the initiative and funding of foreign missionaries and missions. The set-up depended on the availability of funding which could not be sustained with local resources, leading to most TEEs dying or not operating as they should after the departure of the missionaries.

The perceived conflict between
residential seminaries and TEE programmes

The conflict between TEE programmes and residential seminaries has most of the time led to the sidelining and diminishing of the value of TEE. In most cases, emphasis has been placed on the advantages of TEE against seminary training, especially the financial or cost factor. This cost factor understandably causes strong reactions because it was, and still in most cases is, made without a due emphasis on the need for seminary training which is still essential to produce academic and professional theologians.

There was, and still is, a need to emphasise how TEE and theological seminaries are both essential and complement each other in the theological development of both clergy and lay people. The good aspects of TEE (practical work, adaptability to context, cost-effectiveness, etc.) are also required for the seminary, just as the important aspects of the seminary (academic emphasis, high-quality study material, etc.) are also required and must also be emphasised for TEE.

There are a good number of cases in Africa where TEE programmes exist side-by-side with seminaries or theological departments. So, for the situation in Africa, the solution is not theological college OR theological education by extension, but it is theological college AND theological education by extension, because each has a role to play and the focus should be to address the shortcomings and weaknesses of each method. In fact, it is important to note that the start of TEE in Guatemala was a venture where the two co-existed in a complementary way.

Departure from the actual TEE method

Some of the TEE programmes could not survive or operate effectively because they did not maintain the basics of the TEE method. Fremont and Sara Regier observed this in the report of their 1994 Research Project of Africa Non-formal Theological Education (which included TEE). They observe that:

> Much of what is called TEE is a far cry from the classical Ross Kinsler model. TEE originally came out of an era of popular liberation movement in Central America stressing bottom-up theology. Much of the TEE training content in Africa is more top-down. What is called contextualization (making the training relevant to the particular situation and environment) is too often

little more than putting African wraps onto Western thought. Often weekly TEE seminars, intended as facilitated discussion and application sessions, become teaching or even preaching. In too many cases, the local TEE program is not really owned by the local church... Some TEE programs are so strongly focused on evangelism that the equipping hardly occurs.[7]

Following the three important components or pillars of TEE requires a lot of discipline and commitment, and a regular review of progress. TEE is contextual; the details of how the programme is carried out differ from country to country, but when the basics of the TEE method are not followed, the programme does not produce the desired results, and the negative things said about TEE begin to become true and the programme is abandoned or collapses.

The significance and relevance of TEE in training for mission in Africa

A general point on the relevance of TEE for Africa, which caused it to be well received and expand significantly fast, is the fact that conditions in the church in Guatemala which led to the start of TEE also exist in Africa. The type of theological training in Africa is still predominantly that of the western-style seminary or university department of theology. This method is evidently inadequate to serve the needs of training pastors for a rapidly growing African church. Moreover, the church in Africa does not have the required resources to expand the colleges, let alone maintain them. There are also other points of relevance; I wish to raise four of these, two in a more general way and two with a specific emphasis on mission.

Viability

The issue of viability of theological education in general has been a constant concern. But the focus on viability has often been on 'financial viability'. Financial viability is an important issue, and we shall say something about below. But we want to note here first that the issue of viability is much broader. Konrad Raiser, the former general secretary of the World Council of Churches, points out that, 'A viable form of theological education and ministerial formation will... aim at preparing leaders of Christian Communities who are able to inspire new life, to renew and transform the institutional identity of the Church.'[8]

---

[7] Fremont and Sara Regier, *Africa Non-formal Theological Education Research Project* (Newton, KS: Commission on Overseas Mission, General Conference Mennonite Church, 1994).

[8] Konrad Raiser. 'Importance of the Ecumenical Vision for Theological Education and Ministerial Formation', in J. Pobee (ed), *Towards Viable Theological Education; Ecumenical Imperatives Catalyst of Renewal* (Geneva: WCC, 1997).

One of the reasons that led to a search for and development of the TEE method was that the then-existing forms of theological education became inadequate and therefore not viable. It was because of this that the church in Guatemala set out to search for other alternatives to make theological education respond to the challenges of meeting the numerical demand for ministers, as well as the need to train ministers whose theology was tuned into their context because that was where it had been developed. Through its over forty years of existence, TEE has been shown to be a viable means of theological education.

Turning back to financial viability, TEE is financially more viable compared with residential theological training. It costs much less to train a larger number of church leaders and workers through TEE than through residential or seminary training. But as Adrian Chatfield points out, 'This does not mean TEE is cheap.'[9] The development of TEE material which is of high quality can be quite costly. But this cost is often one-off and indeed goes a long way because, once the material is produced, over time it is well used. Because of the nature of the course material, essential revisions are made from time to time in the process of use. In some cases, the misunderstanding that TEE is cheap and does not require much resource is overstressed and leads to the collapse of a programme.

Accessibility

TEE is a very accessible method of education and formation. Ross Kinsler in the introductory chapter to his book *Diversified Theological Education*, points out ten points of access: geographical, economic, cultural, ecclesiastical, gender, race, class, different abilities, pedagogical, and spiritual.[10]

It is the ecclesiastical, economic, class and pedagogical accessibility of TEE that opened it to the African Instituted Churches (also known as African Independent Churches) where most of the leaders did not have access to formal theological training. In November 1978, twenty leaders from eleven African Instituted Churches in eight countries across the continent met in Cairo, at a meeting convened by Bishop Antonious Markos of the Coptic Orthodox Church of Egypt. The meeting established the Organization of African Independent Churches (OAIC) to support and nurture these churches in a variety of ways. In 1980, the OAIC initiated the TEE programme under the leadership of Agustin and Rosario Battle. The programme, continental in nature, produced more than sixty TEE texts in Swahili, English and French.[11] One of the co-ordinators of TEE

---

[9] Regier, *Africa Non-formal Theological Education Research Project*.
[10] Kinsler, *Diversified Theological Education*.
[11] Fareth Sendegeya and Leon Spencer (eds), 'Understanding TEE: A course outline and Handbook for Students and Tutors in Residential Theological Institutions in

Programming for the OAIC in West Africa, the Rev. Helena Hooper, was later to become the first chairperson of the All Africa TEE Association formed at the second All Africa TEE Conference in Livingstone, Zambia, in 2006 in an effort to revitalise and strengthen TEE programmes in Africa.

The accessibility of TEE helps the church to implement the priesthood of all believers, because TEE dares to open quality theological learning to ordinary members of the church, and in this way also opens the church to the critical theological thought and reflection of ordinary members. It is this aspect that makes the method a key factor in ecumenical collaboration and also a vehicle through which the church can respond to the pressing needs of our time.

Class accessibility also deserves a brief comment. At a time when academic education has become a preserve of the powerful and financially able, and therefore a class factor, many people who would otherwise make good church ministers and leaders miss out on good theological education, either because they cannot afford to go to seminary and/or because they do not have the academic qualifications to enter it. This is not to say academic requirements are not important, but in a situation where academia is still so much the banking system and unfairly controlled largely by the 'haves' and the powerful in society, the church ought to think of ways of providing theological education that are academically flexible, which can offer many a chance to develop their God-given potential. Here Paulo Freire's creative thoughts about education (the educator and the learner) come into play. TEE makes theological education accessible even to those with less education without necessarily compromising on quality, but ensuring quality at every level, through the careful and rigorous preparation of the course material.

Providing an alternative to western-style seminary training

One of the significant aspects of TEE is that it challenges western styles or models of education or schooling which have also permeated theological education and are held as the standard model because of inherited traditions, as Norman E. Thomas points out:

> The powerful drive for schooling among people in developing nations too often results in acceptance of the traditional schooling paradigm as norm for ministry formation. After all, we have the weight of tradition behind such models as the monastic discipline of the Middle Ages in Europe, the University based training of clergy, and the denominational seminary model began in North America. But these are not the only viable models.[12]

Africa', in *The Journal of African Network of Institutions of Theological Education Preparing Anglicans for Ministry,* Issue No. 32, November 2001.

[12] N.E. Thomas, 'Partners in Transforming Ministry: Models for a New Millennium', in *Mission and Transformation in a Changing World; A dialogue with*

The dominant feature of seminary theological training normally is its heavy theoretical bias which has been a carry-over from the general model of education. This has been criticised by educators like Paulo Freire[13] as being teacher-centred where the teacher is the only source of knowledge which is passed on or 'banked' in the learners. Through its emphasis on group study and practical work, the TEE method makes possible the 'theology from below' approach where the teacher, tutor or facilitator are open to learning also from the learners.

Theology from below, rooted in the people themselves, is important for the success of Christian mission. One criticism, and also one cause of the failure of some early mission enterprises, was the fact that it was transplanted from the North to the South. While this criticism is often connected with early European missionaries, it is still something to watch out for today when we have local missionaries. We have to be aware of transferring contexts and classes. Mission should be from within, and therefore a training method that encourages theology from below or from within the people will make for strong and effective missiological results.

In fact, the classical or predominant seminary-style theological education, with all its advantages of producing needed theological scholars, had been identified to be the weak link in the chain of Christian mission as early as the 1938 International Missionary Council held in Tambaram.[14] This was because this style of theological education was no longer effective in training future church leaders in the rapidly changing and growing church in the global South. TEE indeed provides a fitting alternative.

Responding to the broader mission paradigm
of fighting the forces of death

The focus of mission has for several years now been understood to be to fulfil Jesus' mission as expressed in John 10:10 – 'to give life in all its fullness'. This mission focus out of necessity significantly requires mission to include the fight against the life-denying forces of poverty, disease, economic injustice, ecological degradation, etc. This inclusion has not formed a major part of mission in the past. As Ross Kinsler aptly observes:

> Many Christians and many churches maintain, as we have suggested, a mission paradigm that is individualistic and pietistic, that gives priority to individual 'salvation' and 'spiritual' or religious practices, and that ultimately focuses upon eternal life after death. We have chosen... to follow a mission

---

Global Mission Colleagues (General Board of Global Ministries, The United Methodist Church 1998).

[13] See the writings of Paulo Freire, especially *The Pedagogy of the Oppressed* (New York: Continuum, 30th Anniversary Edition 1970).

[14] Saint Beagle, 'Outline and evaluate Theological Education by Extension as an appropriate model of training for church leaders in the Global South': http://saintbeagle.wordpress.com/papers/tee-theological-education-by-extension

paradigm that focuses on the biblical mandates associated with the Sabbath Day, the Sabbath Year, and the Jubilee, because they deal with fundamental economic and ecological realities that are pre-eminent in our time, that are the primary threats to life in the twenty-first century, that are largely beyond the reach of traditional mission paradigms, and that are eminently biblical and spiritual matters. This paradigm does not minimize the personal relationship with God, but it may in fact call into question any understanding of salvation that ignores or minimizes these realities. The critical question for this paradigm is, 'What was Jesus' understanding of God's mission?' And this leads to the question, 'What does it mean to follow Jesus in today's world?'[15]

TEE is flexible as a training method that moves 'from outside to the inside', bringing theological thought and reflection from those people on the fringes of what is regarded as mainline theological centres, namely seminaries and theological schools. It is these people on the fringes of society, as experience has proved, who are mostly affected by the forces of death and dehumanisation in society, which are among the key things theology must respond to and address.

Taking his call for a paradigm shift in mission further, Ross Kinsler argues that:

It is evident, for example, that professional, Western models of healthcare will not in the foreseeable future be able to provide adequate services among the expanding poor populations of Africa, where 15,000 children die daily for lack of clean water, basic nutrition, and preventive healthcare. Grassroots health education and community development combined with Theological Education by Extension might transform that situation, if in fact a new holistic vision of God's mission could bring together those three parallel movements that depend primarily on local leaders.[16]

Conclusion

The relevance of TEE has necessitated strong efforts to revive it after a period of regression and in some cases collapse. The effort was sparked at the 'Journey of Hope' meeting which was organised by the World Council of Churches' Ecumenical Theological Education Department, was held in Kempton Park in South Africa. This important meeting brought together people from different fields of theological education, including a number of TEE practitioners from Botswana, South Africa, Kenya, Uganda and Zambia. It was these people that initiated efforts to revive and strengthen the work of TEE in different countries in Africa. They noted that, while TEE was active in the five countries they came from, they had not known about each other until this meeting. It was therefore imperative, they thought, as part of strengthening TEE work, to create a forum for sharing good practice and giving mutual support, as well as a joint effort in

---

[15] Kinsler, *Diversified Theological Education..*
[16] Kinsler, *Diversified Theological Education.*

establishing TEE in countries where none existed but was greatly needed. Thus efforts were started to establish the All Africa Theological Education by Extension which was formally launched at the second All Africa TEE Conference held in Livingstone, Zambia, in 2006.

The Association has since organised two other All Africa TEE Conferences in Dodowa, Ghana, in 2010 and in Addis Ababa, Ethiopia, in 2014. The Association has also supported the revival of TEE in Lubumbashi, Democratic Republic of Congo, after the civil war there, in Msoma, Tanzania, many years after the Mennonite Church Leadership had closed it to channel resources to support the Bible college, which has not fully succeeded; hence the need to revive TEE. The Association has embarked on regional training programmes in areas like writing TEE course material, as a way of supporting TEE.

TEE programmes currently exist in the following countries: Angola, Botswana, Burundi, Democratic Republic of Congo, Ethiopia, Gambia, Ghana, Kenya, Malawi, Liberia, Madagascar, Mauritius, Mozambique, Nigeria, Sierra Leone, South Sudan, Tanzania, Zambia and Zimbabwe. There currently efforts to establish TEE with the Lutheran Church in Senegal.

TEE in Kenya is carried out in separate denominations, with the strongest being in the Presbyterian Church of East Africa based at the East Africa Presbyterian University. TEE in Ethiopia, which is one of the oldest, is also denominationally based in the Mekane Yesus Church. It is well established as a department at the Mekane Yesus Seminary, with programmes covering several districts in Ethiopia. The Ethiopian TEE clearly demonstrates the uniqueness of TEE in that, while it is an integrated department of the Seminary, the seminary also has a distant-learning unit.

TEE in South Africa is also one of the well-established programmes set up in response to the Apartheid system, to provide proper theological education for black pastors who could not be admitted to theological schools because they also admitted whites. The programme is ecumenical and has developed into a TEE college catering for other countries in Southern Africa like Swaziland, Lesotho, Zimbabwe and Mozambique. The college has since developed and attained accreditation with the South African government, becoming the first college to offer a TEE degree.

Another strong programme is Zambia TEE which is solely focused on lay training. It is ecumenical, bringing together nine mainline churches. Like the South Africa TEE, Zambia TEE has introduced it to prisons as a way of helping in the reform process.

TEE is an important and suitable method for theological training for mission in Africa. So we end by echoing Fremont and Sara Regier, who carried out the most extensive evaluation of TEE in Africa in 1994. They conclude their report by making a call for African church leaders to reflect upon the strengths of TEE, to accept it as a meaningful alternative to formal residential studies, and to work to address the challenges and difficulties TEE programmes sometimes face.[17]

---

[17] Regier, *Africa Non-formal Theological Education Research Project.*

SECTION TWO

CRUCIAL ISSUES

THEOLOGICAL EDUCATION
AS MISSIONARY FORMATION

Stephen Bevans, SVD

'Mission is the mother of theology.'

'... theology has exegesis as it starting point and missionary proclamation as its goal.'

'... theology, rightly understood, has no reason to exist other than crucially accompany the missio Dei.'

Introduction

The aim of this chapter is to unpack and reflect on the implications of these three short quotations from the early twentieth-century biblical scholar Martin Kähler, the contemporary systematic theologian and ecumenist Cardinal Walter Kasper, and the great twentieth-century missiologist David J. Bosch.[1] The thesis of this chapter is that any and all theological education at whatever level should be infused with a missionary perspective and be geared to missionary practice. I will argue, in other words that, today especially, theological education should be missionary formation.

My argument will be developed in three steps. A first step will trace how theology began precisely as reflection upon the church's mission, but that, as Christianity became more and more institutionalised, mission itself and reflection on mission became more and more relegated to the theological margins. A second step will examine some 'turns' in contemporary theology towards missionary reflection and will point out several reasons why such a 'turn' is imperative in today's church. A third step of the argument will propose how theological education might be conceived as missionary formation.

---

[1] Martin Kähler, *Schriften zur Christologie und Mission* (Munich: Chr. Kaiser Verlag, 1971 [first edition, 1908], 189. Quoted in David J. Bosch, *Transforming Mission: Paradigm Shifts in Theology of Mission* (Maryknoll, NY: Orbis Books, 1991), 16. Walter Kasper, *The Methods of Dogmatic Theology* (Shannon, Ireland: Ecclesia Press, 1969), 26; Bosch, *Transforming Mission*, 494. Kasper speak about 'dogmatic' (systematic) theology, but I think his point is relevant to the whole field of theology.

From Matrix to Margins

In the first three centuries of the church's existence, what I have called the 'missiological imagination' was what gave it identity and inspired its theology.[2] Theology emerged in the earliest Christian writings as 'an accompanying manifestation of the Christian mission', as Martin Kähler put it. More recently, Martin Hengel has expressed it similarly: 'The history and the theology of early Christianity are, first of all, "mission history" and "mission theology"'.[3] Theology – Paul's letters, the four gospels, the writings of the apologists Justin, Irenaeus, and Origen in the West and Bardasian and Tatian in the East – was reflection that emerged from the matrix of mission.

But, especially in the West, as Christianity became legal in and then the state religion of the Roman Empire, theology was gradually transformed into reflection on Christian life and Christian faith, not so much its dissemination. 'As the culture was "Christianized"', Darrell Guder writes, 'the *theological* relevance of mission appeared to diminish.'[4] Focus shifted from reflecting on the problems and challenges of proclaiming and witnessing to the faith as a minority group, to explaining and defending formulas of faith that were connected with upholding the political unity of the Empire. From the 'Golden Age' of the patristic period, through the Middle Ages and into the eighteenth century, theology was concerned with, as Edward Farley expressed it, 'the knowledge of God and the things of God'.[5] The irony was that, while throughout history amazing theological reflection was indeed being done out of missionary experience – Gregory the Great writing to Augustine of Canterbury, the eighth-century Saxon gospel called the *Heliand*, or the creative efforts of contextual thinking practised by Cyril and Methodius among the Slavs, Matteo Ricci among the Chinese, Alexandre de Rhodes in Vietnam, or William Carey in India – very little of these potentially ground-breaking principles found their way

---

[2] See Stephen Bevans, SVD, 'Wisdom from the Margins: Systematic Theology and the Missiological Imagination,' *Australian e-Journal of Theology* 5 (August 2005): http://aejt.com.au/__data/assets/pdf_file/0006/395502/AEJT_5.1_Bevans.pdf, 1-18. In this section I am following this article rather closely.

[3] Kähler, *Schriften*, 190, quoted in Bosch, *Transforming Mission*, 16; Martin Hengel, 'The Origins of the Christian Mission', in *Between Jesus and Paul: Studies in the Earliest History of Christianity* (London: SCM, 1983), 53, quoted in Bosch, *Transforming Mission*, 15.

[4] Darrell L. Guder, 'Theological Formation for Missional Faithfulness after Christendom: A Response to Steve De Gruchy,' in Werner, Dietrich, David Esterline, Namsoon Kang and Joshva Raja (eds), *Handbook of Theological Education in World Christianity: Theological Perspectives, Regional Survey, Ecumenical Trends* (Oxford: Regnum, 2010), 52.

[5] Edward Farley, *Theologia: The Fragmentation and Unity of Theological Education* (Philadelphia, PA: Fortress Press, 1983), 31, 77. I am following David Bosch's explanation of Farley in *Transforming Mission*, 489-90.

into the thought of the theologians who were shaping the classic works of theology in the West and writing the works that would be used in theological education in the universities and, eventually, seminaries and theological schools in Europe and North America.

In the seventeenth and eighteenth centuries, as theology was influenced – consciously or unconsciously – by the rationalism of the Enlightenment, the mission dimension of theology became even more isolated from mainstream theology. What had been a unified process in the medieval period became subdivided into practical fields necessary for priests and pastors. Moral theology, for example, had already emerged in Roman Catholicism by this time as a particular theological discipline. Dogmatic or doctrinal theology became more and more a 'technical and scholarly enterprise', and theology itself developed into the 'fourfold pattern' of biblical studies, church history, systematic theology, and practical theology – especially in Protestant theology, but influential in Roman Catholic theology as well.[6] Friedrich Schleiermacher wrote of a threefold schema of theological studies consisting of philosophical theology, historical theology, and practical theology, locating missiology in the third area.[7] Theology and theological education in this period, writes David Bosch, were 'thoroughly unmissionary'[8] – despite the fact that the nineteenth century saw an explosion of missionary activity in both Protestant and Catholic churches. Learning theology – whether in Oxford in England, Princeton Seminary in the United States, the Gregorian University in Rome, or the Major Seminary in Vigan, Philippines – was learning what was being thought about and written about in Europe or North America. It had nothing to do with the church's mission, either in a Europe turned upside-down by the Industrial Revolution or colonial expansion, or encounters with new cultural worlds as the church expanded in Asia, Africa or Oceania. What was learned was 'applied' to specific concrete situations; not by any means were questions encountered in the front-lines of missionary and intercultural encounter understood as sources for much theological reflection.

In the late nineteenth century, Alexander Duff and then Gustav Warneck pioneered the new discipline of missiology, and some reflection on mission was introduced into the theological curriculum. Even then, however, there was 'no guarantee that missiology now had a legal domicile in theology'.[9] Duff's conviction was that theological reflection on missionary activity was central to theology. It should be studied not only by those preparing to

---

[6] See Farley, *Theologia*, x-xii; 73-124, referred to in Bosch, *Transforming Mission*, 490.

[7] Friedrich Schleiermacher, *Brief Outline on the Study of Theology*, trans. Terrence N. Tice (Atlanta, GA: John Knox Press, 1966 [originally published 1830]), 102 (#298).

[8] Bosch, *Transforming Mission*, 490.

[9] Bosch, *Transforming Mission*, 491.

minister in 'mission lands', but by those 'whose ministry lay amid highland farms and flocks, Clydeside factory sirens' or among women and men 'stocked with solid comforts of the urban middle class'.[10] Nevertheless, as Andrew Walls tells the story, he could only get approval for his chair of mission at the University of Edinburgh by insisting that what he taught 'would not affect the other branches of the theological curriculum'.[11]

Although the late nineteenth century would see the establishment of chairs of missiology in many major universities in Europe and North America, they were usually treated, as David Bosch wryly describes them, as 'the theological institution's "department of foreign affairs", dealing with the exotic but at the same time – for "real" theology – the peripheral', existing in 'splendid isolation'.[12] It is fascinating to read about the tensions between theological education and missionary preparation in the report of Commission V of the 1910 Edinburgh World Missionary Conference.[13] Such has been the situation to our own day, when we see those chairs and departments of mission being left vacant or changing into chairs of World Christianity, Interreligious Studies or Intercultural Studies. Mission in theological education has gone from the matrix to the margins.

Missionary Formation for a Missional Church

There are two factors, however, that might indicate a reversal of this centuries-old trend to marginalise the place of mission in theological thinking and theological education. The first is a shift in theology itself, particularly in the area of ecclesiology. The second is a shift in understanding the world in which the church ministers today.

Shifts in theology

The shift in theology goes back at least to the 1952 Conference of the International Missionary Council in Willingen, Germany, where – inspired by the theology of Karl Barth and Karl Hartenstein – Wilhelm Anderson proposed a dynamic understanding of God whose very Trinitarian nature is expressed in God's saving involvement with the whole of creation. God, in

---

[10] Andrew Walls, 'Missiological Education in Historical Perspective,' in Dudley Woodberry, Charles van Engen, and Edgar J. Elliston (eds), *Missiological Education for the 21st Century: The Book, the Circle and the Sandals* (Maryknoll, NY: Orbis Books, 1996), 14.
[11] Walls, 'Missiological Education in Historical Perspective,' 17.
[12] Bosch, *Transforming Mission*, 492.
[13] World Missionary Conference, 1910, *Report of Commission V: The Training of Teachers* (Edinburgh and London: Oliphant, Anderson & Ferrier; and New York, Chicago and Toronto: Fleming H. Revell, n.d. [1910]): https://archive.org/stream/reportcommissionv00worliala#page/n5/mode/2up, 35-40.

other words, is a God of mission.[14] In the 1960s, Roman Catholic theologian Karl Rahner sparked a revival in Trinitarian theology by his strong assertion that 'the economic Trinity is the immanent Trinity, and vice-versa'.[15] Any theological understanding of God as such, Rahner insists, must start with women's and men's *experience* of God in history – as God reveals Godself in the divine mission. Especially because of Barth's and Rahner's work, says Catherine LaCugna, contemporary Christian theology's 'only option... is to be trinitarian'.[16]

What it means to be church, then, as Anderson and Willingen explained further, is to be a people caught up in this *missio Dei*, working together with God for the wholeness, healing and fulness – salvation – of all that exists. Some thirteen years later, the idea of the church participating in the mission of God emerged in Vatican II's document on mission. The church, the Council stated, is 'missionary by its very nature' because 'it is from the mission of the Son and the mission of the Holy Spirit that it takes its origin, in accordance with the decree of God the Father'.[17] Such a missionary turn was bolstered as well by the eschatological turn of twentieth-century theology, a turn that emphasised the already-present but not-yet realisation of the Kingdom or Reign of God in the preaching and witness of Jesus.[18] The church began to understand itself not so much as the 'Kingdom of God on earth' as the servant of that Kingdom, of which it is 'the initial budding forth'.[19] Eschatology and Christology revealed the church's provisionary, and therefore missionary, nature.

While this shift in understanding the nature of the church took place principally within the discipline of missiology, it has gradually moved into the mainstream of ecclesiology as well. In his 1975 work on ecclesiology, to give just one example, Jürgen Moltmann noted that 'Today one of the strongest impulses towards the renewal of the theological concept of the

---

[14] See Wilhelm Anderson, *Towards a Theology of Mission. A Study of the Encounter between the Missionary Enterprise and the Church and Its Theology*, IMC research Pamphlet No. 2 (London: SCM, 1955). See also Bosch, *Transforming Mission*, 389-90.

[15] Karl Rahner, *The Trinity* (New York: Herder & Herder, 1970), 21-24, 82-103 (see esp. 22).

[16] Catherine M. LaCugna, *God For Us: The Trinity and Christian Life* (San Francisco, CA: HarperSanFrancisco, 1992), 3.

[17] Vatican Council II, Decree on the Mission Activity of the Church, *Ad Gentes* (AG): www.vatican.va/archive/hist_councils/ii_vatican_council/documents/vat-ii_decree_19651207_ad-gentes_en.html, 2.

[18] See the short summary of twentieth-century eschatological and Christological developments in Anthony Kelly, *Eschatology and Hope* (Maryknoll, NY: Orbis Books, 2006), 30-31.

[19] Vatican Council II, Dogmatic Constitution on the Church, *Lumen Gentium* (LG): www.vatican.va/archive/hist_councils/ii_vatican_council/documents/vat-ii_const_19641121_lumen-gentium_en.html, 5.

church comes from the theology of mission'.[20] This shift in ecclesiology is seen particularly clearly in the 2013 statement of the Commission on Faith and Order from the World Council of Churches (WCC), *The Church: Towards a Common Vision*, influenced, it freely admits, by the WCC's Commission on World Mission and Evangelism 2013 statement on mission, *Together Towards Life*.[21] This document locates the church within the mission of the triune God and declares: 'As a divinely established communion, the Church belongs to God and does not exist for itself. It is by its very nature missionary, called and sent to witness in its own life to that communion which God intends for all humanity and for all creation in the kingdom.'[22] While perhaps more of a mission document, Pope Francis's 2013 Apostolic Exhortation makes a strong plea for a church that is missionary through and through, speaking of Christians as 'missionary disciples'. 'I dream,' the Pope writes, 'of a "missionary option", that is a missionary impulse capable of transforming everything, so that the Church's customs, ways of doing things, times and schedules, language and structures can be suitably channelled for the evangelization of today's world rather than for her self-preservation.'[23] Theological education for such a missionary church needs to be a thoroughly missionary formation.

---

[20] Jürgen Moltmann, *The Church in the Power of the Spirit* (Minneapolis, MN: Fortress Press, 1995), 7. See, for example, Stephen Bevans, 'Missionary Ecclesiology: Reflections on the Church as a Community of Missionary Disciples', in a forthcoming Festschrift for Charles van Engen; from a Roman Catholic perspective, see 'Mission as the Nature of the Church: Developments in Catholic Theology', in *Australian e-Journal of Theology* 21.3 (December 2014): http://aejt.com.au/__data/assets/pdf_file/0011/694298/AEJT_Mission_as_the_Natur e_of_the_Church_Developments_in_Catholic_Ecclesiology_Bevans.pdf, 184-96.

[21] Commission on World Mission and Evangelism, *Together Towards Life: Mission and Evangelism in Changing Landscapes* (TTL), www.oikoumene.org/en/ resources/documents/commissions/mission-and-evangelism/together-towards-life-mission-and-evangelism-in-changing-landscapes

[22] Commission on Faith and Order, *The Church: Toward a Common Vision* (CTCV): www.oikoumene.org/en/resources/documents/commissions/faith-and-order/i-unity-the-church-and-its-mission/the-church-towards-a-common-vision, 13. See Stephen Bevans, 'Ecclesiology and Missiology: Reflections on Two Recent Documents from the World Council of Churches', in *Dialog* (November 2015). See CTCV, 'Historical Note', 46, for the statement of how TTL influenced the document. See also John Gibaut, 'From Unity and Mission to Koinonia and Missio Dei: Convergences in WCC Ecclesiology and Missiology towards Edinburgh 2010', in John Gibaut and Knud Jørgensen (eds), *Called to Unity for the Sake of Mission* (Oxford: Regnum, 2014), 73-88.

[23] Pope Francis, Apostolic Exhortation *Evangelii Gaudium* (EG): http://w2.vatican.va/content/francesco/en/apost_exhortations/documents/papa-francesco_esortazione-ap_20131124_evangelii-gaudium.html, 24 and 27.

An emerging new world

Not only, however, is the shift in theology an indication of a need for theological education to become more missiological. The shape and dynamic of the church itself demand that missionary formation becomes a factor in theological education. Today's church and its ministers exist in a world that has profoundly changed in the wake of the end of nineteenth-century colonialism, two devastating wars in the twentieth century, the demise of the Communist vision in almost every place in which it once had a stranglehold, the ecological crisis, globalisation and its fallout of increased world poverty and human trafficking, and the ascendancy of Islam as the world's fastest-growing religion and menacing radical parties within it. The face of the world has changed, with what many claim is the greatest movement of peoples in the world's history. The amazing development of communications media in the last several decades, with computers, email, mobile phones, Skype, FaceTime, texting, Facebook and Twitter, has made time and space almost irrelevant in today's world. Anyone can virtually be in any place at any time. This is the world in which the church must witness in its life and service, and proclaim a relevant and challenging Gospel message. Such a world demands a missionary church, with ministers educated for mission.

While we can still speak of the distinctiveness of pastoral work, work among people who have ceased practising religion, and primary evangelisation among peoples who have not yet accepted the Gospel, we can no longer divide up the world into places that are evangelised and places that are not. Every church exists in a missionary situation. The centre of gravity of Christianity has shifted to the global South, and yet these vital churches are often without adequate resources and personnel to deal with the immense problems they are faced with. Members of these churches have also migrated to lands where there exist what were formerly considered 'sending churches'. With those migrants have come women and men of other religious ways, and so countries that have been traditionally Christian are no longer overwhelmingly so. Missionaries do not need to cross oceans to engage in primary evangelisation; they need only walk down the streets of their home cities. Missionaries from churches formerly considered 'missions' now arrive to care for those who have migrated to the West and North, and there engage in primary evangelisation or to evangelise or re-evangelise their former evangelisers. As western Christians find themselves in numerical decline, they have come to recognise the need to witness to and preach the Gospel in new ways and with new urgency in the pluralist and secularist societies in which they live. Mission is everywhere. Theological education needs to be missionary formation. What has been marginal to theological education needs once again to be its matrix.[24]

Theological Education as Missionary Formation

What might a theological education that is missionary formation look like? Building on what I have suggested elsewhere,[25] we might think of a theological education that cultivates both particular methods that emerge out of missional practice and a particular content that emerges from such a practice as well. What I would like to sketch out here is only meant to be suggestive of further thinking along these lines, and is limited by my own social location as a white, middle class, North American male. I will focus first on the particular methods to be cultivated, and then outline some of the major features of the content of a theological education that is missionary formation.

Methodological perspectives

A first methodological perspective to cultivate is an understanding of the nature of theology as rooted in and aimed at pastoral and missional practice. The aim of theological education is not so much to learn theology as a *content* – although theological competence certainly includes studying and mastering the riches of the Christian tradition. Emphasis should be placed, rather, on learning theology as a *process*, or in other words learning to *do* theology, to *theologise*. Theological education will not be a process of learning a set content that will then be 'applied' *a priori* to a situation.[26] What it will entail is helping students name and challenge the theologies, biblical interpretations, moral decisions, commitments to justice and spiritual practices that emerge from particular situations themselves. Learning theology, then, will have its starting point in the life of the Christian community as it strives to discern what God is doing in human history and how the church might be a sign and instrument of that saving presence. Like the church that does not exist for its own sake but for the sake of that Reign, so theology will be done not for its own sake but in order better to witness to, serve and preach the already-but-not-yet saving,

---

[24] These last two paragraphs follow closely the conclusion of my article 'New Evangelization or Missionary Church? *Evangelii Gaudium* and the Call for Missionary Discipleship', in *Verbum SVD*. 55, 2-3 (2014): 173-75.

[25] Bevans, 'Wisdom from the Margins,' 9-18.

[26] See Steve De Gruchy, 'Theological Education and Missional Practice: A Vital Dialogue', in Werner et al (eds), *Handbook of Theological Education in Global Christianity*, 44.

healing, and forgiving presence of its Lord. Learning theology in a missional church should be learning theology as practical theology.[27]

Secondly, theological education as missional formation must teach theologising that 'listens to all the voices'. Not only must a missional theology listen to the 'usual' voices – the essential voices of Scripture, the patristic sources, the great theologians like Augustine, Aquinas, Luther, Calvin, Schleiermacher, Barth and Rahner. They need to listen to those sources with a post-colonial consciousness and listen to sources 'beyond the boundary' as well. In the first place, this means listening to theologians in the whole *catholic* church – the Latin American Bishops' important statements at Medellín, Puebla, Santo Domingo and Aparecida; the statements of the Federation of Asian Bishops' Conferences; the theologians like Larenti Magesa from Tanzania, Agbonkhianmeghe Orobator from Nigeria, Maria Clara Bingemer from Brazil, Kwang-Sun Choi from Korea, Estela Padilla from the Philippines, or Jione Havea from Tonga. Second, theologising for missionary formation would listen to subaltern voices in the wider Christian tradition. Rosemary Radford Ruether has suggested that theologians today should listen for the 'prophetic principle' that runs through the Scriptures and the 'countercultural movements' in church history that may have been suppressed by those who hold institutional power.[28] Sarah Coakley has suggested that rich resources for theology are to be found in studying the religious lives of ordinary people in ordinary church congregations.[29] Dale T. Irvin has pointed out that besides the well-known expansion of Christianity westward through Asia Minor and Europe, Christianity also expanded to the East and South, into Persia, Armenia, India and Ethiopia. We find in these places a church that undertook a vigorous mission, despite persecution by and in tension with Islam in particular. Listening to these churches' traditions and voices might offer immense theological resources to a church struggling to find its voice as a minority in secular western cultures and non-Christian cultures as well.[30]

---

[27] See two important books on practical theology published recently in the United States: Kathleen A. Cahalan and Gordon S. Mikoski (eds), *Opening the Field of Practical Theology: An Introduction* (Lanham, MD / Plymouth, UK: Rowan & Littlefield, 2014); and Claire E. Wolfteich, *Invitation to Practical Theology: Catholic Voices and Visions* (Mahwah, NJ / New York: Paulist Press, 2014).

[28] Rosemary Radford Ruether, *Sexism and God-Talk: Toward a Feminist Theology*, Tenth Anniversary Edition (Boston: Beacon Press, 1993), 20-37.

[29] Sarah Coakley, *God, Sexuality, and the Self: An Essay 'On the Trinity'* (Cambridge: CUP, 2013), Kindle Edition, Location 2284-3525.

[30] See Dale T. Irvin, *Christian Histories, Christian Traditioning: Rendering Accounts* (Maryknoll, NY: Orbis Books, 1998), 110. See also Irvin and Scott Sunquist's two-volume *History of the World Christian Movement* (Maryknoll, NY: Orbis Books, 2001 and 2012).

What these first two methodological perspectives point to is the necessity for all theology – across the theological disciplines – to be done as contextual theology. This means several things. It means, first, that theology will take on a strong interdisciplinary character, working not only with philosophy – whether western or otherwise – but with the social sciences, the results of sciences like biology, physics and astronomy, and the arts as well. It also means that doing theology will take on a more 'occasional' character, meaning that what will be taught and learned in theological education will present itself from particular contexts and questions of ordinary Christians or in the course of the practice of missionary service. A context like Latin America, as Chilean theologian Ronaldo Muñoz notes, would wrestle not so much with atheism or unbelief, which was the classic beginning of reflection on God in the wake of the western Enlightenment, but with idolatry. The question is not whether Latin Americans (or many peoples outside the West or migrants form those places) believe in God, but whether the God they believe in is the real God of Jesus Christ, or a God who condones oppression, illicit wealth or innocent suffering.[31] The third consequence of a method of contextualisation is that its questions might come from areas that classical, non-missional theology has neglected or reflected on very little. Popular religiosity, witchcraft and healing, for example, might become major areas of scriptural investigation, or ethical or systematic theological reflection in some contexts, while issues of anthropology and ecology might be central in others. A contextual methodological perspective, in the fourth place, will reveal particular models of doing contextual theology, as I have tried to outline in my book *Models of Contextual Theology*.[32] Fifth, community involvement and collaboration among theologians will be much more prominent in the act of theological reflection. Finally, the shape of theological reflection might be less discursive and more poetic, proverb-centred, or visually oriented. These methodological perspectives should be kept in mind as we survey the content of the theological curriculum in the following paragraphs.

A missionary theological curriculum

As Christopher Wright has argued at length, 'mission is... the major key that unlocks the whole grand narrative of the canon of Scripture'.[33] Theological education as missionary formation will offer courses on Scripture – focusing, of course, on *doing* exegesis rather than learning

---

[31] See Ronaldo Muñoz, *The God of Christians* (Maryknoll, NY: Orbis Books, 1990).
[32] Stephen B. Bevans, *Models of Contextual Theology* (Maryknoll, NY: Orbis Books, 2002).
[33] Christopher J.H. Wright, *The Mission of God: Unlocking the Bible's Grand Narrative* (Downers Grove, IL: IVP, 2006), 17.

content – that will illuminate how God's mission is reflected in the biblical books, from the Pentateuch and historical books through the prophets and the wisdom literature of the Old Testament, and through the literature of the New Testament. Every Gospel reflects the missionary situation of the community out of which it comes. The Acts of the Apostles trace the development of the earliest community through Luke's theology of the continuity between Jesus' mission and that of the early church, and Paul's letters in particular present a model of contextual theologising within communities struggling to live and witness to Christian life.[34] Many themes in mission, for example, contemporary migration or ecological commitment, can also be approached from a biblical perspective.[35]

Systematic theology is transformed when viewed through the lens of mission. The triune God is a God in mission, sending the Spirit into the world at the dawn of creation, becoming incarnate in Jesus of Nazareth, an icon of social justice, dialogue and inculturation. The Holy Spirit, anointing Jesus at his baptism, anoints the followers of Jesus at Pentecost, and forms the hesitant disciples into the church, who as God's new People, the manifestation of Christ's Body, and the Spirit's Temple in the world, share and continue Jesus' mission to all cultures until the Reign of God be fully established. The church is endowed with the missionary marks of apostolicity, catholicity, unity and holiness, and is charged to make those marks visible in the ecclesial community and in the world in which it lives. The nature and elements of mission become a pivotal part of ecclesiological reflection. A missional Christology is developed as a Spirit Christology, focusing on the teaching, healing and reconciling mission of Jesus, who by his cross reveals the very being of God as a God of tenderness, mercy and humility. Christology's major question in this age of interreligious interaction, conflict and dialogue is how God's grace works even outside the boundaries of explicit faith and church membership to bring humanity the fulness of salvation. Wrestling with such questions transforms eschatological reflections on punishment or reward after death, and the eschatological nature of history situates the church's mission as constitutive of the church's identity.[36]

---

[34] On the missionary dimensions of the Bible, see Wright, *The Mission of God*; Donald Senior and Carroll Stuhlmueller, *The Biblical Foundations for Mission* (Maryknoll, NY: Orbis Books, 1983); Lucien Legrand, *Unity and Plurality: Mission in the Bible* (Maryknoll, NY: Orbis Books, 1990); William J. Larkin, Jr. and Joel F. Williams (eds), *Mission in the New Testament: An Evangelical Approach* (Maryknoll, NY: Orbis Books, 1998).
[35] For example, Dianne Bergant, *The Earth is the Lord's: The Bible, Ecology, and Worship* (Collegeville, MN: The Liturgical Press, 1998); van Thanh Nguyen and John M. Prior (eds), *God's People on the Move: Biblical and Global Perspectives on Migration and Mission* (Eugene, OR: Pickwick Publications, 2014).
[36] I have written more at length on this, although still in a rather programmatic way, in 'Wisdom from the Margins, 13-18; see also Stephen Bevans, '"Revisiting

The contextual nature of a theology for missionary formation would result in an ethics that, as one of my colleagues put it, develops women and men as people of *character*, and who are able to assist others in making ethical decisions and commitments. Ethics, like God's mission itself, is about the fulness of life, of cosmic and human flourishing.[37] Ethical reflection and practice will focus in particular on those whom the affluent world marginalises or ignores, being evangelised by them, and committing Christians to work for social and ecological justice, solidarity with those on the margins, and dedication to assisting them to become the subjects of their own history.[38]

Historical studies, as I have mentioned above, will not be confined to a study of the church's western expansion, as traditional, non-missional church history was wont to do, but will look at the entire history of the world Christian movement. A church history that contributes to missionary formation is one that is virtually indistinguishable from mission history, which would mean that special emphasis would be given to Christian growth in the Persian Empire early on, in Africa, and in Asia.[39] It would mean, as Justo González points out, that certain neglected periods in church history would receive new recognition as vital periods, such as the second, seventh and eighth centuries, and the Spanish conquest of the Americas in the sixteenth century, relativising the Protestant Reformation in importance.[40] Attention to mission will also affect the *method* of church history in that equal focus will be placed on the ordinary Christians of history, rather than only on kings and bishops and popes. This will also facilitate the inclusion of women as a vital part of the ongoing history of the church.[41]

Liturgical studies is an area where inculturation and contextualisation are important practices to cultivate and develop, and the skill for this is something that needs to be developed in every minister today. Celebrating liturgy worthily is being recognised more and more today as a missionary act, and every student needs to be formed for this more missional

Mission at Vatican II," Theology and Practice for Today's Missionary Church', in *Theological Studies*, 74, 2 (June 2013): 274-77.
[37] This is the central theme of TTL. See in particular 1.
[38] See TTL 38-42; EG 176-216, esp. 198.
[39] See Irvin and Sunquist, *History of the World Christian Movement*; Andrew F. Walls, *The Missionary Movement in Christian History: Studies in the Transmission of the Faith* (Maryknoll, NY: Orbis Books, 1996); Wilbert R. Shenk (ed), *Enlarging the Story: Perspectives on Writing World Christian History* (Maryknoll, NY: Orbis Books, 2002); Stephen B. Bevans and Roger P. Schroeder, *Constants in Context: A Theology of Mission for Today* (Maryknoll, NY: Orbis Books, 2002).
[40] Justo L. González, *The Changing Shape of Church History* (St Louis, MO: Chalice Press, 2002), 35-44.
[41] See Stephen Bevans and Roger Schroeder, 'The "New" Church History', in *New Theology Review* 16, 4 (2003), 79-81; Susan E. Smith, *Women in Mission: From the New Testament to Today* (Maryknoll, NY: Orbis Books, 2007).

perspective.[42] Preaching, too, is a highly contextual skill, and one that will be transformed by a conviction that every homily or sermon is a chance for deeper or first-time evangelisation. Spirituality studies also need to be infused with an awareness that Christian spirituality, and in particular ministerial spirituality, has to be rooted in one's missionary discipleship.[43]

All these disciplines come together in field education that connect what is learned in the classroom with what goes on in concrete congregations and concrete circumstances. Theological education needs to be a missionary formation that fosters skills of theological reflection and 'reflective believing' across cultures and religious traditions, forming missionary disciples who are deeply reflective practitioners and evangelisers.[44] In many ways, field education becomes the capstone of a theological education that is missionary formation.

Conclusion

Steve De Gruchy writes about the need for a vital dialogical relationship between theological education and missional practice. The result of such a dialogue would be that theological education would be missionary formation. This is what this essay has argued as it has unpacked Martin Kähler's dictum that 'mission is the mother of theology', Cardinal Walter Kasper's conviction that the goal of theology is 'missionary proclamation', and David Bosch's insistence that, unless theology accompanies the church in its participation in the *missio Dei*, it has no reason to exist. Theology only makes sense in the context of a missionary church, and formation for ministry only makes sense in such a church if it is missionary formation. This has long not been the case, but in our day it is becoming more and more evident that it needs to be so. In the 21st-century church, theological education must be missionary formation.

---

[42] See, for example, Ruth A. Meyers, *Missional Worship, Worshipful Mission: Gathering as God's People, Going Out in God's Name* (Grand Rapids, MI: Eerdmans, 2014); *Together Towards Life: Mission and Evangelism in Changing Landscapes*, 74.

[43] *Evangelii Gaudium*, 259-83; 29-35.

[44] See especially Edward Foley, *Theological Reflection across Religious Traditions: The Turn to Reflective Believing* (Lanham, MD / Plymouth, UK: Rowan & Littlefield, 2015).

'OUR FAVOURITE TASK': EQUIPPING THE SAINTS FROM AN ORTHODOX PERSPECTIVE

Eric George Tosi

Introduction

In 1907 as he prepared to return to Russia after a nine-year ministry in America, Archbishop Tikhon (Belavin) charged his American flock to continue the missionary work by exhorting:[1]

> For each of us the dissemination of the Christian faith must be a favorite task, close to our hearts and precious to us; in this task each member of the Church must take an active part – some by personal missionary effort, some by monetary support and service to the "needs of the saints," and some by prayer to the Lord that He might "establish and increase His Church" and that He might "teach the word of truth" to those who do not know Christ, might "reveal to them the gospel of righteousness, unite them to His Holy, Catholic, and Apostolic Church.[2]

This challenge still rings true today. The dissemination of the Christian faith must be the church's favourite task as it is the *raison d'être* of the church. The church exists to be missionary and to live out the truth of the Gospel of Jesus Christ. Anything else is simply a distraction that pulls the church and the faithful away from that singular task. St Tikhon believed that favourite task is the responsibility of all people in the church, not just a few specialists, but all the faithful. If the church is to 'equip the saints' then it must begin with that singular mindset – mission is for all and is all in the church. Fr Alexander Schmemann, a prominent twentieth century Orthodox theologian, writes: 'State, society, culture, nature itself are the real *objects* of mission and not a neutral "milieu" in which the only task of the Church is to preserve its own inner freedom, to maintain its "religious life".'[3]

But the church does not exist in a vacuum as some vague, undefined concept. It is a reality composed of people, of structure and most importantly of worship. The Orthodox Church has consistently taught that

---

[1] Archbishop Tikhon would later be elected the first Patriarch of Russia in over 200 years, only to be later martyred by the Soviet government. He was canonised a saint in 1989. His legacy of missionary work, especially his lessons on 'equipping the saints' remains a powerful paradigm in the Orthodox Church.

[2] John Breck. John Meyendorff and Elena Silk (eds), *The Legacy of Saint Vladimir* (Crestwood, NY: St Vladimir's Seminary Press, 1990), 273.

[3] Alexander Schmemann, *Church, World, Mission* (Crestwood, NY: St Vladimir's Seminary Press, 1973), 216.

the church is a reality that must be lived out and experienced from within. From an Orthodox perspective, that central experience is also the central missionary activity of the church and one that is intimately tied to every activity of the church – that is, the worship. Fr Georges Florovsky, the renowned early twentieth-century theologian, wrote:

> The Church is more than a company of preachers, or a teaching society, or a missionary board. It has not only to invite people, but also to introduce them into this New Life, to which it bears witness. It is a missionary body indeed, and its mission field is the whole world. But the aim of its missionary activity is not merely to convey to people certain convictions or ideas, not even to impose on them a definite discipline or rule of life, but first of all to introduce them into a New Reality, to convert them, to bring them through their faith and repentance to Christ Himself, that they should be born anew in Him and into Him by water and the Spirit. Thus the ministry of the Word is completed in the ministry of the Sacraments.[4]

It is from this perspective that any discussion on the Orthodox Church's approach to missionary training, missionary activity, and, in fact about the very concept of mission itself must proceed. Mission cannot be separated from the church or from worship. Archbishop Anastasios (Yannoulatos), one the greatest modern Orthodox missionaries, writes:

> Orthodox mission – internal or external – is by nature 'ecclesiastical.' It cannot be understood as an individual or a group activity, disconnected from the Body of Christ. For those who work for it; it is the Church that they serve, the Church that they represent; it is the life of the Church that they transplant. No one is saved alone; no one offers Christ's salvation alone. One is saved within the Church, one acts within the Church, and what one lives and offers to others is done in the name of the Church... mission is the extension of the of the love of the Trinitarian God, for the transformation in love of the whole world.[5]

Mission's ultimate goal is renewal of the relationship between a broken humanity and the saviour Jesus Christ. This is accomplished through the sacraments and the liturgical life which reconnects the world. It is the precise entry point for people into the mission of the church and the precise exit point of the church's mission to the world. David Bosch accurately wrote on his own perception of mission in the Orthodox Church: 'In the Orthodox perspective, mission is thus centripetal rather than centrifugal, organic rather than organized. It "proclaims" the Gospel through doxology

---

[4] Georges Florovsky, *Bible, Church, Tradition: An Eastern Orthodox View* (Belmont, MA: Nordland Publishing, 1972), 69 – as quoted in Ion Bria, 'The Church's Role in Evangelism: Icon or Platform?' in *International Review of Mission* 64, No. 255 (July 1975), 244.

[5] Anastasios Yannoulatos, *Mission in Christ's Way: An Orthodox Understanding of Mission* (Brookline, MA: Holy Cross Press, 2010), 220-21.

and liturgy. The witnessing community is the community in worship; in fact, the worshipping community is in and of itself an act of witness.'[6]

Some Theological Perspectives

From an initial viewpoint, this may all seem to be very academic and consisting of some very high theological principles which involve some weighty, if not contentious, discussions on concepts like 'church', 'liturgy', 'sacraments', and of course, 'mission'. From an Orthodox perspective, this discussion can become weighed down with many definitions and practices in which the Orthodox differ from their western Christian counterparts. But rather than get burdened in such discussion, perhaps a foundational question needs to be posed when examining this perspective on mission and equipping the saints. Father Alexander Schmemann posed such a question, 'Can a Church whose life is centered almost exclusively on the liturgy and the sacraments, whose spirituality is primarily mystical and ascetical, be truly missionary?'[7]

The answer to this question is critical in understanding how to 'equip the saints.' Is the church truly expressing its missionary calling through its worship and, if so, is it equipping the members of the church to be missionaries? The answer must be affirmative and must be put into practice in the local worshipping community or else it fades back into theory. Mission is not some intellectual concept but an actual life that is lived by all in the church. There are three ways in which this is realised and, in a sense, which equip the saints in a very real and tangible manner.

First is the liturgical life in the church. This must be the central action of any missionary activity and training. The liturgy is the central focal point in which Orthodox Christians live out their faith in a community, but the liturgy is the truly transforming and missionary event. It was not just a matter of what the church teaches, but how a community lives its sacramental life that is truly missionary. By the very definition, liturgy (Greek *leitourgia*) means 'work'. It is the work of the people and the work of the church. One cannot do the work of the church without actually doing the 'work' of the church. It transforms the individual and it transforms the community.

Fr Schmemann wrote extensively on this meaning of liturgy and its transformative effect on not just the individual and community but on the world. It was the act *par excellence* of humanity, by offering praise, thanksgiving and worship. By living the spiritual life, persons in the community grow more Christ-like through *theosis*, or movement towards God. On another scale, the local community's liturgy reconciles the world

---

[6] David J. Bosch, *Transforming Mission: Paradigm Shifts in Theology of Mission* (Maryknoll, NY: Orbis Books, 1991), 207-208.
[7] Schmemann, *Church,* 210.

with God (2 Cor. 5:19) and through this reconciliation restores humanity through the church. As Fr Schmemann wrote, 'The Eucharist is always the End, the sacrament of the *parousia* (presence or arrival), and yet, it is always the *beginning*, the *starting point*: now mission begins.'[8] So through the Eucharist and through the church and through community as the Body of Christ, true mission begins and a new movement happens, which brings the church into the world and the world into the church. This co-mingling of the church and the world has been popularly phrased as 'The Liturgy after the Liturgy'.

The 'Liturgy after the Liturgy' is a central part of that missionary work. Fr Ion Bria considers that the missionary dimension of the liturgy continues after the community leaves the services as an extension of the liturgy itself.

> The evangelizing and witnessing potentialities of the Eucharistic liturgy extend to other kinds of liturgies and forms of *diakonia* (service to the poor and oppressed) outside the walls of the church. What is at stake here is the continuous building up of the church, the body of Christ, the sacrament of the kingdom of God in history. To strengthen the diaconal role of the worshipping community scattered for daily life, this second movement of the liturgy, the Eucharist has to become 'pilgrim bread', food for missionaries, nourishment for Christians involved in social and moral struggles.[9]

The liturgy feeds and strengthens the community, inspires it to go out into the world to witness to Christ and activates it to be a force of good deeds to those surrounding the community. The 'Liturgy after the Liturgy' is nothing short of realising God's actions in the world through his church. The church 'equips the saints' in a very real manner by participation in and being fed by the liturgical life of the church. This must be done on the local level, in the local parish to the local community. The mission is to the surrounding neighbourhood connecting Christ and his church to the people.

This brings us to the second manner in 'equipping the saints': the local community itself. Christians cannot be Christians by themselves. They need others. A Christian lives in a Eucharistic community which forms the Body of Christ. This term is known as *koinonia* and has been a central element in Christianity from the very beginning. Acts 2:42-47 illustrates *koinonia* in relation to a community: 'They devoted themselves to the apostles' teaching and to the communion (*koinonia*), to the breaking of bread and to prayer... All the believers were together and had everything in common. Selling their possessions and goods, they gave to anyone as he had need... They broke bread in their homes and ate together with glad and sincere hearts, praising God and enjoying the favour of all the people.' Without this *koinonia*, a community is just a group of individuals with the same beliefs, perhaps no different from a local club. However, when it is

---

[8] Schmemann, *Church*, 215.
[9] Ion Bria, *The Liturgy After the Liturgy: Mission and Witness from an Orthodox Perspective* (Geneva: WCC, 1996), 27-28.

found in a Eucharistic fellowship, this gathering of individuals becomes the Body of Christ.

Church theologians recognised the fundamental importance of *koinonia* as a Eucharistic fellowship, especially as the church spreads through the creation of local worshipping communities. Fr John Meyendorff wrote,

> ... a local Church gathered around its bishop for the celebration of the Eucharist: this assembly *is* the Catholic Church... a local Church is not a *part* of the Body, it is the Body itself, which is symbolized most realistically in the Byzantine rite of the preparation of the elements, when the priest places on the paten parcels of bread commemorating Christ Himself, His Mother, all the saints, all the departed and all the living: in this Bread the whole Church is really present together with the Head.[10]

In recent reflection, the understanding of the centrality of the local worshipping community remains foundational. 'Our personal Christian experience,' writes Archbishop Anastasios, 'is made steadfast and strengthened through our *incorporation in the mystical Body of Christ*' [emphasis added].[11] So mission itself must have the central goal of bringing people into that local community, the parish.

However, what is also evident is that this central element is lacking in many parishes. By viewing themselves as a collection of individuals of the same faith and not as members of the Body of Christ, each his own purpose and function actuated and actualised in the Eucharist, these parishes lack the foundation upon which to build. Equipping the saints must focus on incorporating the person into the local community which is the Body of Christ, centralised on the corporate and liturgical life of the community. As Fr Ion Bria wrote, 'Prayer, worship, and communion have always formed the context for the witness of faith, including evangelism, mission, and church life. The missionary structures were built on the liturgy of the word and the sacraments; and since the beginning the great variety of liturgies and rites, creeds and confessions has been due to the diversity of missionary contexts.'[12] This diversity of contexts enables the Body of Christ to extend itself to the community. In other words, diversity of gifts must be part of equipping the saints.

The third manner is using the diversity of the gifts within that worshipping community which is the Body of Christ. Just as no single person can be a Christian alone, likewise each of those Christians has something to contribute to the *koinonia*. The apostle Paul writes in 1 Corinthians 12 about the need for the many parts of the Body of Christ, and again in Romans 12 and Ephesians 4 about how members of the body relate to each other. This is critical in equipping the saints, using all of the gifts of all the faithful who are in the Body of Christ. St Tikhon used such

---

[10] John Meyendorff, 'The Orthodox Concept of Church,' in *St Vladimir's Seminary Quarterly* No. 6 (1962), 61.
[11] Yannoulatos, *Mission*, 113.
[12] Bria, *Liturgy*, 9.

imagery when he first arrived in America in 1898 and gave his inaugural talk to the faithful of his new flock. He requested:

I ask for assistance and co-operation not only from the pastors, but also from my entire beloved flock. The Church of Christ is likened by the Holy Apostle Paul to a body, while a body has not one member, but many (1 Cor. 12:14). These have not one and the same function (Rom 12:4), but each its own: the eye its own, and the arm its own. Each member is necessary and cannot be without the other, they all have concerns for each other, and there is no division in the body (1 Cor. 12:25-26). So you also, my brethren, are the body of Christ, and members in particular (v. 27). And unto every one of you is given grace according to the measure of the gift of Christ (Eph. 4:7), unto the perfecting of the saints, for a work of ministration, for the building up of the body of Christ (v. 12). And for this purpose continue with true love to grow into Him to Whom belongs the whole body, which is built up of and joined through the supply of every joint, according to the working in the measure of each single part, receiving increase for the building up of itself in love (vv. 15-16).[13]

Where is that place for such gifts to be exercised in community? It is the local parish. Fr Bria points to the local parish as both the entry and departures point of mission. 'As a place of gathering for praying and sharing the body and blood of Christ, every local parish is also a point of departure into the world to share the joy of resurrection. The worshipping community is prepared and sent as an evangelizing community.'[14] For Fr Bria, the local parish is essentially the mission community, while the liturgy is the mission event. All are realised and formed, not around an individual action, but rather around a worshipping community gathered together 'to do this in memory of me [Christ]' (Luke 22:19, 1 Cor. 11:24). 'Therefore,' Fr Bria concludes, 'for the Orthodox, the missionary life and structure of every parish is key to practicing the proclamation of Christ today. For the responsibility of every believer does not end at the geographical and cultural borders of the community in which he or she lives, but extends to other communities, including people who do not know the Gospel.'[15]

This connection becomes more understandable in the light of the Orthodox Church's approach to communal life centred on the most basic ecclesial unit, the parish. The foundational concept of the parish itself is ubiquitous as the focal point of all local activity of Orthodox Christians. This is more than just a place for worship; it is the place where parishioners build a *koinonia*. As Fr Thomas Hopko, a prominent recent Orthodox theologian wrote, 'An Orthodox parish, that is, a local community of

---

[13] Tikhon Bellavin, 'My People and My Beloved', as translated in *Alive in Christ*, Vol. XIII, No. 3 (Winter 1997), 36-37, and first published in Russian in *The American Orthodox Herald*, No. 2 (1899), 50-51.

[14] Bria, *Liturgy*, 31.

[15] Bria, *Liturgy*, 31.

Orthodox Christians with one or more priests, has only one God-given reason for being. It exists to be the one, holy, catholic, and apostolic Church of Christ. Whatever the original reasons and conditions for its founding, whatever other services and activities it may provide, whatever other desires and needs it may fulfil for its members, the parish must be Christ's one holy Church. If it is not, then it is neither Christian nor Orthodox whatever else it may be or do.'[16] So despite age and distance, a truly living Orthodox parish converges around the same basic principles. These same principles also lay at the heart of missionary work: to be a worshipping part of the One, Holy, Catholic and Apostolic Church. As Fr John Meyendorff wrote, 'Whenever our parishes – these cells of the Church – really shine with the virtues, the dynamism, the faith of true Christianity, they also perform the mission. This mission – because it is the mission of the Church, and not of an individual, or of a human agency – can take many forms and be performed by a variety of ministries, all equally legitimate.'[17] To properly equip the saints, there must be a properly functioning local parish.

As Fr Hopko details, 'A parish must be *the* Church of Christ and not simply *a* church, because, according to the Orthodox faith, every local community actually is the one Church of Christ.'[18] This understanding of the importance of the local parish as the Body of Christ is foundational. 'Thus every local Christian community, every "parish", theologically, mystically, and sacramentally, is to be "Christ's Body, the fullness of him who fills all in all" (Eph. 1:23). It is to be "the household of God, which is the church of the living God, the pillar and bulwark of the truth" (1 Tim. 3:15). Everything in the parish is to participate in God's fullness and wholeness. Everything is to express it. Everything is to testify to it.'[19] To be truly missionary, the parish, the persons in the parish, the liturgical life of the parish, all of this needs to be functioning so that the Body of Christ is built up in the world. To repeat Bosch's evaluation of Orthodox mission, 'The witnessing community is the community in worship; in fact the worshipping community is in and of itself an act of witness... This is so, since the Eucharistic liturgy is the basic missionary structure and purpose and is celebrated as a "missionary event".'[20]

A note should be added about such organisations as the Orthodox Christian Mission Center as well as other missionary societies which do excellent work throughout the world. Many of these societies concentrate on foreign mission and train people to assist the local church. This training

---

[16] Thomas Hopko, *Speaking the Truth in Love: Education, Mission and Witness in Contemporary Orthodoxy* (Crestwood, NY: St Vladimir Seminary Press, 2004), 86.

[17] John Meyendorff, 'Many Ministries, One Mission', in *Witness to the World* (Crestwood: St Vladimir's Seminary Press, 1987), 180.

[18] Hopko, *Speaking*, 86.

[19] Hopko, *Speaking*, 87.

[20] Bosch, *Transforming*, 208.

is very often in terms of providing linguistic and contextual sensitivity to the culture of the mission. Other traditional methods of training include theological foundational principles. But the real training of the missionary, and the one they bring with them in mission, is primarily spiritual and liturgical. A missionary is taught to pray, to intercede and to bear the light of Christ. A missionary is trained to be a person of worship as the mission is the centre of worship.

The matter of assisting the local community is a critical point (there are cases where they establish new communities but this is always with the blessing and guidance of the local hierarch). They do not go to be outside the community but rather to augment the work in local worshipping communities. They are sent to pray with that community and participate in the sacramental life of that community. This type of activity is within the long tradition of such missionaries from Ss Cyril and Methodius to St Herman of Alaska. Missionaries are sent to be representatives of worship. As such, these societies and missionaries are part of the church, working within the church to bring the worshipping church to the local surrounding community.

To equip the saints in this context is precisely that – giving tools for the people to use and augmenting what they are lacking. These tools can range from providing material and training to educate the leaders and the faithful, establishing health and social programmes to assist the local people, to actually building church and community centres. But the most important contribution is to provide liturgical services to the local community. Churches are set up, services are organised, lay people are trained to lead the worship services. And of course, the sacraments are performed. This is at the heart of every mission, to provide the liturgical and sacramental life for the faithful wherever they may be found and to establish that local worshipping community. This is well within the tradition of Orthodox mission for centuries, that to equip the saints means to provide the tools for a worshipping community.

Conclusion

All Christians are called to be missionaries and to bring the Gospel to a hungry and fallen world. All Christians have a task to perform, whether it is teaching, preaching, serving, supporting or simply praying. St Tikhon exhorted the faithful to remember that very point when he left for Russia and martyrdom. The Church and all the faithful in it must use the God-given gifts to bring light into the world. St Tikhon in his farewell address also went on further to state,

> Christ the Savior said that men lighting a lamp do not put it under a bushel, but on a stand, and it gives light to all in the house (Matt. 5:15). The light of Orthodoxy also is not lit for a small circle of people. No, the Orthodox faith is catholic; it remembers the commandment of its founder: 'Go into all the

world and preach the gospel to the whole creation. Make disciples of all nations' (Mark 16:15, Matt. 28:19). It is our obligation to share our spiritual treasures, our truth, our light and our joy with those who do not have these gifts. And this duty lies not only on pastors and missionaries, but also on lay people, for the Church of Christ, in the wise comparison of St Paul is a body, and in the life of the body every member must take part.[21]

So everyone as the Body of Christ is responsible for the missionary calling in the church. The church equips the saints precisely because it is being the church as it is meant to be: a worshipping community. As Fr Schmemann wrote, 'The Church thus is not a 'self-centered' community but precisely a missionary community, whose purpose is salvation not from, but of the world. In the Orthodox experience and faith it is the Church-sacrament that makes possible the Church-mission.'[22] Archbishop Anastasios reflects, 'The local Church, the diocese, the parish, but also every other form of expression of ecclesial life, such as monasteries, religious organizations, missionary societies, various small informal missionary groups and communities constantly remain open and fulfill their duty within society to radiate the love and glory of Christ to the whole of humanity for the sake of the entire human race (*oikoumene*), always receiving and offering the Gospel.'[23]

Thus, it is more than planting churches; rather, mission is, in a sense, about renewing the relationship between God and man through his church as witnessed by the liturgy. Therefore, the liturgy is the source, the method, and the goal of mission. As Fr Alexander Schmemann succinctly writes, 'The Eucharist is the mission of the Church.'[24] In short, this is what equipping the saints in the Orthodox tradition is about. It is the nurturing and practicing of a faith through the most elemental of church organisations, the parish, which in turn reaches out into the surrounding community. It is worth repeating the observation of Archbishop Anastasios:

> Our personal Christian experience is made steadfast and strengthened through our *incorporation into the mystical Body of Christ*. Our confession draws strength from the experience of the Church. Therefore, in the final analysis, the individual, personal witness for Christ is *ecclesiastical*. When we confess the Lord, we do so mainly as members of a community, the Church which carries on His work. 'Because it is only in the Church that the kingdom of heaven is preached, and every goal of the Gospel of salvation looks thereto.' [Eusebius, *On the Inscription of the Psalms*][25]

Ultimately, a study of mission in the Orthodox Church cannot be divorced from an examination into worship, the community and the persons

---

[21] Breck, Meyendorff and Silk (eds), *Legacy*, 273.
[22] Schmemann, *Church*, 213-15.
[23] Yannoulatos, *Mission*, 149-51.
[24] Schmemann, *Church*, 254.
[25] Yannoulatos, *Mission*, 113.

in that community as they are completely interconnected. Archbishop Anastasios is quoted by Fr Ion Bria,

> Each of the faithful is called upon to continue a personal 'liturgy' on the secret altar of his own heart, to realize a living proclamation of the good news 'for the sake of the whole world.' Without this continuation the liturgy remains incomplete... The sacrifice of the Eucharist must be extended in personal sacrifices for the people in need, the brothers for whom Christ died... The continuation of the liturgy in life means a continuous liberation from the power of the evil that is working inside us, a continuing reorientation and openness to insights and efforts aimed at liberating human persons from all demonic structures, exploitation, agony, loneliness, and at creating real communion of persons in love.[26]

This is the real manner of equipping the saints from the perspective of the Orthodox Church.

---

[26] As quoted in Bria, *Liturgy*, 20.

INEQUALITY IN THEOLOGICAL EDUCATION
BETWEEN THE NORTH AND THE SOUTH

Marina Ngursangzeli Behera

Theological education provides the basis, puts into perspective and gives direction to a person's decision to join the Christian ministry. It is often the starting point in the process of equipping oneself for Christian mission. In the course of a person's theological education, the chances are that the importance of Christian mission might either be brought into sharp focus or sidelined. This education could challenge a person's understanding of what it means to minister, or confirm and strengthen existing preconceptions or prejudices.

The uncertainty and fragility of the outcome of theological education is further accentuated by the fact that worldwide, there are different standards of theological education shaped and influenced by geography, culture, denomination, economics – to name but a few. The notion that theological education will result in open-minded, well-equipped, articulate, knowledgeable, committed and economically independent theologians and missionaries is an utopian idea and ignores the realities in which theological education actually takes place, how Christians – whether theologically trained or laity – live out Christian mission in their daily lives and the dynamics between Christians of different ethnic and economic backgrounds.

Ironically, in an increasingly well connected world where terms such as 'realisation of synergies', 'commitment to co-operation', 'improved optimisation through co-operation', 'collaboration' and 'reciprocity' have become part of the business, and social or political lexicon, nowhere are they more absent than when it comes to defining or characterising global theological education.

How then is theological education to be viewed? Can it be considered one of the prime moving forces of mission, considering that discrepancies in quality and motives worldwide have led to fractured agendas and methodologies of undertaking theological education?

This paper primarily proposes to look at the inequality in theological education between the global North and global South, and examines this inequality from three points of view: (1) Inequality in the availability of resources; (2) Differences in the methodology and pedagogy in teaching theology; (3) Differences in the understanding of the goal and vision for theological education.

Inequality in the Availability of Resources

When one thinks about the inequality in theological education between the global North and the global South, what immediately comes to mind is the inequality or disparity in the availability of resources. This comes out very clearly in the parallel session on Theme 6: Theological Education and Formation, of the Edinburgh 2010 study process which points out 'Disparity in the availability of resources for theological education between the North and the South, and within several regions' as the first point among the most important challenges in relation to the strengthening and reshaping of theological education and missionary training for world Christianity in the twenty-first century.[1] When we talk about resources, it is very important to make a clear distinction between financial resources and human resources which are different from one another and have different implications for theological education. At the same time, we need to recognise the interrelatedness between the two and how one aspect influences the other.

Today, there is a shift in the demographic centre of gravity of Christianity with the growing number of Christians in the global South and the numbers in the global North decreasing. However, though the majority of Christians are now located in the South, the financial resources and material power remain concentrated in the North. How does this influence the inequality of theological education between the North and the South?

Unequal access to theological education and financial support

In the global survey on theological education, it was found that, proportionately, the number of theological schools (including online, extension, and other programmes) in the regions where Christianity is rapidly growing (Africa, Latin America, and parts of Asia) does not quantitatively meet the needs of the people for theological education. In contrast, it was found that in Europe and North America the number of theological institutions more or less quantitatively met the needs of the people.[2] This finding is connected with the second finding on the question

---

[1] Parallel Session on Theme 6: Theological Education and Formation, in Kirsteen Kim and Andrew Anderson (eds), *Edinburgh 2010, Mission Today and Tomorrow* (Oxford: Regnum 2011), 159. Hereafter to be cited as Parallel Session on Theme 6: Theological Education and Formation.

[2] *Global Survey on Theological Education; Summary of Main Findings for WCC 10th Assembly, Busan, 30th October-8th November 2013*, A joint research project by The Institute for Cross-Cultural Theological Education, McCormick Theological Seminary, Chicago; Ecumenical Theological Education Program (ETE), World Council of Churches, Geneva; and The Center for the Study of Global Christianity (GSGC), Gordon-Conwell Theological Seminary, Boston, 2, hereafter cited as *Global Survey on Theological Education.* http://www.oikoumene.org/en/resources/

regarding the financial situation of theological education. Respondents in the global South clearly felt that theological education is financially unstable.[3] We can perhaps infer that the lack of financial resources in the South results in the inadequate number of theological schools to meet the needs of the people. While there are a few respondents from North America and Europe who believe that theological education is financially unstable, though the majority still considers it to be stable, [4] what is consistent in the findings is that there are not enough theological institutions to meet the needs of the people in the South, and that this is closely connected with the lack of or weak financial support for theological education in the South. Another factor that needs to be noted is the status of theological education and theological faculty in the North. Unlike in the South, where most theological seminaries and colleges and faculties are not attached to state universities and do not get any financial support from the state, in the North a number of state universities have faculties or departments of theological studies which in turn guarantee state funding for the teaching faculty, further research and greater accessibility to theological education.

Human resources

There is also unequal availability of human resources in terms of theological teachers or educators in proportion to the number of Christians between the North and South. When there are not enough financial resources for theological education, it has severe adverse effects on the standard and quality of the education that is imparted in theological institutions. This is manifested in different ways. First, theological institutions that are financially poor cannot afford well trained and qualified teaching faculty, who would rather work in places where they would be able to earn more. This also leads to the problem of 'brain-drain' from the South to the North. There are many from the South who have studied or obtained scholarships and have had the opportunity to study theology in the North. A good number then continue in or go back to the North to work in theological colleges, seminaries or universities. While this shows that theologians from the South are also capable and not inferior to those in the North, and have much to offer and contribute towards theological education, it is a pointer to the fact that theological institutions in the South are not attractive for well qualified and well trained theological educators.

We must also keep in mind the need to examine new and authentic models of partnership especially when it comes to developing and sharing human resources. With more Christians in the South and more resources in

documents/wcc-programmes/education-and-ecumenical-formation/ete/global-survey-on-theological-education
[3] *Global Survey on Theological Education*, 2.
[4] *Global Survey on Theological Education*, 2-3.

the North, those in control of this inequality cannot unilaterally decide who comes to the North and who does not, and so become 'experts' on the South.[5] In contrast, in the North there is a decline in the interest in theological education or training, not because of the lack of opportunities and financial resources but perhaps because of the increasingly secularised context.

Unequal facilities and aids

If one considers other forms of education apart from the traditional classroom scenario, such as online education, in the findings of the global survey on theological education we see that the interest in online theological education is very high in North America (76%) with Europe coming in second (39%), whereas only 25 % and 27% in Africa and Asia respectively opt for online theological education.[6] One can assume that the reason why very few in Africa and Asia opt for online theological education is because there is less accessibility to internet facilities and other forms of modern communication technologies. This also means that compared with people in the North, people in the South are less familiar with the communication devices or hardware required to take advantage of such opportunities simply because they have less access to such devices.

Another factor to be taken into account is the lack of good libraries and reading material which are essential for students opting for online courses. While students in the North have access to good libraries and theological books to complement what is offered online or can access materials offered online, a large number of the students in the South do not have access to internet facilities or even own their own computer. Additionally, libraries are often poorly stocked in terms of reading or reference material, and even in terms of offering internet services.

Differences in Methodology and Pedagogy

A major difference in the theological education between the global North and the global South, and which is a major contributing factor to the inequality between the two, would be the methodology and pedagogy followed in theological education. Whereas the methodology of imparting knowledge and learning in the North requires rigorous independent research and personal reflection, the system that prevails in the South is more experiential, and also more of an apprenticeship where the students depend a lot on the teacher. What Gwayakeng Kiki and Ed Parker have observed about the system of learning in the Papua New Guinea context holds true for most of the global South contexts. They state that 'Learning

---

[5] See Parallel Session on Theme 6: Theological Education and Formation, 164.

[6] *Global Survey on Theological Education*, 4.

takes place by observation, imitation, listening and participating. Questions are not often raised, and if they are, it is never as a first option'.[7] Bill Houston succinctly describes what then takes place – dependency of the students on the teacher for their learning:

> Where there are large classes and where the learning resources are in short supply, the easiest solution is to have one person, the lecturer, teach a class of whatever size with notes scribbled up on a chalk board so that diligent student can transcribe the same into their notebooks. Far too much activity in the classroom follows the transmission model in which the lecturer has the knowledge and transmits it in class time to the passive student who is assumed to have learned. One skeptic has defined a lecture as 'The transmission of the lecturer's notes to the student's notebook without passing through the minds of either'![8]

Such a method of study is applicable not only to theological education but is a reflection of the whole system of education in the South, whether secular or religious. In such systems, emphasis is laid more on rote learning and being graded on performance in written examinations, which themselves give importance to how much and how accurately a student remembers classroom lectures and materials in books.

Generally, theological education in the North is done through the state universities of higher or advanced education where there are adequate resources and facilities for higher theological education and research work in an academic setting. While the insights and 'secular' education have their own value to theological enterprise because of the importance of not isolating theological education from other realms of human knowledge, this poses a challenge to theological seminaries in the North which now are at the risk of closure or the dimension of ministerial formation being weakened. The existence of interdenominational theological seminaries are also threatened and in some cases have been closed down.[9] In contrast, in the South, in a majority of cases, theological education is imparted and taught in theological colleges and seminaries and Bible schools which are owned and run by denominational churches, and are considered instruments of training and equipping students for ministry, in line with their respective denominational beliefs and expectations, and are not really considered institutions for rigorous academic undertaking. There are of course theological colleges and institutions which are ecumenical and non-denominational. But more often than not, these institutions face financial

---

[7] Gwayaweng Kiki and Ed Parker, 'Is there a Better Way to Teach Theology to Non-Western Persons? Research from Papua New Guinea that Could Benefit the Wider Pacific', in *Australian eJournal of Theology* 21.2 (August 2014), 108.

[8] Bill Houston, 'The Future is not What it Used to Be: Changes and Choices facing Theological Education in Africa', in Isabel Apawo Phiri and Dietrich Werner (eds), *Handbook of Theological Education in Africa* (Oxford: Regnum, 2013), 109-10, hereafter cited as *Handbook of Theological Education in Africa*.

[9] See Parallel Session on Theme 6: Theological Education and Formation, 163.

challenges as most denominational churches would rather take care of their own denominational colleges and seminaries than institutions that are not exclusively under their care and responsibility.

However, the inequality in theological education between the North and the South cannot be merely encapsulated as something resulting from the inequality in resources and differences in educational systems. There are also several interrelated dimensions that need further analysis and reflection. A pertinent question that needs to be answered is, who decides what is good theological education and what is not? The global survey on theological education referred to earlier concentrates on quantitative and not on qualitative needs, specifically whether existing theological institutions meet the qualitative needs of theological education. This is important since we consider theological education as 'mission formation for all Christians, and missionary formation for mission workers, agencies and churches in changing situation of mission'.

Kiki and Parker explains how for the PNG (Papua New Guinea) Melanesian, life is seen as an interrelated experience where there is no distinction between religious and non-religious experiences, and between knowing and existence or knowing and being. The process of 'understanding and deliberation becomes a moral and or religious process motivated by a practical interest into taking the right action within a particular environment', meaning 'knowledge arises from concrete experience of life rather than philosophy'.[10] Drawing insights from Thomas H. Groom, Kiki and Parker state that knowledge is also not considered as something one acquires for oneself but for it to be lived out in 'shared praxis', and hence is socially distributed and involves 'partnership, participation, and dialogue'.[11] This understanding finds expression in what Kiki and Parker called the 'Wokabaut-Kurikulum: A Papua New Guinean Way of Knowing and Learning', where the physical and the emotional self are not separated, and attention is given not exclusively to the mind and heart in learning, but also reaches out to people and community with its norms, laws, expectations, structures, and traditions – and simultaneously the community also shapes one's perception and meaning.[12] This understanding of learning where an individual does not acquire knowledge as an independent individual but as a member of a community is something that is common in most countries in the South. H.S. Wilson, along the same lines as Kiki and Parker, states how, in Asia, theologically trained leaders cannot be involved in just giving good biblical-theological counsel without

---

[10] Kiki and Parker, 'Is there a Better Way to Teach Theology to Non-Western Persons?', 112.

[11] Thomas H. Groome, 'Shared Christian Praxis: A Possible Theory/ Method for Christian Education', in *Lumen Vitae* 31 (1976), 142-45, cited in Kiki and Parker, 'Is there a Better Way to Teach Theology to Non-Western Persons?', 114.

[12] Kiki and Parker, 'Is there a Better Way to Teach Theology to Non-Western Persons?', 118.

personally engaging in various aspects of community life, including interfaith dialogues and engagements.[13] This communitarian understanding of learning and shared praxis can also be glimpsed in Josè Duqu's description of theological seminaries in Latin America, where theological education is imparted using the metaphor of 'tropical forest'. He states:

> ... there are many different species among the trees of the tropical forest; none will take prominence as the head, or centre, or elite, or more important than the other plants; because they all equally share the task of renewing oxygen, or providing food or energy... a tree by itself does not constitute a forest. A tropical forest is made up of many varieties of species that live in communion; in other words, they make community.[14]

Differences in the Understanding of the Goal and Vision for Theological Education

It is accepted that theological education was introduced and started in the global South by missionaries from the global North. Regardless of Christianity having grown phenomenally in the South, the western world still exercises hegemony over the global church and also in theological education. Wilson, quoting Timothy Tennent, describes how the western church continues to be the centre of gravity for advanced theological education, producing the majority of the theological literature in almost all areas of theology, which has also resulted in the English language becoming important for global theological discourse. Consequently. churches in the South have a double task of rethinking theological education in relation to contextual realities in the South, and also appropriately claiming the space that the shifting of the centre of gravity of Christianity has provided, by transcending the continued hegemonic power of western Christianity.[15]

The issue of language is an important one for the future and accessibility of theological education. The overwhelming use of English in theological education is, on one hand, a reminder of the lack of proper indigenous

---

[13] H.S. Wilson, 'Theological Education and Ecumenical Challenges in Asia', in Hope Antone, Wati Longchar, Hyunju Bae, Huang Po Ho and Dietrich Werner (eds), *Asian Handbook for Theological Education and Ecumenism* (Oxford: Regnum, 2009), 632, hereafter cited as *Asian Handbook for Theological Education and Ecumenism*.

[14] Josè Duqu, ' The Forest of Theological Education', Ecumenical Congress: Mission and Evangelism in Latin America, IX Assembly of the World Council of Churches, 5: https://www.oikoumene.org/en/folder/documents-pdf/WOCATI_2008_-_The_Forest_of_Theological_Education_-_Dr._Jose_Duque.pdf (accessed 10th February 2015).

[15] Timothy C. Tennent, 'New Paradigm for 21st Century: Missiological Reflections in honour of George K. Chavanikamannil', in Simon Samuel and P.V. Joseph (eds), *Remapping Mission Discourse* (Delhi: NTC/ISPCK, 2008), 194-95, cited by Wilson, 'Theological education and Ecumenical Challenges in Asia', 628.

resources for use in theological education and, on the other, automatically excludes vast sections of world Christianity from being involved in, as well as advancing in, theological competence and Christian leadership.[16] This is evident in the African context which suffers from the cultural invasion of the North by the introduction of the cultural and religious values from the home country of every Christian agency. This cultural invasion of Africa is particularly evident among the African elite as a result of schooling and indoctrination through the curricula in schools, colleges, seminaries and universities which are overloaded with cultural values from Europe and North America. Christian instruction and the use of foreign languages as the medium of instruction have reinforced this alienation of African students from their culture.[17] At this point, the words of Bishop Grove are worth pondering and merit quoting:

> In the work of training the native Christians' Churches, and in particular those who are to be the leaders of the Churches, the greatest possible care will have to be taken to avoid the risk of denationalizing those who are being trained. In particular we desire to lay the greatest emphasis on the importance of giving religious teaching, not only of the elementary kind, but as far as possible throughout, in the vernacular. We feel certain that those of our witnesses are right who believe that religion can only really be acclimatised in the heart of the natives of any country if it finds expressions in their native language – the language of their home.[18]

Perhaps what is then not an obvious but nevertheless a very important contributing factor to the inequality in theological education between the global North and the global South is the inevitability as well as the need to contextualise theological education. Sister Virginia Fabella of the Philippines writes under the entry of 'contextualization' in the *Dictionary of Third World Theologies:*

> It has been claimed that all theologies, because they are born out of social conditions and needs of a particular context, are in a sense 'contextual', philosophical abstractions, church doctrines and biblical texts – rather than concrete situations and experiences – were used as starting points of theology. This was true of western theology which was taught as 'universal theology', applicable to all times and contexts.[19]

---

[16] This has been pointed out very clearly in Parallel Session on Theme 6: Theological Education and Formation, 164.

[17] Jesse N.K. Mugambi, 'The future of Theological Education in Africa and the Challenges it faces', in *Handbook of Theological Education in Africa*, 117.

[18] World Missionary Conference, 1910, *Education in Relation to the Christianization of National life*, Report of Commission III (Edinburgh & London: Oliphant, Anderson & Ferrier; New York, Chicago, Toronto: Fleming H. Revell, 1910), 373, cited by David A. Kerr and Kenneth R. Ross, *Edinburgh 2010: Mission Then and Now* (Oxford: Regnum, 2009), 87-88.

[19] Virginia Fabella, M.M. Thomas, and R.S. Sugirtharajah (eds), *Dictionary of Third World Theologies* (Maryknoll, NY: Orbis Books, 2000), 58, cited by David

Kwok Pui-lan describes this reality as 'epistemic colonialism' where many people still harbour the hidden assumption that 'western theology is normative and represents the 'universal', while other theologies – African, Asian, Latin American, black, feminist, womanist, Latino/a, queer, and so forth – are local or contextual, perspectival, and limited'.[20] She also clearly highlighted the challenges of 'Theology from the global South through western eyes' – how a majority of books on 'global theology', 'theology in global dialogue', or 'theology in a global context', are written or edited by white scholars in Europe and North America, filtered through their epistemological frameworks.[21]

Historically too, with regard to systematic and constructive theology, theological institutions in the global South have been obligated for a long time to teach western theological giants such as Augustine, Calvin, Luther, Schleiermacher, Barth, Bultmann and Tillich, dealing with God, Jesus, the Holy Spirit, the church and the world. As a result, there has been little thought or space given to theological pioneers from the global South dealing with theological realities of the South, or using African and Asian philosophical resources or the wisdom traditions of the indigenous people to construct their own theologies.[22] As Houston also points out regarding the African context, many theological colleges there were started as projects from the West with the resources from the West, as a result of which many theological colleges in Africa are still faithfully teaching the knowledge generated in the West. One important factor is the dependency on western and other textbooks which do not reflect African realities.[23] As Pui-lan rightly states, even with the shift of Christian demographics to the global South, 'a closer look at the theological curriculum at many schools clearly indicates that the European and Euro-American traditions are privileged over others', and that 'teaching of theology has not changed to catch up with the new global situation'.[24] Geevarghese Mor Coorilos, while discussing the need for theological space states:

> With a colonial legacy in our minds, our thinking of space is conditioned, influenced, by Western colonial logic. One of the first steps we need to take to develop an Asian theology is to reclaim our Asian sense of space... Every project of colonisation, of imperialism starts with the conquest of space...

Suh, 'An Ethos for Teaching Theology Ecumenically in Asia', in *Asian Handbook for Theological Education and Ecumenism*, 644.

[20] Kwok Pui-lan, 'Teaching Theology in a Global and Transnational World': https://www.aarweb.org/publications/spotlight-on-theological-education-march-2014-teaching-theology-in-a-global-and-transnational-world (accessed 9th January 2015).

[21] Pui-lan, 'Teaching Theology in a Global and Transnational World'.

[22] See David Suh, 'An Ethos for Teaching Theology Ecumenically in Asia', 647.

[23] Houston, 'The Future is not What it Used to Be', 109.

[24] Pui-lan, 'Teaching Theology in a Global Transnational World'.

Our space means our lands, our social relationships, our contexts, our resources, everything.[25]

One of the major difficulties that is prevalent in the global South is running denominational organisations as well as framing the content and goals of theological education, keeping contextualisation in mind. While there has been a certain degree of contextualisation, theological education in the South remains in many respects colonised. This is not surprising considering that denominationalism in most of the countries in the South is after all an extension and a continuation of the denominational schisms that took place in the North. It is only lately that theologians from the South are tracing the east and southward movement of Christianity, while more emphasis is being laid on Christianity as an eastern religion with its message of liberation born out of a specific eastern context, and yet one that is universally recognisable and acceptable.

Where Do We Go from Here?

This paper has attempted to analyse some of the reasons for the inequality in theological education between the global South and the global North. It is hoped that further questions have been raised about how resources and teaching methodologies can be shared and a better understanding arrived at about how different contexts shape the content and goals of theological education. The paper also reminds us that inequality is a consequence of human factors and can therefore be addressed and corrected. The obvious factors that can be corrected constitute the easier part. What is difficult is a change in mindset and perceptions. Are we willing to change syllabus content to accommodate the concerns of Christians living in contexts different from our own? Can we consider African and Asian philosophies in our quest to better understand Christian thought? Conversely, do Greek and western philosophies find resonance with African and Asian philosophies and contexts, or do these continue to be imposed on the global South without consideration for a two-way exchange of information and ideas?

There is an urgent need for a more holistic approach to viewing as well as constructing methodologies for theological education. This must begin with a long overdue acknowledgement from the North that colonialism has left its legacy on theological education in the South. Under the guise of enlightenment and the view to 'civilise' indigenous populations, theological education has used the language of the colonisers, its method of instruction has been modelled on European structures of education, and it has for a long time been identified with the close relationship between

---

[25] Geevarghese Mor Coorilos, 'Theologizing in Asian Context', in *CTC Bulletin*, June 2011, 47-51, cited by Wilson, 'Theological Education and Ecumenical Challenges in Asia', 628.

colonialism and the various global missionary movements.[26] The global South must also acknowledge that there have been sporadic efforts and progress in a search for indigenous and contextual approaches to theological education, and that various church and denominational traditions continue to take refuge in administrative processes and forms and orders of worship introduced by western missionaries.[27]

Theological education must be interdisciplinary in outlook and move beyond the compartmentalisation of theological disciplines. This would encourage integration of academic learning with spiritual growth and the development of pastoral identity.[28] This is especially true when one realises and acknowledges that, more often than not, it is the spiritual life of the teacher that influences students more than what they learn in a formal classroom setting.[29] To take this analogy a step further, Bible seminaries, colleges and universities can also learn from, and be enriched and complemented by, other models of theological learning and teaching, such as the discipleship model of learning theology, monasteries and worshipping communities. Equally important, as Michael Biehl stresses, theological education cannot be a preparation for mission in a vacuum but must contribute to social transformation, leadership capacity-building, and poverty reduction. There is the need to keep in mind the link theological education must have with social, political and economic development and not just with church-related issues. He stresses the need for a closer and more explicit co-operation between theological education and developmental agencies for such a contribution.[30]

Space for equality in theological education between North and South must also be created in terms of widening the scope and ambit of what constitutes theological education. Theologies related to gender, children,

---

[26] For example, John S. Pobee gives a good description of how Christianity in Africa, south of the Sahara, was involved with the two movements – the Christian missionary movement and colonial expansion – which also holds true for other countries in the South. See John S. Pobee, 'Good News Turned by Native Hands, Turned by Native Hatchet and Tended with Native Earth – A History of Theological Education in Africa', in *Handbook of Theological Education in Africa*, 17.

[27] Theological students are impatient to work in ecumenical collaboration, in team research projects that are relevant to local communities, and look to church leadership for vision and integrity. See *Global Survey on Theological Education*, 6.

[28] Cf. Parallel Sessions on Theme 6: Theological Education and Formation, 161.

[29] 80% of the respondents of 'The Global Survey on Theological Education' felt that the 'integrity of Senior leaders' was the most important element in determining the quality of theological education. See *Global Survey on Theological Education*, 6.

[30] Michael Biehl, 'Response to the "Global Survey on Theological Education"', 6. Paper presented during the first session of the Ecumenical Conversation No. 6: Ecumenical Theological Education at the 10th Assembly of WCC in Busan, October 2013.

minorities, refugees, migrants, marginalised people and the voices of the subaltern, often not integrated into the core of systematic theology or biblical studies, must make up what is considered contextual theology, and there must be equal participation and balance between what makes up the universality and the contextuality of theological education.[31]

There must also be space given for ecumenical and denominational theological education. Increasingly, candidates from Pentecostal and emerging churches are joining ecumenical theological centres of education to obtain their theological degrees. This is evident in the African context where more models of theological education can be looked at with the emergence of new African initiatives in Christianity and the Pentecostal charismatic movement. As a result, a variety of traditions in theological education, such as colonial patterns and missionary denominational interests, along with those mentioned above, exist openly alongside each other and make invaluable contributions to a better understanding of what contextual theological education is.[32]

Conclusion

In the ultimate analysis, theological education and all that is understood by and constitutes the term – including the urge or 'calling' of the individual to be theologically educated – must be a mission-oriented activity. As is clearly stated in the Parallel Sessions on Theme 6: Theological education and Formation: 'Educating the whole people of God is a key to mission and Christian mission should be the organizing focus and reference point of theological education.'[33]

While we acknowledge the lack of common quality standards in terms of resources (both financial and human), teaching and study aids, and resources and pedagogical methodologies, the global North which dominates in these must recognise that these are not the be-all-and-end-all for preparing a person theologically for mission. These resources are tools

---

[31] Cf. Parallel Sessions on Theme 6: Theological Education and Formation, 162. See also section 3: Theological Education for the Whole People of God, in 'Magna Carta on Ecumenical Theological Education in the 21st Century', in Mèlisande Lorke and Dietrich Werner (eds), *Ecumenical Visions for the 21st Century: A Reader for Theological Education* (Geneva: WCC, 2013), 340. In line with this thinking, respondents of the 'Global Survey on Theological Education' would like to see subjects such as cross-cultural communication and practical skills added or strengthened in theological education. Additionally, respondents in Africa and Europe indicated more interest in courses in interfaith dialogue than on Biblical studies, while respondents in Africa, Asia and Latin America showed more interest in gender studies than those in Europe and North America. See *Global Survey on Theological Education*, 5.

[32] Pobee, 'Good News Turned by Native Hands, Turned by Native Hatchet and Tended with Native Earth- A History of Theological Education in Africa', 17-18.

[33] Parallel Session on Theme 6: Theological Education and Formation, 160.

in the *missio Dei* and not the yardsticks by which mission must be measured. There must also be a willingness to embrace non-formal and non-residential forms of theological education that also involves the entire human being. An open mind and a willingness to discuss and learn about diverse theological traditions could help in dialogue for mutual understanding, and in overcoming theological perceptions and prejudices over against other traditions. Such an approach will ensure theological education's relevant, vital and life-giving role in shaping mission thinking today for both the churches in the North and South.

If theological education is to contribute more effectively to mission formation, both the global North and the global South must contribute as equals and in equal measure. This search for an effective yet appropriate theological education cannot be the prerogative or the privilege of either side.

GENDERED THEOLOGICAL EDUCATION: A READING FROM INDIA

Atola Longkumer

Introduction

Theological education is many things to many people, in the contemporary complex and multi-context world. For some, it is about equipping oneself for ecclesiastical professionalism, for some it may be a journey into profound philosophical quest, seeking answers to perennial questions of existence; theological education, for some, may yet provide the opportunity towards serving humanity. With its possible multi-purposes and rationales, a fundamental underlying principle of theological education is its centrality to the Christian faith. Theological education is about critical reflection and passionate participation for transformation of humanity from an exclusive and myopic outlook towards a just co-existence and reconciled creation. If education is about imparting knowledge and skills, theological education is about seeking understanding that transcends boundaries and engenders transformation in concrete contexts, rooted in God's love for the creation. In the 2014 Convocation address of the Senate of Serampore College (University), India, Dietrich Werner summed up the core of theological education as 'knowing about God, to meet the totally Other, who is nothing but unconditional love to each and everybody, particularly the vulnerable, is at the core of theological education'.[1] Theological education, understood in this way, serves as an interpretation of God's vision of a just world, where the most vulnerable are included and embraced.

With this premise, that theological education is intrinsically linked with a vision and action towards a just and inclusive world, this essay interrogates the Indian context of theological education and argues that it remains gendered, privileging the parochial social-cultural structures. Consequently, theological education in India remains accountable to the excluded of socio-cultural structures, ecclesiastical hierarchy and politics of the powerful. To recast its role as a medium of transformation of an oppressive socio-cultural matrix, theological education in India will need to develop deliberate policies and radical mechanisms of ensuring inclusive communities.

---

[1] Dietrich Werner, '*Expect Great things from God, Attempt Great things for God*': *The Serampore Vision for Integral Education, the ecumenical search for a theology of life and the future of theological education in World Christianity.* Serampore Convocation Address, February 2014.

Theological education is by its nature primarily related to the Christian community and its tradition and identity. This is, however, not to deny that theological education has its engagement and responsibility towards the larger society, wherein the Christian community is situated. Theological education understood in its specific context is embedded within the Christian community, while theological education defined as a critical reflection on the state of the world in the light of God's vision for a just world, has the 'world as its parish'. Hence, theological education in India is understood as accountable to both the Christian community and the larger society.

A discussion on India needs to underscore the fact that India has a multi-layer of socio-cultural, economic and religious contexts marked by a plurality of peoples, cultures, socio-economic conditions, languages, religions, etc. These conditions of plurality and contradictions have undoubtedly left their imprints on Christianity in India. If the country is not homogeneous, so also Christianity in India is not monolithic in its form and expression in the region. Christianity is observed in diverse traditions and expressions related to different historical periods and in multiple forms of indigenous Christianity. The diversity of contexts of the Christian community is also reflected in theological education in India. Theological education and its relationship with the Christian communities vary from church to church, according to their denominational history, policy and practice. While there are differences in policy, support, funding, role, and even curriculum to some extent, it can be said that there is a commonality shared by all: the recognition, role, support and placement of women in theological education. Put simply, the scenario and experience of theological education for women remains an extension of the larger kyriarchal[2]-patriarchal society: a male-centric environment biased towards producing male professionals for a kyriarchal church.

Reflection on theological education as a missional task of the global church, post-Edinburgh 2010[3] and Together Towards Life[4] – the new mission document prepared by the CWME-WCC – need to be more candid of the church's position and practice in relation to theological education

---

[2] Elisabeth Schüssler Fiorenza coined the term 'kyriarchal' as an analytical term to articulate in a more comprehensive way the systemic oppression of women manifest across the socio-political structure of a complex web of domination than the conventional term patriarchy. Kyriarchy locates sexism and misogyny in a wider spectrum of oppression, as she writes, 'the neologism kyriarchy-kyriocentrism (from the Greek word *kyrios* meaning lord, master, father, husband) seeks to express the interstructuring of domination and to replace the commonly used term "patriarchy" which is often understood in terms of binary gender dualism'. See Schüssler Fiorenza, *Rhetoric and Ethic: The Politics of Biblical Studies* (Minneapolis, MN: Fortress Press, 1999), 5.
[3] www.edinburgh2010.org
[4] www.oikoumene.org

and women. The lopsided understanding and exploits of power is a central theme addressed quite radically in both the documents as exemplified in the following two samplings, 'disturbed by the asymmetries and imbalances of power that divide and trouble us in church and world, we are called to repentance, to critical reflection on systems of power, and to accountable use of power structures...'; in the same vein, the following lines from the Together Towards Life reckon with the failure of the church in mission in relation to power, 'sometimes in practice it [church] is much more concerned with being in the centres of power, eating with the rich, and lobbying for money to maintain ecclesial bureaucracy'.[5]

Radical and candid as these quotations are, they remind us of the churches' unfinished task of being the community that is a foretaste of God's Kingdom, where the barriers and differences between the powerful and the powerless will be no more. The lopsided power structures that the documents critique can be observed in relation to theological education and women. The lament from different quarters seems to indicate that discrimination against women in theological education is an almost global phenomenon, and more acute in India, exacerbated by larger socio-cultural attitudes. To be sure, theological education has contributed to the discourse and the inclusion of women in the life of the church.[6] Articulations of feminist, womanist theologies have sprung from the experience, contexts and consequence of theological education.[7] While theological education creates the space to articulate inclusive theology, theological education apparently is not free of discrimination or exclusion. The following observation made by the study group of Theological Education and Formation attests to the fact:

> While we celebrate the significant changes that have occurred in some contexts with regard to women in theological studies and teaching, it should be emphasised that continuing efforts are needed. In most regions of the world there is still an overwhelming task to be accomplished in terms of encouraging, equipping, and enabling young women theologians to gain access to degree programs, teaching positions, and leadership in churches and

---

[5] Jooseop Keum (ed), *Together Towards Life: Mission and Evangelism in Changing Landscapes* (Geneva: WCC, 2013), 16.

[6] All the following feminist theologians were embedded in theological institutions and articulated their theological discourse for women's liberation and empowerment from their roles as theological teachers: Rosemary Radford Ruether, Letty R. Russell, Elisabeth Schussler Fiorenza, Rebecca S. Chopp, Kwok Pui Lan, Serena Jones, etc.

[7] For a helpful review of theological education as a locus for theological discourse and example of inclusive community, see Rebecca S. Chopp, *Saving Work: Feminist Practices of Theological Education* (Louisville, KY: Westminster John Knox Press, 1995); for an excellent source of analytical research on women in leadership in theological education in the contexts of the USA and Canada, see Barbara Brown Zikmund, 'Three Coins in the Fountain: Female Leadership in Theological Education', in *Theological Education*, Vol. 45, No. 2 (2010): 1-60.

educational institutions. As there are backlash in many regions regarding the presence of women in church leadership and positions in higher education in general, it is very important that women receive strong support at every stage in theological education.[8]

Christian mission that is radically concerned for the flourishing of life needs to reckon with equipping, enabling and embracing women in all facets of theological education in the church. If Christian mission is participation towards a transformative spirituality, then it calls on the churches to participate in constructive theological education that calls for subversion of patriarchal ideologies and practices.[9]

Christian Mission and Theological Education

Central to Christian mission has been the education of the 'natives' as documented in many studies. In a general sense, along with the objective of evangelisation, education of the 'natives' in the mission fields served at least two immediate purposes: to 'civilise/modernise' and to produce indigenous leaders.[10] Pastors, evangelists, translators and assistants were needed in the nascent Christian communities, for which Bible schools and theological seminaries were required to be established. The Report of the Commission III: *Education in Relation to the Christianisation of National Life* of the World Missionary Conference, Edinburgh 1910, attest to this need:

> We wish to lay it down that we believe that the primary purpose to be served by the education work of missionaries is that of training of the native church to bear its own proper witness. And in as much as the only way in which the native church can bear its own proper witness, and move forward to the position of independence and self-government in which it ought to stand, is through native leaders, teachers and officers, we believe that the most important of all ends which missionary education ought to set itself to serve,

---

[8] 'Theme Six: Theological Education and Formation', in Daryl Balia and Kirsteen Kim (eds), *Edinburgh 2010: Witnessing to Christ Today* (Oxford: Regnum, 2010), 159.

[9] Namsoon Kang, 'The Centrality of Gender Justice in Prophetic Christianity and the Mission of the Church Reconsidered', in *International Review of Mission*, Vol. 94/373, April 2005, 279-89.

[10] The topic of Christian mission and education continues to provide a most exciting area of productive and critical analyses for many areas of research, ranging from post-colonial studies to cultural studies to individual biographies. See Maina Singh Chawla, *Gender, Religions and 'Heathen Lands': American Missionary Women in South Asia* (1860s-1940s) (New York: Garland Publishing, 2000); Kwok Pui-lan, *Chinese Women and Christianity 1860-1927* (New York, Oxford University Press, 2000).

is that of training those who are to be spiritual leaders and teachers of their own.[11]

The document on *Leadership Formation in the Changing Landscapes of World Christianity: Ecumenical Covenant on Theological Education* also underscores the pioneering work of Christian missionaries towards theological education and ecumenical leadership formation.[12] Theological education as an agenda of Christian mission has gone through changes over the decades, from the objective of nurturing indigenous leaders to the contextualisation of theological curriculum.[13] In the process, theological education has shaped and helped define the mission of the church, towards evangelisation, translation, contextual theology, ecumenical relationship and ecclesiastical traditions.

It may be noted that, apart from a few, most of the theological colleges in north-eastern India are initiatives by native converts. And theological education continues to be an enterprise of the churches in a complex way, in that some churches have stronger ties, ownership role, and even recruitment policy, while there are other churches where there is little of a direct ownership role within the theological college. While there are no explicit restrictions against acquiring theological education for women and the appointment of women faculty, the challenge for women theological students remains after the completion of their studies, because the church, being a culturally influenced community, has very little opportunity for a woman.[14]

Theological education, in India, is inadvertently linked with the missionary movement and remains a mission concern of the church, to ensure that adequate, inclusive and contextual theological education is imparted. To do this, the church in India needs to understand the stark reality of women's presence and participation in theological education.

---

[11] Quoted in Namsoon Kang, 'Note from the President of WOCATI' in Dietrich Werner and Namsoon Kang, Challenges and Opportunities in Theological Education in the 21st Century: Pointers for a new international debate on theological education: www.oikoumene.org. ETE-WCC-and-WOCATI-Nov09.pdf, accessed 27th January 2015).

[12] 'Leadership Formation in the Changing Landscapes of World Christianity: Ecumenical Covenant on Theological Education', ETE, 2012, in Melisande Lorke and Dietrich Werner (eds), *Ecumenical Visions for the 21st Century: A Reader for Theological Education* (Geneva: WCC, 2013), 382-88.

[13] See David Esterline, 'From Western Church to World Christianity: Developments in Theological Education in the Ecumenical Movement', in Dietrich Werner, David Esterline, Namsoon Kang and Joshva Raja (eds), *Handbook of Theological Education in World Christianity, 13.*

[14] I have discussed this in detail in another essay – see Atola Longkumer, 'Tetsur Tesayula: Christian Mission and Gender in the Ao Naga of Northeast India' in Christine Lienemann-Perrin et al (eds), *Putting Names with Faces: Women's Impact in Mission History* (Nashville, TN: Abingdon Press, 2012), 187-206.

Gendered Theological Education in India

The Edinburgh 2010 thematic study group on Theological Education and Formation pointed out the general malaise of women's position and role in theological education, noting the need of 'continuing efforts' despite the significant improvements since the World Missionary Conference in 1910.[15] The study group also rightly observed the apparent 'backlash' against 'women presence and leadership' in many contexts.[16] The context of Indian theological education can be one such: there is rigid resistance and hence an urgent need for a radical commitment to equip women leaders for church, theological education and the larger society. Given the attitudes and practices prevailing in the churches in India in relation to women's participation and leadership in theological education, it can be stated that theological education in India has unfortunately been gendered, privileging the dominant male for leadership in the ecclesiastical hierarchy and leadership in theological education. At best, there have been some token measures, but a radical shift from a kyriarchal-patriarchal template of the larger socio-cultural society has not taken place. The fact that in a history of almost two hundred years, Serampore has not had any woman leadership in the executive/administrative positions bespeaks of a colossal wall of resistance, reinforced by sporadic tokenisms. Exclusion, resistance and objectification of women are challenges faced by women in many theological institutions. Many churches do not encourage women for theological education; if they can overcome this attitude and pursue theological education, the Eucharistic ministry of the church remains inaccessible for women in many churches, particularly in the northeast India region. Monica Melanchthon writes, 'The plight of women within theological education fills me with feelings of frustration and a sense of hopelessness. I have heard of a woman theologian being paid less than her male counterparts in a Senate affiliated college only because she had a MTh [Master of Theology] in Theology through the department of Women's Studies.'[17]

A common experience across different regions, language groups and denominational identity for women in theological education is one of discrimination. The persistent discrimination begs the question: where is

---

[15] Daryl Balia and Kirsteen Kim (eds), *Edinburgh 2010;* for some specific contexts of women in theological education, see Isabel Apawo Phiri, 'Major Challenges for African Women Theologians in Theological Education', in *International Review of Mission*, Vol. 98, No. 1, 2009, 105-19; Michelle Sungshin Lim, 'A Tragedy of Women's Leadership' in *Theological Education*, Vol. 45, No.2, 2010, 81-84.

[16] 'Theme Six: Theological Education and Formation' in Daryl Balia and Kirsteen Kim (eds), *Edinburgh 2010: Witnessing to Christ Today* (Oxford: Regnum, 2010), 159.

[17] Monica Jyotsna Melanchthon, 'Feminist Theologizing: Rethinking Theological Education in India'. Lecture III *of Bishop and Mrs S.K. Parmar Mission Lectures 2010*, Leonard Theological College, Jabalpur, MP, 2010.

inclusive gender justice that has been in our collective consciousness since the Ecumenical Decade of Churches in Solidarity with Women (1988-1998)? That theological education in India is gendered is also attested to by the assessment provided by Wati Longchar: 'It is a matter of concern that the structure of theological education under SSC is mainly male dominated: 80% theological students; 90% teachers, 90% members of the governing board... it is obvious from our experience that we have not achieved gender justice either in theological colleges or in other forms of Christian ministry.'[18]

In such a scenario of a gendered theological education in India, the church's mission of equipping and enabling leaders for the continuity and relevance of the Christian faith calls for radical, disciplined, prophetic commitment towards an inclusive theological education that participates in a constructive transformation of the creation.

Equipping Leaders and Theological Education: Mission Re-affirmations

The Handbook on Theological Education begins with the following passage:

> Theological education is vital for the future of World Christianity... Theological education has the potential to be the seedbed for the renewal of churches, their ministries, mission, and commitment to Christian unity. If theological education is neglected by church leaders or in funding, the consequences are far reaching; they might not be visible immediately, but they will certainly become manifest over time in the theological competence of church leadership, the holistic nature of mission, and the capacities for ecumenical and interfaith dialogue and the interaction between church and society. Investment in theological education is investment for hope in the future and mission of World Christianity.[19]

Indeed, the vitality and constructive continuity of the Christian community is inevitably influenced by the nature and content of theological education. Theological education ideally upholds the traditions of the faith, provides critical reading of the sacred text, produces organic leaders for the community, and brings together the community for collective lived spirituality, marked by the Gospel's values. In its role as a source for continuity and relevance of the church, theological education holds together the two important facets of the Christian community: its identity as God's people reconciled through Jesus Christ, and its prophetic witness for constructive transformation. Subsequently, the quality and nature of theological education is crucial for the healing of a fragmented and

---

[18] Wati Longchar, 'The History and Development of Theological Education in South Asia', in Dietrich Werner, David Esterline, Namsoon Kang and Joshva Raja (eds), *Handbook of Theological Education in World Christianity*, 416.
[19] Dietrich Werner et al, *Handbook of Theological Education*, xxv.

hierarchical society. It is the task of theological education to develop critical reflection by creative reading of the sacred text to enable the church to be critical of destructive forces and myopic practices. Theological education needs to articulate a transformative radical spirituality of empathy and inclusion in order that the church be renewed in its mission to be the good news of justice in a world of oppressive injustice. Such times and the context of today's globalised world, calls for a spirituality that embraces diversity in all its manifestations, beyond the familiar and the normative as defined by patriarchal cultures.[20]

While theological education has been the harbinger of renewed and contextual interpretation of the Christian faith, it is still accountable to the margins, particularly to women both in the church and the larger society. In the following section some proposals are made towards a theological education in India that is radically missional in its role as a medium of constructive transformation of an existing exclusive and male-centric society. From the perspective of women, who continue to be under-represented and discriminated, unless a deliberate commitment for changes are made, theological education in India will remain a mere apparatus of producing ecclesiastical professionals to maintain the existing kyriarchal-patriarchal socio-cultural structures both within the church and the larger society.

Gendered theological education in India has persisted due to un-interrogated bias and traditions that have undergirded exclusive attitudes. Therefore, to recast its role as a medium of constructive transformation, theological education in India will need to develop deliberate policies undergirded by theological certitude and practical measures. These measures might include the following facets: curriculum, practical experience, mentoring, resource management, ecumenical efforts, collective evaluation, theological foundation, and a prophetic spirituality.

Limatula Longkumer points out the weakness of conventional curriculum, that 'very often women's concerns are placed alongside the main curriculum as an "appendix"'.[21] The content of theological education is crucial to the formation of inclusive spirituality, and the *curriculum* plays an important role in equipping future leaders of the church. A curriculum that is within the framework of critical pedagogy towards construction of inclusive communities is required to go beyond additions. Hence, women's issues, gender justice and feminist theology may be brought to the fore, rather than made convenient additions or sub-points. From the perspective of Christian mission that is radically in solidarity with the margins, a theological curriculum may be called to radical centering of gender justice

---

[20] See Daniel Aleshire, 'Community and Diversity', in www.ats.edu/uploads/resources/publications-presentations/documents/community-and-diversity.pdf (accessed 28th January 2015).
[21] Limatula Longkumer, 'Women in Theological Education from an Asian Perspective', in Dietrich Werner et al, *Handbook of Theological Education*, 70.

and inclusion of women's empowerment. Reverse hierarchy is not the intent; rather it is to have a theological curriculum that locates and excavates the voice of the victims of power and knowledge as the locus of theological education. Such a curriculum might envisage a deliberate encounter with the texts, contexts, history as the launch-pad of critical theological reflection enabling the resistance of selfish desires for exclusion.

Secondly, *practical exposures* may be made a fundamental feature of a theological education in India that is truly missional in its embrace of the margins and the vulnerable. The new mission document, *Together Towards Life*, defines margins as those who are excluded from the centre, where power, influence and possibilities reside. The new India of the globalised world presents unprecedented economic wealth for some. Globalisation, however, that is both economic and cultural, is built on greed and accumulation, and consequently there are victims of a system that favours the powerful. In the context of India, theological education should make deliberate efforts to encounter the margins, not just via narratives inscribed in texts or documentaries but by embedded experience. Undoubtedly, theological education in India has included a praxis dimension of learning; for instance, the revised syllabus of the Board of Theological Education of the Senate of Serampore College (BTESSC) has made practical ministry a core subject. An embedded experience of contexts of marginalisation, particularly of women, such as forced prostitution, human trafficking, migrant labourers, may lead to an understanding of the vicious nexus between a patriarchal attitude and the victimisation of women. A theological education that does not contribute to understanding the web of hierarchy will continue to remain gendered, privileging the existing socio-cultural hierarchies.

Mentoring would be the third proposal towards an inclusive theological education. The fact that there are still few women theological teachers, students, and few women theologians serving in leadership position in India, can be attributed to a lack of mentoring. The patriarchal socio-cultural mentality has impacted the relationship between students and teachers, leaders and learners. Hence, it is more than often the case that a male faculty would mentor a male student, a male church leader would choose to send a male candidate for theological education. The vicious cycle continues: there are fewer women leaders, faculty members, and fewer younger women are mentored to be leaders. Consequently, a gendered theological education is maintained. For theological education to be radically inclusive, mentoring of younger women both as students and faculty members, and as researchers, is necessary. This calls for deliberate practical steps and a planned mechanism for mentoring to take place both in the church and in theological institutions. Identifying, encouragement, guidance, creating networks, enabling, and nurturing of young women students will help to translate the ideal of mentoring towards an inclusive theological education.

Resource management makes the fourth measure that may contribute towards an inclusive theological education. The work of the former secretary of Ecumenical Theological Education, Dietrich Werner, has amply highlighted the importance of resource management of the Christian community in the ministerial formation of leaders. Resource management is vital to ensure that theological education is not gendered in favour of the dominant group. Human resources, funds and assets comprise the resources in theological education. Without adequate resources, theological education will remain mere static or worse, will remain only ideals but not a vibrant instrument to guide the church in its continuity and relevance. If resource management is vital to the life of theological education, a just management of resources is crucial to ensure a theological education that is inclusive. Development of faculty, enrolment of students, undertaking of projects, funds allotment, funds employment and funds accountability must all take adequate steps to include the empowerment and inclusion of women. These measures are recommended and practised in many contexts; however, the dismal figures of women in leadership positions such as principal, dean, board member, and the experiences of women in theological education both as students and faculty members call for persistent support.

Related to the resource management, the fifth proposal towards an inclusive theological education would be *ecumenical efforts*. As some church historians describe the contemporary era in Christianity as a post-denominational era, ecumenical relationships and fellowship are thriving as never before, not only in the sense of structured organisations such as the World Council of Churches, but also in larger fellowships of global Christians, such as the Global Christian Forum. While common witness and expression of a collective voice in common worship are important, it is also important that theological education and its value for the church are kept on the agenda in the common fellowship. Ecumenical efforts towards an inclusive theological education call for more shared efforts and shared resources; for instance, theological institutions that have a denominational history and objectives may be called to share their resources with members of other denominations. Ecumenical efforts in theological education mean going beyond denominational self-centeredness and fragmentation.[22]

The sixth proposal towards an inclusive theological education would be *collective evaluation*. The above-mentioned five proposals will contribute towards a constructive transformation of inclusive theological education when collective evaluation is part of the process of revitalising theological education. Practical measures and inspiring ideals will remain lofty ideals

---

[22] Dietrich Werner, *Theological Education in World Christianity: Ecumenical Perspectives and Future Priorities* (Tainan: Programme for Theology and Cultures in Asia, 2011), 117.

without a commitment for transparent collective evaluation of the recommendations. Collective evaluation calls for a principle of accountability and transparency that is willing to reflect the intentional commitment towards inclusive communities. Commitment towards a mission of equipping leaders for the mission of the church to go beyond mere rhetoric and declarations of policy requires a radical commitment to review the practice and progress towards the stated vision of inclusive community.

A firm *theological foundation* would be the seventh proposal towards an inclusive theological education. A firm theological foundation is characterised by faith derived from the Bible as the word of God, the faith that affirms that God is the creator, who in his grace and love reconciled humanity through Jesus Christ, and continues to transform humanity through the Holy Spirit. A theological education without a firm affirmation of a faith in God who seeks to reconcile, liberate and embrace all creation, would be like any other process of education, that seeks knowledge for professional, economic gains or other social capital purposes.

And, lastly *a prophetic spirituality* undergirds these recommendations towards an inclusive theological education. A prophetic spirituality is a disciplined way of life rooted in the knowledge of the triune God as the source of all knowledge and wisdom and the humility derived from the cross, which exemplifies the ultimate self-emptying for the flourishing of life. A prophetic spirituality combines keen awareness of the triune God as the creator, the beginning and the end, and motivation to live a life that reflects faith in the triune God. Worship, relationship, character, community life, compassion, solidarity, accountability and communion are all facets of a prophetic spirituality. An inclusive theological education is markedly distinct from other processes of education because a prophetic spirituality exists together with the cognitive dimension of learning. The vision shared by an inclusive theological education for a reconciled and just humanity is fed by a prophetic spirituality, without which theological education would be a vacuous exercise.

Conclusion

To conclude this argument that theological education in India remains gendered, and hence a missional commitment for inclusive theological education is needed, a personal experience of theologian Ursula King might encourage one to persevere with hope for constructive transformation. King narrates her experience of being a minority when she began her theological education in the 1970s: 'I remember in my early student years being refused admission to join the courses on Thomas of Aquinas in a German college of Dominicans, only because I was a woman. I also recall the disappointing answer of an eminent British Jesuit whom I consulted about job opportunities... He simply said to me, "I am afraid there is no place for you in England.'" To this experience of exclusion and refusal, King states, 'a remark never forgotten, and a prediction proved entirely wrong', as she chaired a department of theology and religious studies, and was governor of a Jesuit theological college.[23]

There have been undoubtedly significant changes in women's participation and leadership in theological education;[24] however, theological education remains gendered. Therefore, King's wise insight towards a renewed and relevant theological education by a community of men and women needs to be heeded: 'Engendering theology is an urgent task and requires much transformation of traditional theological perspectives and approaches. This can only be achieved through women and men working closely together, by integrating their respective experiences and ways of thinking in a new manner. This requires working as friends and partners in communion empowered by the powers of love, the presence and fire of the spirit. The hope for possibility of such communion offers a vision of great hope for the churches and the world.'[25]

---

[23]Ursula King, 'Journey Thus Far: An Overview of Feminist Perspectives From around the World', in LWF, Engendering Theological Education for Transformation: www.lutheranworld.info/What_We_Do/DMD/DMD-Documents/ EN/DMD-Engendering-Theol_Education.pdf LWF, 2001 (accessed, 28th January 2015).

[24] The report of the project on women's leadership in theological education in the USA and Canada indicates encouraging trends; for instance, in 2007, out of 252 theological institutions there were 63 women leaders of the institutions. See Barbara Brown Zikmund, 'Three Coins in the Fountain: Female Leadership in Theological Education', in *Theological Education.*

[25] King, 'Journey Thus Far', 41

THEOLOGICAL EDUCATION, BIBLE AND MISSION: A LAUSANNE PERSPECTIVE

Chris Wright

The Lausanne Movement, historically, is committed to world evangelisation. It interprets that last phrase in holistic terms, as including all that is involved in the broad task of Christian mission in the world. While the task of discipling new believers has always been included in that understanding, the specific work of theological education has not been much to the fore. At the Third Lausanne Congress, in Cape Town in 2010, however, a small group representing the interests of theological educators globally, sought to ensure that theological education should be perceived as an integral part of the teaching ministry of the church and therefore included within the terms of the so-called Great Commission. The group included Paul Sanders (then Director of the International Council for Evangelical Theological Education), David Baer (President of Overseas Council), and myself (International Director of Langham Partnership). We held a series of dialogue session under the title, 'Every Paul needs an Apollos'. The concerns expressed in that track are summarised in the *Cape Town Commitment*, IIF.4 – 'Theological Education and Mission,' which reads as follows:

> The mission of the Church on earth is to serve the mission of God, and the mission of theological education is to strengthen and accompany the mission of the Church. Theological education serves *first* to train those who lead the Church as pastor-teachers, equipping them to teach the truth of God's Word with faithfulness, relevance and clarity; and *second*, to equip all God's people for the missional task of understanding and relevantly communicating God's truth in every cultural context. Theological education engages in spiritual warfare, as 'we demolish arguments and every pretension that sets itself up against the knowledge of God, and we take captive every thought to make it obedient to Christ'.[1]
>
> a. Those of us who lead churches and mission agencies need to acknowledge that theological education is intrinsically missional. Those of us who provide theological education need to ensure that it is intentionally missional, since its place within the academy is not an end in itself, but to serve the mission of the church in the world.
>
> b. Theological education stands in partnership with all forms of missional engagement. We will encourage and support all who provide

---

[1] 2 Corinthians 10:4-5.

biblically faithful theological education, formal and non-formal, at local, national, regional and international levels.

c. We urge that institutions and programmes of theological education conduct a 'missional audit' of their curricula, structures and ethos, to ensure that they truly serve the needs and opportunities facing the church in their cultures.

d. We long that all church planters and theological educators should place the Bible at the centre of their partnership, not just in doctrinal statements but in practice. Evangelists must use the Bible as the supreme source of the content and authority of their message. Theological educators must re-centre the study of the Bible as the core discipline in Christian theology, integrating and permeating all other fields of study and application. Above all, theological education must serve to equip pastor-teachers for their prime responsibility of preaching and teaching the Bible.[2]

We may reflect on those paragraphs with three words: What, Why, and How.

THE WHAT:
What is our fundamental purpose?
We need a *reminder* of the goal of theological education.

What is the fundamental purpose of theological education? What is it we are trying to do? To answer that question biblically, we have to ask further questions, answering them as the *Cape Town Commitment* does above:

Who is theological education for? Biblical answer – for the church, to serve the life, growth and mission of God's people, both in training its pastor and leaders, and in helping *all* believers to 'be transformed through the renewal of their minds' (Rom. 12:1-2).

But for what does the church exist? Biblical answer – in the present era, for the sake of participating in the mission of God in the world. Therefore theological education must serve the church in its mission.

The Great Commission includes in its mandate, 'Make disciples... teaching them to obey all that I have commanded you.' So, theological education, as part of the teaching work of the church, is intrinsically missional. It is Great Commission work.

How then can theological education serve the mission of the church? Primarily, in my view, by training those who will equip the saints for *their* ministry.

One of the more destructive inward-turns that theological education took was when it came to be regarded as more or less exclusively committed to the task of training men (and it usually was men) 'for the ministry'. And of course, 'the ministry' meant the ordained pastoral ministry within church

---

[2] 2 Timothy 2:2; 4:1-2; 1 Timothy 3:2b; 4:11-14; Titus 1:9; 2:1.

congregations. You got called 'into the ministry', and then you went to seminary to get 'trained for the ministry'. And when you came out, you 'entered the ministry', and led churches, preached, pastored, baptised, married and buried people, etc. Since those activities are predominantly what 'the ministry' was, it unavoidably shaped what theological education was thought to be.

But that was not how Paul saw the task of pastoral ministry. The role of the 'pastor-teacher' was not to 'do the ministry', but to equip the rest of the church for *their* ministry. 'Christ himself *gave* the apostles, the prophets, the evangelists, the pastors and teachers, *to equip his people for works of service.*' Those words from Ephesians 4:11-13 (my italics) ought to govern our goals in theological education.

Doubtless some young graduates come out of theological education thinking they are God's gift to the church! Well, they are right – but not in the sense they may imagine. They are not so much gifted, as *given*. God has not *given to them* all the gifts to do all *the* ministry themselves; rather he has *given them as people* (with their particular gifts) to equip others for their ministry.

So, the job of pastor-teachers, according to Paul, is precisely to equip the rest of the people of God (the saints) for *their* ministries – their many ways of serving God in the church and in the world. So, in theological education, we do not train people for a clerical ministry that is an end in itself, but for a *servant* ministry that has learned how to train disciples to *be* disciples in every context in which they live and move. Congregations need to be told that they do not come to church 'to support the pastor in his / her ministry'. Biblically, it is the opposite. The pastor comes to church to support and equip the people for *their* ministry. Are we training future pastors to think like that, and to shape their preaching and teaching ministry for that goal – to be equippers of the saints for *their* ministry?

This is a perspective that John Stott repeatedly pointed out through fifty years of writing (sadly, it fell on largely deaf ears). He insisted that, in biblical terms, pastoral ministry is not *the* ministry (certainly not the only one), nor are pastors the only people who 'do ministry'. Although Stott had a very serious personal commitment to the biblical validity of ordained pastoral/teaching ministry within the church, he passionately believed that it was damagingly unbiblical to confine the concept of 'ministry' to the clergy. He affirmed that ministry and mission were the calling of *all* disciples of Christ – in all their varied vocations.

> We do a great disservice to the Christian cause whenever we refer to the pastorate as 'the ministry', for by our use of the definite article we give the impression that the pastorate is the only ministry there is... I repented of this view, and therefore of this language, about twenty-five years ago... The fact is that the word 'ministry' is a generic term; it lacks specificity until we add an adjective.

There is a wide variety of Christian ministries. This is because 'ministry' means 'service', and there are many different ways in which we can serve God and people. [There follows a discussion of the events in Acts 6.] ... It is essential to note that both distributing food and teaching the word were referred to as ministry (*diakonia*). Indeed, both were Christian ministry, could be full-time ministry, and required Spirit-filled people to perform them. The only difference between them was that one was pastoral ministry, and the other social. It was not that one was 'ministry' and the other not; nor that one was spiritual and the other secular; nor that one was superior and the other inferior. It was simply that Christ had called the Twelve to the ministry of the word and the Seven to the ministry of tables.

It is a wonderful privilege to be a missionary or a pastor, *if God calls us to it*. But it is equally wonderful to be a Christian lawyer, industrialist, politician, manager, social worker, television script-writer, journalist, or home-maker, *if God calls us to it*. According to Romans 13:4, an official of the state (whether legislator, magistrate, policeman or policewoman) is just as much a 'minister of God' (*diakonos theou*) as a pastor.

There is a crying need for Christian men and women who see their daily work as their primary Christian ministry and who determine to penetrate their secular environment for Christ.[3]

And consequently, there is also a crying need for institutions of theological education, insofar as they are engaged in training future pastors, to train them to be *equippers* – to have a high view of the calling and ministries of *all* God's people, including the vast majority (98%) who are *not* pastors, etc. but are out there as salt and light in the world.

This is a concern that the *Cape Town Commitment* expresses in an earlier section about the responsibility of Christians to live out the truth of God in the workplace. Theological education needs to equip pastors to equip others in this missional understanding and practice.

In spite of the enormous evangelistic and transformational opportunity of the workplace, where adult Christians have most relationships with non-Christians, few churches have the vision to equip their people to seize this. We have failed to regard work in itself as biblically and intrinsically significant, as we have failed to bring the whole of life under the Lordship of Christ.

We name this secular-sacred divide as a major obstacle to the mobilisation of all God's people in the mission of God, and we call upon Christians worldwide to reject its unbiblical assumptions and resist its damaging effects. We challenge the tendency to see ministry and mission (local and cross-cultural) as being mainly the work of church-paid ministers and missionaries, who are a tiny percentage of the whole body of Christ.

> a. We encourage all church members to accept and affirm their own daily ministry and mission as being wherever God has called them to work. We challenge pastors and church leaders to support people in

---

[3] John Stott, *The Contemporary Christian* (IVP, 1991), 140-42, italics original.

such ministry – in the community and in the workplace – 'to equip the saints for works of service [ministry]' – in every part of their lives.

b. We need intensive efforts to train all God's people in whole-life discipleship, which means to live, think, work and speak from a biblical worldview and with missional effectiveness in every place or circumstance of daily life and work. (*CTC* IIA.1)

THE WHY:
Why should the Bible be at the heart of theological education? We need a *re-centring of the Bible* in theological education.

The *Cape Town Commitment* calls for this, quite emphatically, twice:

> We long that all church planters and theological educators should place the Bible at the centre of their partnership, not just in doctrinal statements but in practice. (*CTC* IIF.4.d).

> We long to see a fresh conviction, gripping all God's Church, of the central necessity of Bible teaching for the Church's growth in ministry, unity and maturity. We rejoice in the gifting of all those whom Christ has given to the Church as pastor-teachers. We will make every effort to identify, encourage, train and support them in the preaching and teaching of God's Word. In doing so, however, we must reject the kind of clericalism that restricts the ministry of God's Word to a few paid professionals, or to formal preaching in church pulpits. Many men and women, who are clearly gifted in pastoring and teaching God's people, exercise their gifting informally or without official denominational structures, but with the manifest blessing of God's Spirit. They too need to be recognized, encouraged, and equipped to rightly handle the Word of God. *(CTC IID.1.d.1)*

So the *Cape Town Commitment* brings theological education into the sphere of Christian mission, and then urges that it should be biblically rooted and centred. Why should this be so? Let me suggest three reasons: *the biblical mandate, the global need and the pastoral priority.*

The biblical mandate

The teaching of God's word is integral to the growth and mission of God's people. Teaching, as we saw above, is included within the Great Commission itself. Theological education (as one dimension of the church's broader teaching ministry), is therefore an intrinsic part of the missional life and work of the whole church. The Bible provides robust support for this conviction.

THE OLD TESTAMENT

'The Old Testament is the oldest and longest programme of Theological Education.' This remarkable affirmation was made by Professor Andrew Walls in a presentation given at the Mission Leaders' Forum at the

Overseas Ministry Study Center, New Haven, Connecticut. Throughout the whole Old Testament, for a millennium or more, God was shaping his people, insisting that they should remember *and teach to every generation* the things God had done ('what your eyes have seen') and the things God had said ('what your ears have heard'). He gave his people priests as teachers of the Torah, and prophets to call them back to the ways of God, and Psalmists and wise men and women to teach them how to worship God and walk in godly ways in ordinary life. When reformations happened in Old Testament times (e.g. under Jehoshaphat, Hezekiah, Josiah, Nehemiah-Ezra), there was always a return to the teaching of God's word. God's people were supposed to be a community of teachers and learners, shaped by the word of God, as we see so emphatically in the longings of the author of Psalm 119.

JESUS

So when Jesus came, he spent years doing exactly the same – constantly teaching his disciples as the nucleus of the new community of the Kingdom of God. Even as a twelve-year-old boy he showed that he was rooted in the Scriptures and was able to engage with the rabbis in the temple. And in the Great Commission, he mandates his apostles to teach new disciples to observe all that he had taught them. Teaching was at the heart of Jesus' mission and ministry.

PAUL

The importance of biblical teaching in the missionary work of Paul can hardly be missed. There is his personal example of spending nearly three years with the churches in Ephesus, teaching them 'all that was needful' for them, as well as 'the whole counsel of God', and combining that with systematic teaching in the public lecture hall (Acts 19:8-10, 20:20, 27). There was his personal mentoring of Timothy and Titus to be teachers of the Word. There was his mission team, including Apollos whose primary training, gifting and ministry was in church teaching. His missional curriculum in Corinth included Old Testament hermeneutics, Christology and apologetics (Acts 18:24-28). And Paul insisted that his own work as a church-planter and Apollos's work as a church-teacher (watering the seed) 'have one purpose' (1 Cor. 3:8). Evangelism and theological education are integral to each other within the mission of the church.

The Bible as a whole, then, highlights the importance of teaching and teachers within the community of God's people – teaching that is rooted in, and shaped by, the Scriptures and which in turn brings health and maturity to God's people and shapes them for their life in the world.

So, to be very frank at this point, whenever theological education neglects or marginalises the teaching of the Bible, or squeezes it to the edges of a curriculum that has become crammed with other things, it has itself become unbiblical and disobedient to the clear mandate that we find taught and modelled in both testaments. Theological education which does not produce men and women who know their Bibles thoroughly, who know how to teach and preach the Scriptures, who are able to think biblically through any and every issue they confront, and who are able to feed and strengthen God's people with God's Word – whatever else such theological education may do, or claim, or be accredited for – it is failing the church by failing to equip the church and its leaders to fulfil their calling and mission in the world. That is why the *Cape Town Commitment* makes its strong plea for the re-centring of theological education around the Bible.

The global need

The *Cape Town Commitment* goes on to identify several of the most disfiguring aspects of 21st-century evangelicalism. It confesses that we are not always particularly attractive in the way we live and behave, and that we simply do not look like the Jesus we proclaim.

> When there is no distinction in conduct between Christians and non-Christians – for example, in the practice of corruption and greed, or sexual promiscuity, or rate of divorce, or relapse to pre-Christian religious practice, or attitudes towards people of other races, or consumerist lifestyles, or social prejudice – then the world is right to wonder if our Christianity makes any difference at all. Our message carries no authenticity to a watching world.

> We challenge one another, as God's people in every culture, to face up to the extent to which, consciously or unconsciously, we are caught up in the idolatries of our surrounding culture. We pray for prophetic discernment to identify and expose such false gods and their presence within the Church itself, and for the courage to repent and renounce them in the name and authority of Jesus as Lord. (*CTC IIE.1*).

But what lies behind these areas of failure? Is not the moral confusion and laxity of the global church a product of a *'famine of hearing the words of the LORD'* (Amos 8:11)? – the lack of biblical knowledge, teaching and thinking, from the leadership downwards? As in Hosea's day, are there not multitudes of God's people who are left with *'no knowledge of God'* – at least, no adequate and life-transforming knowledge, and for the same reason as Hosea identified the failure of those appointed to teach God's word (the priests in his day) to do so (Hos. 4:1-9)?

Decades ago, John Stott believed that it was this more than anything else that was to blame. And he believed that the key remedy, 'the more potent medicine' as he called it, was to raise the standards of biblical preaching and teaching, from the seminaries to the churches. Here is an extract of a document I found among his papers, dated 1996, expressing his personal vision for the work of *Langham Partnership* (which he founded) and the need for it:

> All sorts of remedies are proposed for the reformation and renewal of the church, and for its growth into maturity. But they tend to be at the level of technique and methodology. If we probe more deeply into the church's sickness, however, we become aware of its need for more potent medicine, namely the Word of God.
>
> Jesus our Lord himself, quoting from Deuteronomy, affirmed that human beings live not by material sustenance only, but by the spiritual nourishment of God's Word (Deut. 8:3; Matt. 4:4). It is the Word of God, confirmed and enforced by the Spirit of God, which effectively matures and sanctifies the People of God.
>
> If God reforms his people by his Word, precisely *how* does his Word reach and transform them? In a variety of ways, no doubt, including their daily personal meditation in the Scripture. But the principal way God has chosen is to bring his Word to his people through his appointed pastors and teachers. For he has not only given us his Word; he has also given us pastors to teach the people out of his Word (e.g. John 21:15-17; Acts 20:28; Eph. 4:11-12; 1 Tim. 4:13). We can hardly exaggerate the importance of pastor-preachers for the health and maturity of the church.
>
> *My vision, as I look out over the world, is to see every pulpit in every church occupied by a conscientious, Bible-believing, Bible-studying, Bible-expounding pastor. I see with my mind's eye multitudes of people in every country world-wide converging on their church every Sunday, hungry for more of God's Word. I also see every pastor mounting his pulpit with the Word of God in his mind (for he has studied it), in his heart (for he has prayed over it), and on his lips (for he is intent on communicating it).*
>
> *What a vision! The people assemble with hunger, and the pastor satisfies their hunger with God's Word! And as he ministers to them week after week, I see people changing under the influence of God's Word, and so approximating increasingly to the kind of people God wants them to be, in understanding and obedience, in faith and love, in worship, holiness, unity, service and mission.*

But if that is the need, and that is a major factor in the necessary solution, then pastors need to be trained in how to preach and teach the Bible to their people. And for those pastors who are trained in seminary (granted only a minority globally), this should be one of the priorities of such training – which leads us to:

The pastoral priority

Seminaries exist mainly for the training of future pastors (not exclusively of course, but historically they have been 'invented' to serve the church by training those who will serve in ordained pastoral ministry).

But *what should a pastor be able to do*? What should a pastor-in-training be trained and equipped for? We should start to answer that question by consulting the list of qualifications that Paul gives for elders / overseers in the churches he had founded which were now being supervised by Timothy and Titus. We find extensive lists of qualities and criteria in 1 Timothy 3:1-10 and Titus 1:6-9. What is striking is that almost all the items Paul mentions are matters of character and behaviour – how they live and conduct themselves and their families. Pastors should be examples of godliness and faithful discipleship. Only one thing could be described as a competence, or ability, or skill – *'able to teach'*. The pastor above all should be a teacher of God's word, able to understand, interpret and apply it effectively (as Paul further describes in 1 Tim. 4:11-13; 5:17; 2 Tim. 2:1-15; 3:15-4:2). In fact, the pastor's personal godliness and exemplary life is what will give power and authenticity to this single fundamental task. The pastor must live what he or she preaches from the Scriptures.

So then, if seminaries are to prioritise in their training what Paul prioritises for pastors, they ought to concentrate on two primary things: personal godliness and ability to teach the Bible. Now, of course, there are many other things that pastors have to do in the demanding tasks of church leadership. They will need basic competence in pastoral counselling, in leading God's people in worship and prayer, in management and administration of funds and people, in articulating vision and direction, in relating to their particular cultural context, etc. But above all else, Paul emphasises what they must *be* (in godliness of life), and what they must commit themselves to *do* (the effective preaching of God's Word).

All that is taught and learned (formally and informally) in seminary should contribute to producing those who can preach the Word. Now, immediately I would add, this is NOT to say that the Homiletics Department takes over the curriculum (any more than to say that all that a seminary does should be 'missional' means that the Missions Department takes over the curriculum)! Rather, it means that every part of the curriculum should deepen, enrich and resource the life and mind and skills of future pastors for their preaching ministry. When a pastor comes to preach a biblical text, he or she should be able to draw not only on the resources of the Biblical exegetical courses they may have done, but also on the riches gleaned from Systematic and Historical Theology, from the lessons of Church History, from the insights and applications of Cultural or Anthropological or Religious Studies. All of this can give depth and breadth to the preaching of the Bible. 'It takes a whole seminary to raise a preacher.'[4]

---

[4] A comment by Paul Windsor, Programme Director for Langham Preaching (one of the programmes of Langham Partnership), echoing, of course, the African proverb, 'It takes a whole village to raise a child.'

THE HOW
How can we put the Bible at the centre of theological education?
We need a *re-integration of biblical hermeneutics*
within the whole curriculum.

By which I mean *both* an integrated way of reading, teaching and studying the Bible, *and* an integrated way of using the Bible in relation to all other areas of study. The *Cape Town Commitment* does not have anything on the mechanics of this, other than its exhortation, but some further points can be made.

Integrating biblical studies

Even Biblical scholars – members of departments of Biblical Studies – in many theological education institutions lament the fragmentation of the discipline into Old Testament and New Testament, then into further sub-sets of those, then into the various critical disciplines, etc.

It is sadly possible for students to gain great expertise in various parts of the Bible, without having a thorough grounding in an integrated understanding of what the Bible is as a whole. They need to be constantly reminded that the Bible is:

- not just a book full of *doctrines*, inconveniently unsorted, for systematic theologians to rearrange;

- not just a book full of *promises*, on which students can peg their spiritual formation and pastoral care;

- not just a book full of *rules*, for some kind of ethical applications to the problems of life around us, by whatever system of hermeneutics we use to extract our ethics from the Bible.

Rather, the Bible is essentially a story. It constitutes *the* grand narrative of God and the world. The Bible can be read as a drama in six 'Acts'.[5]

1. Creation – 2. Fall – 3. O.T. Promise –
4. Gospel – 5. N.T. mission – 6. New Creation

Reading and studying the Bible with this overarching framework in view at all times keeps us working with the 'grain of the text', and *aligned with the mission of God* (which is why it has been broadly adopted by those seeking 'a missional hermeneutic').

So while, of course, it is necessary to get down deep into the exegesis of biblical texts from every part of the canon – with all the specific and detailed work that this requires, and with all the disciplines we can bring to

---

[5] See, for a good exposition of this perspective: Craig G. Bartholomew and Michael W. Goheen, *The Drama of Scripture: Finding our Place in the Biblical Story* (Grand Rapids, MI: Baker, 2004).

bear on the task – we must bring students back to the surface often, to survey their text within the wider flow of the whole narrative. What has already come before this text, where is it leading, where does it fit, how is it integrated into the whole story?

This integrated reading of the Bible as a whole has several important impacts.

IT TELLS US THE STORY WE ARE IN

We are *in* the story of the Bible – participating in Act 5, and doing so in the light of all we know from Acts 1-4, and in anticipation of what God will do at Act 6. So the hermeneutical task is not just a matter of working out how a particular text applies to one's life, but rather, asking how one's present life as a believer fits into this great drama of which one is part, in a way that is consistent with the story itself.

IT SHAPES OUR WORLDVIEW

Worldviews are basically shaped by narrative. Worldviews answer four basic questions:

- *Where are we?* (What is the nature of the world / universe we live in?)
- *Who are we?* (What does it mean to be human?)
- *What's gone wrong?* (Why is the world in a mess, and why do we even perceive it as a problem?)
- *What's the solution?* (What needs to be done to solve the mess we're in?)

The Christian faith, as a coherent worldview, answers all these questions from within the Bible story – as a whole (from creation to new creation, with Christ at the heart of it). Once again, the *Cape Town Commitment* emphasises this narrative and missional nature of biblical revelation and theology.

> *The story the Bible tells.* The Bible tells the universal story of creation, fall, redemption in history, and new creation. This overarching narrative provides our coherent biblical worldview and shapes our theology. At the centre of this story are the climactic saving events of the cross and resurrection of Christ which constitute the heart of the gospel. It is this story (in the Old and New Testaments) that tells us who we are, what we are here for, and where we are going. This story of God's mission defines our identity, drives *our* mission, and assures us the ending is in God's hands. This story must shape the memory and hope of God's people and govern the content of their evangelistic witness, as it is passed on from generation to generation.
>
> (Cape Town Commitment I.6B)

So, then, the Lausanne-encouraged task of 're-centering the Bible in theological education', means that we use every part of the 'Biblical Studies' curriculum to enable students

- to inhabit the Bible story, and see it as *The Story* within which we live, whatever story the world around us tells about itself.
- to adopt the Bible's wordview – in marked contrast to the worldview of whatever cultures surround us.

That may be done by some kind of 'orientation to the Bible' course, to help students realise, up front, that they need to do this kind of integrative work in all their biblical studies classes. But it would be even better if *all Bible teachers* in our seminaries would take time regularly in their courses, to find ways to remind students of this broad, whole Bible, integrative background to whatever small slice of the canon they happen to be studying.

Integrating the Bible as a whole into all other studies and issues

This may seem the more challenging task, since it is inviting those who are not biblical specialists, but teachers of systematic theology, ethics, church history, pastoral studies, etc. to see the overall biblical narrative as the framework, governing paradigm, for their disciplines. This does not mean that the Biblical Studies department simply takes over all the rest! Rather, it means that all disciplines (including Biblical Studies) organise their objectives, content and learning outcomes with deliberate awareness of the overarching framework of Christian confession, shaped by the grand narrative flow of the Bible, and then 'live' within that paradigm.

This means, for example, that teaching of *doctrine* seeks to show how the grand house of Christian theology in fact reflects the implications of every part of the revelation contained within the great Bible story.

It means that *church history* is seen as the outworking of God's mission in Act 5 of the Bible story – and is assessed in terms of its faithfulness or otherwise to the patterns already set in Acts 1-4 and the expectation of Act 6.

It means that in *ethics*, we help students, not merely to weigh up the different systems of ethics (whether theological, philosophical or ethical), but to bring every ethical issue into the light of every part of the Bible story – what light is shed on the issue by the implications of the great facts and truths of each section – all six Acts.[6]

---

[6] There are some institutions of theological education that are seeking to implement such an integrative, Bible-centred and mission-oriented curriculum. One such is the Arab Baptist Theological Seminary in Beirut, Lebanon. The story of their radical, missional audit and the reshaping of their whole curriculum is written up in the fine book, Perry Shaw, *Transforming Theological Education: A Practical Handbook for Integrative Learning* (Carlisle, UK: Langham Global Library, 2014).

We need to teach people how to *think biblically* about any and every issue that will arise. They need to have learned how to bring every issue into the light of all the key points along the Bible narrative and how to hear the major 'voices' of the biblical canon. I would love to see such a 'whole-Bible approach' become characteristic of all theological education – across all disciplines. We should be learning together to read the Bible as a whole and to root our theology and our practice deeply and scripturally (with Paul) in the 'whole counsel of God'. We need to help our students see that the Bible is not just an *object* of their study (limited to when they are doing 'Biblical Studies', but the subject of their thinking – about everything. That is to say, the Bible is not just something we 'think about', but rather something we 'think with'. The Bible informs and guides the way we think about everything else – whether in the classroom or in all the rest of life in the world.

Conclusion

I'd like to say, 'I have a dream...' At least, I once *had* a dream, which I used to muse upon when I was the principal of All Nations Christian College in the UK. I dreamt of a 'Bible College' which would be exactly and only that – a place where we would teach and study only the Bible together in depth, sequentially from the very beginning, and let everything else flow out of the exegesis, interpretation and application of the biblical text. And immediately you would be forced not only to be rooted confessionally in what the Bible says, but also to be engaged missionally with all the *issues that the Bible itself engages with*. Then you would draw in, of course, the expertise of our systematicians and historians and ethicists, missiologists, etc. You would have to deal with the uniqueness of biblical monotheism and the nature of God, cosmology, issues of science and faith, the nature of humanity, sex and marriage, the problem of evil, gender relations and disorder, creation care and ecological challenges, violence and corruption, ethnic diversity and conflict, urban development and culture, ageing and death... and that's before you even get past Genesis 1-11.

MISSION SPIRITUALITY FOR LEADERS IN A MISSIONAL CHURCH

Knud Jørgensen

One of the aims and outcomes of the Edinburgh 2010 study process has been to affirm that mission is a key integrating element for ecclesiology and theology, and that we need a new vision for theological education within a missional model. The listening group at Edinburgh 2010 said that:

> This is particularly the case where growing tension is experienced with regard to ministerial and spiritual formation versus academic preparation. Teachers are to be spiritual mentors, and there still are needs to further develop education and training which are rooted in the local and regional context, resisting the impact of western models on a non-western context.[1]

I shall in the following search for answers to the questions:

- How may the formation of missionary spirituality become integrated into theological education?
- In which ways are missionary spirituality and missional leadership interconnected?

The word 'missionary' refers to the specific mission activities of the church, whereas the word 'missional' is related to the nature of the church, as being sent by God to the world.

What is Missionary Spirituality?

The Edinburgh 2010 study track on Mission Spirituality and Authentic Discipleship struggled hard to come up with a definition of 'mission/missionary spirituality'.[2] The assignment given to the study track and study group was 'to articulate a motivation and dynamic for mission that is rooted in the Kingdom of God. It will draw on the experience of Christians in the South and will seek to understand mission in relation to such concepts as new creation, spiritual gifts, renewal, reconstruction, identity, service and holism'.[3] At the outset, mission spirituality was understood as essentially Christian spirituality lived in and fuelled by awareness of the *missio Dei*; such mission spirituality will result in tangible

---

[1] Kirsteen Kim and Andrew Anderson (eds), *Edinburgh 2010. Mission Today and Tomorrow* (Oxford: Regnum, 2011), 316.
[2] Wonsuk Ma and Kenneth R. Ross (eds), *Mission Spirituality and Authentic Discipleship* (Oxford: Regnum, 2013), 5ff.
[3] Ma and Ross, *Mission Spirituality and Authentic Discipleship*, 3.

mission practice in the world. In the course of its work, the group looked for answers to the question: 'What motivates and sustains us in mission?' since it believed that the answers would point to a fuller understanding of missionary spirituality. Answers are collected in Wonsuk Ma and Kenneth R. Ross, *Mission Spirituality and Authentic Discipleship*;[4] they show the great variety across the globe and confessional backgrounds – there cannot be one prescribed discipline for a missional spirituality since spirituality has to be context-sensitive. In addition, the answers show that spirituality is not a solitary enterprise: it has to do with a spiritual life lived in community, rooted in common worship, and sustained by the prayer and encouragement from our local Christian community.

Missionary spirituality suggests 'that Christian mission begins with the spiritual activity of discerning the spirits (according to the revelation of Jesus Christ) in order to discover the movement of the Spirit of God in the world and join in with it'.[5] In this way it recognises that God is already working, and has been working within all cultures, revealing Godself.[6] This implies that spirituality is not 'an additional dimension of mission to be considered when all the doctrinal and practical apparatus is already in place. Rather, the spiritual dimension is the first thing around which everything else ought to revolve'.[7] God is the primary agent of mission and he works through the power of the Holy Spirit. Openness to the Spirit – *joining in with the Spirit* – is therefore what mission is about: '... it is through awareness of the work of the Holy Spirit that Christian mission finds its true character and has its authentic impact.'[8]

As the study group met in Edinburgh 2010, they came up with additional statements. One of these emphasises the dynamic of missionary spirituality:

> Mission spirituality is the ongoing inspiration of the Holy Spirit that moves us to witness to the good news of God's love in Jesus Christ's life, suffering, death and resurrection with the aim to bring together God's family in a loving household, share a sense of God's call, live life in humility and fulfil God's will on earth.[9]

Here movement and witness are joined together, with an echo of Jesus' prayer in John 17 that 'they all may be one so that the world will believe'. At the end of the process, the group contributed a statement which eventually became the ninth point in the Edinburgh 2010 Common Call:

> Remembering Jesus' way of witness and service, we believe we are called by God to follow this way joyfully, inspired, anointed, sent and empowered by the Holy Spirit, and nurtured by Christian disciplines in community. As we

---

[4] Oxford: Regnum, 2013.
[5] Kirsteen Kim, 'Mission Spirituality', in *Religion in Geschichte und Gegenwart* (4th edition) (Tubingen, Germany: Mohr Siebeck, 2007).
[6] Balia and Kim, *Edinburgh 2010. Witnessing to Christ Today*, 241.
[7] Ma and Ross, *Mission Spirituality and Authentic Discipleship*, 9.
[8] Ma and Ross, *Mission Spirituality and Authentic Discipleship*, 9.
[9] Kim and Anderson, *Edinburgh 2010. Mission Today and Tomorrow*, 184.

look to Christ's coming in glory and judgment, we experience his presence with us in the Holy Spirit, and we invite all to join with us as we participate in God's transforming and reconciling mission of love to the whole creation.[10]

But why single out 'missionary spirituality'?[11] May it not be claimed that Christian spirituality is missionary spirituality since it is the same Spirit that makes possible life in Christ and that empowers the church to witness and serve? In this way, Rene Padilla claims that Christian spirituality is a gift and a task:

> It requires communion with God (contemplation) as well as action in the world (praxis). When these two elements are separated, both the life and the mission of the church are deeply affected. Contemplation without action is an escape from concrete reality; action without contemplation is activism lacking a transcendent meaning. True spirituality requires a missionary contemplation and a contemplative mission.[12]

I use the term 'missionary spirituality' to focus on a view of God as an actively sending God (*missio Dei*). *Christian* spirituality points to the Christian's awareness of and response to the presence and acts of the triune God in one's life. *Missionary* spirituality goes a step further: It is the Christian's, and the Christian community's, awareness of and response to the work of the triune God to become the God of mercy, justice, reconciliation and healing in us and through us, for all humankind and for the whole of creation. It is 'to search for our place in God's work for the redemption of the earth and humankind.'[13]

As we strive to make visible the holistic character of theological education, we also strive to integrate a holistic theology with a holistic spirituality – a spirituality where we return to the classical Christian spiritual disciplines: the practice of daily Scripture reading and meditation, prayer and solitude; a spirituality where mission and evangelism, worship and the use of the gifts of the Spirit, go hand-in-hand with a concern for justice, human rights, and caring for creation.

---

[10] Kim and Anderson, *Edinburgh 2010. Mission Today and Tomorrow*, 2.
[11] I use the term 'missionary spirituality' where Ma and Ross (and Kim) use the term 'mission spirituality', in order to ensure that the specific mission activities of the church are kept in sight.
[12] C. René Padilla, 'Spirituality in the Life and Mission of the Church' (2009, paper submitted to Edinburgh 2010 Study Group 9).
[13] Tore Laugerud, 'Mission and Contemplation: Mission Spirituality in the 21st Century', in Tormod Engelsviken, Ernst Harbakk, Rolv Olsen and Thor Strandenæs (eds), *Mission to the World. Communicating the Gospel in the 21st Century* (Oxford: Regnum, 2007), 131.

Rediscovering the Missional Nature of the Church

The concept 'missionary spirituality' grew out of the rediscovery of the missional nature of the church. *Lumen Gentium* from the Second Vatican Council expresses for the first time that the church is by nature a missionary church. From this document, missionary spirituality found its way into all the other Vatican documents. Walther Buehlmann says that 'the church now has missionary spirituality and mission commitment as an essential dimension'.[14] Also in the 1960s, the ecumenical movement initiated a study and a focus on the missionary nature of the church in which spirituality played a central role.

The term 'missional church' is based on different streams from Orthodox, Roman Catholic, ecumenical and evangelical theology and practice, and in that way represents a joint ecumenical concern which has often been running parallel with the concern for unity and common witness.[15] The term itself came out of *The Gospel and Our Culture Network*, which was initially established in England in 1989, and soon exported to North America and elsewhere. The network was inspired by Lesslie Newbigin and his early books *The Open Secret* (1978), *Foolishness to the Greeks* (1986) and *The Gospel in a Pluralist Society* (1991).[16]

The vision to be a missional church is born out of a critique of the western concept of church. The response to a mission situation is not to initiate efforts to 'communicate with modern man', but rather it is to ask what is wrong with today's church since the Gospel appears so irrelevant to so many. The features of the Constantinian church are similar to a Lutheran/Protestant conception of the church as the place for preaching the Gospel and administering the sacraments. A missional church is where the people of God participate in God's mission through being, word and deed, in their daily lives. The symbols of the Constantinian church are the place,

---

[14] Walbert Buehlman, 'Missionary Spirituality', in *New Missionary Era* (Maryknoll, NY: Orbis Books, 1982), 113-18.

[15] See Knud Jørgensen, 'Biblical and Theological Foundations: The Triune God and the Missional Church', in John Gibaut and Knud Jørgensen (eds), *Called to Unity – For the Sake of Mission* (Oxford: Regnum, 2014), 33-45.

[16] The influence of Newbigin's theology of cultural plurality on these missiological streams has been documented by George R. Hunsberger in *Bearing the Witness of the Spirit* (Grand Rapids, MI: Eerdmans, 1998). The American version of the network also pays tribute to Newbigin; at the same time, it is very preoccupied with its own North American context. This is illustrated by the fact that all the books on the topic mention North America in the titles, for example *The Church between Gospel and Culture. The Emerging Mission in North America* (George Hunsberger and Craig Van Gelder, 1996), *Missional Church. A Vision for the Sending of the Church in North America* (Darrell Guder, 1998), and *Confident Witness – Changing World. Rediscovering the Gospel in North America* (Craig Van Gelder, 1999). The focus on context is a common feature within missional church thinking: What does our mission context require in terms of calling, tasks and witness? And what kind of leadership does this context call for?

the temple, the Word, the sacred – whereas the symbols of the missional church are the way, discipleship, wholeness, spirituality, common witness and everyday life. Likewise, one can distinguish between the custodians of the Constantinian church: a clerical hierarchy of static institutions, and the custodians of the missional church: lay people, who dynamically live out their faith in everyday situations (= missionary spirituality). This does not rule out the ordained ministry, but sees its role in equipping God's people for service (Eph 4:11ff).

In the midst of this paradigm shift the question is: how to be God's church in our time? This question in turn leads to a number of new questions – about everything we are and do as Christians and as church, and particularly about theology and theological education. This is not a matter of new methods or models. When encountering the challenges of a changing society, westerners tend to think in terms of analyses, solutions, projects – new church models, electronic church, reshaped worship, and evangelisation efforts – but the shift we experience today raises more radical questions about theology, missiology and spirituality. We are forced to re-read the Scriptures about what it means to be God's people in the world, and about being signs of the Kingdom of God through who we are, what we do, and what we say.

The missional church concept tries to capture the old truth that mission is part of the church's *esse*. Without mission there is no church. It lies in the genes of the church to be missional, and any ecclesiological discussion without this point of departure will necessarily derail and end up speaking of something other than the church. Therefore, mission should not be reduced to a task or a programme; it is primarily the nature of the church – a nature that grows out of God's nature. In the midst of the crisis that the established church of the West experiences, what will remain is a missional fellowship of people who lives by and demonstrates the Gospel of the Kingdom of God through being, word and deed. Such was the ecclesiological paradigm of the Early Church and such should any new paradigm be. This is a matter of finding the right balance between the nature of the church (what the church is), its tasks (ministry: what the church does) and its structure (how the church organises itself).[17]

We are challenged to be what the church has always been: people of flesh and blood carrying the reality of the Gospel within them, communicating it through missional being and action. For that reason, it is likely that the famous, but seldom realised, priesthood of all believers will become the basic church and mission structure. Together with this structure, one may hope for a rediscovery of the gifts of the Spirit, in a broad biblical perspective, as that which equips the missionary congregation in a post-modern reality. Our ability to be magnets attracting

---

[17] Craig Van Gelder, *The Essence of the Church* (Grand Rapids, MI: Baker Books, 2000), 31, 37.

people to Christ becomes important, as it is in our sister churches in the global South. A missional church will therefore often emphasise meditation, spirituality, presence, genuineness and lifestyle. Modelled on our brothers and sisters in the South and East, we may in a new way become personal carriers of the spiritual reality the world longs for. Before becoming centrifugal, we need to return to the centre – to live centripetally.

The rediscovery of the missional nature of the church calls for a new and integrated understanding of theology and mission. Theological education participates in the task of equipping people for God's mission in today's world; by its very nature, all theological education is contextual and no particular context may exercise dominant influence over the church or over theological education; missionary/missional ecclesiology requires the teaching of missiology, intercultural theology, ecumenics and world Christianity. Central to this new understanding is the interaction and interconnection between theology and spirituality. This also calls for an emphasis on character and spiritual formation, good governance, and appropriate codes of conduct for church leadership in theological education.[18]

Missional Leadership[19]

Developing alternative leadership is a central concern within this missional thinking. The theme is dealt with in much of the literature.[20] The reason is that leadership is the key towards forming missional fellowships: 'Leadership is a critical gift, provided by the spirit because, as the Scriptures demonstrate, fundamental change in any body of people requires leaders capable of transforming its life and being transformed themselves.'[21] These are the words of the chief leadership-ideologist within missional church thinking, Alan Roxburgh.

The division between *clerici* (priests) and *idiotes* (lay people) belongs to the Constantinian church tradition. Breaking this tradition will imply a dramatic change with regard to the role and work of a pastor – in accordance with the biblical model where the people of God is the true

---

[18] Balia and Kim, *Edinburgh 2010. Witnessing to Christ Today,* 155.

[19] See for the following Knud Jørgensen, *Equipping for Service. Christian Leadership in Church and Society* (Oxford: Regnum, 2012), 68ff.

[20] Darrell L. Guder (ed), *Missional Church: A Vision for the Sending of the Church in North America* (Grand Rapids, MI: Eerdmans, 1998), 183ff. Alan Roxburgh, *The Missionary Congregation. Leadership and Limininality* (Valley Forge, PA: Trinity Press International, 1996). Alan Roxburgh, *Leading through Transition: Leadership in a Time of Change* (unpublished manuscript, 1999).

[21] Guder, *Missional Church: A Vision for the Sending of the Church in North America,* 183.

priesthood. All who are baptised are priests, said Martin Luther.[22] The main task of a biblical leadership (evangelist, prophet, teacher, apostle, pastor) is to equip for service (Eph. 4:10-16). Darrel Guder says: '... we have forgotten how to read the New Testament as it was intended to be read, as the equipping of God's people for mission. When that interpretive key is missing in our biblical study, then every aspect of our ministry is reductionist that is captive to a reduced and diluted version of the gospel.'[23] To rediscover the pre-Constantinian Gospel implies going beyond our western reduction of church and leadership, towards a biblical understanding of a servant leadership in the midst of God's priesthood.[24]

This critique of the Constantinian priest model (which in the Roman Catholic context was combined with the focus on Holy Communion as a sacrificial meal – which in turn, so to speak, transformed the priest into a *sacerdos* or sacrificial priest) leads to a critical view of standard theological education. Does it not equip people for a consumer church which traditionally consists of 1% paid staff, assisted by 19% voluntary staff who help with various tasks – with the aim of serving 80% of the congregation who as consumers want to have their spiritual needs satisfied to ensure continued support? On the whole, the traditional route to ecclesial leadership – an academic environment based on competition and individual effort – should be critically reviewed in the light of the great demands for character formation, relational abilities, ministry competencies and a living faith.[25]

The traditional Protestant model has had an overwhelming emphasis on imparting information and knowledge so that the pastor may serve as teacher, communicating knowledge and wisdom through sermons, Bible studies and other classes. The concern of the missional church goes further than imparting theological content. Here 'intake' is as important as 'output'. Knowledge might be made an end in itself. An alternative training model will give priority to reflection, spirituality, presence, genuineness and lifestyle.

The missional church is in need of leaders who are role models rather than performers and managers. Missional leadership needs to emphasise particularly the credibility which grows out of personal discipleship, a genuine faith and a whole personality. By the same token, there should be less focus on the church as institution or a business company, and more on

---

[22] This does not imply that all who are baptized are pastors; the role and function of the pastor remain part of a fivefold ministry (Eph. 4).
[23] Darrell L. Guder, *The Continuing Conversion of the Church* (Grand Rapids, MI: Eerdmans, 2000), 188.
[24] Michael Frost and Alan Hirsch, *The Shaping of Things to Come. Innovation and Mission for the 21st-Century Church (Peabody: Hendrickson Publishers, 2003)*, 172.
[25] Eddie Gibbs, *Leadership Next. Changing Leaders in a Changing Culture* (Downers Grove, IL: IVP, 2005), 41.

the church as an egalitarian fellowship of closely connected people, who are missionaries through their personal and collective testimonies in a multi-society. In this perspective, spiritual leaders are not just or the only professionals of the church, but also lay people who faithfully live, work and witness. The basic contextualisation of the Gospel is not just the task of the pastor; rather it is born out of a process where the local church shapes and interprets the Gospel.

Some will in this connection warn against 'American models', where success becomes important and the Gospel becomes merchandise that needs the right marketing (see Gibbs' critique of these models[26]). There is no quick fix to our crisis and problems of being church in a post-modern era. Instead, we need to take seriously that we live in *liminality*[27] – in the midst of a transition in a time of change. This process may be characterised as a tunnel experience – liminality marks the space between *separation* and *re-aggregation* in a sort of rite of passage situation. As a church, we have gone through a separation phase and are now caught in between the phases. There is no return to the 'good' old days, and we don't know what the new phase will look like. We are in the desert like God's people on the way from Egypt to Canaan, or in a Babylonian exile with no promise of a return to the land that flows with milk and honey. This requires a leadership that is not prone to return to the fleshpots of Egypt, which is patient and does not jump to quick-fix conclusions, because this in-between period is also 'a time of immense opportunity. The potential for something new to emerge is great. The reality of this in-between phase is the tension between these two options: to recapture what has been lost or to risk the discovery of a new future'.[28] The desert might become a fertile place because it is here that God teaches us to listen in vulnerability. The exile could become a creative period because we are being changed through God taking us aside. Thus, the role of the leader is to create a safe place for his sojourners, to reflect and to experiment, to test and to fail.

Roxburgh makes use of an illustration of the leader as *cultivator*. This term is borrowed from agriculture and is related to organising processes for which I am not the engine: some sow, some water, and some tend and weed: how can we as leaders cultivate groups of God's people who live their lives in a continuous conversion to the Gospel and to the mission context in which they find themselves?

Roxburgh also speaks of the leader as a *poet*. The leader converts the emotions of his time into words – poetic leadership helps us to rediscover our identity and finds a way in a situation of loss and grief caused by the collapse of old paradigms. The poet helps us understand and tolerate how we are. Furthermore, we need leaders who are *prophets,* who communicate

---

[26] Eddie Gibbs, *Church Next. Quantum Changes in Christian Ministry* (Leicester, UK: IVP, 2001), 41ff.
[27] Roxburgh, *The Missionary Congregation. Leadership and Liminality,* 57ff.
[28] Roxburgh, *Leading through Transition: Leadership in a Time of Change,* 2.

God's call to conversion in today's context. This function is important with regard to the church's separating itself from dying paradigms. Without prophetic leadership we might become unable to break up and move forward. Prophetic leadership is also related to daring to carry out powerful and sensational symbolic acts. Finally, Roxburgh speaks of the leader as *apostle* – the visionary and the one who turns vision to reality and everyday life by painting the vision before our eyes and making it more attractive than the old world.[29] The apostle leader is in front in the encounter with the surroundings and culture; the primary task is to form congregations in such a way that they become missional and missionary. This function has therefore to do with crossing boundaries – pioneers on the way to new people. Gibbs uses the term 'ground breakers'.[30]

These functions are not exclusive, but overlap. And the functions should not be limited to a special leadership; they belong to the whole church. Some of the pertinent Bible passages, like Ephesians 4, therefore need a two-dimensional reading where one dimension describes the leader matrix while the other describes the service of the entire congregation. The entire missional congregation has an apostolic task at the same time as some are called to be apostles.

Vocational Spirituality and Missionary Spirituality

Spirituality has to do with the life and struggle of faith in the encounter with God and my neighbour. I believe that Martin Luther wanted to say the same when he underlined that 'no one becomes a theologian except through prayer, meditation and contestation/temptation' ('Oratio, meditatio et tentatio faciunt theologicum'). Luther here speaks from his own theology tradition as an Augustinian monk where the focus was less on 'developing' the Christian faith than on becoming so absorbed in it that life in Christ grew stronger. In the language of mysticism it has to do with choosing 'the inner road' – the road with its four stations: solitude, prayer, meditation and contemplation.

In this light, I believe that Luther would have agreed with the Latin American liberation theologian Jon Sobrino when he views spirituality as the integrating dimension in (liberation) theology:

> ... spirituality is a dimension as original and necessary as liberation, and these two demand each other... [liberation theologians] believe, moreover, that spirituality is best understood not only as a dimension of theology, but as the integrating dimension of theology itself.[31]

---

[29] Roxburgh, *The Missionary Congregation. Leadership and Liminality*, 61ff.
[30] Eddie Gibbs, 'Preparing Leaders for an "emerging" Church', in Engelsviken, Harbakk, Olsen and Strandenæs (eds), *Mission to the World*, 338.
[31] Jon Sobrino, 'Spirituality and the Following of Jesus', in I. Ellacuria and Jon Sobrino, *Mysterium Liberationis* (Maryknoll, NY: Orbis Books, 190/1993), 679.

In my view, there is here also a bridge from the broader missionary spirituality to what one may call 'a vocational spirituality' – a spirituality which has to do with the personal formation for service and ministry. This formation is essential for all believers and for those with a special call (*vocatio*) to spiritual leadership.[32] This spirituality begins by learning to live in the sight of God in such a way that this becomes my existential basic position: who am I when God sees me – all of me, all of my life with sorrow, longings, sin and hope?

Secondly, vocational spirituality reflects what Paul says to Timothy: 'Watch yourself and watch your teaching (or your service)...' (1 Tim. 4:16). Watching oneself means to become acquainted with oneself. There must be a single room in my life where I confront myself and dialogue with myself – about my self-image, self-confidence, and feelings. Henri Nouwen uses the expression 'the ministry of presence' in contrast to 'a ministry of absence'.[33]

Thirdly I need 'a space between' where I may become visible to another person, speak truthfully about my life and make use of confession. The Norwegian author Sigurd Hoel is quoted as saying that 'man never lies so badly as when he is to be honest with himself'. Kvarme underlines in the same way that 'we still need to develop a culture and instruments in our church and parish life that provide companionship and counsel to young and old struggling with or reflecting on God's calling to them'.[34]

These perspectives are decisive for the development of a broad missional leadership. In a way different from the Constantinian model, the missional leader is totally dependent on disciplined prayer, fasting, regular Scripture reading ('immersing oneself in Scripture') and spiritual mentoring in fellowship with a friend, colleague or spiritual mentor. Here is the foundation for modelling a spirituality which makes visible Christ-joy and Christ-dependence.

This is a matter of both liturgy and closet. We need the interaction between liturgy's large perspective and the small perspective of solitude. The God whom we in the liturgy praise as Creator of the universe and Lord of history, is the same God to whom I pray in my closet – he who has created me, sees me, loves me and cares for me. Using fixed prayer hours may here be helpful. Beginning the day with confessing the creed and taking time for meditation and retreat are valuable options. Today the church sorely needs the missional imagination of God's people.[35] Such imagination is a fruit of vocational and missionary spirituality.

---

[32] Ole Christian Kvarme, 'Formation for Ministry and Mission. Reflections on Vocational Spirituality', in Engelsviken, Harbakk, Olsen and Strandenæs (eds), *Mission to the World*, 375-81.
[33] See Henri Nouwen, *In the Name of Jesus. Reflections on Christian Leadership* (New York: The Crossroad Publishing Company, 1989).
[34] Kvarme, 'Formation for Ministry and Mission', 379.
[35] Gibbs, *Leadership Next*, 206.

Conclusion

In this chapter I have tried to show how the formation of missionary spirituality may become integrated into theological education. This calls for a clear understanding of what is meant by 'missionary spirituality': Christian mission begins with the spiritual activity of discerning the spirits in order to discover the movement of the Spirit of God in the world and join in with it. In this way it recognises that God is already working, and has been working within all cultures, revealing Godself. Spirituality is therefore not an additional dimension of mission, but the first thing around which everything else ought to revolve. God is the primary agent of mission and he works through the power of the Holy Spirit. Openness to the Spirit – joining in with the Spirit – is therefore what mission is all about: it is through awareness of the work of the Holy Spirit that Christian mission finds its true character and has its authentic impact.

Secondly, I have aimed at showing the interconnection and interaction between missionary spirituality and missional church. The concern of the missional church goes further than imparting theological content. Here 'intake' is as important as 'output'. Knowledge may easily be made an end in itself. An alternative training model will give priority to reflection, spirituality, presence, genuineness and lifestyle.

Such alternative theological education should include a vocational spirituality – a spirituality which has to do with personal formation for service and ministry. This formation is essential for all believers and for those with a special call (*vocatio*) to spiritual leadership. It begins by learning to live in the sight of God in such a way that this becomes my existential basic position: Who am I when God sees me – all of me, all of my life with sorrow, longings, sin and hope?

As I have been writing this paper, I have had in my mind a prayer by the 13th century English bishop, St Richard of Chichester:

> Thanks be to Thee, my Lord Jesus Christ
> For all the benefits Thou hast given me,
> For all the pains and insults Thou hast borne for me.
> O most merciful Redeemer, friend and brother,
> May I know Thee more clearly,
> Love Thee more dearly,
> Follow Thee more nearly.[36]

Some may remember the text and the prayer more vividly from the musical Godspell in the 1970s:

> Day by day
> Day by day
> Oh dear Lord
> Three things I pray
> To see thee more clearly

---

[36] www.ifl.org.au/blog/?p=931

Love thee more dearly
Follow thee more nearly
Day by day.

In my view and in my life, this simple prayer brings together sound spirituality and missional theology in a life of genuine discipleship.

RE-WIRING THE BRAIN: THEOLOGICAL EDUCATION AMONG ORAL LEARNERS

Jay Moon

I walked towards the lone lantern, optimistic and excited to meet this group of new believers. The only light for miles, the weak kerosene flame wobbled in the cool night air, flickering shadows against the mud hut structure that served as a church. The chilly weather was unusual for this African savannah, and the ground was still damp from the rainy week.

Bending my head down, I stepped through the door of the church and was greeted by a large gathering anticipating my arrival. The group began to settle – some leaning up against the walls, others sitting on shaky wooden benches. I stepped to the front of the room, armed with prepared lessons on sin, salvation and how to walk in this new-found faith. It was the method I learned when I first accepted Christ – I was eager to teach, and they were excited to hear.

Well, at first they were.

It wasn't long before I noticed their eyes started shifting, eyelids started to droop and this energetic room that I walked into was now – and I cringe to say it – completely bored.

'How is this possible?' I thought. I considered pushing forward, like forcing someone to eat the peas on their plate – they may not like it but it's for their own good! Seeing the downward spiral that I was falling into, a young pastor stepped forward and began with a proverb,

'*Fi mabiik dan bo cham zuk, fi kan de teng chainya.*'

'If your relative is at the top of the sheanut tree, you do not have to eat the sheanuts that lie on the ground.'

He continued, 'What the white man is trying to explain is that Jesus sits in the top of the tree, right next to God. You can call on him in prayer and be assured that he will hear you. The idols in our homes are like sheanuts that have fallen to the ground. Why would you want these bruised fruits when Jesus provides the good fruit at the top of the tree?'

Smiles and laughter burst forth, and the audience was once again energised. Even more important, they were learning and growing in a way that connected deeply within them.

The pastor continued with a local story, and ended with a locally composed song. The drums burst forth and people danced in a circle, as they belted out words like, 'Jesus is a lorry. Enter in and he will take you to heaven.'

In closing the lesson, the pastor asked them to recall what they learned. I was amazed at how the group recounted the biblical lesson in sharp clarity, drawing from their local proverbs, stories and songs.

This chapter explores the oral learning preference described above by summarising:

1. Fundamental differences between how print and oral learners receive, conceptualise, remember, and then recreate messages.
2. Available genres for teaching among oral learners.
3. Questions to consider when teaching theology in an oral culture, particularly for educators who have been trained using the medium of print.

If you prefer a bored audience, read no more. But if you want to inject some Red Bull into your teaching among oral learners, continue on – it may 're-wire' your teaching.

Re-wiring the Brain

If you have ever read a book that was so good you felt it literally changed your life, science says you may actually be right. Through the use of imaging techniques that map brain activity, neurologists[1] are discovering that the process of learning to read is a transformative act that actually re-wires the brain. The literacy process not only changes the way people receive messages, but also the way they conceptualise, remember and recreate messages for someone else.[2] In fact, the printing press has changed the way people think more than any other single invention.[3]

Print learners,[4] then, have very different thinking patterns from oral learners, from start to finish (see table overleaf).

Consider the initial example of my efforts in Africa. I initially assumed (as I was taught) that words are the main carrier of meaning; therefore, I spent a great deal of time carefully preparing the proper words to share in a three-point message approach. My assumption was that good learners would take notes on the main points, principles and definitions.

---

[1] R. Douglas Fields, 'Genius across Cultures and the "Google Brain"', in *Scientific American Guest Blog*, 20th August 2011: http://blogs.scientificamerican.com/guest-blog/2011/08/20/genius-across-cultures-and-the-google-brain

[2] Charles Madinger, 'A Literate Guide to the Oral Galaxy', in *Orality Journal* 2, No. 2 (2013), 13-40.

[3] W.J. Ong, *Orality and Literacy* (London, UK: Routledge, 1982), 78.

[4] While this article positions print vs. oral learning, both print and oral approaches usually coincide. This article emphasises oral learning since theological educators have largely overlooked it in the past, in favour of print methods. The author advocates a healthy balance of both.

Process	Print	Oral
Receive message	Words carry meaning. → Teacher carefully prepares and reads words.	Mental images, symbols, gestures carry meaning. → Teacher paints mental pictures and creates an experience.
Conceptualise message	Learners take notes on main points, principles, definitions.	Learners see self and participate in metaphors, mental pictures.
Remember message	Learners review notes, written handouts.	Learners review mnemonic devices (music, proverb, story, symbol, ritual, dance).
Recreate message	New teacher refers to written outline.	New teacher guides a journey using story board, memory palace, 'chunk' information.

Table 1. Print vs. Oral learning preferences

Knowing his audience, the African pastor took a different approach. Instead of relying on words to communicate meaning, he created mental images that the community could participate in. Through carefully chosen proverbs (open-ended metaphors), songs and dance, the pastor used mnemonic devices to make the message stick. At the end of the gathering, the learners were able to recall the lessons with ease, using techniques such as:

- *Storyboard:* Maps out the story sequence
- *Memory palace:* Puts objects in different rooms of a house to trigger the memory
- *Chunking:* Consolidates information into one place. An example of chunking is the proverb, as one sentence contains a large volume of content to share.

Treasure Chest of Genres

There is a misconception that orality is just story-telling – but truthfully, orality encompasses so much more. Language can be divided into different genres or types, with each genre offering its own unique perspective of reality in a culture (see Table 2 overleaf).

Bakhtin[5] explains, 'Each genre provides "a specific way of visualizing a given part of reality" since the different forms explore "specific blindnesses and insights".'[6]

---

[5] Bakhtin's works were originally in Russian, which were later translated into English. The translators acknowledged that Bakhtin's writing style was difficult to

Genre	Unique Contribution
Proverbs	The wisdom of many, by the wit of one
Songs	You become what you hum
Stories	Portray it, not just say it
Symbols	Something seen pointing to something unseen
Rituals	Drives meaning deep to the bone
Drama	Words stand on their feet
Dance	Full body participation

Table 2. Genres available in oral cultures with unique contributions

While language unifies a people and their perspective of reality, genres also serve to stratify language and culture so that each different genre provides a different perspective.[7] When genres are combined, a more complete picture of the cultural worldview is evident.

Combined, all different genres form a set of blueprints,[8] or mental maps,[9] that provide a 'guide for acting and for interpreting our experience' – each drawing in the set of blueprints 'purports to give us true information, but only about some part of reality'.[10]

Understanding and then applying these genres takes time but their long-term impact is significant among oral people, as the following example portrays.

Scene One: West African Village (Primary Oral Context)[11]

There was no lack of laughter and excitement around the circle as they sat in the shade of the great baobab tree. The group quieted down as Kofi, a

---

translate but they did their best with English concepts. That is why quotes from Bakhtin are cited differently by different translators.

[6] G.S. Morson and C. Emerson, *Mikhail Bakhtin: Creation of a Prosaics* (Stanford, CA: Stanford University, 1990), 275–276.

[7] M. Holquist, *The Dialogic Imagination: Four Essays*, University of Texas Press Slavic Series, No. 1 (Austin, TX: University of Texas Press, 1981), 429.

[8] P.G. Hiebert, *Missiological Implications of Epistemological Shifts: Affirming Truth in a Modern/Postmodern World*, ed. A. Neeley (Harrisburg, PA: Trinity Press International, 1999), 76-81.

[9] J.P. Spradley, *The Ethnographic Interview* (New York: Holt, Rinehart, & Winston, 1979), 7.

[10] Hiebert, *Missiological Implications of Epistemological Shifts: Affirming Truth in a Modern/Postmodern World*, 80.

[11] The author was an SIM missionary doing church planting, theological education, and water development among the Builsa people in Ghana, West Africa from 1992-2001. Some of the stories and quotes in this chapter are detailed in the book: W. Jay Moon, *African Proverbs Reveal Christianity in Culture: A Narrative Portrayal of Builsa Proverbs Contextualizing Christianity in Culture*, Vol. 5, American Society of Missiology Monograph Series (Eugene, OR: Pickwick Publications, 2009).

church leader, took his place in the centre of the circle. A hush settled as the group prepared to hear the proverb that most defined his faith:

'Nurubiik a labri ka kpiak kawpta po,' he said.

'A human being hides in the feathers of a chicken.'

It was a dramatic pause with a very puzzling ending. Joe, the missionary present at the time, thought, 'Really? What does a chicken have to do with Christianity?'

Kofi continued, 'In the life of the Builsa people, fowls are used to hide shame from problems. If someone has money troubles, they can sell some of the fowls at market and then use the money to solve the problem. If someone has sickness, infertility, drought or famine, the traditional Builsa culture allows sacrifice of fowls to the ancestors or earth shrines. Growing up, I knew that we were always protected from shame as long as we had fowls, because we could always hide inside their feathers.'

'They also help us initiate friendships,' Kofi said. 'If I want to start a friendship with someone, then I offer them a chicken for us to share a meal together, or I give him a chicken to take home.'

'Now that I am a *Kristobiik* [Christian], I feel that *Yezu* [Jesus] is the chicken that I hide under. When problems come, I can run to *Yezu* in prayer and ask him to cover my shame and protect me. He will bear the full impact of the problem that has come upon me, and I can safely rest in His feathers.'

Another Builsa Christian, Immanuel, chimed in, 'When we rest in the feathers of *Yezu*, then we no longer need to have charms, *juju*, or any other black medicine to protect us. The feathers of *Yezu* will cover us – our relationship with Him assures us that He will cover us with His wings. *Naawen Wani* [the Bible] says that *Naawen* [God] will "cover you with his feathers and under his wings you will find refuge; his faithfulness will be your shield and rampart"' (Psalm 91:4).

Immanuel continued, 'This proverb has touched me deeply and it helps me to understand the heart of *Yezu*. When I hear this proverb and read Matthew 23:37, I can feel *Yezu's* heart and desire for us Builsa people. *Yezu* says, "How often I have longed to gather your children together, as a hen gathers her chicks under her wings?" That is *Yezu's* desire for us – to protect us, cover our shame and bear the brunt of our difficulties. That is a closer friend than I have ever known!'

Another Builsa Christian chimed in, 'Do you remember how Ruth was a widow? Like our widows here, she had little hope for the future. When she placed herself under *Naawen's* feathers, *Naawen* brought about a wonderful blessing. Listen to the praise she received from Boaz in Ruth 2:12, "May you be richly rewarded by the Lord, the God of Israel, *under whose wings you have come to take refuge*".'

The lively conversation around chicken theology continued with a recounting of the following story:

A man rested his hoe against his shoulder as he walked towards his bush farm to prepare the ground for planting. When he returned home that night, his heart sank from afar as he saw only the scorched remains of his house. He forgot his weary arms and legs as he sprinted to his home, heart pounding.

The earth, his hut, and his animals were covered in black embers. Everything had been destroyed by fire.

Angered over his loss, he kicked the black scorched body of a lifeless chicken that lay amidst the ground. He screamed and raised his fists in the air to try and stop the all-consuming panic. As he sat in the deathly stillness, he heard a faint sound.

He stopped.

Bending over, he picked up the dead chicken to find live chicks under her limp wings. It was only then that he realised how the mother hen saw the approaching fire and gathered the chicks under her wings. Sitting on top of the chicks, the fire burned the mother hen while the chicks remained safe – and that is what it means for Christians to hide under the feathers of Jesus. He takes the fire as we remain protected and safe.

Spiritual Engagement

This chicken theology was so vivid and concrete that it was easy to remember – in fact, impossible to forget. Months later, Joe would remember this lesson as harvest-time approached. Sitting in his house, Joe heard a sound from far away, 'Waaaaa-hoo.' Gradually, the sound increased in volume as people from neighboring houses used this call to drive away a *sakpak* [witch] that was said to wander in the high millet.

'WAAAAA-HOO' – the shout came from Joe's neighbours as they provided the traditional response to shout and push the *sakpak* away from the house. Joe was reminded of the proverb 'Humans hide under the feathers of a chicken', and his faith strengthened as he began to sing the song he learned in church,

Wa [Yezu] chawgsi mu, Wa chawgsi mu, Wa chawgis mu.
Wa chawgsi mu, Wa sum jam chawgsi.
Wa chawgsi mu, Satana yaa de mu,
Wa chawgsi mu, Wa sum jam chawgsi.
He [Jesus] wraps me tightly, He wraps me tightly, He wraps me tightly.
He wraps me tightly, He really does wrap me tightly.
He wraps me tightly, even though Satan wants to destroy me,
He wraps me tightly, He really does wrap me tightly.

As he continued to sing, his faith strengthened and the fear subsided. Instead of shouting, 'WAAAAA-HOO', hiding under the feathers of Jesus provided a powerful response to this serious spiritual issue. The proverb, the story and the song combined to address this intense discipleship issue.

The above example portrays how various genres can usefully be applied to foster learning for primary oral learners. Chicken theology described above shows that theological education among oral learners has a different starting point from that used among print learners.

Starting points for oral learners

Since the starting point for theological education is different for oral learners from what it is for print learners, print learners who first learn about orality often attempt to adapt to oral cultures by jumping headlong into story-telling. While this is a helpful attempt in contextualisation, many oral cultures do not start or rely primarily on story-telling for discipleship.

My eyes were opened to the powerful use of symbol, ritual and dance in Native American culture. For many Native Americans on the Rosebud reservation,[12] spirituality is intimately connected with their rituals. Zahniser[13] noted that discipleship in other (oral) cultures will most likely start with critically contextualising the existing rituals. The following example describes one such ritual, along with the building blocks of positive rituals – symbols.

Scene Two: Native American Context (Secondary[14] Oral Context)

Standing in shorts and bare feet, participants tentatively wait in single file. Quietly, they approach a stick with an eagle feather tied at the top, blowing gently in the wind.

'If you have any animosity or resentment with someone, you must confess it here,' Randy[15] explains. 'Then, you are ready to go inside the sweat lodge. We will wait until you are ready,' his voice trails off.

As each person approaches the feather, their face reveals deep reflection and honest soul-searching.

Some pray longer than others.

---

[12] Based on the author's observations and discussions during a ten-year partnership on the Rosebud Lakota-Sioux reservation in South Dakota.

[13] A.H.M. Zahniser, *Symbol and Ceremony: Making Disciples Across Cultures* (Monrovia, CA: MARC, 1997).

[14] While primary oral learners cannot read, secondary oral learners have the ability to read but they prefer to learn or process information by oral rather than written means, as described in G. Lovejoy and D. Claydon, 'Making Disciples of Oral Learners', Lausanne Occasional Paper 54, *2004 Lausanne Forum Occasional Papers*, 2005, 63-64: www.lausanne.org/documents/2004forum/LOP54_IG25.pdf

[15] Randy Woodley, President of Eagles' Wings Ministry, first exposed me to this powerful ritual, during a class at Asbury Theological Seminary when he invited the class to participate in this contextualised ritual. The late Richard Twiss (Wiconi International Ministries) invited me and seminary students annually to the Rosebud Lakota-Sioux reservation in South Dakota in order to experience and discuss contextualisation. Among other events, the students participated in the Lakota-Sioux *Inipi* ceremony.

Just prior to entering, Randy offers burning sage to anyone who desires to 'smudge' with the sage smoke, a symbol of God's presence that cleanses sacred spaces.

Bending down, they each crawl on hands and knees to find a spot to sit inside the small circular enclosure. With the entrance still open, light peeks through, revealing anxiety on the faces of the participants. Can I endure the heat? Will I be frightened by the darkness? Is it safe here? Questions like this race through their minds.

FLLLPPP. The entrance flap is closed. It is pitch dark. Huddled close to each other, some of the women instantaneously grab each other's hands for support. This is spontaneous *communitas* created by this liminal condition. After hot rocks are ushered into the middle of the floor, Randy starts with a song. The small tent-like enclosure is filled with praise. Following a few choruses, he gives the opportunity for anyone to offer a song to God.

Round two. More rocks come in. More heat. More steam. 'Pass this dipper of water to the person on your left,' Randy explains. 'When you receive it, drink all of it. Then, you can offer some words to the group. The only stipulation is that they must be words that have come from your heart,' he concludes.

Veiled by the darkness, deep thoughts and feelings emerge from the participants, one by one. These feelings have been bottled up for a long time. Perhaps they went Sunday to Sunday, hoping to share them with someone at church but never having the opportunity. These intimate issues do not simply go away. The last person drinks the water.

Round three. As more rocks enter, the heat and steam accumulate. Sweat pours from their bodies. Randy now offers words of encouragement and advice. Using Scripture and wisdom accumulated over the years, he addresses the individual issues that people had earlier revealed. The liminal condition prepares people to listen closely without distractions, and they take the words to heart. It has been ten years now, and I can still remember the words that Randy spoke to me.

FLLLPPP. The flap is opened again. Light and refreshing air flood the enclosure. After approximately one hour, one by one, we crawl out of the enclosure, ready to move on to the next stage.

Re-incorporation. Catching our breath and drinking water like a horse, we slowly stagger towards the house for a home-made potluck meal. Sitting at the table, I notice how we feel much more connected with each other. Like a family who has been through tough times, we now feel bonded. While this *communitas* wafts throughout the atmosphere like the smell of fresh coffee, I realise that I have just had a powerful encounter of Christian community. I have also just experienced a deep and personal touch with God concerning an intimate issue that had been in the back of my mind for a long time. Deep community. Deep transformation.

I overhear comments like:

'I now feel stronger in my faith – God met me in the sweat lodge.'

'I had my most intense encounter of Jesus in the sweat lodge!'

I realise that I was not the only one that experienced a significant learning moment as a result of the contextualised sweat lodge ritual. Months pass, and I find myself outside a new hospital in Sioux Falls, South Dakota, for the building dedication. The Native American spiritual leader fans the smoke from the burning sage towards the building and audience. Native dancers enter the courtyard and glide across the ground to the beat of the drum.

Finally, the spiritual leader says, 'We are finished. You are now welcome to enter the building.'

The gathered crowd seemed a bit confused since they were waiting for the dedication prayer.

What they failed to realise about oral cultures was that Natives can 'dance their prayers'.[16] For Native Americans, dancing is deeply connected with spirituality. Hascall notes, 'The drum, dance and song are central to our worship.'[17]

After observing and then participating in a Crown Dance, Little[18] describes her experience: 'When the dances began at sunset, the songs were so beautiful, so prayerful. I had never seen the Crown Dance performed in such a prayerful manner. I can't explain. It was very moving and a very spiritual experience for me.'

The Native American context described above portrays the effective use of symbol, ritual and dance for theological reflection. Neglecting these genres in theological education overlooks the very heart of theological reflection for this secondary oral context. After teaching ten years in North American seminaries, however, there are striking similarities and implications for theological education there to consider as well.

Scene Three: North American Seminary (Digit-Oral Context)

Papers shuffled and nervous looks were exchanged as the seminary class was about to begin. This was the big day that students were to make oral presentations in class. David submitted a written paper ahead of class, mistakenly thinking that both a written and oral presentation were required. As my eyes scanned his writing, I was not sure if he really read and

---

[16] R. Twiss, *Dancing Our Prayers: Perspectives on Syncretism, Critical Contextualization, and Cultural Practices in First Nations Ministry* (Vancouver, WA: Wiconi Press, 2002).

[17] John S. Hascall, 'The Sacred Circle: Native American Liturgy', in James Treat (ed), *Native and Christian: Indigenous Voices on Religious Identity in the United States and Canada* (New York: Routledge, 1996), 181.

[18] Juanita Little, 'The Story and Faith Journey of a Native Catechist', in James Treat (ed), *Native and Christian: Indigenous Voices on Religious Identity in the United States and Canada* (New York: Routledge, 1996), 212.

understood the material. It was not written well and the reflections seemed a bit scattered. He would likely obtain a low 'C' grade for this assignment.

When I asked for the first volunteer, however, David eagerly shot to his feet. I could not believe the difference that I now saw before me. He summarised the reading assignment well, engaged the class in a short and meaningful discussion, and then summarised with a very witty and appropriate metaphor. Several students were amazed and commented on how this metaphor helped unlock some barriers to their own understanding of the reading assignment. David admitted his own amazement: 'That metaphor simply came to me as we were discussing the material. I would never have thought of this simply sitting in my dorm room writing a paper.'

Now it was my turn to be confused. Clearly, this oral presentation deserved a high 'A' grade. Yet, his written assignment deserved a low 'C' grade. What grade then did he earn on the assignment? It largely depended on whether he was assessed using print or oral assignments. Furthermore, if David's theological education continues to be assessed by his written work alone, then he will receive low marks and eventually assume that he may not be that smart or gifted. Unfortunately, formal theological education can easily assess how well a student conforms to the print learning preference of the professor instead of assessing how well the (oral) student is actually learning.

In this increasingly technological world, David represents a 'new' learning preference that is beginning to emerge. It looks strangely familiar, though. David is learning very differently from when I attended seminary. The heavy reliance upon digital media affects students such that they exhibit more characteristics of oral learners than print learners. Sachs coined the term 'digit-oral' to describe this learning preference shift.[19] To determine if David is simply an anomaly or if he is indicative of a wider trend, I conducted research on seminary students' learning preferences.

Over a period of nine years,[20] I used a Learning Preference Assessment[21] instrument and found the following:

- 54% of the students tested exhibited an oral learning preference. Keep in mind that these are graduate students at accredited theological institutions. After 16-plus years of schooling, the majority still prefer oral learning!

- The percentage of oral learners went from 42% to 62% over the nine-year span, predicting that this learning preference is on the rise in US seminaries.

---

[19] Jonah Sachs, *Winning the Story Wars: Why Those Who Tell (and Live) the Best Stories Will Rule the Future* (Boston, MA: Harvard Business Review Press, 2012).
[20] W. Jay Moon, 'I Love to Learn But I Don't Like to Read: The Rise of Secondary Oral Learning', in *Orality Journal* 2, No. 2 (2013), 55-65.
[21] L.L. Abney, 'Orality Assessment Tool', 2001: http://fjseries.org/low/Orality_Assessment_Tool_Worksheet.pdf

- When I tested 32 undergraduates at LeTourneau University, a whopping 78% tested as oral learners, indicating that this learning preference change is not going away any time soon.

These results suggest that it is not just theological educators in the African or Native American contexts that need to understand and apply oral learning approaches. This also applies to a highly literate digit-oral generation.[22] Incorporating this sensitivity to oral learning within formal missiological education would better equip and prepare future theological educators in mission elsewhere. Maybe, this would have helped me to avoid boring Africans during my first exposure to oral learners!

Conclusions

From a missiological perspective, the topic of orality is not simply for theological education that is done 'over there' or in the bush. Instead, a nuanced understanding of oral learning is increasingly relevant in western digit-oral contexts, as well as primary and secondary oral contexts worldwide. To effectively reach oral learners, the application of story-telling alone is not enough; rather, we need to adopt a different paradigm.

In the movie 'The Matrix',[23] Morpheus offers a simple choice between two pills as he explains,

> This is your last chance. After this, there is no turning back. You take the blue pill – the story ends, you wake up in your bed and believe whatever you want to believe. You take the *red* pill – you stay in Wonderland, and I show you how deep the rabbit hole goes. Remember: all I'm offering is the truth. Nothing more.

To further explore the rabbit hole of oral learning, educators should consider the following questions:

1. *Start with the learners in mind.*[24] Observe and ask, 'How do they prefer to receive information, conceptualise it, remember it, and then pass the message on to others?' Consider what the majority learning preference is[25], then consider, 'How can this guide my teaching and assessment?'

2. *Learn the indigenous genres.* Resist the temptation to assume that story-telling is the 'silver bullet' for oral learners; instead, ask,

---

[22] This is described further, along with suggestions for educators in digit-oral contexts in W. Jay Moon, 'Understanding Oral Learners', in *Teaching Theology and Religion* 15, No. 1 (January 2012), 29-39.

[23] Andy Wachowski and Lana Wachowski, *The Matrix* (Warner Bros, 1999).

[24] Charles Kraft described this process as 'receptor-oriented' in C.H. Kraft, *Christianity in Culture: A Study in Biblical Theologizing in Cross-Cultural Perspective*, revised volume 25th anniversary (Maryknoll, NY: Orbis Books, 2005).

[25] Along with participant observations, a good starting place is for students to take the Learning Preference Assessment by Lynn Abney at: http://fjseries.org/low/Orality_Assessment_Tool_Worksheet.pdf

'Which genre does the audience appreciate the most? Which genre do they most connect with spirituality? Which genre do you know the least about? How can you learn more about this genre? What particular view of reality are you missing with this genre? How can you learn and experiment with each one (proverbs, song, story, symbol, ritual, dance, drama) at some point in your ministry among these people?'

3. *Observe an effective oral communicator in the host culture.* How do they combine oral genres? How do they paint mental images, use symbols, create experiences, invite audience participation/ engagement, etc.?

4. *Consider a combination.* How can oral teaching methods be combined with print teaching methods to increase the learners' transformation? What oral AND print assessments can be used to assess student learning more accurately?

5. *Prepare an Oral Learning Experience.* Consider the role that the following play in the learning experience you are designing, based on the acronym CHIMES:

   1. Communal: How can you encourage the group to learn from each other (e.g. small groups, group discussions, panels, visits, rituals, etc.)?

   2. Holistic: How can you connect what they are learning with other areas of life so that you are adding to and critiquing what they already know?

   3. Images: What images, symbols and object lessons can be used so that words are not the only communicator of meaning?

   4. Mnemonics: What genres can you use to 'hook' the audience and then form memory 'triggers' for later recall?

   5. Experiential: How can learners experience something and then later reflect on it? Consider the use of exercises, activities, field trips, rituals and festivals that engage the learner through participation.

   6. Sensory: How can the senses be engaged to encourage deep learning? Turner[26] describes how symbols are uniquely suited to connect the senses with an ideology to foster deep learning.

---

[26] V. Turner, *The Ritual Process: Structure and Anti-Structure* (New York: Aldine De Gruyter, 1995).

Section Three

Case Studies

A TRANSFORMATIVE MODEL OF MISSION TRAINING: A CASE STUDY FROM ALL NATIONS CHRISTIAN COLLEGE, UK

Ruth M. Wall

The need for 'new forms of theological education' is highlighted in paragraph 6 of the *Edinburgh 2010 Common Call.*[1] In this call, new forms of education need to be predicated upon the assumption that 'we are all made in the image of God' and therefore, a prerequisite for designing learning is that it 'involves the entire human being'.

Balia and Kim express the vision for theological and mission education, emerging from Edinburgh 2010, as the education of;

the ear to hear God's word and the cry of God's people;
the heart to heed and respond to suffering;
the tongue to speak to both weary and arrogant;
the hands to work with the lowly;
the mind to reflect on the good news of the Gospel;
the will to respond to God's call;
the spirit to wait upon God in prayer, to struggle, and to be silent, to intercede for the church and the world;
the body to be the temple of the Holy Spirit.[2]

This is a vision of Spirit-filled thinking, attitudes and relationships that lead to Spirit-led actions in our world. It is a call for whole person transformation. The idea of whole person training is not new but perhaps the lack of progress in achieving this vision is because practitioners are not yet clear what 'involving the entire human being' actually means in practice. How can we understand whole person learning and what kinds of model are needed to nurture whole-person transformation that leads to action?

This chapter presents a case study of mission training to explore how whole person transformation may be fostered. It draws from current education thinking and mission training practice centred round the assumption articulated at Edinburgh 2010 that learning 'involves the entire human being'. This chapter presents a new, transformative model of mission training that has emerged from my doctoral research conducted at

---

[1] www.emw-d.de/fix/files/Common_Call_final.pdf
[2] D. Balia and K. Kim (eds), *Witnessing to Christ Today* (Oxford: Regnum, 2010), 153.

All Nations Christian College (UK) in conjunction with University College London (ULC) – Institute of Education.[3] The model presented in this chapter is theoretically informed by contemporary adult education theories of transformative learning and is thoroughly tested in mission training practice and through a rigorous process of critical reflection on that practice. A transformative learning lens is used to study a mission training course called En route. Drawing from the extensive literature of transformative adult learning, I define transformative learning as follows:

> Transformative learning engages learners in constructing new ways of thinking and being, and is fostered by a purposive and social process that supports the whole person.[4]

The En route mission training course is a ten-week residential course that has been delivered three times each year since January 2007 to more than 350 adults from over thirty nations and representing more than forty mission agencies and church denominations.

This chapter is divided into four sections:
1. Identifying some education issues
2. Introduction to the En route course
3. Introducing a new model for mission training: the Transformative Learning Triangle (L^3)
4. Implications of the L^3 model for mission training practice and policy

Identifying Some Education Issues

Unexamined assumptions that underpin mission training

Designing and delivering mission training is predicated on a wide range of assumptions about adults, about teaching and learning and about the purpose and intended outcomes of the training. Educators' assumptions about teaching and learning are largely shaped by their culture and experiences of learning. Assumptions about teaching and learning may be uncritically absorbed into their practice as mission educators. Though invisible, these assumptions will influence every aspect of how training is conceived, developed and delivered. Therefore, mission educators must critically reflect and understand the underlying assumptions that underpin their practice.

If the aim is to design and deliver training that may be transformative for the whole person, then mission training practice will need to be embedded

---

[3] Ruth Wall, *Preparing adults for crossing cultures. A study of a transformative approach to Christian mission training* (PhD thesis, UCL – Institute of Education, London, 2015).

[4] Wall, *Preparing adults for crossing cultures*, 49.

in a transformative framework. Mission training practice that is not rooted in a transformative framework is what Edward Taylor calls 'rudderless' teaching.[5] Without a consciously adopted theoretical framework, teaching is likely to float adrift on the currents of trainer's preferred approaches.

Not enough attention to the learning process and learning relationships

The literature on mission training focuses on getting the right content and there is less debate about *how* to engage learners with the content. For example, there are a number of publications describing core competencies for missionaries[6] and broad agreement on areas for inclusion in mission training curricula.[7] In 2003, mission trainers within the International Mission Training Network (IMTN)[8] highlighted character formation as an essential aspect alongside other key competencies for ministry in another culture, and this emphasis on personal and spiritual development is corroborated by other bodies.[9] Furthermore, different kinds of learning – such as knowledge, attitudes or ministry skills are understood to be better fostered in different learning contexts – be they formal, informal or non-formal.[10] However, there is little published about *how* learning actually takes place in these contexts, especially the kinds of learning that foster character development. It is on this question of *how* to nurture whole person transformation that my research has focused.

Mission educators may rightly agree that it is essential to have clearly defined purposes for training, and select content that is relevant to these purposes, but we also need to carefully consider the processes of learning. It is essential to understand *how* to engage learners in learning that may transform. How can adults develop into lifelong, relational learners,

---

[5] J. Mezirow and E. Taylor (eds), *Transformative learning in practice* (San Francisco, CA: Jossey-Bass 2009), 5.

[6] For example, 129 competencies for missionaries set out in 14 key training areas identified in the Latin American context. See W.D. Taylor, *Internationalising Missionary Training* (Pasadena, CA: William Carey Library, 1991), 130; M. Hedinger, *Towards a paradigm of integrated missionary training* (PhD thesis, Portland, OR: Faculty of Western Seminary,2006), 32; J. Lewis, 'In search of a Curriculum in context', in *Training for Cross-Cultural Ministries* (WEA Mission Commission, September 1991), 3; S. Hoke and W.D. Taylor, *Send Me! Your Journey to the Nations* (Pasadena, CA: William Carey Library, 1999).

[7] David Harley, *Equipping for ministry and mission* (Edinburgh: 2010): www.oikoumene.org

[8] IMTN (International Mission Training Network) is a global network of the World Evangelical Alliance-Mission Commission (WEA-MC).

[9] See, for example, R. Brynjolfson and J. Lewis (eds), *Integral Ministry Training. Design and Evaluation* (Pasadena, CA: William Carey Library, 2006); D.L. Whiteman, 'Integral Training Today for Cross-Cultural Mission', *Missiology: An International Review,* 36 (1) (2008), 5-16.

[10] Brynjolfson and Lewis, *Integral Ministry Training.*

competent and open to entering, learning and relating within another culture? It is time for a recalibration in focus from testable and measurable outcomes to more attention to the process and relationships of learning.

Lack of real engagement with community and transformation

Higher education contexts in the UK and North America have increasingly focused on adult education concepts such as learner-centred teaching, formation of learning communities and using transformative learning approaches. For example, in the UK the 2012 Quality Code,[11] (a set of national benchmarks for teaching and learning in *all* higher education institutions) assumes that a transformative learning approach is used. However, many higher education institutions – including Christian ones – have no developed understanding of the assumptions and practices required to foster transformative learning, and pay lip service to concepts such as 'transformative learning' and 'learning communities'. Terms such as 'community' and 'transformation' are in danger of becoming vacuous, nothing more than 'floating signifiers',[12] meaning whatever we want them to mean.

Learning that is situated in a genuine community of learners may well foster transformation, but simply attaching labels of 'learning community' and 'transformative learning' to teaching that is teacher-centred and to curriculum that is largely instrumental will not educe lasting change in learners. A new kind of engagement is needed. Mission educators need to engage with the challenging, unpredictable and messy process of forming communities of learners – whether the learning context is formal, informal or non-formal. If mission educators lack necessary understanding, attitudes and experience to build authentic learning communities, their teaching practices are more likely to equip disciples of Jesus for competition than collaboration.

Educators also need to learn how to deliver the curriculum in ways that will develop the learners' ability to reflect critically, to engage in dialogue, and to take transformative action. These three, reflection-dialogue-action, are the core processes of transformative learning. If mission educators lack expertise required to build reflection, dialogue and action, the course content may mould missionaries into unreflective 'experts' who are not able to examine their own ego- and ethno-centrism and are poorly prepared to learn from others. This is not a question of humility or of good intention. These are not in doubt! Mission training needs a new kind of approach to teaching and learning, and out of years of reflection, it is my conviction that

---

[11] QAA UK Quality Code for Higher Education, *Learning and teaching:* 2012.
[12] 'Floating signifier' is a term that originates with Levi-Strauss and is borrowed by Knud Illeris, *Transformative Learning and Identity* (Abingdon, UK: Routledge, 2014). A floating signifier refers to terms that do not have agreed meanings and may be interpreted in many ways.

a transformative learning approach is well suited to preparing adults to cross cultures.

Need to reconceptualise the 'head-heart-hands'/ 'know-be-do'

The 'head-heart-hands' or 'know-be-do' slogans are well known around the world as a description of holistic or whole person learning. [13] The 'head' signifies knowledge, the 'heart' signifies attitudes/ character, and the 'hands' signify skills. Importantly, this slogan ensures that mission trainers recognise that learning is not solely a cognitive process leading to knowledge acquisition but must include the development of right attitudes and appropriate skills. The head-heart-hand/ know-be-do motif rests on Bloom's [14] description of learning domains in which he describes cognitive, affective and psycho-motor domains. It is of note that Bloom developed his description of learning domains within the context of academic institutions in North America. At that time and in that context, it was a valuable way of moving thinking about adult learning forward. Since the 1950s and 60s, the situated nature and social dimension of learning has been recognised. The head-heart-hand motif ignores this crucial social dimension of learning. Another problem with the head-heart-hands slogan is that it over-emphasises the cognitive dimension since both knowledge and skills are cognitive processes. I suggest that 'head-heart-hands' as it has been understood is not an adequate description of whole person learning. I prefer Illeris' 2002 description of learning as:

> an entity which unites a cognitive, an emotional and a social dimension into one whole. [15]

Drawing from Illeris' work, [16] learning may be understood as combining the cognitive, emotional and social dimensions through a process of acquisition that is interactive with others. Therefore, I offer a reconceptualisation of head-heart-hands where 'head' signifies cognition/thinking (knowing and doing), 'heart' signifies emotion

---

[13] For example, see the All Nations Christian College website: www.allnations.ac.uk

[14] Benjamin Bloom, *Taxonomy of Educational Objectives, the classification of educational goals – Handbook I: Cognitive Domain* (Vol. 1, New York: McKay, 1956) and B. Bloom, B. Masia and D. Krathwohl, *Taxonomy of educational objectives: The classification of educational goals. Handbook II: The affective domain* (New York: David McKay & Co, 1964).

[15] Knud Illeris, *The Three Dimensions of Learning. Contemporary Learning Theory in the Tension Field between the Cognitive, the Emotional and the Social* (trans. D. Reader and M. Malone, Roskilde University Press, 2002), 227.

[16] Illeris, *Transformative Learning and Identity*.

(feeling/attitudes), and 'hand' signifies relating.[17] This may be represented in figure 1 below, adapted from Illeris:[18]

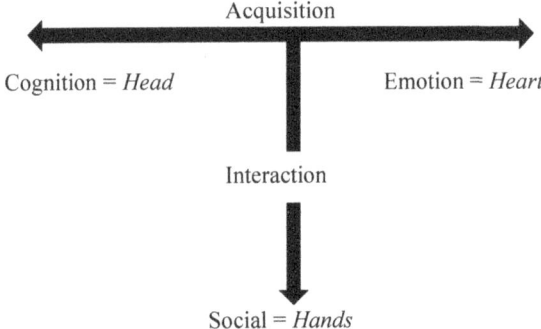

Figure 1: Three learning domains, adapted from Illeris, 2002

To represent whole person learning, I use the symbol H^3 where the H signifies head-heart-hands (thinking-emotions-relating), and the superscripted^3 denotes the possibility of transformative whole person learning when these three dimensions are addressed together. Transformation may be possible when there is integration of our thinking, our emotions and our relationships.

The two learning processes of *acquisition* and *interaction* are crucial aspects of theological education and mission training, namely, learning to learn and learning to relate. Therefore, we can conceptualise theological and mission training as having two crucial aspects that are inseparable: the development of thinking and attitudes that will enable adults to be lifelong learners, and the relational development that will enable adults to be build healthy, resilient relationships with God, self and others. Being able to learn and being able to relate are indivisible and together represent whole person learning.

Introduction to the En Route Course

The En route course was developed in 2006 with the aim of equipping adults to be effective carriers of the Gospel across cultures. It is a ten-week residential course[19] and therefore cannot cover the breadth or depth of

---

[17] Wall, *Preparing adults for crossing cultures*, 171.
[18] Illeris, *The Three Dimensions of Learning*, 19.
[19] All Nations Christian College also has an online, introductory version of the En route course called Explore. The online Explore course is designed to engage a community of learners virtually. The course content is uncovered over thirteen

content covered in a 1-3 year undergraduate programme. However, it is believed that in three months it is possible to provide learning experiences that may be transformative. The En route course aims to develop adults as lifelong learners and mature, relational disciples of Jesus Christ. This is achieved through immersion in an experience of learning that fosters critical reflection, dialogue and action within a community of learners.

Before students arrive, they are asked to reflect on and share their own personal expectations and goals for the course, and these are shared with the community of learners. Throughout the ten weeks, students are encouraged to learn how to learn from others. This requires the classroom to be a hospitable place. Openness and acceptance are key to developing trust.[20] Trust is needed to build a sense of community.

The En route course is made up of five modules. Students complete all five modules, together with all the related assignments. The five modules intentionally build on each other and integrate the learning in three fields of study, namely, spiritual and personal development, Biblical and theological understanding and intercultural awareness. Explicitly connecting theory with practice and integrating the fields of study was found to foster learning that could be transformative.[21]

En route module	Purpose of module
Module 1: Who am I?	To lay a foundation for all learning and relating. It explores our identity in Christ and how to nurture our relationship with God. It provides a starting place to set personal goals for the course as we discover our learning preferences, personality type and preferred team roles. It builds understanding about transition and equips for resilience in faith and character.
Module 2: The Bible and Mission	To answer the question, What does the Bible say about mission? This module explores the Bible's macro narrative and overviews mission in the gospels, the early church, across the centuries and in our world today. It considers current trends in mission and how we, as Gospel carriers, relate in our world today.
Module 3: Culture and Religion	To answer the question, Who is my neighbour? This module develops understanding of culture, worldview and religious traditions. It provides tools

weeks with weekly discussion forums, reflective workbook questions and a personal tutor to provide feedback.

[20] Openness and acceptance are key elements to developing relationships of trust that enable cultural understanding to emerge. See Duane Elmer, *Cross-Cultural Servanthood* (Westmont, IL: IVP, 2006).

[21] This concurs with Perry Shaw. For example, Perry Shaw, *Transforming Theological Education: A Practical Handbook for Integrative Learning* (Carlisle, UK: Langham Global Library, 2014).

	for dealing with culture shock and explores how we can work well in cross-cultural teams.
Module 4: Relating and Integrating across Cultures	To answer the question, How can we work well with people of other cultures? This module deals with the practical issues of relating and integrating across cultures equipping students with the tools for cross-cultural living, whether a single person, married or a family. It deals practically with language acquisition, whole health, suffering and persecution, security and communicating with supporters.
Module 5: Integral Mission	To bring together all the learning and asks, How can we share the good news of Jesus Christ in our world? It explores contextualised evangelism and discipleship, church building and community development. It enables students to articulate their personal vision for mission and to share their research with one another.

The emphasis is on participation within a learning community. Teaching and learning employ a range of methods including lectures, discussion, case studies, small group assignments, role plays, simulations, videos and use of media, research, guided reading, directed reflection and regular feedback.

The emphasis is not on academic achievement, grades and formal assessment but on engagement with the learning, reflective application of learning to real-life situations and to personal and spiritual development.

My research found that this kind of learning is challenging: cognitively, emotionally and relationally. Therefore, students need to be supported within the learning community and by tutors capable of handling strong emotions. Support and mentoring are provided by the En route course tutors and within the All Nations tutorial system, where every student is part of a small group of staff and students who meet together each week to worship and learn. Students meet one-to-one with a tutor two or three times during the course to set personal learning goals, discuss progress, pray together and give feedback on assignments.

The focus on whole person learning runs through all the All Nations programmes so that adults taking the three-year BA programme and one-year Master's programme are also offered an experience of learning that may be transformative.

A New Model for Mission Training:
the Transformative Learning Triangle (L^3)

Since 2010, a dialogue between adult education theories of transformative learning and the experiences of students on the En route course has led to the conceptualisation of a new model for Christian mission training.[22] I call

---

[22] Wall, *Preparing adults for crossing cultures*, 189.

this model *The Transformative Learning Triangle* denoted by the symbol L^3. The symbol '*L*' is for 'Learning' and the superscripted ^{3} signifies the transformative nature of learning that may be possible when the model is applied. To quote from the research;

> The purpose of the [L^3] model is pragmatic, to provide a relevant and useful way to think about fostering transformative Christian mission training. The model extends understanding of whole person learning... and focusses practically on addressing the gap in the literature about **how** transformative learning may be fostered...[23]

The L^3 model connects three key themes in designing and delivering mission training and enables educators to connect these themes into a unified approach to learning while at the same time differentiating between them. Without this differentiation, the danger is that trainers will focus solely on course content. The L^3 model may be presented as a triangle where each corner of the triangle represents one theme, as shown below:

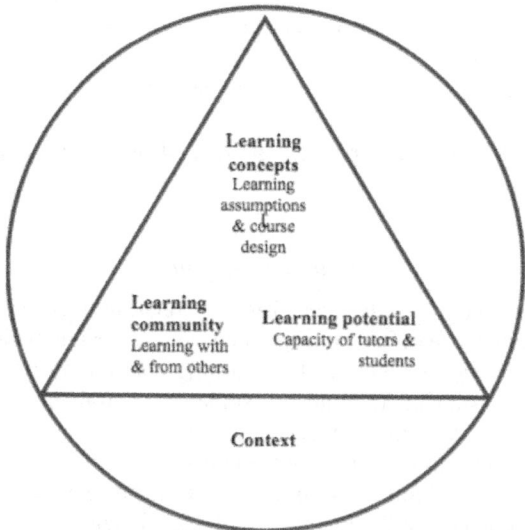

Figure 2: The L^3 model of mission training, Wall, 2015

The three core themes in the L^3 model are the learning concepts, the learning community and the learning potential. These themes will be briefly presented.

---

[23] Wall, *Preparing adults for crossing cultures*, 188.

Learning concepts

The theme of *learning concepts* deals with all the assumptions of learning and the design of the training. It is not enough to adopt a few new techniques in the classroom (whether that is physical or virtual). Underlying assumptions about adult learners, whole person learning and the development of lifelong learners may need examining and transforming. It is only when we have transformed concepts that we will shape the course design in ways that will foster transformation.

Course designs that are intentional about whole person learning need to:

- Recognise who the learners are and be flexible
- Connect content to the learners' contexts and questions
- Engage and challenge the whole person (head-heart-hands) through designing learning tasks that connect thinking and emotions and challenge learners relationally
- Build reflection, dialogue and action through participatory learning
- Employ the whole curriculum – the formal (explicit) curriculum and the informal (hidden) curriculum of attitudes, values and relationships
- Integrate the content so that one module builds and connects to another
- Connect theory and practice so that ideas can be applied to real situations

Learning community

The L^3 model recognises the crucial role of relationships in learning. The L^3 model connects learning concepts and course design with the second theme, the *learning community*. The learning community refers to *all* the relationships – student to student, students to trainers and, between students, trainers and the subject – so that a sense of community is established and nurtured throughout the course.

Relationships are built on values that are made explicit. These values include reciprocity, individuality[24] and accountability. These values encourage mutuality in learning, recognise each individual as uniquely shaped by their experiences, personality and culture, and expect that learners and trainers are each accountable to God, self and one another.

Openness and acceptance are needed to establish safety and trust within this community. Where safety is experienced and trust established, students and trainers will be able to learn together and from one another.

---

[24] Individuality recognises each person as uniquely made in God's image, and therefore one size does not fit all.

My research corroborated the findings of MacMillan and Chavis[25] that a sense of community is built where there is

- a sense of belonging,
- each member has influence,
- needs are met, and
- deep connections are made.[26]

Establishing a sense of community is an intentional process that needs to be made explicit to all, both trainers and students. The learning space needs to be experienced as a hospitable one, where openness and acceptance are clearly demonstrated by the trainers. Mission trainers need to create space in the curriculum for the sharing of stories and events.

Learning potential

The L^3 model recognises that fostering transformative learning requires certain key *capacities* in trainers and in students. I refer to the *learning potential* within the community as the capacity of the educators combined with the capacity of the students.

Students need to be open to God, self, and others, and open to new ideas and ways of expressing ideas. Students need to learn to reflect and be able to dialogue. They will need to be effective, cross-cultural listeners. When resistance is experienced, students need to be able to handle strong emotions and be open to exploring the underlying premises of resistance.

Theological and mission educators need a mature self-understanding and the capacity to guide the learning process. They need to be able to handle strong emotions. Educators also need to develop their own capacity for critical reflection and be able to model praxis. They need to relate the course content to the learners' goals and questions.

Learning context

Learning does not take place in a vacuum. Therefore, in designing and delivering training, educators must understand and engage with the context in which the training is taking place. The context may inhibit transformation and therefore mission educators must first understand and engage with the assumptions and values in the context. For example, if the assumption of an institution (or church) is that the educators are experts who possess knowledge that needs to be transferred to students, then training will be designed to effectively transfer knowledge and to test whether the transfer has been successful. In such a context, whole person

---

[25] D.W. McMillan, 'Sense of Community', in *Journal of Community Psychology*, 24 (4), 1996, 315-25; D.W. McMillan and D.M. Chavis, 'Sense of community: A definition and theory', in *Journal of Community Psychology*, 14 (1), 1986, 6-23.
[26] Deep connections are spiritual, emotional and ideational.

learning will not be fostered because learning is assumed to be the acquisition of knowledge, rather than the transformation of thinking, attitudes and relationships.

The contextual nature of the L^3 model is represented by the circle that surrounds the triangle in figure 2.

Implications of the L^3 Model for
Mission Training Practice and Policy

If the L^3 model provides a useful and relevant lens through which to look at mission training and if the L^3 model is adopted by mission trainers (and by theological educators), then there are implications for mission training practice and policy. Three implications will be presented here.

Training designs

More dialogue is needed in developing course designs. The L^3 model suggests that course design is a crucial aspect of fostering transformation. Course design is more than getting the right content or planning the timetable. It may be expedient to share curricular materials but transformative designs need more than a collection of documentation. We need to go beyond the sharing of curricula documents, especially those that have been developed in western contexts, and actively engage with one another to address *how* to develop training designs that are appropriate to the learners' context and that are intentional about fostering new ways of thinking and relating.

Wycliffe/SIL's 'Learning that LASTS'[27] draws from the ideas of Paulo Freire,[28] Jane Vella[29] and Global Learning Partnerships.[30] These educators provide a framework for course designs that emerge from a transformative learning lens and provide an excellent starting point for developing mission training.

Mission educators

Mentoring is needed for mission educators. Important as academic excellence and cross-cultural experience are, it is the ability to model

---

[27] Wycliffe, SIL and their partners have been delivering Learning that LASTS workshops since 1998. LASTS is an acronym for Learner Centred, Action with reflection, Solving problems, Teamwork, Self-discovery / self-direction.

[28] Paulo Freire, *Pedagogy of the Oppressed* (Penguin Group, 1972).

[29] Jane Vella, *Learning to Listen, Learning to Teach: The Power of Dialogue in Educating Adults* (San Francisco, CA: Jossey-Bass, 2002); Jane Vella, *On Teaching and Learning: Putting the Principles and Practices of Dialogue* (San Francisco, CA: Jossey-Bass, 2008).

[30] Global learning partners: www.globallearningpartners.com

praxis, to demonstrate openness to learning from others, to communicate acceptance and build relationships, and to demonstrate integrity (thinking-emotions-relationships) that is crucial for mission trainers.

Mission trainers need mentoring to develop understanding of how to nurture transformative learning, but they also need the ongoing work of personal transformation. This requires being open and accountable to God, self and others for their own development as disciples.

Length of training

In the ongoing debate about the length of time required to prepare adults for crossing cultures, the experience of the En route course should be considered. Ten weeks is certainly a limited time but it has been found to provide a foundation for serving cross-culturally. Three months may be sufficient to provide a map that will then guide the adventurer in their lifelong journey of learning. In a survey carried out a year after the En route course, students perceived that their learning had transformed thinking, emotions and relationships and the learning had endured.

With the burgeoning workforce being sent from the global South and East, perhaps now is the time to focus on what *can* be done to provide training that may *begin* a lifelong process of whole person learning and transformation.

INFORMATION TECHNOLOGY FOR MISSION IN THE 21ST CENTURY: THE GLOBAL DIGITAL LIBRARY ON THEOLOGY AND ECUMENISM

Stephen Brown

While only two percent of all Christians lived in Africa in 1910, now nearly one in four Christians in the world is African. Europe and North America accounted for 80 percent of Christians in 1910 but only 40 percent a century later, when the 'statistical centre' of Christianity was to be found near Timbuktu in Mali. Christianity is also seeing dramatic growth in Asia, where, during the past century, it has increased at twice the rate of overall population growth.[1] Moreover, much of the growth of Christianity has been in Charismatic, Pentecostal, Evangelical and non-denominational forms of expression,[2] while in the former heartland of western Europe and North America, the mainstream denominations that were the bedrock of the 20th-century ecumenical movement are being eclipsed. This intersection between the post-Christian West and non-western Christianity will be a 'defining ecumenical characteristic' of the 21st century.[3] Such shifts in world Christianity have also called into question an understanding of Christianity based on Roman Catholicism, Orthodoxy and what has been called 'mainline' Protestantism. While half a century ago, the member churches of the World Council of Churches accounted for roughly as many members as the Roman Catholic Church, today some estimates suggest that WCC members now make up only a quarter to a third of world Christianity.

At the same time, through global population movements and the global communication and media infrastructure, religious pluralism has become a global reality. Religion itself is increasingly prominent in world affairs, yet often perceived as a factor of international conflict and of societal disturbance, or as a counterpoint to the claimed 'progress' of modernity.[4]

---

[1] Wesley Granberg-Michaelson, *From Times Square to Timbuktu: The Post-Christian West Meets the Non-Western Church* (Grand Rapids, MI: Eerdmans, 2013), 8. See also the source for these statistics: Todd Johnson and Kenneth Ross, *Atlas of Global Christianity: 1910-2010* (Edinburgh: Edinburgh University Press, 2009).

[2] *Global Christianity: A Report on the Size and Distribution of the World's Christian Population* (New York: Pew Research Center, 2012), 67-69.

[3] Granberg-Michaelson, *From Times Square*, 150.

[4] See, for example, Konrad Raiser, *Religion Power Politics* (Geneva: WCC, 2013), esp. 11-12.

Through these population movements, the religious face of the West is also changing. Alongside people who simply do not belong to any religion, and communities of other faiths, global migration has led to the growth in what are variously called black-led churches, migrant churches, or churches with a migration background,[5] often only with local leadership structures. Meanwhile, a wider shift in the balance of power at the global level away from western Europe and North America towards Asia in particular, is accompanied by increasingly apparent contradictions of the form of globalisation that emerged at the end of the 1980s, despite its neo-liberal underpinnings remaining extraordinarily resilient.

Such developments are changing the context for mission. The new ecumenical affirmation on mission and evangelism, *Together towards Life,* underlines the need for a shift of the mission concept from 'mission *to* the margins' to 'mission *from* the margins', moving away from a concept of Christian mission that has been characterised in the past 'by conceptions of geographical expansion from a Christian centre to the 'unreached territories', to the ends of the earth'.[6] The shifting centre of gravity of Christianity to the global South and East, it states, represents a challenge 'to explore missiological expressions that are rooted in these contexts, culture and spiritualities', strengthening mutuality and partnership and affirming interdependence within mission and the ecumenical movement.[7]

Such mutuality, partnership and interdependence need also to find expression within theological education that, in the words of the Edinburgh 2010 Common Call, is able 'to shape a new generation of leaders with authenticity for mission in a world of diversities in the twenty-first century'.[8] Yet, as the study group on theological education and formation organised in advance of Edinburgh 2010 noted,[9] the changing patterns of world Christianity are making visible the unequal allocation of resources for theological education between the South and the North. While the 'absolute majority' of resources for theological education are located in the North, the greatest needs are found in the South. Access by scholars from the South to the resources of the North such as PhD scholarships, research visits and theological libraries is increasingly difficult, not least because of visa restrictions. At the same time, while theological knowledge from the Anglophone North is readily disseminated within the South, it is much

---

[5] See Amélé Adamavi-Aho Ekué, 'Migration and the Challenges for Christian Communities', in Stephen Brown (ed), *Churches Speaking Truth to Power: Christian Communities as Agents of Justice* (John Knox Series 21), Geneva: John Knox International Reformed Center, 2012).

[6] Jooseop Keum (ed), *Together Towards Life: Mission and Evangelism in Changing Landscapes – with a Practical Guide* (Geneva: WCC, 2013), 5.

[7] Keum, *Together towards Life*, 38.

[8] www.edinburgh2010.org/en/resources/papersdocumentscc36.pdf

[9] 'Theological Education and Formation', in Daryl Balia and Kirsteen Kim (eds), *Edinburgh 2010: Witnessing to Christ Today* (Oxford: Regnum, 2010), 161-66.

more difficult for theological insights and research results from the South to be assimilated in the North, or even within the various regions of the South. Such tendencies within theological education are further exacerbated by the more general global knowledge divide. Structures of commercial academic publishing mean that access to scientific and academic publishing resources is expensive if not impossible in many parts of the global South. On the other hand, knowledge production in general from within the global South has often been marginalised and overlooked at a global level, not least because of the Science Citation Index, including its derivatives, which has become 'the universal yardstick by which the value of a researcher's output is measured', and has had 'a hugely chilling effect on the growth of and access to research in [the] developing world'.[10]

The Global Digital Library on Theology and Ecumenism (GlobeTheoLib), launched in September 2011 under the URL www.globethics.net/gtl, is one attempt to respond to these shifts in global Christianity, missiology and theological education. GlobeTheoLib is a multi-lingual online library offering free-of-charge access to more than 750,000 full-text articles, journals, books and other resources, with a focus on theology, ecumenism and religious studies within world Christianity. It has been developed as a joint project between the World Council of Churches, represented by its programme on Ecumenical Theological Education (ETE), and Globethics.net, a global ethics network based in Geneva that launched a Global Digital Library on Ethics (GlobeEthicsLib) in 2008.[11] This ethics library provides free-of-charge access to hundreds of thousands of documents and articles on ethics, as a means of helping to ensure that 'people in all regions of the world are empowered to reflect and act on ethical issues', and promoting 'more equal access to knowledge resources in the field of applied ethics [to] enable persons and institutions from developing and transition economies to become more visible and audible in the global discourse on ethics'.[12]

Using the same infrastructure as GlobeEthicsLib, GlobeTheoLib can be seen as a response to the issues related to theological education raised in the context of Edinburgh 2010. These include bridging the divide of unequal accessibility of theological education, developing innovative forms of theological education and formation for ministry, and creating new models

---

[10] Leslie Chan, Eve Gray and Rebecca Kahn, *Open Access and Development: Journals and beyond* (Brighton, UK: Institute of Development Studies, 2012), 7: www.ids.ac.uk/files/dmfile/Open-AccessandDevelopmentJournalsandBeyond_Nov2012_Gray_et_al.pdf

[11] Christoph Stückelberger and Amélie Vallotton, 'The Future Role of Online Libraries: Globethics.net's Innovative Model', in Werner, Dietrich, David Esterline, Namsoon Kang and Joshva Raja (eds), *Handbook of Theological Education in World Christianity: Theological Perspectives, Regional Survey, Ecumenical Trends* (Oxford: Regnum, 2010), 307-11.

[12] www.globethics.net/about-us/portrait

of online education and e-learning, recognising the impact of information and communication technologies (ICTs) have had on education, while affirming that 'theological education is about communicating God's good news and creating new abilities to communicate this good news in today's world'[13] – including web-based study courses, internet-based research groups, distance degree courses, and electronic library and other data resources.

GlobeTheoLib is an attempt to use ICTs to respond to the needs of theological education that in many parts of the South is unable to keep pace with demand, with a proliferation of new colleges and Bible schools often without libraries, developed curricula or a consistent educational framework, as well as an increase in non-formal and non-residential forms of theological education. As the report from the Edinburgh 2010 event underlined,[14] patterns of theological formation are changing, sometimes without requiring formal study at seminaries or a seminary degree, accompanied by a weakening of interdenominational co-operation or joint programmes, while migrant churches have new needs for theological training programmes.

GlobeTheoLib is supported by a consortium made up of associations of theological seminaries and theological libraries, Christian world communions, and regional ecumenical organisations, to support the project through conceptual and strategic guidance, networking and promotion.[15] The aim is to develop a resource including all currents of world Christianity, beyond those represented by WCC member churches, to use the possibilities offered by ICTs to address strategically the challenge of a more balanced theological knowledge transfer between churches and institutions of theological education in the North and South, East and West; to provide a common platform for existing digital resources and theological libraries in the world; and to promote the sharing of expertise in theological research and education – to counter some of the imbalances at work in the present state of world Christianity and of theological education systems worldwide.[16]

GlobeTheoLib aims to empower people from all regions of the world, especially in developing and transition countries, for interreligious and intercultural dialogue, theological reflection and action between East and West, North and South by:

- Providing access to knowledge resources on theology and ecumenism;

---

[13] Balia and Kim, *Witnessing to Christ Today*, 170.
[14] 'Theological education and formation', in Kirsteen Kim and Andrew Anderson (eds), *Edinburgh 2010. Mission Today and Tomorrow* (Oxford: Regnum, 2011), 161.
[15] The full list of Consortium members can be found at www.globethics.net/web/gtl/consortium-and-structure
[16] www.globethics.net/web/gtl/about

- Enabling the authentic theological voices of churches and marginalised groups of Christians and churches from the different continents of this earth to be heard by creating a new quality of mutual connectivity;
- Facilitating networking on theology and ecumenism with an online community of persons and organisations;
- Stimulating global collaborative research on selected fields such as contextual theology, ecumenical theology and interreligious dialogue.[17]

Content for GlobeTheoLib comes from four main sources:

- *Commercial providers:* GlobeTheoLib makes commercial content accessible to individual registered participants in the framework of institutional subscription fees or content purchase through negotiation with publishers.
- *Open repositories:* GlobeTheoLib harvests documents from among the roughly 2,500 existing Open Access repositories from throughout the world.
- *Partner institutions:* GlobeTheoLib offers partner institutions the opportunity to submit their own documents to the online library and to build specialised collections.
- *Individual participants:* GlobeTheoLib allows registered participants to submit their own documents to the online database.

GlobeTheoLib thus offers a single portal with a unified search system for material from a diversity of sources. Moreover, since GlobeTheoLib is directed towards individual registered participants, its resources are available to anyone with access to the internet and not only those who work in or are linked to institutions. GlobeTheoLib not only offers access to information through its online library, but, using the platform of Globethics.net, seeks to promote networking and collaborative research by registered participants.

While content from the Open Access repositories may be accessed by any visitor to the GlobeTheoLib site, viewing content from commercial publishers requires (free) online registration. As of September 2014, there were more than 30,000 registered participants of which roughly three-quarters come from the South (Asia 52.7%, Sub-Sahara Africa 10.4%, Middle East and North Africa 7.5%, and Latin America 3.6%).

From the very beginning, as part of a commitment to cross-cultural understanding, GlobeTheoLib has underlined the importance of a multi-lingual approach to theological resources, with its portal available in six languages (Chinese, English, French, German, Indonesian and Spanish). At the same time, there is a concerted attempt to work with partners, particularly in developing countries, to ensure that their production of theological knowledge resources is available at the global level, while

---

[17] www.globethics.net/web/gtl/vision-and-mission

individual participants and researchers are encouraged to upload their own papers and research to the library.

Since GlobeTheoLib shares the same database, infrastructure and software as GlobeEthicsLib, while each library has a distinct identity, it is possible to search both libraries at the same time and using the same tools, allowing interconnections between the libraries and their holdings. As such, the online libraries help those from religious, academic, policy and media institutions to deepen their interdisciplinary understanding of the role of religion and ethics in the world today, and to link this knowledge to a range of policy issues and interreligious dialogue and actions.

GlobeTheoLib is not intended simply as a technical tool in isolation, but to be embedded in a wider community of sharing and ecumenical learning. The preparatory workgroup for Edinburgh 2010 made a distinction between *Christian education, theological education, ministerial formation, lay formation* and *theological education by extension.*[18] To this may be added the need for *ecumenical education*, as described by Konrad Raiser, WCC general secretary from 1993 to 2003. This does not mean absorbing items of information about global problems, but 'to enter into the reality of the larger household of God's oikoumene'.[19] This concept of ecumenical learning, according to Raiser, 'challenges the tendency to consider the identity and tradition of one's own community as something to be preserved and defended against influences from outside by pointing to the fundamental insight that all Christian identities and traditions have been shaped by processes of continuous learning and exchange'. Such an understanding of 'ecumenical learning' which has absorbed other concepts such as 'intercultural learning', 'global learning' and 'interfaith learning' thus reflects:

> ... an invitation and an impelling imperative for churches and educational institutions facing growing globalisation and pluralisation today to deliberatively relate contents and methodologies of education to a genuine encounter with the 'otherness' of different religious, cultural and social identities which global migration has brought right in the midst of any learning situation of churches in today's world.[20]

This has consequences for theological education, for while ecumenical learning 'reaches beyond the forms and structures of theological education and goes to the very self-understanding of the churches as a community of learning', theological education plays a significant role in assisting the churches to respond to the ecumenical imperative. Such a role is

---

[18] *Witnessing to Christ Today*, 151-52.
[19] Konrad Raiser, 'The Future of Theological Education in Central and Eastern Europe: Challenges for Ecumenical Learning in the 21st Century', in *International Review of Mission*, 98.1 (April 2009), 59.
[20] Dietrich Werner, 'Ecumenical Formation in Theological Education: Historical Perspectives', in Dietrich Werner et al (eds), *Handbook of Theological Education in World Christianity* (Oxford: Regnum, 2010), 107.

particularly important given what Raiser describes as the 'renewed denominational orientation' of theological education, where the ecumenical dimension is being weakened again.[21]

GlobeTheoLib is thus also an attempt to respond to the need to reinforce the ecumenical dimension in theological education and learning: ecumenical in the sense both of transcending denominational perspectives and standpoints and of linking the local to the global within the worldwide *oikoumene*. ICTs become a means of linking the local with the global, and creating an awareness of the links between communities in different parts of the world. The description of the 'essential marks' of ecumenical learning in theological education and Christian education contained in a 'Magna Carta on Ecumenical Formation in Theological Education in the 21st Century',[22] presented to the 2008 congress of the World Conference of Associations of Theological Institutions (WOCATI) could serve also as a guide for the mandate of GlobeTheoLib. Picking up the recommendations of the WCC's 1983 assembly in Vancouver, it underlined that ecumenical learning (a) transcends barriers, (b) is action-oriented, (c) is done in community, (d) means learning together, detecting the global in the local, (e) is intercultural, promoting the encounter of different cultures, traditions and forms, (f) is a total process: social and religious learning are not separated from each other but constitute a unity.[23]

Developing GlobeTheoLib, however, also poses challenges for a genuine global theological and missiological sharing.[24] The first of these is the danger of *cultural centrism*. GlobeTheoLib has harvested (or imported) more than 700,000 documents from the more than 60 million documents in the 2,500 repositories worldwide, selecting those documents that are particularly relevant to theology and religious studies. This requires a sophisticated set of queries and keywords to identify the repositories and specific documents required. In part, this is a technical issue of identifying those repositories and sub-repositories that have genuinely open content (the contents of many repositories are accessible only from within the institution concerned). More importantly, it is a matter of developing a series of keywords and queries, as well as the overarching subject classification, to harvest what is seen as the most relevant content for the online libraries. This, however, is a crucial issue, for who defines what is 'relevant'? As an internal Globethics.net discussion paper has noted, 'Knowledge mapping, terminology, thesauri and classification systems are

---

[21] Raiser, *The Future of Theological Education*, 63.

[22] Dietrich Werner, 'Magna Charta on Ecumenical Formation in Theological Education in the 21st century – 10 Key Convictions', *International Review of Mission*, 98.1 (April 2009), 161-70.

[23] Werner, *Magna Charta*, 166.

[24] The section that follows draws upon Stephen Brown, 'The Global Digital Library on Theology and Ecumenism', in Odile Dupont (ed), *Libraries Serving Dialogue* (IFLA Publications Series 163: Berlin/Munich: De Gruyter Saur, 2014), 112-25.

deeply related to the *Weltanschauungen* of their authors', alongside the unconscious process of selection that might take place when queries and keywords are drawn up by a single individual, or even a group from a similar cultural context. It is for this reason that GlobeTheoLib seeks to work with advisory groups with people drawn from various continents. In drawing up the subject classification for the online library, for example, it became clear that it would not be possible simply to adopt a classification of church history in which 'Church History in the Non-Western World' was seen as a sub-category of Church History.

A second danger is the issue of the *ownership of knowledge production*, and specifically the danger of appropriating content and knowledge from the global South in order to package and to commercialise it in the North. In response to this concern, the GlobeTheoLib project leadership group drew up a 'Policy Document on the Sharing and Ownership of Theological Knowledge',[25] which sets out a set of affirmations on the 'sharing and ownership of theological knowledge'. Among other things, these affirmations state that, 'given the present imbalances and inequalities in terms of access to and visibility of theological knowledge from the different world regions, the mission of GlobeTheoLib is particularly directed and committed to empowering regions marginalised and sidelined in the mainstream of international discourse to raise their voice and to increase their visibility via GlobeTheoLib'. As the policy document notes, 'since GlobeTheoLib is neither exclusive nor one-sidedly selective in terms of a preference for a particular tradition, the process of maintaining and establishing a proper balance between different realms of theological knowledge within GlobeTheoLib is to a large extent also an issue and a challenge for its users. Their readiness and commitment to contribute from their denominational and geographical contexts and their efforts to enlarge the relevant scope of theological content presented within GlobeTheoLib is decisive for the participatory and liberative nature of the whole project of GlobeTheoLib'. In this common task, the policy document refers to the seven fundamental values on which GlobeTheoLib is based:

> *Sharing:* GlobeTheoLib promotes the mutual sharing of global and contextual Christian theological concerns and perspectives as a contribution towards overcoming religious fundamentalism and strengthening world peace;
>
> *Respect:* GlobeTheoLib respects and affirms the dignity of every person and the diversity of all Christian denominations, different cultures and world religions;

---

[25] GlobeTheoLib Project Leadership Group, 'Policy Document on the Sharing and Ownership of Theological Knowledge', December 2011: www.globethics.net/ documents/2781038/ 13471567/PolicyPapersAndReports_PolicyDocumentOnTheSharingAndOwnership OfTheological Knowledge_201112.pdf

Unity: It serves the unity of Christian churches and solidarity with all people of goodwill in the service of peace, justice and integrity of creation;

Participation: GlobeTheoLib values the participation of people from all regions and denominational backgrounds of the world, including representatives from other religious traditions;

Responsibility: GlobeTheoLib encourages responsible use of and responsible contributions to its knowledge resources and network;

Transparency: GlobeTheoLib is committed to building trust through honesty, openness, transparency and accountability;

Quality: GlobeTheoLib is committed to providing and promoting high-quality resources and scholarly contributions to theology and religious studies.[26]

In reflecting on the missionary tasks of theological education in the 21st century, such a set of seven fundamental values – sharing, respect, unity, participation, responsibility, transparency and quality – may be of wider relevance and application.

---

[26] www.globethics.net/web/gtl/vision-and-mission

EQUIPPING FOR MISSION IN THE 21ST CENTURY: UNITY IN DIVERSITY IN YWAM/UNIVERSITY OF THE NATIONS

Steve Cochrane

What does 'equipping for mission in the 21st century' mean to a mission consisting of over 200 nationalities and dozens of denominations? In short, the answer is a complexity of objectives and approaches held together by relationships, values and principles. Youth With a Mission (YWAM) began in 1960 and includes within its ranks the above diversity with a variety of ministries globally as well. In 1978 Loren Cunningham and Dr Howard Malmstadt co-founded the Pacific and Asia Christian University (PACU) in Kailua-Kona, Hawaii, which in 1988 was re-named the University of the Nations (U of N), reflecting the growth of courses to more than 600 locations in 160 nations. A passion for mission was inherent in the choice of Kona as the initial location, as reflected upon by Loren Cunningham: 'We found ourselves particularly intrigued by the idea of the lighthouse for the Pacific and Asia. For some time, we had grown increasingly aware of the great needs of that area, for it was the least evangelized region in the entire world. Sixty percent of the earth's population lived there, yet only one percent of Asians claimed a personal relationship with Christ.'[1]

Though Kailua-Kona was the initial location for PACU/U of N, training in YWAM had actually begun in Lausanne, Switzerland, at the end of 1969. A year earlier, Loren and Darlene Cunningham had moved there with a desire to start what became YWAM's first school, a School of Evangelism, equipping young missionaries for service.[2] The School was originally fourteen months in duration that included a three-month 'field trip' to the Middle East. Elements like visiting speakers, living in community while learning, and practical outreach that developed in these early years, would later become foundational in U of N courses.

From the early equipping efforts in Switzerland and then Hawaii, the importance of 'learning by doing' was emphasised. As missionaries emerged from these training schools, more locations were established all over the world. Training took place not just at one location, but was

---

[1] Loren Cunningham, *Is that Really You, God?* (Seattle, WA: YWAM Publishing 1984, 2001, 2nd edition), 150.
[2] The School of Evangelism (SOE) is still run in YWAM/U of N today, but the foundational school is the Discipleship Training School (DTS) which started in the 1970s.

integrated on a YWAM 'base'. Without a central campus but with
campuses of varying sizes that were usually also the mission's training
'bases', there was also no physical centre for administration.[3] Due to this
ongoing symbiotic relationship between campuses and bases, this chapter
will use both YWAM and U of N interchangeably as is often the case in
practice internally in the organisation.

The U of N is organised into seven colleges and offers a 'live-learn'
approach with communities of learners in a mission environment.[4] The
'live-learn' approach emphasises the importance of the formation of
students taking place in an environment where application of learning in a
community of relationships is foundational. Many of the courses of the U
of N also have a practical field assignment following a more traditional
classroom experience, often served in a cross-cultural situation. While the
strong emphasis is on sending out students into practical short- and long-
term mission opportunities upon completing courses, there is also a
possibility of doing not only Associated of Arts degrees (two years) but
also a Bachelors of Arts (four years), and in some of the colleges even a
Master's degree is offered. Future vision in the U of N also includes being
able to offer doctoral degrees, with all of these degree programmes
designed for deepening excellence in any particular area of service.

In the 2002-2011 sessions, there were 241,591 students that finished at
least the foundational Discipleship Training School (DTS), with many
going on to do further courses as well. These DTS and other courses were
offered at more than 550 locations around the world.[5] To illustrate the
nature of the campus/mission training base synergy, 49 of the largest
YWAM/U of N bases trained 52.4 % of these students over these ten years.
Within that 49, the 12 largest bases trained more than 2,500 students each
over this period and 28.2 % of the total. In 2011 alone, there were students
in U of N schools from 169 nations. The top five nations in terms of
students were the USA, South Korea, Canada, Brazil and India.

With students coming from such a wide diversity of nations, it may
provide more insight to look region-by-region at locations of training. At
six training bases in the Pacific there were 11,242 students, at eight bases in

---

[3] The largest campus is still in Kailua-Kona, Hawaii. Being the original location as
well as the residence of the co-founders of YWAM, Loren and Darlene
Cunningham, it is often identified as the primary campus of the University of the
Nations.
[4] These seven are the College/Faculty of Christian Ministries, College/Faculty of
Counseling and Health Care, College/Faculty of Science and Technology,
College/Faculty of Humanities and International Studies, College/Faculty of
Education, College/Faculty of Communication, and College/Faculty of Arts and
Sports. For a complete listing and description of these colleges as well as centres
linked with the U of N, see: www.uofn.edu
[5] Statistics on the time frame of 2002-2011 are from an unpublished
report/presentation given by the U of N leadership team in 2013 in Kona, Hawaii.

Latin America there were 11,086, in Africa at six locations there were 8,922, and in Asia at five campuses there were 7,418 students. Thus, in regions of the global South there were 25 training bases with approximately 39,000 students in 2011. In Europe and North America there were fifteen bases with approximately 19,000 students. The sheer numbers of those in the global South receiving training in YWAM/U of N schools over those in the West parallels similar dynamics in mission training of other institutions. Since 2011 when these statistics were compiled, the disparity in numbers in YWAM/U of N has likely further increased based on rates of continued growth, particularly in areas of Asia like India and East Asia.

Linking these thousands of students and hundreds of campuses/bases together is a records system that is understandably daunting in its complexity, and a leadership structure that is closely aligned with YWAM's geographic networks. A student can do courses on several continents and complete a degree programme with a unique blend of academic experience and cross-cultural dynamic. Communicating this plethora of courses and opportunities for mission resulting from them is a global catalogue that is produced every three years, now also in an online format.[6]

Perhaps not surprisingly, in an organisation with little centralisation, there is no top-down definition of how to equip for global mission. YWAM itself has people involved in both many forms of evangelism and church planting as well as mercy ministries, including some among Muslims, Hindus and Buddhists, but also is concerned with equipping students to be engaging in societal change among the seven 'spheres' that the colleges of the U of N reflect.[7] As related by Loren Cunningham in his first book, he was with Dr Howard Malmstadt in 1978 in Hawaii and sharing that 'God had been leading us to start a university. It would be a very special kind of spawning place – a place that would teach young people how to know God intimately and then make Him known in the influential areas of society'.[8] The response of Dr Malmstadt, a 'leading scientist and professor at the University of Illinois in Urbana when I first met him',[9] was that he had the same guidance, establishing a partnership that would continue until Malmstadt's death in 2003.

This commitment in YWAM/U of N to both the least-evangelised as well as seeing transformation of areas of society contributes to a wide-ranging diversity of approaches to the task and goals of mission in the

---

[6] University of the Nations catalogue 2014-2016, publ 2013 by University of the Nations: www.uofn.edu

[7] These seven spheres or areas of society include the Church, Arts and Entertainment, Business, Education, Media and Sports, Science and Technology, and the family. Similar terms for these areas are used at times internally in YWAM/U of N as well as externally in missions globally.

[8] Cunningham (1984:158).

[9] Cunningham (1984:158).

organisation itself. Tensions do sometimes result with such a variety of strategic objectives, but freedom is given in the mission for initiatives consistent with Scripture and values. YWAM/U of N provides an example of a global mission that embraces far-ranging objectives, yet with an emphasis on local initiative in developing strategies for the context around them. The strong emphasis on cross-cultural dimensions to every course, whether in the classroom or practical outreach afterwards, provides a foundation that is inherently global while relevant locally.

In using YWAM/U of N as a case study in this chapter, four resources will be used to describe a holding together in unity with a complexity of diversity. The first is the foundational Discipleship Training School (DTS) which all YWAM staff must complete and which is the entry course for other U of N courses. The second is Scripture itself, where a metaphor of the apostle Paul provides an apt description both of the diversity and outworking of YWAM approaches to training for mission around the world. The third resource will be from the mission's values, perhaps the most important tool providing coherence globally apart from the DTS. The fourth resource considered is the 'Founding Principles' of the U of N. These four resources discussed below provide a way of examining the topic of equipping for mission from different perspectives.

DTS Model in Equipping for Mission in YWAM/U of N

In the University of the Nations, the foundational course that all must do first in order to join secondary courses (and as noted earlier to join YWAM staff as well), is the Discipleship Training School (DTS). While not of course a perfect model of adaptation at the global level, the DTS after starting in the early 1970s has grown to be in 160 nations and 97 languages at more than 600 locations. The DTS seeks to provide a five-month intensive experience (three months of lectures from visiting speakers and two months of practical outreach with an option for a further month) that equips the student, using the motto of YWAM: 'To know God and make Him known.' While a speaker may occasionally lecture via Skype or another web-based tool, students must be doing the DTS in a 'live-learn community' referred to at the beginning of the chapter. In this environment, they experience day by day the ups and downs of physical and emotional relating to others. Students often also experience learning and living with those from another culture. Perhaps this cross-cultural dynamic is one of the most important aspects of equipping for mission in the 21st century that goes on in the DTS and other courses.

While many experiences in mission training globally now involve on-line learning, the power of the DTS and further courses in the U of N involve in part this daily mixing and learning from others for an intensive six months. The strength of a 'cohort' that meets several times a year – as many on-line training programmes do, including the U of N's growing

Master's degree opportunities – is no substitute for a 'live-learn' foundation, often in a cross-cultural context. One of the unique features of the U of N globally is the entry programme of the DTS which functions as a doorway into all seven colleges and corresponding courses in these colleges.

With the diversity of nations and languages involved in the DTS, the curriculum is the same throughout the world. This is maintained by regular meetings, internationally and regionally, of the DTS leaders and staff, organised by one of the centres of the U of N, the Centre for Discipleship Training Schools. The Centre's purpose is to 'maintain and enhance excellence in DTS programmes worldwide in accordance with the DTS purpose, curriculum and guidelines set by the international leadership of Youth With a Mission and the University of the Nations'. It also seeks 'to serve DTS leadership by providing encouragement, support, and expertise in programme, leadership and resource development'.[10]

Recognising the growth of this global diversity in students and locations, in recent years the DTS Centre has developed also a 'Centre Network' that includes an International Committee based all over the world. Of the 51 members of this group, 28 of them are focused on or from the global South. The DTS continues to evolve in its adaptation to local contexts of culture and learning styles. As an example, one of the International Committee members is currently involved in a Master's thesis research project with the U of N, adapting the DTS into an oral learning context. How the DTS as the foundational entry programme into YWAM, as well as further U of N courses, continues to change and adapt, while maintaining its core purposes and aims, will be an important part of the future of the U of N in its 21st century equipping of new missionaries.

As one of the goals for this 'Centre Network' in equipping students through the DTS, a commitment to 'Strategic Multiplication' emphasises again the global mission purpose of the training. This goal states the desire to 'promote the pioneering of new DTS and Field Assignments/Outreaches in the ten major language groups and the least evangelized nations of the world'.[11] In the section on the DTS's foundational purposes, the first one states the desire to 'gather and challenge people to worship, listen to and obey God, releasing them (in the context of the DTS) to serve through evangelism, intercession, acts of compassion, and other expressions of God's heart for the world, possibly even pioneering new ministries'.[12] This commitment to prayer and worship in every DTS intends to establish a lifestyle for the student that will continue long after the course ends.

In the next section, under the aims of the DTS, the concern to equip students with a heart for the world is again declared, that graduating

---

[10] U of N Catalogue, 155-56. Also included here are the purposes of the DTS, the aims for graduating students, and the goals of the DTS Centre Network.
[11] Cunningham, 156.
[12] Cunningham, 155.

students may be those 'who are growing in understanding of the breadth and depth of God's character and ways, and in particular of His great love for every person and culture'.[13] Other similar aims include training students 'who can share the Gospel with the lost and have a lifelong commitment to do so', and 'who have a commitment to continue to be involved in some way with God's work among the nations, including unreached people, the poor and needy and in spheres of society'.[14] The DTS is a foundational equipping course in 'Knowing God and Making Him Known', reflecting YWAM's founding motto.

Diversity of the Gifts

Another resource for examining the unity and diversity in equipping for mission is from two letters by the apostle Paul. The first of two passages from these letters highlighted in this chapter is in Ephesians 4:11-13:

> And His gifts were that some should be apostles, some prophets, some evangelists, some pastors and teachers, to equip the saints for the work of ministry, for building up the body of Christ, until we all attain to the unity of the faith and of the knowledge of the Son of God, to mature manhood, to the measure of the stature of the fulness of Christ.

This passage from Ephesians includes the understanding that the five different gifts listed are meant to be exercised to 'equip the saints for the work of ministry' and 'for building up the body of Christ'. The five particular gifts according to Paul are designed to help bring the body to a unity of faith and to 'mature manhood'. While the teaching gift in equipping is normally associated with an educational institution, and often attracts those identifying with this gift, the U of N developed from and within the calling of a mission movement. The apostolic gift, meaning 'sent one' or 'special messenger', is an equipping gift often associated with sending out missionaries.

The calling of a mission like YWAM is apostolic in nature, and the fact that the U of N continues to function in a symbiotic relationship with the mother mission movement, keeps the apostolic call at the heart of the University. In Paul's fivefold equipping gifts, there was not a separation or division, as happens at times in Christian education involvement. The apostolic and teaching gifts were together. A strength of the U of N being within the mission movement of YWAM is that there is an integration of both gifts within a larger context of a commitment to 'building up the body of Christ' and attaining the 'unity of the faith'.

In 1 Corinthians 12:4-31, the apostle Paul describes the church as the Body of Christ. Functioning in ways similar to the human body, he begins his discussion in verse 4 observing that there are varieties of gifts, but the

---

[13] Cunningham, 155.
[14] Cunningham, 155.

same Spirit; varieties of service, but the same Lord; varieties of working, but the same God who inspires all of them. This diversity of gifts is later compared in the passage to the diversity of parts of the human body, all different and uniquely valued yet needing to work together. A diversity of gifts is inspired, however, by one Spirit that gives to each member varying gifts according to their faith. Though this passage does not specifically refer to equipping for ministry as Ephesians 4:11-13 does, the emphasis on the varieties of service and ministry provides an important scriptural foundation for seeing YWAM/U of N's multiple ways of training for mission in the 21st century.

An extremely broad expression of nationalities and ministries enables a corresponding breadth and depth of possibilities for equipping approaches. When this is truly global in nature and not only branches of a particular group of nations and cultures, there can be the opportunity for fresh eyes and voices to emerge and shape the courses and outcomes. Unfortunately, even a mission as diverse as YWAM or the global church more generally does not always take enough time to listen to the breadth of voices and learn from them in order to affect practice in equipping for ministry. What can be more common is for one nation or a denominational preference or approach to take dominance. Then methods in training become hued with those colours, instead of the richness that is actually available. This 'ethno-centrism' or 'denominational-centrism' then ends up being the opposite of the rich diversity of the body metaphor in Ephesians 4 and 1 Corinthians 12.

One model of training that has worked in a particular context at a particular time in history becomes the favoured one thought to have continued applications everywhere. Instead of an openness to new approaches based in the context of the newer sending nations, there is at times a reliance on old models that worked in the country of origin. In the previous section on the DTS training in YWAM/U of N, this danger of an old model being restrictive to adaptation in new contexts and cultures was addressed by an openness to other voices from other nations being involved in a shaping and transforming. An old model can be combined with new life and approaches. In the final section of this chapter, old and new power paradigms are discussed that have application to equipping frameworks in the 21st century.

Values as a Foundation for Equipping for Mission

Another perspective on how a group like YWAM/U of N looks at approaches to equipping for mission in the 21st century is provided from their own Foundational Values.[15] Founded in 1960 by Loren Cunningham from within the Assemblies of God denomination and Southern Californian

---

[15] For all YWAM's Foundational Values see www.ywam.org

culture, YWAM has now grown to be much more diverse over half a century later. Of the eighteen values that help unite the mission, and indeed are called the DNA (using another body metaphor), the seventh value is that the mission is 'broad-structured and decentralized'. This decentralisation offers the opportunity for a variety of theological reflections and expressions of ministry. As noted at the beginning of the chapter, there is not one organisational headquarters or central training campus that controls the rest. At times a potential recipe for chaos and anarchy, this decentralisation and broad-structured leadership, more often than not, actually gives greater room for other approaches and models to emerge and flourish. Experimentation in ministry and training for mission can occur without a corporate manual having to be consulted, or emails sent off to a central campus gaining approval for an innovative idea being implemented.

There is however a complex mix within the U of N of standards related to course content and degree requirements. The decentralisation is combined with a globally linked 'broad structure' that provides accountability for students and faculty both in their ongoing learning experience and goals leading to ministry placement. It is often not an easy fit to combine this accountability with the freedom to innovate both in course content and resulting mission opportunities. This is accentuated with the diversity of nations, both in origin of students and faculty as well as location of campuses and courses, reflected in YWAM's commitment to the eighth value, being 'international and interdenominational'.

One of the challenges represented in this value as applied to equipping for mission in the 21st century is the question of accreditation for the U of N's courses and degrees. Though YWAM originated in the USA, from the beginning there was a desire and expectation for staff from other nations. Indeed, as noted earlier in this chapter, the first courses YWAM began were located in Lausanne, Switzerland, with practical field experiences in the Middle East region. The U of N has resisted pressures to yield to a particular system of accreditation based in one nation. Though in the short term it may provide a certain degree of acceptance in secular or denominational training circles, it could be limiting and perhaps even crippling when the longer-term and international diversity is considered. According to a section in the U of N catalogue on 'Considerations about Accreditation', the 'U of N recognizes the value of accrediting agencies in maintaining predictability in quality of education. Therefore, U of N will complete the application process with a global accrediting association in the near future. However, this association is in its early stages of development, and will have to go through its own processes of recognition'.[16]

---

[16] U of N Catalogue, 24-25. Several reasons are then given for this stance on accreditation.

A larger discussion in the church needs to continue, related to the future of accreditation and mission equipping in the 21st century, in the light of the globalisation and diffusion of centres for training in the global South. Methods of verifying the quality of courses and instruction from only certain parts of the world will be inadequate for this growth, as in some contexts there is a rapid expansion of new ways of equipping for mission. As part of this, recognition is needed that the buildings and institutional frameworks required for the equipping of missionaries are not ultimately the most important elements. As Cunningham writes of the early beginnings of the U of N: 'Instead of waiting for a new campus and buildings, we started *where we were*. The buildings were only tools, after all. So, the University of the Nations began. We rented a room here, a meeting hall there, an apartment somewhere else, and began teaching.'[17]

Importance of Founding Principles

The fourth resource is the importance in the U of N of a set of Founding Principles that guide the equipping of missionaries in the 21st century.[18] These principles, in alignment with the values of the mother movement of YWAM, provide another element of cohesiveness for the staff and students of the U of N. They are 'founded upon biblical principles' and enable the U of N to 'fulfill its commitments to Christ and His Great Commission by equipping men and women with spiritual, cultural, intellectual, and professional training, and inspiring them to continually grow in their personal relationship with God while also seeking to make Him known among all peoples in all nations'.[19]

As seen in the above preamble to these principles, the U of N has a commitment to equipping students for mission. In the next section, after quoting Christ's command in Matthew 28:19-20 to 'make disciples of all nations', the mission mandate of the university is further clarified: 'Special priority for service is given to nations, cities, and people groups which have had the least access to the message of the gospel. An integrated approach to ministry, including evangelism, training, and the meeting of physical needs, is presented biblically and worked out practically.'[20]

While there is in the U of N an equipping for mission to those with 'least access to the gospel', in the next section there is stated in addition the desire to 'broaden the scope of evangelistic endeavors by equipping students to serve in all spheres of society, in all nations, in response to Jesus' declaration that we are the salt and light of the world'.[21] In these sections, the call to reach the unreached in evangelism, training and

---

[17] Cunningham, 184.
[18] For a complete list of these Founding Principles, see U of N Catalogue, 11.
[19] U of N Catalogue, 11.
[20] U of N Catalogue, 11.
[21] U of N Catalogue, 11.

meeting physical needs reflects YWAM's three priorities of ministry; evangelism (and church planting where there is no church), training, and mercy ministries. Added to this in the U of N principles is the commitment to be 'salt and light' in every area of society.

The next few sections of principles involve the U of N approach to education: 'Character development' is an 'integral part of the curriculum', and 'educational excellence' is also part of the commitment in equipping students for ministry. The commitment to academics is combined with an emphasis on spiritual formation 'through an emphasis on knowing and loving God and seeking His revelation and guidance'. This formation takes place with students in 'every course' being involved in 'regular times of intercession and worship' as well as living in community with others, as discussed earlier in this chapter.

The final section of the Founding Principles declares that every course in every College/Faculty of the U of N should be a 'multiplier for missions', and should equip and send workers to the mission field. As part of that commitment, every student experiences 'field assignments with cross-cultural experiences' that are a 'fundamental feature of the University training programmes'. These U of N Founding Principles, when placed alongside the YWAM Foundational Values, ensure a cohesiveness of unity to the international diversity of students and courses, and provides a framework of accountability as well. The range of mission objectives, from more traditional approaches in evangelism and church planting to being 'salt and light' for societal transformation, is encompassed in a complexity of methods and goals. The equipping of students from all nations, going to all nations with all potential approaches, reflects the increasing diversity of the global context in the 21st century.

The Rest of the 21st Century

In the remaining eighty-five years of the 21st century, equipping for mission will continue to take place in a context marked globally by an increasingly diverse group of students. The values of YWAM/U of N in their emphasis on international and denominational diversity, as well as decentralised structures, should lend themselves well to this context. The challenge of holding together equipping mechanisms for mission across wide geographic and cultural gaps will continue to be evident for the U of N and all institutions/missions involved in training.

In recent research on understanding the nature of power in the 21st century, the idea of 'new power' is contrasted with 'old power'.[22] 'Old power,' write the authors, 'works like a currency, held by a few and jealously guarded.' 'New power', however, is 'like a current: open,

---

[22] Research was recently published by Jeremy Heimans and Henry Timms in the *Harvard Business Review*, Dec 2014 (accessed: 4th December 2014).

participatory and peer-driven'. It has an emphasis on 'co-ownership', represented by the models of Wikipedia and Alpha courses worldwide, and has a 'special emphasis on collaboration'. The shift to these new power dynamics is being led particularly by those under 30 (over half the world's population) where the 'common assumption is emerging that we all have an inalienable right to participate'.

The authors postulate that, while 'power is shifting in the world', 'society's old power superstructures' have been harder to change. This includes educational systems, which have remained 'largely unchanged, with school timetables still built around family lifestyles of the 1800s'. While the authors are writing in a context of secular education, it is also true in global mission education, where outdated models are at times used without reflection or evaluation.

In this article, Heimans and Timms provide some 'essential tasks' for 'traditional organizations' that want to develop a 'new power capacity'. They must 1) evaluate their role in a context of shifting power, suggesting that groups do a 'power audit'; 2) listen to critical voices, engaging in 'painful conversations' both internally and externally; 3) increase their ability to mobilise more people to be involved by developing a 'movement mindset'. How is YWAM/U of N currently doing with these three tasks, and what is the prognosis for the next decades of the century?

With this case study of YWAM/U of N, and how students are equipped for mission in the 21st century, the coming years of the century will continue to see the importance of collaboration globally in a variety of contexts and cultures. There will need to be a complex synergy of 'old power' and 'new power' models in values and approaches. Heimans and Timms propose that today 'the right strategy for the moment is to go bilingual, developing both old and new power capacities'. YWAM/U of N, with a blend of mission strategies and approaches as well as degree programmes and adapted accreditation, could provide a possible and important model as the 21st century unfolds. As seen in the section in this chapter on the DTS model, an 'old' model of training is being evaluated and adapted into very diverse contexts, yet keeping its purposes and aims intact. Critical listening will continue to be crucially important in the coming decades in this changing global context.

In closing their article, the authors write that 'the greatest test for the conductors of new power will be their willingness to engage with the challenges of the least powerful'. In equipping for mission in the 21st century, an emphasis on those having 'least access to the message of the Gospel', as evidenced in the U of N Founding Principles, must be a strong priority for churches and mission training programmes. This may require a closer evaluation of what approaches to training are currently being used and a willingness to change and adapt them where needed. The change in context of a world now involving a mission sending paradigm as diverse as

Mongolia to Bolivia requires old approaches to be combined with new ones.

NETWORKING FOR THE SAKE OF MISSION IN THEOLOGICAL EDUCATION: THE CASE OF ACTEA AND THEOLOGICAL EDUCATION IN AFRICA

Emmanuel Chemengich

Introduction

In this article, I seek to highlight networking for mission in sub-Saharan Africa in a two-pronged approach. In the first place, I show how the Association for Christian Theological Education in Africa (ACTEA) has shaped the collaborative and networking nature and goals of mission for the African church through its mission and services to theological institutions. By its very nature, ACTEA is a networking organisation for member theological institutions in Africa, and subsequently plays a vital role in shaping the unfolding landscape of the church's mission to the African society and beyond.[1] In this regard, I will state how ACTEA is equipping institutions for mission at their leadership and learners' levels. And finally, I present two case studies of ACTEA's member institutions that exhibit unique models that reflect on and equip its students for mission.

But before we proceed, it is necessary to define and clarify two terms used extensively in this article, 'mission' and 'theological education'. We use 'mission' here in the context of every individual being called by God, but also collectively together as the church, to a specific calling that fulfils God's agenda to the world. Subsequently, we are here referring to 'mission' entrusted to individuals and specific church ministries. Thus, we shall be looking at the mission of the African church as a strand within the larger, universal mission of the Lord's global church, in which God is using her to reach out and transform African society and the entire world.

And we use the term 'theological education' in reference to the formal theological training that leads to an award of a recognised academic credential such as a 'Certificate', 'Diploma', 'Degree', etc. and not in the informal training format often offered outside training institutions (e.g. churches or mission centres), such as is done by Theological Education by Extension (TEE). For this reason, we shall limit ourselves to theological training programmes offered within formal theological institutions.

---

[1] For more information on ACTEA, visit www.ACTEAweb.org

Understanding ACTEA and its Networks

ACTEA stands for Association for Christian Theological Education in Africa (formerly, Accrediting Council for Theological Education in Africa). ACTEA is a project of Association of Evangelicals in Africa (AEA) and was founded in 1976 in Nairobi, Kenya, by Dr Byang Kato, then AEA's General Secretary. The primary mission of ACTEA is 'to promote quality evangelical theological education in Africa by providing supporting services, facilitating academic recognition, and fostering continental and inter-continental co-operation'.

ACTEA is the only network and support service for evangelical theological education throughout Africa. It seeks to assist evangelical theological schools and programmes throughout Africa in their quest for excellence and renewal. Since its founding in 1976, ACTEA has become widely accepted as the most active service body for theological education on the continent. Dr Paul Bowers observes: 'When a history of evangelical theological education in modern Africa comes to be written, it will doubtless take as a defining moment the founding in 1976 of the Accrediting Council for Theological Education in Africa... For it was with the emergence of ACTEA that evangelical theological education in Africa first gained that sense of common identity, that sense of community, of shared values promoting quality evangelical theological education in Africa, that has so bonded and energized the movement to a degree that we almost take for granted today.'[2]

Christian universities are mushrooming in Africa, but this is believed to enhance the significance of ACTEA rather than diminish it. For one thing, due to lack of theological knowledge and expertise in government accrediting agencies, Christian universities in Africa need ACTEA as much as theological colleges and seminaries do.

At the global level, ACTEA was a founding member of the International Council for Evangelical Theological Education (ICETE) in 1980. And through ICETE, ACTEA is linked with regional bodies around the world.[3] ICETE is a Global Partner with the World Evangelical Alliance (WEA).

---

[2] Paul Bowers. 'Theological Education in Africa: Why Does It Matter?' (unpublished paper presented at AIM-SIM Theological Education Consultation, Honeydew, South Africa, 19th-23rd March 2007): www.theoledafrica.org/OtherMaterials/Files/TheologicalEducationInAfrica_WhyDoesItMatter.pdf

[3] These regional bodies include the Asia Theological Association (ATA), the Caribbean Evangelical Theological Association (CETA), the Association for Biblical Higher Education [North America] (ABHE), the Association for Evangelical Theological Education in Latin America (AETAL), the European Evangelical Accrediting Association (EEAA), the Euro-Asian Accrediting Association (E-AAA), and the South Pacific Association of Bible Colleges (SPABC).

Importance of theological education in equipping for mission in the Africa context

The African continent has abundant natural resources, not least in its people. Yet ironically, it is a continent that is constantly facing myriad problems and an uncertain future. African nations are beset by social, religious, political and economic problems that are overwhelmingly huge and complex. Among these nations are Egypt, Mali, Central African Republic, Nigeria, Democratic Republic of Congo, Libya, Somalia, Sudan, South Sudan, Eritrea, Zimbabwe, Tunisia, Mozambique, Guinea-Bissau and Ethiopia – to name but a few.

Granted its historical profile, its current presence in the continent, and its core mandate of transforming humanity for God, Christianity can and must play a central role in any change that needs to take place in Africa. Despite the fact that Christianity has been in existence in some parts of Africa for more than 1,800 years, its contribution to socio-political and economic transformation, and moral and intellectual progress, remains woefully inadequate.

It is in the midst of this unfortunate state of affairs that African churches must be equipped to play a central role in addressing these many problems in African society. Equipping African churches means building their capacity to gain greater strength, depth and maturity with regard to its mission mandate to African societies in their current state of instability. Strong and mature churches must uphold the highest moral and ethical standards that are biblically shaped and guided. Consequently, empowered African churches must become models to society because they are demonstrating themselves as credible entities. The result of all this is that churches can influence and transform society for the better.

African churches can achieve strength, depth and maturity through quality and relevant theological education that produces transformed Christians that are both thinkers and doers. In many African nations, there is a constitutional right to freedom of religion. Many of the churches are experiencing remarkable growth. There is also economic growth, even though not widely and evenly spread across the continent. All this presents African churches with an opportunity to impact society through leadership and scholarship that are creative, biblical, contextually relevant and thoroughly informed by a transforming vision of God's purpose in and for the world. ACTEA exists to help institutions to achieve this vision.

Networking for Mission: How ACTEA Reflects on and Equips for Mission

In this section, I show how ACTEA is equipping institutions at their leadership and learners' level for mission through its networking and accreditation services respectively.

Mission in ACTEA networking services

The church's mission plays a crucial role in ACTEA's networking services. Through its mandate to offer support services to member institutions, ACTEA has partnered with like-minded organisations in building the capacity of leaders and faculty of theological institutions in mainstreaming the church's mission into their training programmes. With these partners, ACTEA facilitates workshops and conferences at regional, continental and international levels. ACTEA's key partner in facilitating capacity-building forums that prioritise the church's mission is the Overseas Council International (OCI), and the forums include: 'Institutes of Excellence', 'Global Associates for Transformational Education' and 'International Program for Academic Leadership (IPAL)'. Some of the topics and themes in the recent workshops and conferences include: 'Spiritual Formation in the Seminary'; 'Effective Teaching and Learning'; and 'Curriculum Design and Contextualization'.

Mission in ACTEA accreditation services

In many African nations, ACTEA is the only source of international academic recognition available for evangelical theological education. Some institutions that have obtained government recognition also continue to look to ACTEA for recognition of the academic quality and evangelical ethos of their theological training programmes.

ACTEA Standards for accreditation were last revised and edited in 2011 to make them more relevant and effective in influencing and shaping the perspectives and content of theological education programmes and their effects on graduates in all its member institutions. While other aspects of ACTEA Standards deal with five key institutional operations – that is, administration, facilities, staffing, academics and students, I will make selective reference to only those aspects from these sections that directly impact the equipping of theological learners for the church's mission to the world. As a result, except for administration and staffing, most of my selected Standards fall within the nature and design of institutional academic programmes that include the nature of library holdings, curriculum design, supervised field experiences, and requirements for individual student graduation.

What follows is a presentation of ACTEA's Standards that are geared towards shaping theological education for mission.

ACTEA STANDARDS ON ADMINISTRATION:

On funding of theological institutions, the Standard on finances reads in part:

'More than half of the institution's annual operational expenditure related to theological education should be derived from within the continent. Where this is not yet the case, there must be in operation a realistic plan to increase locally-derived support to that level.'

The rationale informing this Standard is for theological institutions to ensure they do not wholly or continually depend on their well-endowed western partners or collaborating agencies in funding institutional operations. Granted the restrictive nature of donor funds, dependence on external funds can cripple an institution's ability to prioritise and be good stewards of its financial resources, and can tilt the institutional mission to the donor's priority.

ACTEA STANDARDS ON STAFFING:

Here, the Standards on staff read in part:

'The institution must evidence achievements in Africanisation of the governing board and of the senior administrative positions, or responsible efforts towards Africanisation wherever an African majority is not already present.'

Further, on preparing non-African teaching staff:

'For non-African staff there must be evidence of adequate orientation in the African setting.'

This Standard ensures that theological institutions intentionally recruit Africans for key administrative and teaching positions in order for them to make significant contributions from and for their own cultural settings. The purpose of this Standard is to promote contextualisation of administrative and teaching staff with regard to the community served by the institution. Among other benefits, this action eliminates the cross-cultural barriers that often hinder non-African staff from addressing the core needs of learners. And finally, Africanisation of an institution's staff protects it from continued reliance on missionary personnel and initiatives from the West that has left western-founded churches in a state of immaturity with regard to their stewardship of personnel, as well as inability to prioritise the unique mission agendas of their immediate contexts.

ACTEA STANDARDS ON ACADEMIC PROGRAMMES:

(a) Standards on Library Holdings:

The Standard on Library holdings reads in part:

'The holdings should represent both breadth and concentration; breadth with reference, for example, to academic levels, theological orientations, and subjects covered; concentration with reference, for example, to the theological orientation of the institution, the geographical and cultural context of the institution, and the subjects of instruction at the institution. The reference collection and periodicals received should manifest a similar blend of general breadth and specific concentration.'

This Standard articulates the important role the library plays in availing a knowledge database to the learning community of the institution, but with special focus on both the breadth and depth as well as sufficiency and rate of accessibility to the readers. In addition, this Standard seeks to ensure that library stocks are well oriented and relevantly confronting and speaking to the immediate context (geographical, cultural, and religious) of the learners.

(b) Standards on Programme Integration and Graduation Requirement: The Standard on Curriculum Integration reads in part:

> 'The institution's theological education programmes, including non-residential programmes, programmes offered through modular or block scheduling, and/or distance programmes, should evidence a holistic approach, combining both curricular and extracurricular activities in an educational plan which embraces concern for the students' spiritual and vocational as well as academic development. Thus worship, community life, work, sports, social activities, practical Christian service, and so forth, should be intentionally and manifestly shaped to further the institution's objectives for theological education. Institutions are also encouraged to develop co-curricular enrichment programmes for theological education, such as lectureships, workshops, and field trips.'

The purpose of this Standard is to ensure a holistic approach to prepare and mould learners for the wider context that forms an important part of their pastoral and congregational ministries. This Standard also affirms the importance of the student's spiritual and vocational development as essential in forming a well-rounded Christian leader with the capacity for effective societal transformation.

It is worth noting here another related Standard on graduation requirement because it affirms and supplements the importance of this stated integrated curriculum, and reads in part: 'The institution must demonstrate that consideration of the spiritual and vocational as well as the academic development of the student is an integral part of the evaluation procedures which determine the student's suitability for graduation from its theological education programmes.'

(c) Standards on Curriculum Relevance:
The Standard on Curriculum Relevance reads in part:

> 'The theological education curriculum as a whole and the syllabus for each individual course subject should show that the institution has not merely borrowed these from elsewhere, nor simply allowed them to develop on an ad hoc basis, but that the institution has carefully planned the curriculum and each syllabus to meet its own particular objectives, for the specific Christian community it is serving, for the specific vocations for which the students are being prepared, and for the specific cultural context in which the students will minister. Classroom interaction and course assignments should encourage students to relate each course subject to the students' cultural, church and

community contexts. Selection of textbooks should also show sensitivity to contextual relevance.'

This Standard helps highlight the importance of relevance in the study programmes offered in a theological institution. Relevance is often evaluated and measured by the effectiveness of these curricula to help learners engage and confront the context in which they are being prepared to serve. In addition, member institutions must show commitment to this Standard by providing for ongoing, periodic reviews and evaluations of its curriculum in the light of ever-changing contexts of ministry and societal realities.

(d) Standards on Curriculum Balance:
The Standard on curriculum balance reads in part:

> 'The content of the theological education curriculum of the institution must be justified in relation to the normal spread of subjects in post-secondary theological curricula, with regard to Biblical, theological, historical, practical, and general areas of study. There must also be neither significant omission nor undue overlap in the overall body of knowledge and skills being conveyed.'

The goal of this Standard is to ensure theological curricula in all member institutions operate within an agreed spread of specialised study areas in theological education, such as biblical, theological, historical, practical and general areas of study. This balance in theological study programmes exposes learners to the diverse dimensions of theological scholarship and the way it interfaces with other related study disciplines. Consequently, it is in reviewing the 'general studies' section that many of our member institutions have introduced courses that interface with theology and the pastoral mission of the church, such as Psychology, Sociology, Community Development, and Interreligious Studies.

(e) Standards on Guided Practical Experience:
The ACTEA Standard on supervised practical experience reads in part:

> 'For theological education programmes which are focused on vocational preparation (e.g. pastoral training), institutions shall incorporate into the requirements for graduation arrangements for guided practical experience in the specific vocations in which the individual students are being prepared. This may, for example, take the form of an internship programme. Institutions are strongly encouraged to incorporate similar arrangements for guided practical experience into the graduation requirements of any other theological education programmes it offers, in the specific curriculum areas in which the individual students are being prepared.'

The primary purpose of this Standard is to expose students to practical and pastoral experiences in order to assist them in integrating the knowledge learned in classroom settings with practical aspects of the church's missional context. This Standard helps institutions provide a mechanism that fosters healthy relations and involvement of their students with the local community they are being prepared to serve. In addition, this emphasis on supervised and assessed field experiences guarantees graduates that are well equipped to engage in the mission work of the church.

Mission in African Theological Institutions: Case Studies of Two Institutions

In this section, I present two ACTEA member institutions as case studies to demonstrate the direct impact of the above standards in shaping their unique models for training and equipping African Christian and church leaders for mission. These two African institutions have intentionally placed mission at the centre of, not only their curriculum, but also their practice of theological education. While the first institution has put mission at the centre of its programme design through implementing an in-service training model, the latter has designed its curricula to intentionally apportion a higher proportion of it to mission-oriented courses.

Africa Theological Seminary (ATS), Kenya

Africa Theological Seminary (ATS) is an interdenominational institution located in Kitale, Kenya, and is owned and managed by International Christian Ministries (ICM), a para-church organisation serving several countries in Africa.[4] ATS offers programmes at undergraduate levels in two departments, namely, the Theology and Counseling Departments. Thus the seminary awards Diploma and BA degrees in both 'Bible and Theology' and 'Counseling'. In addition, ATS has a 'Christian Leadership Institute' (CLI) which serves as a key resource centre in providing required field education materials for the students' Field Practicum. CLI has materials that include the following: Bruce Wilkinson's 'Walk Thru the Bible'; John Maxwell's 'Purpose-Driven Materials'; and Bruce Wilkinson's 'Teach the Nations'.

With regard to its educational philosophy and approach, ATS believes that effective learning takes place within the context of the mission in which the students are serving. It should be noted that, to make this arrangement possible, ATS admits only students involved in ministry. Thus they train 'in ministry' and not 'for ministry'. The driving motto of ATS is clearly expressed in its philosophy: 'Training the Mind; Instructing the Heart; and Empowering the Hands'.

In order to ensure students learn and continue applying what they learn in their ministry settings, ATS has a unique programme design that is 100% in-service or modular. In this modular design, learners come to the seminary for residential classwork for a period of three to four weeks, three

---

[4] For more information on ATS, visit its website, www.atseminary.ac.ke.

times a year. Thus it is a trimester system where they are residential for one month for classroom work to cover three to four courses, and return back to their mission stations for three months of ministry work before returning back for residential lectures for the next month. And this goes on until completion of their studies.

For all courses, 80% of the course work (lectures, exams, presentations, group work) is completed during the one-month residency period, while the remaining 20% is done and completed in the context of their ministry during the three-month non-residential time referred to as 'Field Assignment'. The Field Assignment is a written assignment which must be contextual because it should relate to the relevant aspect of the student's current ministry involvement.

In addition to the course work (residential and field assignment), all ATS students are required to complete Field Practicums before graduating. In order to fulfil this requirement, ATS students select materials from the CLI Resource Centre and teach them in the context of their ministry with on-site supervision provided by an appointed faculty or ATS representative (mostly ATS alumni). The student completes the Field Practicum by submitting a written paper detailing the content of the Field Practicum (following a format guideline), his/her personal experiences, and what they learned from the same.

Through this in-service/modular delivery system, ATS has successfully designed a model which permits learners to integrate what they learn in the classroom within the context of the learners' mission contexts. In doing this, ATS has allowed knowledge learned in class to address the realities of the mission work of its students. In this way, ATS has not only contextualised lessons learned in class to the learners' contexts, but has also succeeded in placing mission at the centre, not at the end, of the theological training process by making students lifetime learners and reflective ministry practitioners.

Jos ECWA Theological Seminary (JETS), Nigeria

Jos ECWA Theological Seminary (JETS) is an institution located in Jos, Plateau State, Nigeria, serving the Evangelical Churches of West Africa (ECWA).[5] JETS offers theological diploma and degree programmes distributed into three study disciplines: pastoral ministries, teaching ministries, and communication ministries. In addition, JETS offers summer classes through its 'Institute of Pastoral Studies' to meet the continued needs of pastors, and special programme for wives of JETS' diploma and degree students through its 'Women's Institute'. Successful completion of

---

[5] Information on JETS contained in this article is sourced from Robert W. Perris, *Renewal in Theological Education: Strategies for Change* (Wheaton, IL: Billy Graham Center, 1990), 79-89.

these two programmes leads to an award of a 'Certificate in Church Ministries' and a 'Certificate in Bible' respectively.

Most training programmes at JETS have been developed in direct response to the needs of constituent ECWA churches through a request from them for a particular educational service and professional skills for ministry. Thus JETS reviews and evaluates its curriculum periodically in order to incorporate the desired changes into it. The overriding purpose of all these reviews is the strong conviction and desire for the contextualisation of a theology that is predominantly western-oriented into the African setting.[6]

With regard to its educational philosophy and approach, JETS combines classroom teaching, field education, advice from faculty, and personal discipleship. Field education includes training in evangelism and discipleship, and each student is given placement in a local church or Christian ministry setting under direct field supervision. Further, in its curricula, JETS has intentionally assigned a high number of courses to the 'Ministry Skills' division for all the BA study programmes it offers. This amounts to 27.5% for BA in Pastoral Ministries, 45.6% for BA in Communication Ministries, and 46.2% for BA in Teaching Ministries.

The biblical and theological divisions are covered during the first two years, while the third and fourth years are reserved for the division on 'Ministry Skills' for the professional development of learners. In adopting this curriculum strategy where a high ratio of course work is dedicated to professional development, JETS has demonstrated not just its sensitivity to the missional agenda and issues of the church, but also prioritised it through practically amending its curriculum design to cater for the same.

In implementing a mission-sensitive and skill-oriented approach through reformatting its curricula, JETS has both successfully implemented a contextualisation of ministry training that is responsive and relevant to its constituents, and significantly placed the mission of the church at the centre, and not at the end of the theological training process.

Conclusion

We have examined here ACTEA's work on mainstreaming the church's missional agenda into theological training through both its accreditation processes, and its networking and support services. By intentionally incorporating the mission of the church into capacity-building workshops and conferences with participants from member institutions and in its Accreditation Standards, and ensuring member institutions implement them in the light of their specific institutional objectives, ACTEA has inspired member institutions, as shown in the two case studies in this article, to

---

[6] Robert W. Perris, *Renewal in Theological Education*, 83-84.

prioritise and mainstream the mission of the church into its theological training processes.

The two case studies show how the two institutions have mainstreamed mission into the centre and not at the end of their theological programmes. Thus, Africa Theological Seminary (ATS), through its in-service/modular study programme design, has succeeded in integrating theory and practice in mission, and subsequently placed mission at the centre of its theology training. And Jos ECWA Theological Seminary (JETS) has satisfactorily integrated the missional agenda into its theological training curricula. In both cases, we get two unique and exemplary models to inspire us all to be intentional in prioritising and integrating the mission of the church into theological training at the curricula and programme delivery design levels.

ONLINE EDUCATION MISSION
IN AN INTERNET WORLD

Richard Hart

Two of the most important divisions of Online Mission are Online Mission Proclamation, OMP, and Online Mission Education, OME. Two important perspectives on OMP and OME are the viewpoints and intentions of the website providers, and the viewpoints and desires of the online website users or visitors.

Online Mission Proclamation concerns itself with four Gospel-centred focuses. Each focus is important and all are necessary.

- First, OMP web designers seek to present the Gospel of our Lord Jesus Christ. Gospel presentations are done in ways that help the site visitor understand what it means to be a follower of Jesus Christ. Such websites try to create a welcoming climate that encourages repeat visits.

- Second, OMP provides information and perhaps classes that train a person in becoming better at communicating the Gospel.

- Third, OMP provides the viewer with information on people who are involved in Gospel-sharing and thereby help to widen the viewers' network.

- Fourth, OMP includes the developers of software that enables Gospel-sharing believers to develop and store teaching materials for online and offline use. Online Mission Proclamation is carried out by churches and para-church providers.

These features describe for the most part the perspective of the OMP providers. But what are the perspectives of the people who visit the website? What are their desires? And how do they learn about the OMP web presence of OMP providers?

Website visitors usually visit a new site on the basis of referral from someone, or after doing a keyword search through a search engine, or seemingly by chance. OMP sites seek to draw web surfers. When visitors arrive at the website and look around, their search is based on their own particular interests. Sometimes they visit the website on the basis of or curiosity about the topic. Their curiosity may be guided by positive, negative or neutral feelings towards the topic.

OMP websites may offer two kinds of use. One will be for general use for everyone. A second option requires a user login and a user password. When users choose to create a personal login with usernames and passwords, they do this because they want more interaction and or greater access to the information services of the website.

Some visitors may become daily users of the website until their need to know more about the topics presented diminishes. Other visitors, because of their dislike of the website and its topics of discussion, may be adversarial and seek to find ways to undermine the website. Another kind of visitor is the neutral person. This individual may look deeper into the website topic or surf to somewhere else. They may or may not remember the website. Some neutral visitors will become curious enough to consider a return visit.

Online Mission Proclamation providers seek to create links that will encourage continuing connections with the visitor to their website. Ongoing communication may occur through chat rooms, emails and sometimes on paper through postal mail. OMP websites evaluate themselves based on numbers of visitors, and perhaps more importantly, on the development of ongoing relationships with their website visitors.

Online Mission Education focuses on training disciples to become effective in the proclamation of the Gospel. OME takes place through websites, online courses and study programmes. OME is provided by organisations and institutions.

OME users are normally referred to OME sites by friends, pastors or advisors. OME users usually have a good idea of what they want. They may be looking for mission education information or they may want to connect with a study programme that gives credit and helps them gain a credential. OME sites that are connected to higher education institutions offer classes for credit and not-for-credit. Users make choices based on the amount of time they want to invest.

Both OMP and OME leaders seek to heighten the desire of website visitors to learn about the Gospel and live out its implications. OMP and OME communicators try to help people online discover ways in which the Gospel gives guidance for the challenges and choices of modern life.

Many of the characteristics of OMP and OME are similar. OMP focuses more on serving users who are looking for truth to live by. OMP providers seek to help new believers in the Lord Jesus Christ deepen their discipleship to him. Online Mission Education seeks to provide training for disciples who want to learn how to do evangelism and train others to do the same. Since there is a strong relationship between OMP and OME, we will look at twelve characteristics they share. We will also use the term Online Mission as a term that includes both OMP and OME.

1. Online Mission is motivated by a sense of urgency to make the Gospel of Jesus Christ known. Life as God meant it to be is revealed in the Gospel of the Lord Jesus Christ. In the Gospel, men and women have the opportunity to experience spiritual rebirth that starts in the present with effect for all eternity. The Gospel makes it clear that refusing its message leads to darkness and doom in this life, and in the life to come after death.

As people embrace the Gospel of the Lord Jesus Christ, they come alive to God. They begin to see the world through the principles and promises of God. By faith, they submit to the good news of the Gospel and find God the Holy Spirit living in them. With this experiencing of God, there grows a profound desire to please God and to learn more about him.

2. Online Mission points to the transformational elements of the Gospel. A wholesome fellowship with God results from knowing, believing and accepting the Gospel of the Lord Jesus Christ. This relationship with God through the Gospel produces an urgent desire to tell others the Gospel. The Gospel communicator seeks to make the message so clear that others in every culture will start to experience the rebirth the Gospel brings.

Springing from the Gospel are the intangibles of hope, confidence and certainty. In discovering God's personal presence in one's life, there emerges a strong sense of purpose and calling. Life becomes something to be shared more deeply with others. People, who previously thought only of themselves, become care-givers for others.

3. Online Mission providers emphasise values. These are formative values that are also found in approaches to non-formal education, like Theological Education by Extension (TEE). The four key values are accessibility, servant orientation, focus on the Bible-in-context, and church relatedness.[1]

Access, both for the OMP and OME communicators as well as the message recipients, is greatly increased through internet communication. For the OMP and the OME communicator, the investment of funds is relatively small. Similarly, on the receiving end, a simple hand-held device may be enough for the user to receive and send.

Online Mission communication rapidly adapts to changes in technology because of the urgency of getting the Gospel message out to its potential audience. Online Mission communication is often at the leading edge of technological innovation with solar-powered devices and satellite phones that operate without a microwave tower system. All of this is in the name of access.

Online Mission providers are characterised by a servant orientation. They have a deep desire to serve the people with whom they seek to communicate. Providers communicate a generosity of spirit. They share technical help free of charge. Every effort is made to accommodate the needs of the site visitor. Email and Skype-like communication provide direct communication between the site user and site managers.

Online Mission providers promote two-way email traffic, not because they are trying to sell a product or make money, but because they have a genuine concern for the enquirer. Interactive web sites are provided for

---

[1] Robert W. Ferris, 1986: 'Accrediting TEE: Steps Toward Understanding and Practice' (a paper presented at the 1986 Annual Meeting of the Philippine Association for Theological Education by Extension (PAFTEE), held at Sacred Heart Novitiate, Novaliches, Quezon City, 29th-31st January 1986), 6-8.

chatting. Providers point enquirers to other resources that might be able to help in the respondent's search for answers.

Online Mission websites seek to maintain politeness, regardless of the sorts of comments that are posted for public viewing. The approach comes from a desire to live out the Royal Law of the Bible to 'Love your neighbour as yourself'. Politeness contributes to return website visits. Online Mission users are additionally served when their internet conversations are encrypted.

Online Mission seeks to help visitors to come to understand the Bible in its context and ways it may be applied to the contexts of site visitors. In a world of multiple cultures, languages and politics, Online Mission seeks to communicate the Biblical message of the Gospel of Jesus Christ with clarity to the people of the varied audiences it serves.

Church relatedness is a fourth value on which Online Mission is based. Here the understanding of church is believers in groups worshipping, praising, studying and serving together. Online Mission helps web visitors find groups (churches) that may help them grow in their understanding of the Gospel.

4. **Online Mission encourages collaborative innovation.** Creating Gospel web-based deliverables for Online Mission continues to be characterised by pioneer efforts and innovation. As new technologies emerge onto the market, Online Mission remains at the leading edge of experimentation.

A wholesome element of online education is that it gathers educators from many perspectives. Each contributor has some understanding of educational theory. As educators consider how best to create online education, they find themselves in conversation with one another.

This attitude leads to a healthy emphasis on collaboration. Sharing and co-operation of the internet world breeds *camaraderie*. Together, co-operating colleagues overcome technical and programming challenges. With this sharing comes a sense of group and individual ownership of the internet and its possibilities. These traits of the internet world at large are heightened in Online Mission.

5. **Online Mission depends on privacy.** Online Mission, although it uses public radio waves, delivers its message privately. Internet users connect with the website through their own personal internet identity or their phone. Users need not share anything about themselves when they visit the website. Privacy is an asset that enables the web visitor to visit websites with freedom.

In some places, exploring the truth of other groups is frowned upon. Sometimes this includes learning about the Gospel of Jesus Christ. Online Mission communicators seek to provide information on the Gospel that will point people to Christ in kind and gentle ways. The privacy of these encrypted internet accounts permits these conversations to occur.

6. **Online Mission is resource-friendly.** One of its attractive features is the immediate availability of complementary resources that can be found

quickly on the internet. These resources are usually in colour and come from various regions of the world. Users can find and listen to films through YouTube and other media providers that enhance learning. Colleagues can also prepare and post films that can be shared instantly. Online resources also include the people with whom one might chat. Ideas can be rapidly exchanged. Users may find that the best resources on the internet are the people they discover who have similar interests.

7. Online Mission may or may not be revenue-neutral. Online mission has an integrating idea that makes it different from most other forms of online information and education. Online Mission does not promote business ventures for making money. Online Mission is not conducted so that shareholders gain any benefit. Revenue and profit-taking is not the goal.

Since the beginning of the internet revolution, entrepreneurs have been exploring ways to make their internet efforts make them a profit. Whether the online activity sells consumer products, provides news and entertainment, or offers stand-alone courses or university degree programmes, a principal reason why these online providers maintain their internet presence is to increase the revenue of their company or institution.

Online Mission is different. Online Mission proclamation does not expect to earn revenue through its programming. It expects to attract interest through its interviews, drama, news reports, lectures and streaming video. It hopes to develop in viewers the desire to repeatedly return to the website for more discovery experiences of the Gospel of the Lord Jesus Christ in all his glory. Online Mission Education may or may not charge fees.

Online Mission is usually supported by donations from website visitors and by sponsoring companies that share the values of the Online Mission providers. When Online Mission services develop, they may become not-for-profit companies, cultural societies or churches. They develop a donor base of individuals and organisations that pay the costs of running the Online Mission entity. Internet writers, producers and technicians are paid out of these funds.

8. Online Mission seeks to be open to all. One can visit and enter into the activities of the website without needing previously earned certificates, diplomas or degrees. Web deliverables may be prepared for oral learners and readers. All viewers, whatever their educational background, are welcome. Discussions will often occur between people of different ages, backgrounds and nationalities. Everyone learns from one another. In OMP these characteristic are especially evident.

9. Online Mission may be non-credentialling or credentialling. Unlike much of theological education, OMP does not give academic or professional licensing certificates. Online Mission seeks to model Gospel sharing and holy living. The content providers seek to introduce the visitor to better discipleship practices. Evaluation is usually self-assessment. But

when OME is connected to institutions, it often helps with the credentialling of graduates.

10. Online Mission is energised by love for God and love for neighbour. What is it that keeps Online Mission supporters, providers and technicians going when there may be no money to pay them? It is evident that they keep on serving because of their love for God and their love for their neighbours who need the touch of the Gospel. This application of the Royal Law – as it is called in the Letter of James (James 2:8) – is an essential part of the ethos of Online Mission.

11. Online Mission sees itself as a partner with others. When the Lord Jesus Christ sent his disciples into the world to disciple, baptise and teach others the Gospel, he did not send them as lone workers. He sent them as partners in service. In his three years with them in partner-building, he showed them how they needed to work together if they were to succeed as his disciples. Throughout the New Testament, we see believers seeking other believers for help in making the Gospel known.

Online Mission developers eagerly seek to engage with others of similar conviction and purpose. Together, Online Mission colleagues are able to stimulate one another to achieve the innovations needed to maintain their active web presence.

12. Online Mission creates networks of helpers. Online technologies are complex. When people work in Online Mission, nearly every problem that is faced has already been experienced by someone else. As one works in the online environment and becomes acquainted with others in the same field, people begin to share the ways they solved their internet communication problems. When solutions are shared, discussions start and best practices emerge. Some Online Mission providers develop a niche of helping others achieve their goals.

	Characteristic	OMP Church	OMP Parachurch	OME Organisation	OME Institution
1	Motivated by an Urgency to Make the Gospel Known	Yes	Yes	Yes	Yes
2	Points to the Transformational Elements of the Gospel	Yes	Yes	Yes	Yes
3	Emphasises Christian Values	Yes	Yes	Yes	Yes
4	Stimulates Collaborative Innovation	Yes	Yes	Yes	Often
5	Depends on Privacy	Yes	Yes	Yes	Yes
6	Resource-Friendly	Yes	Yes	Yes	Yes
7	Revenue-Neutral	Yes	Yes	Often	No
8	Open to All	Yes	Yes	No	No
9	Credentialling	No	No	No	Yes
	Non-Credentialling	Yes	Yes	Yes	No
10	Energised by Love for God and Love for Neighbour	Yes	Yes	Yes	No
11	Sees Itself as a Partner with Others	No	Yes	Yes	Yes
12	Creates Networks of Providers	No	Yes	Yes	No

Characteristics of Online Mission Providers

Online Mission Made Practical

The reader has observed that there are at least twelve traits that characterise Online Mission. We will look at two different Gospel-strengthening ministries that may be seen as examples of Online Mission. Each group demonstrates many of the twelve traits discussed earlier.

Online Mission Growth Opportunities

For centuries, Christians have lived and been a part of society in eastern Mediterranean nations. Moving across North Africa in a westerly direction, however, the situation of Christian witness was until recently quite different. Christian disciples in western Mediterranean countries were rare. Now, many in North Africa are finding hope and rebirth in the Gospel.

Libyans, Tunisians, Algerians and Moroccans are discovering and accepting the Gospel of the Lord Jesus Christ. They are looking for ways to grow. They are seeking to know Christ better.

As eastern Mediterranean friends met these new followers of Christ from the western Mediterranean, a natural bond quickly developed. The Royal Law, 'Love your neighbour as yourself,' (James 2:8), energised the easterners to look for ways to help their western Mediterranean friends deepen their knowledge. Easterners in consultation with westerners began to develop a plan.

Evangelical leaders who were related to member institutions of the Middle East Association for Theological Education (MEATE: www.meate.org) and media specialists with the Middle Eastern broadcasting network known as SAT-7 formed a partnership.

The common goal was to help western Mediterranean followers of Christ deepen their understanding of the Gospel and discover ways to enhance their gospel ministry. The project was funded by donor organisations that shared these common goals.

The leaders of MEATE, SAT-7 and the donors established a project and named it TEACH–LEARN (Theological Education for Arab Christians at Home – Leadership Education and Resource Network). The partners consulted together and through their various committees created a learning stream aimed at blending into the contexts of western Mediterranean followers of Christ. Project management was placed under the direction of one of the MEATE institutions. Staff members were hired and trained for preparing project outputs.

Project management invited theological scholars in Arab theological education to submit book texts. Writers from Bible colleges and seminaries in Lebanon, Jordan, Palestine and Egypt prepared study materials. Once the texts were completed, they were given to script writers for SAT-7 television programming, and also to course writers for internet web-based delivery. The goal was culturally relevant TV programming with Bible-in-context web-based deliverables. Both the TV programming and the web-based courses would be freely given to users.

During a five-year period, scholars and their institutions, project managers and e-learning writers developed 33 courses for the online environment. All the courses became available free to Arabic speakers everywhere. In addition, students from any MEATE institution were able to study the same courses online or in their homes.

The project successfully brought together human resources from many institutions. Scholars, writers, producers, technicians and managers worked together to produce context-friendly learning materials. More online courses continue to be prepared. The number of Online Mission students is increasing. Believers in churches large and small are being drawn into TEACH–LEARN. Every day, the Online Mission platform of TEACH–LEARN encourages believers as they deepen their commitment to sharing the Gospel of the Lord Jesus Christ in their contexts.

A user interface was created by the TEACH–LEARN team in co-operation with the Bible Society of Lebanon. The site is called Bounian (www.bounian.com). Users can study all the TEACH–LEARN courses in the Arabic language free of charge in an online environment wherever the user happens to be. All the same courses are also available through MEATE member institutions. Courses can be taken for credit or not-for-credit.

Online Mission Strengthening Resources

An array of service providers appear in Online Mission efforts. Some focus on the online infrastructure with its internet accessing hardware. Others, like TEACH–LEARN, assemble scholars, script and course writers, producers, e-learning experts and managers to provide online programming and study materials.

Another group in the Online Mission field are those who come alongside the Online Mission community to help providers enhance their service. Sometimes this means helping providers simplify online software tools aimed at the end user. One such entity is MAF–*LT*, Mission Aviation Fellowship–*Learning Technologies*.

MAF is best known for its aviation services to church and mission personnel in remote areas of the world. Over the past ten years, however, MAF has positioned itself in a way that describes what it has always done well, but now opens up opportunities to add service alternatives to its creative and effective ministries. Stating their focus in one sentence, we can say MAF seeks to 'overcome barriers' in order to 'transform lives' to help in 'building God's Kingdom'.

MAF–*Learning Technologies* (MAF–*LT*) is one of those service alternatives that has become an important part of the organisation. MAF–*LT* develops software products for computers and mobile phones that bring

Online Mission resources to pastors and church workers wherever they live. These church workers are able to download the tools and create context-specific learning for their church members.[2] While many people have easy access to the internet, most people for various reasons do not. MAF–*LT* seeks to find offline ways to help end-users whatever their situation might be.

In addition, MAF–*LT* has developed a software product that enables the person living in locations where internet service is not reliable to produce lessons for teaching in their churches and ministries. The software programme MAF–*LT* has produced for this purpose is called Lumin and is a free download at www.maf.org/lumin. MAF–*LT* personnel will assist local curriculum writers in mastering the software. The goal is for local people to develop lesson materials for their own contexts. With these skills, writers can create, use, evaluate, revise and train others to do the same.

Another free software application developed by MAF–*LT* is called Estante which is an Android™ app. With this phone app, pastors may store digital resources that can be kept for use and sharing at any time. The user may store a whole library of resources on his mobile phone. Books, films and presentations can be viewed at any time and anywhere. Lessons developed on Lumin may also be stored on mobile devices with the Estante app.[3] This app is also available at www.maf.org/estante.

MAF–*LT* works in partnership with other Online Mission providers. Together, they are able to do what they cannot do alone. As a result, hundreds of pastors in rural and remote locations are being provided with resources that are enabling them to serve their churches more effectively.

Many pastors, church leaders and their congregations are oral learners. They may or may not be able to read. Resourcing these ministry colleagues means that teaching by story is needed in order to serve these contexts. MAF–*LT* also has produced story-telling software called Story Fire that can be used to teach the skill of story-telling and discussion-leading for people who learn best orally.[4]

The resources produced by MAF–*LT* are free for others to use simply by downloading them from the internet. With USB thumb drives or microSD cards, one can save the software and add it to the computer or mobile device at a later time. MAF–*LT* continues to develop and improve the software it produces. Training in the use of the software is available. The desire of MAF–*LT* is to serve the global church through the resources it provides in partnership with others.

---

[2] https://www.maf.org/about/lt#.VRpl0o4W6ZE (accessed 31st March 2015).
[3] https://www.maf.org/about/lt#.VRpl0o4W6ZE (accessed 31st March 2015).
[4] https://www.maf.org/about/lt#.VRr9MY4W6ZF (accessed 31st March 2015).

The Future

Encyclopædias share with us what has happened in the past and what the situation is at present. We do not know what the future will bring. But as we look at how processes and products develop, we expect that Online Mission will play an important role.

We expect that Global Mission partners will continue to develop simple software that may be easily used by pastors, teachers and youth workers around the world. Mobile devices will become the main learning-teaching tools for most youth and adults. In every region, believers will be empowered to develop training materials in their own languages for their own people.

As individuals share files through their hand-held devices, they will stimulate discussions that lead to learning, teaching and growth. Self-discipline will still be required. The challenge will be to choose, from all the available learning alternatives, the ones that are best suited for one's group. With this in mind, we will continue to ask Online Mission leaders to point us in directions that will result in nourishing us as local church leaders.

More voices will be heard. More will join the conversation because of global access to oral communication devices. Audio and video resources will become as important as written ones. Audio books will likely be in greater demand.

Although internet and mobile device communication will increase, we will still need to hold one another accountable for sharing the Gospel with our neighbours nearby and far away. May future generations out-perform past generations in sharing the Gospel in the cultures and contexts of all.

CMS PIONEER MISSION LEADERSHIP TRAINING – A NEW PATHWAY

Jonny Baker

To Make a Way Where There Is No Way

In the summer of 2014, we had our first graduation of students from the Church Mission Society (CMS) pioneer mission leadership training course in Oxford.[1] It was a wonderful occasion which we called 'To make a way where there is no way'. We gave students an object to symbolise the call, gift and journey of being a pioneer in mission. To produce these, we worked with a sculptor Iain Cotton who designed and made them. The objects were slate tiles in which a new unique path had been hewn to make a way where there was no way. The path was carved with a hammer and chisel, metaphorically making a way across a new landscape. The path also looks like a letter or script, and plays with the notion of a new language that is found in the journey. He described it on his write-up as speaking in tongues, a language of the Spirit. They look amazing and they really are a powerful sign of the gift that pioneers bring, and the journey that they make to share the Gospel of Jesus Christ with those beyond the margins of the church, joining in with God's mission of healing and transforming creation.

In the first term of the pilot year, I remember being surprised how much 'imagination' was the topic that students kept bringing up and talking about. As a result, *The Prophetic Imagination*[2] became a favourite text of that first group of students with its themes of prophecy, newness, grief and amazement. When there is no path, it has to be dreamed against the odds, seen and imagined. This act of radical imagination prefigures a world and a church that is not already here.[3] It requires a suspension of the normal to explore and entertain other ideas, and possible worlds and ways of doing things. Those seeing a new path need to hold open a space and let go of what is familiar and known and, whilst doing so, silence their inner or outer

---

[1] See http://pioneer.cms-uk.org
[2] Walter Brueggemann, *The Prophetic Imagination* (Minneapolis, MN: Augsburg Fortress Press, 1978).
[3] I came across the notion of prefigurative research in Max Haven and Alex Khasnabish, *Radical Imagination* (Halifax and Winnipeg: Fernwood Publishing, 2014), where they advocate designing research not based on the universe that currently exists but on the one that they imagine will exist in the future – i.e. their research prefigures that which is not already here. This seemed to me to be a helpful way of thinking about both church, the world and mission education.

critics listing the reasons why it can't be done. It is often nurtured in the face of resistance from the 'powers that be' who, on the one hand, say they want something new but, when push comes to shove, gravity seems to pull back in the direction of business as usual, of what we already know works. It's best nurtured in communities. Alongside this gift of seeing and imagination, the path in stone has to then be built and it's difficult to hew. The path in slate is a reminder that the gift that pioneers bring is not just about dreaming, it's about doing and building, making a way where there is no way, and finding the resources to make happen what is seen.

When the Spirit is given on the day of Pentecost and the apostles speak in tongues, the people gathered from many nations are amazed when they hear the message in their own native languages. This is an early indication that the relationship between Christian faith and culture is one that takes seriously the expression of that faith within local language and cultural forms – this process of inculturation then comes with the gift of the Spirit. This symbol, then, is a sign of seeing and imagining a way where there is none, of building and making something new happen, and of a new speech of the Spirit that is not in the language of the culture the pioneer has come from. but is inculturated in the language of those to whom they are sent. It embodies the essence of the pioneer gift.[4]

Pioneering in mission is not new. The church in mission has always had pioneers. Indeed, most of the saints remembered in the church were pioneers of one sort or another. But the current use of the term in the UK has risen to the surface in the last decade, largely thanks to the Church of England. Following a pattern of significant decline in church attendance over a series of decades, mission has come to the fore as something that the church needs to focus on for the way forward. There has been a growing realisation that the UK is a mission context, and the imagination, skills and lens of cross-cultural mission that is nurtured when a missionary travels to a country or culture elsewhere in the world is precisely what we need in our own context. Several waves of experimentation took place around the edges of the church in the UK over a period of around thirty years. In 2004, the Church of England published a report which described these as 'fresh expressions' of church and advocated for a mixed economy of church into the future which could hold both traditional and newer forms of church[5]. One of the recommendations in the report was that the church should identify, select and train 'pioneers and mission entrepreneurs'. Subsequently the Church of England recognised a new designation which joined the word 'pioneer' together with 'ministry', calling this vocation 'ordained pioneer ministry', which was a descriptor for people who could develop fresh expressions of church with those beyond the reach of existing

---

[4] I have expanded on the notion of what the pioneer gift is in Jonny Baker and Cathy Ross, *The Pioneer Gift* (London: Canterbury Press, 2014), chap. 1.
[5] Graham Cray (ed), *Mission-Shaped Church* (London: Church House Publishing, 2004).

churches. The church in the West has a tendency to focus on paid ordained leaders, but this movement has largely been lay-led with many of those volunteers or part-time rather than paid.

Theological courses and colleges quickly had to adapt to offer training for ordained pioneer ministers – in the Church of England colleges, sadly, lay pioneers don't get thought about or resourced in the same way – which is curious as they offer a very hopeful and economically viable way forward for the church as part of the mix of leading the church. The approach that many took was soon being described as 'priest plus', which refers to the assumption being that these pioneers need all the training of a parish priest, and then pioneering on top. This was partly because they only had two or three so they could not afford to create a pathway solely designed for pioneers. Two reviews highlighted the shortcomings of this approach and the frustrations of pioneers.[6] Some of the headlines were that there needs to be training in missiology, inculturation and new ecclesiology, those training should remain within their context and be trained on the job, that the mission communities or sodalities[7] of the church such as CMS are a good resource to draw on, and that the church needs not to neglect the recognition and training of lay pioneers. Reflecting on the experience of both recruiting and training pioneer ministers, the Church of England Ministry Division invited CMS to consider training pioneers and to do something imaginatively different from other pathways. CMS has been discerning, selecting, training and sending pioneers in mission into a whole range of contexts around the world for over 200 years. Pioneering is one of the CMS community's four values, and resourcing pioneer leaders in mission is one of the three aims of the community. We simply had to say yes!

Prefiguring –
Training for a World and Church that Is Not Already Here

Following the initial invitation, we took some time as a team to dream and design a new approach. One of the challenges in training leaders in today's church is that the church and world that we have known is rapidly changing, indeed disappearing. So rather than training leaders for the church as it has been, we need to design mission education that prefigures a

---

[6] These were Beth Keith, *The Fresh Expressions Report on the experiences of pioneers* (Fresh Expressions, 2010), and David Holbrooke and Kerry Thorpe, *The Church of England Ministry Division's review of pre-ordination training for ordained pioneer ministers* (2011).

[7] Ralph Winter, *The Two Structures of God's Redemptive Mission,* in Missiology: An International Review, 2.1, 121-39, explores how the mission of the church is best carried by two structures of the church as modality and sodality. Modality is geographically gathered and sodality is a spread-out mission community that is ecclesially gathered around a second-order commitment to mission or discipleship.

church and world that is not already here – or at least training that enables leaders to both draw on the tradition but in such a way as to be creative, adaptable and flexible enough to navigate new worlds. We also searched for anyone who had written about or taken a different missional approach to see what we could glean.[8] We researched various training pathways and courses to explore whether anything already existed which we could use as a vehicle rather than having to design everything from scratch. We landed on using a local university, Oxford Brookes, as they had a very flexible foundation degree in ministry which was modular and designed for in-context training, and which was used by a number of other colleges and dioceses in our region who were extremely helpful and welcoming to us when we were getting started. It was surprisingly easy to take the modules and adapt the teaching and assessment for pioneering mission based on what we had dreamed up. We were able to do all the teaching ourselves at our own site with our own teaching staff. Crucially, it also had creative possibilities for assessment by portfolios of evidence in which students demonstrate that they have fulfilled a gift and competency. Typically, a competency requires evidence of knowledge, experience, skills, and reflection on practice. Two years in, we also added in an MA as we had graduate students asking for it. It took longer than anticipated to do the paperwork and be approved by for the Church of England, but two years in we also took in our first group of pioneer ordinands.

We also formed a partnership with Ripon College Cuddesdon, a Church of England theological college close by that uses the same university awards. For students training for ordained pioneer ministry, they do a series of weekends each year with the college alongside training with us to give them a wider experience of formation for ministry which is not just with pioneers. This combination is ideal formation for leaders in a mixed-economy church as it enables students to gain experience of two different learning communities with quite different cultures, pedagogies, ecclesiologies and theologies. Some students find this challenging at first but grow to appreciate the gifts in both. It has been made easier because Cathy Ross, who leads the MA, is also part-time on the staff at the college. Along with many others, we are now in the midst of a process of transition to accrediting through Durham University but hope that we are able to retain the flexibility and creativity we have developed so far.

---

[8] For example, Robert Banks, *Re-envisioning Theological Education: Exploring a Missional Alternative to Current Models* (Grand Rapids, MI: Eerdmans, 1999); Parker Palmer, *To Know As We Are Known* (San Francisco, CA: Harper & Row 1983); Perry Shaw, *Transforming Theological Education* (Langham Global Library, 2014); Darren Cronshaw, 'Re-envisioning Theological Education, Mission and the Local Church' in *Mission Studies*, Vol. 28, No 1 (2011).

Every course or college is orienting in a particular way. Mission is our true North,[9] orienting everything around the magnetic pull of the *missio Dei* as we seek to join in with God's transformation of the world. Whilst others orient around World Christianity or Intercultural Studies or Practical Theology, we at CMS love mission in spite of the baggage that can be associated with the word. This pull has three aspects: the first is that mission itself is a lens through which everything is taught and integrates – so if we are teaching pastoral care or ethnography or worship, they lean towards mission. The second is the practice of mission. This sounds so obvious and so simple that I hardly dare write it down, but it strikes me that there are lots of places where theological education, missiology and, dare I say, even practical theology can be strangely disconnected from practice. All our students are engaged in pioneering mission. They typically come to us for one day a week so the questions and challenges they face are brought into the conversations and study, and generate what we sometimes refer to as 'heat in the room' that we welcome and work with. The action/reflection is on real questions.

We also value practice through bringing practitioners to contribute to every module and through hosting training weekends in pioneer communities to learn in their context. These have been some of the richest learning experiences. This is not to devalue the academic – in many ways, the practice encourages engagement with learning to better reflect on what is happening on the ground.

The third way in which we are oriented around a true North of mission is the particular focus on pioneering as described above. It is an amazing privilege to have a learning community of pioneers. They bring an amazing gift. Whilst leading the course has been demanding in lots of ways, it's also the most rewarding thing I have done in my life, and that is entirely due to the people themselves. It's easy in education to focus on the curriculum and think that the important thing is the content of the modules, but our discovery is that the learning community itself and the conversations and friendships found there are where as much formation and learning is taking place.

Contours of a Curriculum

I was very reassured reading Comprehending Mission[10] in which Stanley Skreslet maps the field of study of missiology. He groups mission education under particular themes, and whilst our curriculum is organised in slightly different categories, we touch on all the same areas and

---

[9] I have elaborated on this notion of true North in a forthcoming chapter in Jason Sexton and T.A. Noble (eds), *Doing Mission For the Church's Theology* (Ada, MI: Baker Academic, 2015).
[10] Stanley Skreslet, *Comprehending Mission* (New York: Orbis Books, 2012).

recognise the integrative nature of missiology which he describes. These are some of the contours[11] we navigate that help pioneers develop the ability to imagine and build:

- Every pioneer is in a context. The reorientation to context in global Christianity is massive. To make sense of that context will involve, for example, exploring notions of identity, reading cultures, economics, religion, locale, myths, texts, symbols, power relations, gender, ethnicity, contextual and local theologies.

- Each pioneer is unique, and has particular gifts and calling that they will relate to the context, so we spend time working on who you are. That includes personality, calling, story, identity, brokenness, character, posture, self-awareness. One of the most common pieces of feedback we get from students who train with us is that they have grown in confidence in who they are. Pioneering mission happens best when it flows out of who you are rather than trying to fulfil an expectation of what you think a pioneer ought to be.

- We study mission – this is such a rich vein for pioneers with its themes of ecology, liberation, hospitality, the five marks of mission,[12] discernment and joining in with God's mission, evangelisation, reconciliation, inculturation, migration, healing, prophetic dialogue, ecclesiology, mission theology(ies) and so on. The breadth of mission can be a challenge but we have found that it gives a lot of avenues for students to open up their pioneering beyond mere evangelism and church planting. We do have many students who have started new missional communities and churches, and are sharing the Gospel with those outside the church. But mission as a framework has enabled others to advocate for those at the edges, to campaign to end the practice of female genital mutilation (FGM), to develop a new approach to renewing town centres, to begin social enterprises and so on.

- To both see and build something requires tools and skills such as theologising, reading culture, crossing cultures, resourcing, strategies and tactics, communication, pastoral care, fund-raising. Some of those skills will relate to particular aspects of pioneering such as church planting or building social enterprise – our missional entrepreneurship module has proved to be one of the most popular with students doing individual modules.

- They are not the first people to do such a thing so there is a lot to learn from history, including various paradigms of mission, both good and bad, imperialism, contextual approaches, stories,

---

[11] See also Ross and Baker, *The Pioneer Gift*, 6-7.
[12] This is a way the Anglican Communion has conceived of mission – see: www.anglicancommunion.org/ministry/mission/fivemarks.cfm

ethnography, tradition as local theologies, women's movements, CMS, doctrine.

- The Bible is an amazing resource for understanding God's mission in the world and for working creatively to communicate that story in the contexts that pioneers are in.

- The romantic ideal of pioneering is not quite like the actual experience on the ground, so they need to work out how to fuel a life of mission with support, friends, prayer, spiritual direction, retreat, appropriate rhythms – a mission spirituality.

Learning about Learning

Since setting the course up, we regularly discuss how learning is taking place and what we are learning about learning, what the pedagogy might be undergirding what we are doing. I have written about this elsewhere but wanted to offer a couple of thoughts in this area.[13] The first is the importance of creating the kind of environment in which learning takes place. I suspect multiple factors are involved and it's hard to pin down what those might be. One is being hosted at CMS in a mission community, which is so affirming of pioneers and connected to the global church. Another is the team who host and create an atmosphere of hospitality. Unsurprisingly, research into what makes a good teacher shows that one of the key things is the quality of relationships with students – that it is hospitable.[14] The teacher is able to create an environment of openness, trust, welcome, to value student's contributions and lead the way in vulnerability and honesty, making a space that is safe and real. This goes alongside being qualified and competent to teach in a particular subject. At CMS we have a sense of being in it together with students as learners ourselves, and with whom in an appropriate way we are also a community of friends. A student who visited for a term from New Zealand wrote a reflection for his college in which he said that he was struck at CMS how it became easy to forget who were staff and who were students, as those teaching might be leading in one class and listening in another. Once a term we host a dreaming space, 24 hours in which a mix of teaching staff, students and others in our wider network gather to reflect on a particular question or issue we are wrestling with. This too, I think, contributes to this overall sense of a learning and hospitable environment.

In spite of all the contemporary theories about learning which in different ways show that learning is not just cognitive, and certainly not best done through an expert passing on content to a student to download, you could easily get the impression in many universities and theological

---

[13] Baker in Sexton and Noble, *Doing Theology for The Church's Mission.*
[14] Shaw, *Transforming Theological Education,* 262.

colleges that really it's all about head knowledge.[15] So, secondly, we have determined to fight for learning that is not just taught and assessed in a traditional fashion. It sometimes feels this is going in the opposite direction to gravity – if you want to do creative assessment or integrated learning, there is always a strong pull in the other direction. Our response to this has simply been to try to stick to our approach and to value creative and artistic practice alongside written work. In our experience, a portfolio of evidence demonstrating knowledge, skills and application lends itself well to this. In portfolios, we have had students submit video animation,[16] liturgy, poetry, journal entries, evidence of mission they have participated in, theological reflections with a mission community, grant applications, strategies for mission, essays exploring themes that have arisen in their mission context, reflections on cross-cultural experiences, and reworking of Scripture passages in a way that would resonate with that context, exploration of spiritual practices and retreat. Of course, there is also always written work which engages with the subject at hand. But even this seems to come alive most when it is addressing live questions. Perhaps a couple of examples will help. One student working with spiritual seekers who struggle to feel valued and acceptable submitted a couple of portfolios exploring the theme of shame which included an essay on shame, a creed written with a group of women, a Eucharistic prayer, a sermon on the woman with the issue of blood who comes to Jesus, and the idea of developing shame-resilient communities. Another student who is training whilst working full-time with us explored the doctrine of salvation. He opened it up as the healing of creation, and as a result has realigned some of his work towards renewing town centre high streets for which he has since won a national award. His written piece on salvation was an interview with an imagined other, laying out the themes and objections he would have encountered in his church tradition. Both of these portfolios were excellent pieces of work engaging with plenty of theological and missiological texts, but in a way that enabled connections to be made with their pioneering practice. One has since been published in a book.[17] That's not to say we get it right all the time. It reminds me of Daniel and his friends eating vegetables and asking for time to see whether that formed healthy individuals or not. The results were persuasive. I sometimes feel we are saying the same thing to university and church as we seek to embody a holistic approach to learning. I was

---

[15] For example, Bloom's cognitive, affective and behavioural domains; Heron's addition of an intuitive or gut dimension, Gardner's multiple intelligences, Kolb's learning cycle, Knud Illeris' triangle of content, incentive and environment. All are referenced in Knud Illeris (ed), *Contemporary Theories of Learning* (London and New York: Routledge 2009).

[16] See https://www.youtube.com/watch?v=97sgcQo4GRw for an animation of the Bible story.

[17] Andrea Campanale, 'A Gospel That Overcomes Shame', in Baker and Ross, *The Pioneer Gift*, chap. 10.

encouraged to see that the paper from Edinburgh 2010 on theological education and formation takes a similarly broad and holistic view.[18] The majority of students training at CMS are not getting ordained and are paying their own way. We are also ecumenical, with students from several denominations. For some, they are training while doing their daily work either full-time or in most cases part-time. And some have raised funds through charities or churches or individuals to support their training, often in a mix with some work. Whilst the Church of England has opened up a pathway for pioneer ordinands, in practice, numbers of pioneer ordinands are currently very low indeed. It feels as though the church is still in two minds about whether she needs or can resource those who will do something new outside the tramlines of what currently exists. I hope that this increases and certainly think the church needs more ordained pioneers, but whether it does or doesn't, it's hugely exciting to have created a training pathway where so many people are training as lay pioneers. CMS is a religious community of the Church of England, and because of that we have been able to use the guidelines of the church to recognise CMS pioneers as lay workers within the church who can then be licensed locally by a diocesan bishop. Whilst for some this might not seem relevant or important, for others it has given a very helpful way for how CMS pioneers connect with the way the church operates and understands ministry and mission. At our first graduation, we admitted eight CMS pioneers to the order of lay worker. As this continues, there might well be a hundred CMS pioneers in a decade or so able to be licensed for pioneer ministry in the church in this way.

Formation for Mission

My background is not in education so it has been a steep learning curve for me designing a course. I have come to it as a practitioner who loves learning and practice, and the relationship between the two. One of the words that tripped me up early on was 'formation'. I kept hearing it being used in contexts where I found it difficult to pin down what was being described. It's a good word, I think, because it moves education beyond head knowledge into questions of being formed as a person in the likeness of Christ, in character, in discipleship. I began to ask people what they understood formation to be and got a whole range of answers which helped me realise that there is a variety of formations and not just one type – it's contested. Some were quite negative from those on the receiving end of being formed, seeing formation as a control word in an overly parental

---

[18] Kirsteen Kim and Andrew Anderson (eds), 'Parallel Session on Theme 6: Theological education and formation in Edinburgh 2010', in *Mission Today and Tomorrow* (Oxford: Regnum 2011). Here theological education is described as supporting the whole of Christian mission through education of ear, heart, tongue, hands, mind, will, spirit, body.

church conforming leaders to a particular mould. Others were much more positive, seeing it as being along the lines of developing mature followers of Christ through practice. I ended up being most helped by Gerald Arbuckle where he contrasts formation in cloistered monastic communities with spread-out mission communities who live in the world rather than in the cloister.[19] For the former formation requires living together, and calls for stability and routine. For the other the purpose of formation is inculturation which requires flexibility and adaptability. Whilst both are being formed as disciples of Christ, they are quite different. At CMS the purpose of formation is like the spread-out mission communities – to inculturate the Gospel creatively and imaginatively beyond the edges of where the church is currently active.

Returning for a moment to the path in the slate tile, we hope that the CMS pioneer training is forming pioneers who can imagine and build a new path and find a new language to do so.

---

[19] Gerald Arbuckle, *From Chaos to Mission: Refounding Religious Life Formation* (London: Geoffrey Chapman 1996).

KOREAN PERSPECTIVE ON MISSIONARY TRAINING

Tim Hyunmo Lee

Approximately a century ago, Samuel Austin Moffett, a Presbyterian missionary to Korea, was invited to the Edinburgh 1910 World Missionary Conference as a representative of the Korean Church. It took him one month to reach Edinburgh by the Trans-Siberian Railway. He presented a paper at the conference, 'The Place of the Native Church in the Work of Evangelization' which introduced the Korean Church as a good model of the 'receiving church'. A century later, the present article is now addressing the Korean Church as a model of the 'sending church'. We are astonished at how much things have changed. Within the last 100 years, the Korean Church has grown by the grace of God to be self-supporting, as well becoming a partner of the worldwide churches that send missionaries.

By the end of 2013, the Korean Church had deployed 25,745 overseas missionaries to 169 countries.[1] Bearing in mind that only 93 missionaries were deployed from Korean in 1979, the growth in numbers achieved within such a short period is astonishing.[2] Missionaries in the early days manifested pure enthusiasm and strong commitment, but the supporting systems or mechanisms were ineffective and poor. Above all, the lack of missionary training was a serious problem. During the past thirty years of sending missionaries, the Korean Church has made important progress, especially in the area of missionary training. The current report on the progress and current state of missionary training by the Korean Church can therefore serve as a good case study, especially in the light of the present need to train and support missionary resources which come from the southern hemisphere.

A Brief History of the Korean Church and its Current State

Korea was forgotten by the western world for a long time; it was one of the last countries in Asia to be able to access the message of the Gospel.

---

[1] This figure is net, excluding the number of missionaries with dual affiliation. The other research institution, Krim, reported that 20,085 Korean missionaries were deployed in 171 nations at the end of 2013. The difference of numbers comes from different methods of research. Krim excluded missionaries who were sent by individual local churches, and who had foreign citizenship or pastored a Korean congregation.

[2] Marlin L. Nelson, *A List of Korean Mission Agencies, Missionary Training Institutions, and Missionaries* (Seoul: Basile Publishing, 1989), 203.

Korean church history is also unusual because the first churches were not planted by foreign missionaries but by national converts.

Even the Roman Catholic Church, which was very active in missionary outreach, did not work out a plan to deploy missionaries to Korea until the latter part of the 18th century. The first Korean Catholic Church came into being spontaneously. Around 1770, a Korean envoy to China, Chung, Tu-won, brought back to Korea a copy of Matteo Ricci's book, *The True Doctrine of the Lord of Heaven*. A group of pragmatic Confucian scholars began to study this book and to follow its doctrines which were significantly new and different from existing culture. In 1783, the group sent a representative to visit the Catholic missionaries in China to learn more about this new western religion. Yi, Seung-hun, who was sent by this group, sought out a Jesuit missionary and was baptised. He returned to Korea and, with a handful of others in this group, founded the first Roman Catholic parish in Korea in the mid-1780s without the presence of the officially ordained priests or missionaries. By 1795, there were 4,000 Catholics in Korea; by 1801, the number had grown to about 10,000. A Chinese Catholic priest, Zhou Wen Mo, came to Korea in 1795 and was martyred in 1801. The first western Catholic missionary, Pierre Philibert Maubant from the Paris Foreign Missions Society, came to Korea in 1836.

Furthermore, it was not until 1885 when the first protestant missionaries came to Korea. Horace G. Underwood, a Presbyterian missionary, and Henry G. Appenzeller, a Methodist missionary, arrived in Korea together on Easter morning. Just like the Roman Catholic Church, the first Protestant church in Korea was also started by Korean converts in 1877. Suh, Sang-ryun and Suh, Kyung-jo were converted to Christianity after hearing the Gospel from John Ross from China, who was translating the Bible into the Korean language. In 1884, when they returned to Korea, carrying parts of the translated New Testament, they immediately started a church in So-rae, in Whang-hae province. Later, when they were ready to be baptised, they invited missionary Underwood to their church. In 1887, when Underwood baptised them at So-rae church, there were already about 70 members attending the worship service.

The story of the Korean Church sounds like the stories in the Book of Acts, in which believers who had heard the Gospel on the day of Pentecost returned to their home towns and planted churches. The Korean Church had experienced the Pyoung-yang revival, which was the closest equivalent of the Great Awakening of the United States in the 18th century. Since then, the Korean Church has not ceased to grow during the last 100 years, except during the period at the end of Japanese colonial rule and the Korean War. Currently, the Korean Protestant Church has more than 55,000 congregations and 9.2 million believers (18.3%), and the Korean Catholic

Church has 5.5 million believers (10.9%).[3] The percentage of Protestant Christians of Korea is the highest among Asian nations.

From the early days, the Korean Church became conscious of overseas missions. In 1906, the Church of Christ in Korea, which was an earlier form of the Korean Baptist Church, decided to join in overseas mission work and deployed five missionaries to Manchuria in north-east China. In 1907, Korean Presbyterians deployed Lee, Ki-poong who was one of the seven first-generation graduates of Pyoung-yang Seminary, to Jeju Island, where cultural differences were significant enough for it to be considered a cross-cultural mission field. This missionary endeavour was followed by a number of waves of immigrants to Mexico, Japan and different parts of the United States, Los Angeles and Hawaii.[4] However, as the churches went through periods of hardship from the end of colonial rule till the Korean War, the spirit of mission decreased due to financial difficulties, and confusion and conflict in national politics. In the 1970s, the missionary challenge issued by the Lausanne International Congress on World Evangelisation and the growth of the Korean Church reignited missionary enthusiasm. In the early 1980s, missionary resources from para-church groups in Korea began to be deployed to international mission agencies. Gradually denominational mission agencies took part in missionary endeavours. Since the 1990s, denominational agencies began to take a lead in overseas mission work.

Historical and Current Missionary Training in the Korean Church

In the history of missionary training in Korean Church, we can observe a similar pattern to what we have seen in western nations. The report on missionary training done by Commission V of the 1910 Edinburgh World Missionary Conference revealed that missionary training in western churches in the past runs a parallel course with theological education. Missionary training programmes were not specialised, nor were they distinguished from theological education. Although training done in America was better than that of Europe, missionary candidates in both places received their theological education together with the seminary students who were being equipped for home ministry.[5] In other words, both groups were 'products' of a common theological curriculum, the only exception being that missionary candidates received a little additional training from mission agencies. Moreover, the content of the additional

---

[3] This figure is an official government statistic. However, Protestant churches in Korea reported different statistics quoted from Korean Gallop Poll: Protestants 21.5% and Catholics 8.2%.
[4] David Tai-woong Lee, 'The Korean Mission Movement: A Descriptive Analysis' (unpublished article), 1.
[5] Someone, however, points out that, in Europe, some mission seminars were often structurally divided from theological faculties in the 19th and 20th centuries.

training was of a mainly theoretical and cognitive nature, such as comparative religion or the history of missions. Consequently, at the 1910 Edinburgh Conference, it was concluded that missionary training must be distinguished from the kind of training and education received by candidates who would minister in national churches, for they needed to be equipped with specialisations that required independent training.[6] From then on, much discussion took place through which various missionary training programmes progressively developed more specialised and practical training for international missions.

In Korea, even as late as the mid-1980s, no systematic missionary training was being offered by mission agencies. Missionary candidates believed that, if they were equipped as ministers and acquired viable skills in foreign countries, they were ready to be deployed to mission fields. These early missionaries belonging to denominational agencies as well as independent missionaries were deployed without training. Gradually, however, the Korean Church began to recognise the need for missionary training before deploying them. Since the 1980s, therefore, denominations and independent mission agencies began to establish missionary training centres. Specifically, the International School of Mission operated by East-West Center for Missions Research and Development, founded by Cho, David Dong-jin in 1968, functioned as the forerunner in providing missiology classes as intensive programmes. This school contributed greatly in producing excellent mission leaders. The centre's programme, however, was deficient in the area of cross-cultural training, for its curriculum resembled too closely traditional mission education rather than that which was specifically suited for missionary training.

Interdenominational mission agencies linked with international agencies had become more active in Korea by the 1980s and deployed more missionaries. Denominational agencies also grew rapidly and were able to catch up with interdenominational agencies in the 1990s; they became dominant in overseas missionary work. Missionaries serving in international agencies were able to receive some level of training overseas, i.e. outside Korea, before deployment. The General Assembly of the Presbyterian Church in Korea (Hap-dong), which thus far has deployed the largest number of missionaries among Korean churches, was the first to set up the MTI (Missionary Training Institute) in 1982. More importantly, after the establishment of GMTC (Global Missionary Training Center) in 1986, the concept of integral and communal missionary training began to be widely recognised. By December 2013, 255 mission agencies (39 denominational agencies and 216 interdenominational agencies) and twenty specialised missionary training centres were operating in Korea.

---

[6] W. Douglas Mackenzie, 'The Preparation of Missionaries', 22nd June 1910, Report of Commission V, Edinburgh World Missionary Conference.

Especially significant were the consultations for designing missionary training curriculum carried out by the World Evangelical Alliance Mission Commission (WEA MC) and their proposals for profiling model, for they exerted a far-reaching influence in Korean training institutions.[7] In 1989, the WEA MC took the initiative in holding the first international missionary training conference in Manila. Subsequently, the International Missionary Training Fellowship (IMTF) was formed to further discuss, encourage and help other training programmes around the world, particularly the Two-Thirds World training centres.[8] Subsequent meetings continued to study how to design a curriculum specifically tailored for the Two-Thirds World missionary training, and finally a 'Consultation for the Two-Thirds World Missionary Training Curriculum Design' was held in Pasadena, California, in 1994. The Consultation introduced essentialist concepts of pedagogy and grafted profiling concepts onto missionary training. As a result, a missionary training model that included profiling concepts was introduced to the Korean Church and exerted a positive effect. Profiling concepts were further developed to produce the idea of integral missionary training. Currently, many training centres in Korea aim to carry out the model of integral training, although not many training centres seem to be achieving this goal effectively.

WEA MC published another important report in 1997: *Too Valuable to Lose* is a report of the 'Reducing Missionary Attrition Project' (ReMAP) that researched reasons for missionary attrition by major missionary-sending countries. The reasons for missionary attrition were reflectively considered and the ideas by which the problem might be prevented or reduced were incorporated into the new training curriculum. The report contributed significantly to changes being brought about in the content of existing training curricula and being adopted to suit the specific needs of the fields. 'Problems with peer missionaries' was considered the most serious reason for attrition among Korean missionaries in this report.[9] Ever since the report, building interpersonal relationships and conflict management have been of high importance in training.

---

[7] 'Profiling model' is a method which uses profiling in curriculum design. Profiling involves two essential parts: establishing entry levels of knowledge, skill and maturity, and identifying desired exit competencies or outcomes. Profiling defines the specific learning steps to bridges the 'gap' between two levels. Steve Hoke, 'How to transform Commitments and Objectives into Curriculum for Training' (paper presented at the Missionary Training Consultant Seminar, Pasadena, 22nd-26th February 1994).

[8] William D. Taylor, *Internationalizing Missionary Training* (Grand Rapids, MI: Baker Book House, 1991), ix-xii.

[9] Steve Sang-cheol Moon, 'Missionary Attrition in Korea: Opinions of Agency Executives', in *Too Valuable to Lose*, William D. Taylor (ed) (Pasadena: William Carey Library, 1997), 136-37.

Features and Directions of Missionary Training in Korea

Missionary training has to do with a level of development of missionary work. Training for pioneering work, training to be deployed to the mission fields where mission boards are in operation to provide care and management, and training for workers serving in international agencies must differ. Pioneering work refers to missionary work operating without any support systems (such as mission boards) in the fields. In this case, the missionary has to cope with tasks by himself. Missionaries who plan to work at a pioneering stage need more extensive and comprehensive training because they will be the first and/or alone in the field. Such missionaries are expected to be people of greater ability. But missionaries who are going to be deployed to fields that have adequate support systems need not pass through such a long training session in the home country, because they will be cared for through proper management. They can avoid unnecessary trials and errors in the field. For this reason, American mission agencies which are equipped with stable field mission boards provide only a short period of training at the orientation level before deployment. Missionaries to be deployed by international mission agencies usually receive training in a foreign country in addition to in-country training. However, it is highly recommended that missionaries go through the basic training in culture, language and mission policy before being sent out. Because the Korean Church has a comparatively short history in missionary work, most of the training programmes were established for pioneering work. Accordingly, missionaries are often required to go through a longer period of training than those from western nations. The level and period of training can be adjusted according to the changes occurring in mission fields, and the state or condition of ministries.

The second consideration has to do with the change in what the Korean Church expects from missionaries. More than two decades ago, in the early part of missionary endeavour, the general impression of missionaries was appreciation for the sacrifices they made. Because of the missionary family's sacrifice to leave their home, the churches appreciated them without reservation. Therefore, even if there were not much fruit in their ministries, the sending church continued to support and extended goodwill towards the missionary. However, in the last twenty years, living conditions on mission fields have changed dramatically. Of course, a few mission fields still remain in destitute circumstances, but the living conditions of many urban areas of mission fields have improved remarkably. The church's attitude towards missionaries therefore has changed, now requiring them to be more strictly responsible rather than giving them unconditional appreciation. There are two expectations for missionaries from the Korean Church: one is competence in ministries and another is integrity in life. Those who fall short of these expectations will be weeded out. Therefore, the content and quality of training have to be changed according to such change in expectations.

The third point has to do with a generational perspective. Kath Donovan and Ruth Myors point out in their article, 'Reflections on Attrition in Career Missionaries: A Generational Perspective into the Future', how different cultural perspectives as a result of generation gaps can affect missionary work.[10] The authors also comment that their research deals with western perspectives, and therefore does not indicate the implications of their study in non-western settings. However, similar tendencies often have been found in non-western nations as well. Generational conflicts were shown in Korea. The matter of generation gaps exerts a serious impact on missionary training. For contemporary missionary candidates who are quite different from those who were deployed twenty years ago, traditional patterns of missionary training can no longer be applied. This trend should be recognised as an indicator for making changes in the content of training.

Mission Education and Missionary Training

We need to distinguish between mission education and missionary training. Mission education means the activity of teaching mission-related lessons in order for participants to understand what mission is all about. Missionary training denotes an attempt to nurture or change the missionary's life, attitudes, value systems, and competence. Whereas the goal of mission education is understanding, the goal of missionary training is producing desired changes in the trainee. Therefore, missionary training is a comprehensive concept that includes mission education. Mission education by itself cannot satisfactorily fulfil the ultimate goal of missionary training.

Missionary training is operating in the Korean Church mainly in three formats. The first one is the mission school for mobilisation at a local church level. The second one is missiological education at the seminary level. The last one is missionary training offered by specialised missionary training centers.

Most of the mission school models provided by local churches assume a module type of mission education which is usually offered once or twice a year. A typical model of this format is LMTC (Local Missionary Training Course) operated by the General Assembly of the Presbyterian Church of Korea. This training programme conducts two-hour meetings for 24 weeks (sometimes four hours for twelve weeks) and one mission trip overseas. Graduates are qualified to be deployed as short-term lay missionaries. The content of the curriculum is flexible, but is mainly parallel with the curriculum of *Mission Perspectives* or *Mission Exposure* with supplements in 'mission history of Korean churches', 'missionary approaches to world

---

[10] Kath Donovan and Ruth Myors, 'Reflections on Attrition in Career Missionaries: A Generational Perspective Into the Future', in *Too Valuable To Lose*, 41-73. The writers use terms for the generational classification in the article: boosters, baby boomers, and busters.

religions', and specific situations found in mission fields. Currently, GMS (Global Mission Society) is operating 39 local courses in Korea. The substance of the programme is closer to education than to training, and is directed towards mobilising lay Christians for mission endeavours.

Another model is the 'In2Mission' programme carried out among Baptist churches. The denominational missionary training centre, WMTC, supervises this programme, despatching speakers to local churches for ten weeks. After the ten weeks' training, a mission trip opportunity is offered. Its curriculum is made up of biblical understanding of mission, introducing various mission activities, intercessory prayer, mission field stories, and the mission policy of the denomination. Mission professors of Korea Baptist Theological Seminary and missionaries join as speakers. After the completion of this training, the graduates are qualified as intern missionaries and are able to serve for one year. The content of this course is close to education.

The second format is missiological education done by seminaries. More than ten seminaries have established graduate schools of mission and offer ThM or MA in mission. The greater part of these graduate schools of theology offer doctoral degrees majoring in mission. Most seminaries require missiology as a compulsory subject and offer many mission-related subjects as elective courses. Mission faculty is plentiful. More than 100 persons who have earned PhD in mission or DMiss are teaching in seminaries.

Most of the specialised training centres require a community type of training. Most of the denominational or interdenominational agencies demand more than four weeks of community training. Some of them require additional training to be done in foreign countries.

Three formats of missionary training need to be acknowledged, not as separate training programmes, but as comprehensive and consecutive training. The comprehensive training concept is more effective in equipping for competence in the fields.

Models of Missionary Training

Training based on the integral training concept

With regard to the International Missionary Training Network (IMTN) led by WEA MC, some of its major concerns deal with integral missionary training. A typical book showing the integral training concept is *Integral Ministry Training* (2006) by Robert Brynjolfson, the first full-time representative of IMTN.[11] Integral training denotes a learning experience

---

[11] Robert Brynjolfson and Jonathan Lewis (eds), *Integral Ministry Training: Design & Evaluation* (Pasadena, CA: William Carey Library, 2006).

that targets the needs of the whole person, including character and spiritual formation, development of ministry skills and self-understanding. It intends to keep a balance among three elements: being, doing and knowing. Trainers have to orchestrate formal, informal and non-formal educational methods in order to combine learning academic theories, practising skills and transforming characters.

GMTC (Global Missionary Training Center) was the first training institution to adopt the integral training concept and profiling system. From the beginning, GMTC followed the suggestion of the Missionary Trainers' Consultation led by the WEA Asia Mission Commission which was held at Manila in 1993, in their process of designing curriculum and training methods. GMTC has nine subjects to achieve the goals of integral training, these being: i) spiritual maturity; ii) integrity of character; iii) stable family life; iv) resilience in emotional and physical health; v) relational skills; vi) basics in biblical and theological knowledge; vii) understanding missiology; viii) cross-cultural ministry skills; and ix) practical life skills. Various detailed lessons and seminars are designed to achieve the respective goal of each subject.

Missionaries who are going through the above training learn the meaning of culture, to cope with culture shock and how to overcome it, methods for language acquisition, in order to communicate in different cultures, minister in a cross-cultural situation, and cope with stress in a different culture. In addition, some of the theological issues in going into a cross-cultural situation and the biblical and theological basis of cross-cultural mission are also on the learning agenda. Towards the end of the programme, an emphasis is made on acquiring cross-cultural ministry skills. Cross-cultural discipleship training, cross-cultural exegesis and homiletics, and cross-cultural church planting are some of the sub-topics.

Each seminar is four days long and usually a number of tutors team-teach it. In addition, a number of case studies from different cultures are presented, usually by returning graduates. A group project is required for each seminar. For example, for cross-cultural exegesis and homiletics, four or five trainees form a team and choose a particular target culture. The team is then led to work on at least two cross-cultural sermons: one sermon on nurture and the other on evangelism. The prepared sermons are delivered in the classroom and the participants in the class are invited to offer critique.

Another significant part of training has to do with offering counselling to missionary candidates, for some or many of them will have had scarring experiences in their lives. A tremendous amount of counselling is needed to help heal whatever they have suffered from previously in their lives; the training session is an excellent period for dealing with the experiences and bring them out into the open. Normally at GMTC, every Friday morning is set aside for Life Formation. The session is usually divided into two parts. One is a class session. A part of this session is scheduled for helping trainees to integrate missiological information with devotional and spiritual life experiences. All of these help the trainees to think about themselves and to shape their lives to move closer to the end-profile that they have shaped with their tutors at the beginning of the training programme. The other part is a tutorial session meeting in a small group setting. There is a theme, such as self-discipline, personal piety, meditation, and the meaning of wholeness of persons to discuss. In reality, however, this is an open session when trainees can freely share anything that is on their minds in a small group setting.

WMTC is a training institute of the Korea Baptist Church that also follows the recommendation of WEA MC's training and curriculum design consultation. WMTC used profiling methods in the initial stage of its curriculum design. It spent more than one year to establish an end-profile. If too high a level of the end-profile is set, a lengthy period of training is needed, but if it is projected too low, the training has no effect. The beginning-profile is set as seminary graduates, because it functions jointly with its denominational seminary. Comparing these beginning- and end-profiles, the trainers come up with details of the training content to fill the gaps between the two profiles in six subjects; those subjects are: i) spiritual formation; ii) character formation; iii) missiological knowledge; iv) cross-cultural ministry skills; v) language acquisition; and vi) mental and physical health.

WMTC provides a communal-type missionary training programme for thirteen weeks. Training progresses in three different stages, each under respective subjects. The 'being'. dimension of the integral training concept is emphasised in the first half of the training period, which is gradually reduced in the subsequent stages. The 'knowing' dimension is less emphasised in the first half but is increased in weight in the middle part, and reduced in the latter part. The 'doing' dimension is increased in its weight as the training moves towards the latter part. The important fact is that the dimensions of being, knowing and doing should not be separated, but harmonised in order to generate integrative results. While formal, informal and non-formal educational concepts are applied evenly, the knowing aspects adapt a more formal pattern of education, while the doing aspects use a more informal pattern, and the being aspects make use of a more non-formal pattern.

The WMTC curriculum reflects attempts to prevent or circumvent the indicators dealing with the major reasons of missionary attrition in the ReMAP report. Therefore, it gives more weight to the matter of character-building, which was pointed out as one of the major weaknesses of Korean missionaries. Three counselling staff personnel spend much time with the missionaries in training during their whole period of training. The trainees are examined through several personality tests such as TJTA (Taylor Johnson Personality Analysis), MMPI (Minnesota Multiphasic Personality Inventory), and Family Relationship Scale. The trainers use the results of the above personality tests effectively, and minute the observations made in counselling. Counselling often brings about big changes and sometimes results in revocation or postponement of deployment.

GMTC and WMTC are typical models of the training institutions which have applied integral missionary training concepts.

Training for non-traditional missionaries

Today, various kinds of missionaries differing from the role of a traditional missionary have appeared: tentmakers, business missionaries, short-termers, strategy co-ordinators, diaspora ministers, senior missionaries ('silver missionaries'), etc. Different kinds of missionaries require different patterns of training.

A typical training model for tentmakers or business missionaries in Korea is GPTI (Global Professional Training Institute). It provides training programmes for professionals preparing to be deployed. Because these trainees are workers with specific jobs, their training programme is offered on Saturdays, meeting from afternoon to evening for 22 weeks. There is also a community-type training for two weeks. Mostly resembling the existing mission education model, the curriculum consists of basic mission studies, professionals' ministries, cross-cultural ministries, and life formation. During the past twenty years, GPTI has produced more than 1,600 graduates. Among them, about 600 have been deployed to mission fields, and more than 100 graduates are serving as mission leaders or mobilisers in local churches and mission agencies.

The term 'senior (or silver) missionary' refers to a person deployed for the first time to a mission field after the age of 50; most senior missionaries are people who have retired or retired early. Senior Mission Korea and many other senior mission schools offer training for such candidates. Most of the training consists of a ten-week programme. The content of training is similar to that offered by local church mission schools, emphasising peculiarities of senior missionaries and various mission opportunities for the seniors.

Training as self-directed learning

Until now, missionary training has been primarily operating as a closed learning or training system. However, as training experiences are accumulated, we are recognising that there is a felt need to develop a self-directed learning pattern of training. Traditional training concepts distinguish trainees from trainers, and trainers take leadership throughout the training process. In this pattern, the planning of the curriculum as well as the implementation and evaluation of the training are done in a single direction. As such, when the programme is over and the trainees are no longer engaged, the learning itself ceases. In new models, trainees become trainers in self-directed learning. That is to say, trainees are trained to discipline themselves to strengthen their competence as missionaries. The advantage of the self-learning model is that it allows missionaries to continue in their learning process even after completion of the training programme. Indeed, the preparation of missionaries requires more and more extended periods of time because of rapidly changing situations around the world; this kind of self-directed learning therefore becomes essential in missionary training.

Missionary training is not a marginal issue in missionary endeavour. It is one of the most serious tasks of the mission agencies' home office to recruit competent candidates and to train them thoroughly before deployment. As a responsible partner of world churches, the Korean Church must be mindful of its responsibility to study and develop more enhanced and relevant models of missionary training to serve the Lord.

AFRICAN PERSPECTIVES ON
THEOLOGICAL EDUCATION FOR MISSION

Ben Y. Quarshie

Introduction

Mission is essentially a matter of gospel and culture engagement. The good news embodied in the person of Jesus Christ, God who has become flesh (Jn. 1:14), can make its divinely expected transformative impact only by being incarnated into the cultures of targeted people groups or 'nations' (Mt. 28:19-20). Any other approach will make Jesus, and thus the Gospel, basically alien and therefore unwelcome to the given people group and their cultural context. The mandate that Christ has given to the church for mission (Mt. 28:16-20) demands that those who carry out mission should be equipped to be able to transmit Christ and him crucified (1 Cor. 2:2) in a manner that, in co-operation with the recipients, facilitates Christ and the good news he offers being incarnated in specific cultural contexts.

The African context is diverse, but there are many common cultural elements that make it possible to speak of 'African perspectives' in theological education for mission.[1] Theological education in Africa must be for mission because the church in Africa, indeed the global church, cannot afford ivory tower theologising or a theological academy interested only in the promotion of the careers of theologians.[2] Mission is God's mission, *missio Dei*, and thus should be the church's raison d'être. If theological education is to serve the church, therefore, it must be totally missionary, ready to engage with culture, rather than be self-serving. Culture entails the totality of a people's life, and so gospel and culture engagement in mission has not only religious and moral ramifications but also political, social, economic and ecological or environmental implications as well.

This paper deals with the general state of the theological academy in Africa, with a specific focus on mission, and highlights some multi-dimensional perspectives that are critical for formation for mission in Africa today. These perspectives are to some extent embodied in the work

---

[1] For unity in the diversity in African culture(s), especially Africa's religious heritage, which of course in Africa has implications for all aspects of life – political, social and economic – see, for example, John Mbiti, *African Religions and Philosophy* (London: Heinemann, 1969).

[2] See, for instance, the lamentations of A.F. Walls over the state of the western academy in 'Christian Scholarship in Africa in the Twenty-first Century', in *Journal of African Christian Thought* 4.2 (December 2001), 44-52.

of some theological institutions associated with the African Theological Fellowship,[3] but particularly of Akrofi-Christaller Institute of Theology, Mission and Culture (ACI), whose name clearly indicates that the institution's starting point is God (theology) before the move into mission that then involves engagement with culture and its political, social and economic ramifications.[4]

Theological Education for Mission in Africa

Lack of African perspectives

Theological education in Africa has for a very long time been driven by perspectives from the western theological academy. There are still many theological institutions in Africa that are simply carbon copies of their western counterparts.[5] Many reasons account for this. First, many of these institutions were established by western missionaries, who could offer only what they had – western theology; and they did so without any serious attempts to engage with African cultural resources, which almost invariably they condemned in derogatory terms.[6] Secondly, where the missionaries left off, their chosen successors have continued to operate in the same

---

[3] See G.M. Bediako, 'The African Theological Fellowship – an Innovative Model for Evangelical Theological Education', in Isabel Phiri & Dietrich Werner (eds), *Handbook for Theological Education in Africa* (Oxford: Regnum, 2013), 947-55. See also G.M. Bediako, 'The Akrofi-Christaller Institute, Ghana, as an Innovative Model of Theological Education in Africa', in Isabel Phiri & Dietrich Werner (eds), *Handbook for Theological Education in Africa* (Oxford: Regnum, 2013), 930-46.

[4] ACI, until 2006 when it gained a Presidential Charter to award its own degrees, was called Akrofi-Christaller Memorial Centre for Mission Research and Applied Theology. Until then, ACI had collaborated with the then University of Natal in South Africa to run its academic programmes.

[5] This generally acknowledged fact has become obvious in interactions with institutions that have sought affiliation with ACI for mentoring purposes, and also in consultancy work of over two decades for the National Accreditation Board of Ghana. These experiences have consistently confirmed a lack of African perspectives in the curricula of many theological institutions in Ghana. This is the case in other parts of Africa as well. See the entries in 'Part I: History of Theological Education in Africa', in Isabel Phiri & Dietrich Werner (eds), *Handbook for Theological Education in Africa* (Oxford: Regnum, 2013), especially those of J.S. Pobee, James Kombo, Bill Houston and Jesse Mugambi.

[6] The missionary rejection of African culture is a well established fact. Kwame Bediako asserts, 'That Western missionaries, on the whole, took a negative view of African society and its values – religious and cultural – cannot be evaded.' See his *Christianity in Africa, The Renewal of a Non-Western Religion* (Edinburgh: Edinburgh University Press, 1995), 78. See also, for example, S.G. Williamson, *The Akan Religion and the Christian Faith – A Comparative Study of the Impact of Two Religions* (Accra: Ghana Universities Press, 1965).

manner that the missionaries did. Moreover, some current western-trained African theologians who have returned home have somehow not seen it fit to take cognisance of the African context and culture in their theologising. Thirdly, the explosion of Christianity on the continent continues to attract foreign Christian groups who come every year to 'train' and ordain freelance pastors. Such training is often for a short period, in some cases a total of a mere three weeks. The implications of such activities for mission in Africa are enormous, considering that for decades, even people who have undergone a full three- or four-year ministerial training, have come out into the field to work, only to realise that, in order to make headway in ministry, they have to discard many of the things they learnt in seminary.

This unfortunate situation is true of theological education in Africa generally, but even more so when it comes to training for mission. ACI did not start off with the running of academic programmes.[7] It initially concerned itself with the running of various continuing educational – church-related and ecumenical – programmes. One such programme was the 'Mission Fields Conference'. This was designed for agents of the Presbyterian Church of Ghana (PCG) who served in the 'mission fields' of the church as pioneers but had had no training at all for such cross-cultural mission work. As noted by Kwame Bediako, founding Director/Rector of ACI, with regard to this annual conference, 'It was the first time ever that the PCG mission fields had been taken seriously as distinctive and significant entities in the life of the church and therefore as requiring a unique vision and formation, as well as particular skills for ministry.'[8] This apparent disregard for ministerial formation for mission was not unique to the PCG but was rather a pronounced phenomenon all over Africa.[9] Hence a critical look at many of the theological institutions in Africa indicates a general lack of African perspectives in theological education and in most cases, no real interest in mission studies as such, even to talk about African perspectives in that specific area.

African perspectives

Theological education in Africa is often understood only in terms of formation for the ordained ministry. Right from the beginning, however, this has not been the case at ACI. As its vision statement indicates, both lay and ordained are needed for mission, and thus both require theological

---

[7] See Bediako, 'The Akrofi-Christaller Institute, Ghana', 941.
[8] Kwame and Mary Bediako, *'Ebenezer, This is how far the Lord has helped us (1 Sam. 7:12)', Reflections on the Institutional Itinerary of Akrofi-Christaller Memorial Centre for Mission Research and Applied Theology (1974-2005)* (Akropong: ACMC in-house publication, 2005), 13.
[9] The ecumenical seminary that trains PCG ministers also trains ministers for the major Protestant churches in Ghana, and has trained ministers for churches in other parts of Africa.

training.[10] In 'training Christian workers and leaders for effective mission in the African context', certain perspectives are discernible in ACI's approach, perspectives that, we believe, should characterise all theological education (for mission) in the African setting. We discuss these perspectives in three main areas: language, worldview, and values.

LANGUAGE AND COMMUNICATION/TRANSLATION

Language is grammar, morphology and syntax and is a necessity for communication. It is thus a requirement for mission. Language is, however, more than just a tool for social interaction and the basis of various communication theories. Language is also the very means for the transmission of culture and as such a key factor when it comes to a person's self-identity. It is mainly through language that socialisation takes place, and cultural values and other indicators of self-identity are passed on from one generation to another. For a people to lose their language is therefore to lose a prime element that defines them.

Language is also the means for the apprehension and experience of reality. As Aloysius Pieris has said, 'Language is the "experience" of reality, religion is its expression.'[11] This means that it is through language that any people experience reality, and for the Christian the ultimate reality is God himself. Thus, a people's language must be a critical factor when it comes to their apprehension and experience of the transcendent.

Finally, language is a means for the articulation and expression of what a people group have understood and experienced of the transcendent. More than any other language, it is a person's mother tongue that affords them the greatest opportunity and freedom for true expression of experiences (of the transcendent) that others may not readily appreciate or understand.

On the basis of what has just been outlined, language should be a critical element in any missionary enterprise because it is a tool not only for communication but even more so for translation, which is communication at a much deeper level.

Today, many people in Africa insist that to participate in the global village demands the use of international languages to the detriment of local language use. These international languages, such as English, French and Portuguese, were introduced into Africa by missionaries, traders and colonialists. These languages have come to stay and remain important on the continent. Theological education is carried out in these languages, in most cases to the total neglect of local languages. It is, however, significant that it was also missionaries, critically assisted by native people though,

---

[10] The ACI vision is 'to be a pacesetting academic and pastoral institution, training Christian workers and leaders for effective mission in the African context.' See the ACI website at www.acighana.org

[11] Aloysius Pieris, *An Asian Theology of Liberation* (Edinburgh: T & T Clark and New York: Orbis Books, 1988), 70. See also Bediako, *Christianity in Africa*, 175.

who were in the forefront in the reduction into writing of many African indigenous languages.[12] Unfortunately, those efforts have not always been sustained and in some cases have actually been truncated. Much of the theologising in Africa takes place in foreign languages, and that, as acknowledged by J.S. Pobee, enables such theologising to gain a wider audience. In reality, however, articulating theology in foreign languages is only second-best to theologising in indigenous languages.[13]

In Africa, the languages used by the majority of people, especially those on whom Christian mission efforts focus, are mother-tongue languages. The majority of Christians are also mother-tongue speakers who experience and articulate their faith in the mother tongue. Hence as agents of mission, they could best be equipped for service by being trained in the use of the mother tongue for mission work. This presupposes the translation of the Bible into African languages, something that is ongoing. The translation of the Scriptures into African languages is a major factor in the phenomenal growth of Christianity in Africa.[14]

If, as has been argued, language is so critical for theological education, and even more so for theological education for mission, then mother tongues must feature prominently in the theological curricula in Africa. This must be seen in terms of engagement with indigenous songs and hymnody, prayers, and poems and writings in local languages, but above all the Bible in the mother tongue. The use of the Bible in the mother tongue must be built into the theological curriculum, and equipping people to think and operate in the mother tongue should be a *sine qua non* for potential and aspiring missionaries in the African context.

At ACI, mother-tongue use is of crucial importance for research and training. It is an area of great research interest that has resulted in various works and publications on indigenous songs and hymnody as well as publications in indigenous languages.[15] When it comes to the Bible in the mother tongue, ACI works very closely with Bible translation agencies in

---

[12] In Ghana, for instance, the Basel missionaries were critical for the development of local languages. Johannes Zimmermann and Johannes Christaller, with assistance from natives, translated the Bible into Ga and Twi respectively in the nineteenth century.
[13] John S. Pobee, *Toward an African Theology* (Nashville, TN: Abingdon Press, 1979).
[14] Bediako, *Christianity in Africa*, 62. See also Ype Schaaf, *On their Way Rejoicing, The History and Role of the Bible in Africa* (Akropong: Regnum Africa, 2002), and Lamin Sanneh, *Translating the Message – the Missionary Impact on Culture* (New York: Orbis Books, 1989).
[15] See, for example, the Institute's *Journal of African Christian Thought* 16.1 (June 2013), which was dedicated to the theme 'Theology, Spirituality and Mission in Africa'. The Gbotsui Series of the ACI publishing wing, Regnum Africa, is dedicated to publications in the local languages. On the other hand, the Nyamedua Series is for African mother-tongue theology. Recently, research into 'Indigenous Christian Hymnody' resulted in the launch of a CD of such indigenous hymns.

Ghana and beyond.[16] ACI in fact runs an MTh track in 'Bible Translation and Interpretation', an area that can also be pursued at PhD level. In the life of ACI itself, the mother-tongue Bible occupies a very prominent place. The use of the mother-tongue Bible characterises all courses that involve the use of the Scriptures. It is for this reason that the admission letter to any applicant to ACI contains this penultimate paragraph: 'All students whose mother tongue is not English should bring along with them a copy of their mother tongue Bible or any Ghanaian (or indigenous) language Bible they are most familiar with.' Furthermore, at ACI devotions that begin and end the working day, the local language, Twi, is used together with English. In the morning, the Bible and the commentary on a given passage are read in both languages. Prayers (on various topics and for all members of the ACI community based on a prayer calendar) are said in any of the many languages represented at ACI. Finally, all MTh and PhD candidates are required to produce their dissertation or thesis abstracts not only in English but also in their mother tongue.

The conscious emphasis on the mother tongue at ACI is not meant to suggest that international languages are not important. They remain important, and English is the medium of instruction at ACI. When, however, it comes to mission in the African context, which is to predominantly people who use mother-tongue languages, it is vital that aspiring missionaries are trained and equipped to be able to use and operate with the local languages. It is a crucial factor in any attempt at planting the Christian faith in African soil and being in a position to unearth and share true African theological insights with the global church.

WORLDVIEW AND UNDERSTANDING

The second area for discussion is worldview. Worldview is a people's map of the universe, how it operates, as well as their place or role in that universe.[17] A given people group's worldview provides a way for other people to understand it as a people group. Worldviews as maps of the universe may be re-drawn, and aspects may shrink or be reduced, but they are never annihilated.[18]

Every people group has its own worldview, and for anybody to be able to communicate with it effectively, that person will have to understand the people group's worldview and be ready to engage with it and seek to reach the people through it. To disregard a people's worldview or attempt to

---

[16] ACI has close working relations with the Bible Society of Ghana, the Ghana Institute of Linguistics, Literacy and Bible Translation, as well as their international collaborators.

[17] See, for example, A.F. Walls, 'Introduction: African Christianity in the History of Religion', in C. Fyfe and A. F. Walls (eds), *Christianity in Africa in the 1990s* (Edinburgh: Centre of African Studies, 1996), 1-16.

[18] Walls, 'Introduction: African Christianity in the History of Religion', 6-11.

impose a foreign worldview on any people group will render ineffective any attempt at communication and translation.

Mission as gospel and culture engagement is often cross-cultural in character; hence a failure to engage with a people's worldview will undermine the missionary enterprise. As a result of the Enlightenment, the western map of the universe that dichotomises the sacred and the secular, plus the spiritual and the physical, has held sway over the western theological academy. The involvement of the spiritual in daily life is deemed mythological and has virtually been rejected. What is real is what can be seen and touched, the object of scientific enquiry. Effectively speaking, life has been divided into two parts, spiritual and physical, and these are held in different and separate compartments with very minimal contact between them. Unfortunately, as mentioned earlier, there are many theological institutions in Africa which still operate with this western model, and it is little wonder that they are not making any lasting impact.

In Africa, the dominant worldview remains primal.[19] The primal worldview sees life as being completely one. No sharp division exists between the spiritual and the physical; there is constant interpenetration of the spiritual into the physical world. Nothing happens in the physical world that does not have spiritual undertones. In fact, for the African, what is real is rooted in the spiritual. This worldview persists even in the face of modernity. Theological education for mission in Africa must therefore take seriously the primal religions and the primal imagination or primal religious consciousness that remains so dominant in Africa. Failure to do so is a sure recipe for ineffective mission. What makes this even more significant is that this primal worldview is also the worldview reflected in the Bible such that, as Mbiti said decades ago, 'The man of Africa will not have very far to go before he begins to walk on familiar ground.'[20] Life is one integrated whole, just like the human being.

ACI appreciates the importance of the continuing primal religious consciousness for theological education for mission. There are courses on primal religions/spirituality and the Christian faith and a conscious engagement with the primal in the various courses of the institute. This awareness of the primal imagination has implications for constant prayers and total dependence on God in all things, spiritual and physical. It also underscores the importance of the translated Bible and how it speaks to the circumstances (both spiritual and physical) of the African today. The primal is a reality that cannot be discarded. Andrew Walls has said that everybody

---

[19] For the meaning of 'primal' and how it persists in Africa and elsewhere, see A.F. Walls, *The Missionary Movement in Christian History: Studies in the Transmission of Faith* (New York: Orbis Books, 1996), 120-21; see also Bediako, *Christianity in Africa,* 91-108, and Walls, 'Introduction: African Christianity in the History of Religion'.

[20] John Mbiti, 'Christianity and East African Culture and Religion', in *Dini na Mila* 3.1 (May 1968), 4.

is a primalist underneath,[21] and so the African emphasis on the primal in theological education for mission should be relevant to the western theological academy.

VALUES AND ETHICS

Values have to do with issues of morality and therefore of ethics. Values involve questions of what is right or wrong; what deserves commendation or reward and what calls for punishment or sanctions. Every people group is made up of individuals and, as a result, various relationships are defined, especially in terms of how the individual relates to the group and vice versa. What are rights of the individual vis-à-vis the community? Questions of this nature undergird the value system of the given people group that may be the target group for mission. Thus, for any mission effort to make the necessary impact would require knowledge of and engagement with the values and ethical system of a given people group. A failure to engage and instead to simply import into the mission context an alien value-setting system would spell disaster for the mission enterprise.

Mission cannot proceed without a sense of what is right or wrong in any given mission setting. Missionary work in Africa for a very long time did not see anything good in anything indigenous. African values were therefore not appreciated, leading to attempts at imposing western values on the African, some of which were completely at variance with African and indeed Christian values. Western society is highly individualistic, and given the long history of Christianity in the West, individualism has come to be seen as virtually a Christian value. Related to this is another value that is very pronounced in western society, especially when it comes to ethics, and that is relativism. In many areas of life in western society today, what is right is in the hands of the doer. On several fronts, when it comes to societal values, many things have become relativised. The (human) rights of individuals have whittled away communal rights in many areas of life. The scenario on values is, however, very different when it comes to Africa, in spite of continuing efforts at blindly exporting western values into Africa.[22]

In Africa, communal values remain very important. There is a strong sense of community, and fellow-feeling is a characteristic feature of good traditional societies. The sense of right and wrong is still communal in outlook. Still relevant is the popular view of Mbiti: 'I am because we are and, since we are, therefore I am.'[23] Furthermore, the African community is also quite significantly a multi-religious one. There are people of different

[21] Walls, *The Missionary Movement in Christian History*, 121.
[22] See, for example, Abamfo Atiemo, *Religion and the Inculturation of Human rights in Ghana* (London: Bloomsbury Academic, 2013).
[23] Mbiti, *African Religions and Philosophy*, 108-109.

faiths seeking to live in community, and mission and preparation for mission must always be sensitive to this reality.

In the face of the continuing communal sense of values in a multi-religious Africa, theological education for mission in the African context cannot afford to disregard this communal sense, and import instead western individualism and relativism into Africa. Doing so would have serious negative implications for mission. Mission cannot afford to target individuals as if they live in isolation or are islands; mission must target communities, 'nations' (Mt. 28:19), and hence always deal with individuals as parts of communities. It is noteworthy that the product of mission in the New Testament, the church, was a community that sought to operate as such (Acts 2–8). It is not for nothing that St Paul applied the body metaphor to the church (1 Cor. 12–14) and consistently called upon his various addressees to eschew individual and selfish ambition, and instead seek at all times to serve others the way Christ himself did (Phil. 2:1-11; Gal. 6:1-2; 2 Cor. 8:9; cf. Mk. 10:45).

In its work, ACI runs courses that highlight values that it seeks to live by. There are courses that deal with ethical issues from an African point of view, and issues of holistic mission and development as well as theology, human need and the environment. Also of importance are courses that concentrate on people of other faiths and how to relate to them. The attempt to promote a sense of community in its own life is seen in the ACI's daily communal worship devotions and the wearing of the same uniform by all staff members as one way of underscoring the fact that as a microcosm of the body of Christ, every ACI member's contribution is needed for the well-being of the community as a whole. Conscious efforts are made to promote academic work as a vocation and spiritual discipline in which one and all join hands in co-operation rather than in competition to seek the truth. Mutual support in academic pursuits is the order of the day. At ACI, therefore, there is an attempt to model the kind of community that should result from mission when it succeeds.

Conclusion

The perspectives that have been identified and discussed are in reality not to be isolated one from another. They are intertwined. Life in Africa is one integrated whole and these perspectives must be seen in the same way. At ACI, in pursuing the integrated view of life, there is a conscious effort to move away from the well-known demarcated areas of academic specialisation. ACI's integrated approach means focusing on the collective preparation of mission practitioners so that they can pursue a holistic, integrated approach to mission that transforms the totality of the person in community with others. ACI remains in mission itself, in that its location, Akropong, is the seat of the paramount chief of Akuapem. As such, Akropong continues to present, day in and day out, issues of gospel and culture engagement. Mission must seek to make a difference in the day-to-day lives of ordinary people. If it fails to engage on that level, then it is no mission at all. Theological education for mission, like all forms of theological education, must serve the church, and it can do so only by drawing people to Christ and into the church, and in turn equipping them for transformative mission in fulfilment of Christ's mandate to the church (Mt. 28:16-20).

FORMATION FOR MISSION: MISSIOLOGY MEETS AUSTRALIAN CATHOLIC EDUCATION

Therese D'Orsa

What are the essential goals, tasks and processes in mission formation today? The answer to that question seems to depend on the way in which 'mission' is construed, and how one reads the context in which 'mission' functions.

'Mission' can be construed in either a narrow sense, which shrinks the notion of mission formation, or in a broad sense, which expands it. Taken in the broad sense, mission is the project of a faith community committed to making the Kingdom of God present both within the community itself, and also within the broader society and culture of which any particular faith community is a part. In recent decades, it is the broader understanding of mission that has been developed within the magisterial documents of the Catholic Church reflecting the broadening consensus of engaged leaders across the globe. It is this understanding which frames the discussion which follows.[1]

The demands of mission arise from a faith community's collective immersion in its historical and cultural context. Reading the context and assessing its multiple demands are preconditions to any effective mission response – that is, to any initiative which makes God's Kingdom present in concrete and helpful ways. This is true of all the communities that now constitute the church, be they parishes, schools, welfare groups, prayer groups, etc.

The Mission and Education Project (MEP)

The MEP discussed here was established in response to the question posed at the beginning of this chapter. Its goal is to support the work of leaders and teachers in Catholic schools, but it is already proving influential in other sectors, particularly as leaders access theological courses focused on leading for mission.

---

[1] For an interpretive summary of the development of official church teaching on mission and evangelisation, see Jim and Therese D'Orsa, 'Securing Mission at the Heart of the Australian Church', in Neil Ormerod, Ormond Rush, David Pascoe, Clare Johnson, and Joel Hodge (eds), *Vatican II Reception and Implementation in the Australian Church* (Mulgrave, VIC: Garratt Publishing, 2012), 240-57.

A further question has driven the MEP: how does one help leaders, and then followers, to develop the conceptual tools to respond to the imperative of mission – to engage in what is termed in the MEP as 'mission thinking'?[2] In no way does the use of this phrase within the project imply that the approach to education and formation is solely or predominantly a cognitive one. Rather, mission thinking is contrasted with strategic and operational modes of thinking which tend to dominate in church institutions in response to the complexities of providing services such as education or health. This is so because they respond to the survival challenges of those who find themselves accountable to both church and society for their ministries.[3]

Strategic thinking and operational thinking are sourced successfully from the contemporary culture which has produced considerable wisdom in these domains of organisational life, whereas in a Christian agency, mission thinking is discerned primarily from the wisdom of the faith community now and across time. The phrase 'mission thinking' encapsulates the responsibility borne by leaders both to conceptualise mission clearly, and also to consider deeply what the nature of the educative/formative task in regard to mission actually is. Furthermore, it is the dialogue between the two sources of wisdom – faith and culture – which is at the heart of the Mission and Education project and, it is argued, must find a central place in any successful formation for those engaged in mission in the world. This dialogue is pursued, formally and informally, through processes of theological reflection of which there are a variety available (see below).

Catholic education is one of the major ways in which the Catholic community carries out its mission within Australian society and its way of life (culture).[4] A perduring issue for Catholic education's leaders and sponsors is the effectiveness of this vast enterprise in carrying out the mission of Jesus in the highly secularised, pluralised and globalised society which is contemporary Australia. The times and context demand a radical rethinking in terms of mission as it applies in Catholic education. With good reason, informed observers speak of a time of 'refounding'.[5] Clearly,

---

[2] Jim and Therese D'Orsa, *Leading for Mission: Integrating Life, Culture and Faith in Catholic Education* (Mulgrave, VIC: Garratt Publishing, 2013), 247-55.

[3] The demand for accountability in exercising such public ministries as education, health and some aspects of welfare comes, not only from the fact that public money is usually involved, but also from the fact that the institutional church is an identifiable element of society and subject to the expectations which govern all institutions in public life.

[4] Catholic schools educate approximately 20% of Australian children in over 1,700 schools. According to the National Catholic Education Commission's 2012 annual report, there are in excess of 735,000 students being educated by over 57,000 teaching and 27,700 support staff (headcount includes part-time staff. Full-time equivalent staff is 67,709): www.ncec.catholic.edu.au

[5] A number of contributors to the fourth exploratory study in the Mission and Education series – *New Ways of Living the Gospel: Spiritual Traditions in Catholic*

such refounding requires work on many levels, and some quality projects are already bearing fruit.

Catholic Education as Bridgehead

Catholic education is a frontier project in that, while many Catholics have lost faith in church leadership as a result of the clerical abuse scandals and negative experiences of clerically dominated parish structures, they have retained confidence in Catholic schools. Hence the latter become something of a bridgehead if Christian mission is to find expression in the homes and milieus of the baptised, and through them to move the social and cultural contexts into closer alignment with the Kingdom of God. Implied here is a starkly different understanding of mission from the one which most present-day clergy learned as a result of their theological education, an understanding which features neat and deep divisions between pastoral theology and mission theology. These divisions make little sense in the light of 'Kingdom of God' missiology.

The imperative for renewed 'mission thinking' to drive effective leadership and formation has been recognised by the twenty Catholic education systems which support the Mission and Education project both financially and through the willing participation of their staff.[6] Without this renewal, leaders and followers run the risk of losing focus in the multi-faith, multicultural, globalised context in which Catholic schools now operate. Moreover, the context yields such a diverse social pattern of participants in the average Catholic school community that both leaders and staff have to be able to do their mission thinking largely *in situ*. Mission thinking is essentially local.

In many Catholic dioceses, missiologists and school educators rarely work together. However, when they do, they find they share much in common. The Catholic educator is concerned to help students integrate life, culture and faith in developing the worldview with which they engage with

---

Education (Mulgrave, VIC: Garratt Publishing, 2015) – drew on the notion of 'refounding' to appropriately describe what they believe to be the necessary response to the current situation facing Australian Catholic education. See Gerald Arbuckle's *Catholic Identity or Identities? Refounding Ministries in Chaotic Times* (Collegeville, MN: The Liturgical Press, 2013*)*.
[6] Since the inception of the programme, the Mission and Education series has received financial support from a number of Catholic education diocesan authorities as follows: Brisbane, Cairns, Rockhampton, Toowoomba, and Townsville (QLD); Armidale, Broken Bay, Maitland-Newcastle, Parramatta, Sydney, Wagga, Wollongong (NSW); Canberra-Goulburn (ACT); Ballarat, Sale and Sandhurst (VIC); Adelaide and Port Pirie (SA); Hobart (TAS); Darwin (NT). Also from Good Samaritan Sisters, Marist Brothers (Sydney Province), Marist Brothers National, Edmund Rice Education Australia, and De la Salle Brothers (Religious Congregations).

the challenges and problems that shape their lives (*The Catholic School* #37).[7] The missiologist is concerned that the message of the Gospel penetrates and shapes human cultures by building on what is already there. Both missiologists and Catholic educators acknowledge the importance of culture and its impact on both faith and human experience, but come at it from different perspectives. Hence, they make potentially good dialogue partners when they engage with each other. The MEP has sought from the outset to foster such engagement. The project has its own narrative, which is now outlined briefly.

Narrative of the Project

There are few people in senior leadership positions in Catholic education who have had the opportunity to study missiology in depth, and who have also had sufficient experience in educational leadership in schools and school systems to be able credibly to promote a grounded 'conversation' between missiology and education. Since my husband, Dr Jim D'Orsa, and myself are privileged to be among that number, we felt impelled to ask ourselves whether we were prepared to contribute a number of years to such a project. A further question was: could we generate the interest and academic support to make such a project viable? Both questions have been answered in the affirmative. The Broken Bay Institute, a dynamic national provider of theological education, staffed and led predominantly by a core staff of lay theologians, and embracing an outstanding wider network of religious and clerical theological and Biblical scholars and teachers, provided the opportunity to begin work as a particular focus within its programme of missiological teaching and research.

If we were going to invite other Catholic educators to join us in this exploration, it was clear that we would first of all have to engage in some 'heavy lifting' ourselves. The scope of the field needed to be opened up. Because both missiology and education are broad areas of study rather than disciplines in any narrow sense, the work was intellectually very demanding. We began to read and research intensively in current missiology, theology, a range of social sciences including especially cultural and social anthropology, hermeneutics, curriculum, leadership and pedagogy. A major area of study was mission in Scripture. Key themes such as emerging dimensions of secularisation, pluralisation and globalisation impacting on the social context in which mission occurs, were also specifically researched. We were aware of the many specialist studies occurring in Catholic education as scholars continued in increasing numbers to produce helpful doctoral work. Clearly, one element of the

---

[7] Congregation for Catholic Education, *The Catholic School*, 1977. This is the foundational post-Vatican II document on the identity of Catholic schools. All magisterial documents are downloadable from the Vatican website.

Mission and Education project would be to invite scholars working in both education and spirituality to consider their particular topics of research within a missiological framework, and to collaborate when their work interfaced with one of the topics approved for exploration by the project's Editorial Board.

Thus we embarked on the most demanding intellectual journey of our lives. The initial study resulted in *Explorers, Guides, and Meaning-makers: Mission Theology for Catholic Educators* published in 2009, the first in what was to become a series of exploratory studies into mission and Catholic education.[8]

As we progressed, we recognised that we ourselves were essentially engaging, albeit in a particular way, in a process of theological reflection. The importance of this became clearer as we proceeded with specific educational topics. In fact, we came to recognise that the capacity to do what we called 'grassroots theology' and the skills and processes for engaging in this work of integrating life, context (including culture) and faith in local situations, is the essence of what the project is essentially about. Further, we came to see theological reflection as a crucial capacity by which missional leaders chart their engagement in God's mission. This insight brought greater clarity to our understanding of what 'mission thinking' involves.

A second volume followed in 2011, entitled *Catholic Curriculum: A Mission to the Heart of Young People.*[9] Although the topic has been under consideration by Catholic educators for decades, the work responded to major developments in school curriculum being initiated by the Australian government, developments which projected into sharp relief the need for a serious exploration into the nature of curriculum suited to Catholic school students.

This was followed in 2013 by a third – *Leading for Mission: Integrating Life, Culture and Faith in Catholic Education.*[10] At this stage, the Mission and Education project was well enough established to attract five other senior leaders to contribute reflective 'guest' chapters on important initiatives in leadership development, whole school development, hermeneutics, and formation in charism, as examples of work 'on the ground' which illustrated what can and does happen when leaders engage in 'mission thinking'.

---

[8] Jim and Therese D'Orsa, *Explorers, Guides and Meaning-makers: Mission Theology for Catholic Educators* (Mulgrave, VIC: Garratt Publishing, 2009).
[9] Jim and Therese D'Orsa, *Catholic Curriculum: A Mission to the Heart of Young People* (Mulgrave, VIC: Garratt Publishing, 2011).
[10] Jim and Therese D'Orsa, *Leading for Mission: Integrating Life, Culture and Faith in Catholic Education* (Mulgrave, VIC: Garratt Publishing, 2013).

A fourth volume, *New Ways of Living the Gospel: Spiritual Traditions in Catholic Education*,[11] has been released. It deals with the creation and sustaining of spiritual traditions as vehicles for mission in Catholic educating communities. To our delight, we were able to attract fourteen other scholars and practitioners, including one bishop, to work with us on what is essentially a 'snapshot in time' dealing with how the charisms which shaped teaching congregations have developed within the church, and are further developing to meet the needs of students and teachers today. The study also includes new spiritual traditions being developed within and across whole dioceses, and in one case in a newly established diocesan secondary school which, under the leadership of the charismatic founding principal, developed a spiritual tradition around the saint after whom the school was named – St Peter. All of these contemporary examples are the result of the work of outstanding educational leaders thinking, and then acting, missionally.

In 2014, the decision was taken by the Editorial Board to expand the scope of the MEP and to produce a second series of shorter practical works focused particularly on teachers, and showcasing some of the work teachers are doing in terms of new missional responses. The aim is to introduce mission thinking to people operating at the 'coalface'. The first, dealing with *Catholic Identity* and written by a diocesan Director of Catholic Education working closely with school-based colleagues, is due for release in 2015.[12]

Theological Reflection – a Formation Process Par Excellence

Our experience in working with educators at all levels of school systems has convinced us that the capacity to reflect theologically – that is, 'to do theology' – now needs to become a major priority in mission formation. Theological reflection provides the person preparing for mission, or the one already engaged, with the capacity to focus on a situation, read it accurately, and then determine what could, and then should, be the response. We stress the point that theological reflection is a priority in formation that has to be co-ordinated with other important priorities. However, our experience in the MEP as well as graduate programmes is that, as the mission experience continues to change and its demands expand, the skills of theological reflection become more obviously essential if leaders are to take added responsibility for mission – for creating

---

[11] Jim and Therese D'Orsa (eds), *New Ways of Living the Gospel: Spiritual Traditions in Catholic Education* (Mulgrave, VIC: Garratt Publishing, 2015).
[12] Dr Paul Sharkey, then Director of Catholic Education in the Adelaide Archdiocese. The volume is being published by Garratt Publishing.

'Kingdom spaces'[13] – in their particular milieus in what is an increasingly complex environment.

Theology is too often understood as a product, while the processes by which it is created go largely ignored. A consequence is that, although 'doing theology' is a skill that is integral to religious meaning-making, it has been undervalued in theological education and formation. In teaching cohorts of Catholic educators, we have become aware that, standing behind their sense of theology as 'product', is an understanding of theology based on a classicist view of culture,[14] one which sees theology as something one learns in a fairly context-free way, rather than something one engages in within a dynamic cultural context. Learning theology, therefore, runs the risk of being an exercise in religious consumerism in which 'more' is seen as 'better'. Such an approach is of little help in linking mission and education, or in forming disciples for mission.

While there are many ways of 'doing theology', our aim has been to provide an explicit method readily accessible to Catholic educational leaders, and to help them reflect theologically on their experience of *engaging in mission*. Theological reflection is best pursued within a *framework* or model that gives it meaning, and by using a *process* that enables the insights contained in this framework to be translated into effective action steps. While a framework can give rise to a number of processes, we have come to focus on a particular process which has proved its value as a good starting point for Catholic educators. It uses a number of specific insights culled from methods readily available in the literature. The outcome of learning to work confidently with a method is that a person or group develops their own capacity for integrating life, culture and faith so that it becomes a habit of mind and heart. As confidence grows, people lose their reliance on the process, becoming able to move in and out of the 'moments' of theology as questions present, data is gained, discernment occurs, and decisions are taken.

See-Judge-Act as Overall Framework

Theological reflection was reclaimed as an important element in theological education in the late twentieth century. This development began in Catholic circles under the rubric of pastoral theology, and in Protestant circles under the rubric of 'practical theology'. It is now an established part of ministry training in both Catholic and Protestant churches.[15]

---

[13] This is a phrase we often used in working with leaders. See *Leading for Mission*, 246-47, 249.
[14] Bernard Lonergan, *Method in Theology* (London: Darton, Longman & Todd, 1972). Lonergan describes theology in terms of mediation between 'a cultural matrix and the significance and role of a religion in that matrix' – Introduction, xi.
[15] See, for instance, Australian Catholic theologian Terry Veiling, *Practical Theology 'On Earth as it is in Heaven'* (Maryknoll, NY: Orbis Books, 2005), and

The See Judge Act (SJA) approach associated with Cardinal Cardijn of Belgium and the Young Christian Workers movement is well known in this country, particularly to older Catholics who were formed for social involvement during their university days in the decades before and immediately following the Second Vatican Council (1962-65). It has undergone some development, particularly in regard to greater sophistication in its three major 'steps', and is still used effectively today.[16] SJA has a long pedigree in Catholic social thought. It was endorsed by Pope John XXIII in his 1961 encyclical *Mater et Magistra* (#236) as a means of 'reading the signs of the times', which in Catholic discourse is often longhand for 'doing theology'.

As is the case with many models of theological reflection, the emphasis is on applying faith to life. This is good as far as it goes. However, many models ignore or take for granted the role culture plays in how people make sense of life. There is a major danger in taking culture for granted. When this occurs, processes of theological reflection ignore the biases (good and bad) that culture brings to any discussion. Cultural biases shape how a leader 'reads' situations – what he or she sees, or fails to see.

In a secular society such as Australia, culture provides people with a default frame of reference that is essentially secular. As such, secular culture comes to define what people see as 'common sense',[17] the starting point for how most people interpret situations, framing what they see and do not see. Theological reflection invites those engaged to acknowledge this, and critique its adequacy as a starting point. It does this by exploring what the wisdom of our faith tradition has to say. However, the wisdom of our faith tradition also has its limitations. Its expressions contain biases which are cultural in origin, since faith always develops within culture and has to be expressed through the medium of culture.

The dialogue between faith and culture therefore needs to be two-way. Theological reflection opens up the possibility that this can occur, and that faith can grow and culture be improved *as human concerns are addressed*. For this to happen, it is necessary to 'befriend' both the wisdom of our faith tradition and the wisdom of our cultural tradition – that is, to engage with them critically, but loyally.[18] This 'befriending' process is a preliminary to effective mission thinking.

---

from the UK, Elaine Graham, Heather Walton and Frances Ward *Theological Reflection: Methods* (London: SCM Press, 2007).

[16] While the method originated in Europe, its nature and outcomes correlate closely with others originating elsewhere, for example, in Latin America.

[17] Cf Bernard Lonergan, *Method in Theology* (London: Darton, Longman & Todd, 1971), 81-84.

[18] James and Evelyn Whitehead, *Method in Ministry* (Washington: Rowman & Littlefield, revised edition, 1995), 9.

The process we have employed in the MEP owes much to the work of Richard Osmer[19] (Protestant) and Patricia O'Connell-Killen[20] (Catholic). Following Osmer, we break the process of theological reflection into 'moments'. We have added an extra 'moment', the 'focusing moment', which is pivotal in the work of O'Connell-Killen.[21] Few, if any, of the methods available provide an epistemological justification of the sequence of steps they follow. Thus their value has to be determined pragmatically: do they lead to useful missional outcomes? The method featured here as a kind of illustration of how the strengths of available methods can be accessed.[22]

Some of the issues which students have chosen as the focus of their theological reflection include the following: pluralism in faith stances and stages among school staff; tensions arising when the religious education co-ordinator and parish priest operate out of different assumptions about the mission of the Catholic school; addressing an inward-looking dynamic in the school community versus the imperative of mission to engage the wider society; and determining who actually are the 'marginalised' in the school.

The MEP process featured below can be used by the leader or a leadership group in attempting to make sense of a complex situation. We have imposed the SJA framework over the model to show the points of connection.

Outline of Method[23]

See

- **Step 1: The Descriptive Moment** (What is going on here?)
  Comment. In this pre-critical stage, the aim is to describe in non-judgemental terms the situation, including the feelings generated among the participants, and the values at play. Most people find that this is quite difficult. Usually they impose value judgements on their interpretation of events.
- **Step 2: The Interpretative Moment** (Why is it going on?)

---

[19] Richard Osmer, *Practical Theology: An Introduction* (Grand Rapids. MI: Eerdmans, 2008).
[20] Patricia O'Connell Killen and John De Beer, *The Art of Theological Reflection* (New York: Crossroad Publishing Company, 1994).
[21] O'Connell and De Beer, 63.
[22] Although discussion of the correlation with Lonergan's work in *Insight* lies outside the scope of this chapter, we believe the method developed does correlate closely. See Bernard Lonergan, *Insight: A Study of Human Understanding* (Toronto: Lonergan Research Institute, 1992).
[23] For a fuller exposition of the processes and questions associated with this method, see *Leading for Mission*, 232-43.

Comment. This is the critical stage in which faith, culture and life have to be brought into dialogue. It seeks to surface the initial bias resulting from a secular frame of reference, and to critique it, not first with reference to faith, but with reference to what else the culture might have to offer. Having established this, Step 2 then brings faith into play as a qualifying factor. The wisdom of our faith tradition – that is, both Scripture and the wisdom of the faith community generated across time – has something more or different to offer which may be helpful.[24] This creates the possibility of dialogue between faith and culture in making sense of human situations. Theological reflection seeks practical outcomes using the best resources available.[25]

Judge

- **Step 3: The Evaluative Moment** (What should be going on? i.e. what is the preferred future we should strive to achieve?)

  Comment. The aim here is to bring imagination and feeling (in the form of hope) into the reflection so that it can move from the head to the heart. Most people bring to the discussion some conception of what should be going on, usually based on their experiences. This could be a resource, but it needs to be tested. One way of doing this is to see if it will facilitate movement towards what people imagine the preferred outcome to be. Again, having established what culture has to offer, the process provides a challenge to the imagination, while bringing the wisdom of faith to bear as a qualifying factor. The genius of Jesus' Kingdom of God motif is that it remains a permanent challenge to the human imagination.

- *Step 4: The Focusing Moment* (What precisely do we need to respond to?)

  Comment. Any process of theological reflection involves discernment, in which there is a sorting out of the essential from the non-essential. O'Connell-Killen calls this 'getting to the heart of the matter'. Discernment involves seeing through symptoms to causes, so that actions can be directed to what really counts. In this, the leader has to be prepared to sense that God is at work when people of goodwill set out to address significant human issues. Prayer has an important place in theological reflection. It often gives leaders the confidence to trust their intuition in discerning what lies at the heart of complex issues. Patricia O'Connell-Killen suggests a fruitful method of discernment: sit with the results of Steps 1 to 3 and wait

---

[24] This wisdom includes, but is not confined to, magisterial church teaching.
[25] This orientation is why it often carries the name 'practical theology'.

for an image to arise, then put questions as to why that particular image arises. This can be quite powerful.[26] Having discerned what the heart of the matter is, it is important also to discern what the first step should be in addressing it. Sometimes this involves estimating people's readiness to respond. Readiness often requires consciousness-raising.

Act

- **Step 5: The Response Moment** (What do we need to do?)
  Comment. The aim in this step is to identify the steps that have to be taken to arrive at the 'preferred future'.
- **Step 6: The Review Moment** (How effective has our response been?)
  Comment. All interventions have an outcome, and this needs to be assessed in the light of original intentions. This can then be used to reformulate the intervention.

In addition to reviewing the process and revealing the sometimes unstated assumptions that lie behind it, the last step also leads back to the first.

Important Features of this Model

- It is essentially practical. The reflection grows out of and takes forward real issues confronting the missional leader.
- It draws attention to the innate biases leaders often employ in reading 'the facts of the matter' (Step 1).
- It seeks to 'get to the heart of the matter', since the presenting face of an issue is often not the 'heart'.
- It brings together the resources of culture and faith. The process does this at two important levels. First, in making sense of the situation (Step 2), and secondly, in determining the criteria required to frame an adequate response (Step 3).
- It brings imagination to bear both in framing a preferred outcome and in getting to the heart of the matter.

Major Insights from Working with Leaders

The experience of MEP personnel in working with a variety of Catholic leaders has itself generated a number of insights:

(i) Catholic school leaders generally operate from a notion of culture as classical rather than empirical, and therefore subject to ongoing change,[27]

---

[26] See O'Connell Killen re the role that feeling and image play in theological reflection, 37.

[27] Jim and Therese D'Orsa, *Explorers, Guides and Meaning-makers: Mission Theology for Catholic Educators* (Mulgrave, VIC: Garratt Publishing, 2009), 44-46.

giving rise to a notion of theology as a product rather than a process. This view of culture is an impediment to be overcome if leaders are to develop skills in missional thinking.

(ii) Leaders are generally not familiar with the church's teaching on mission and evangelisation. This means that when they ask questions about what the faith community has to say, they find they have much exploration to undertake to answer the questions which theological reflection poses. Participants generally demonstrate preparedness to undertake further exploration.

(iii) The issue of Scripture is a major one for Catholic educational leaders. Students generally tend to be unaware of their own hermeneutic when it comes to dealing with Scripture. Our experience has been that most often they operate from a 'proof-text' hermeneutic seeking to apply Scripture quotations to already-determined positions. Alternatively, students may simply use Lonergan's 'commonsense' approach, assuming that what the author of a particular book of the Bible intended is what the text conveys to the unprepared reader today. In addition to introducing students to the fundamentals of Biblical interpretation, they must be invited to enter into the very process of Scripture itself. This is an ongoing deepening of a community's faith in the midst of life's journey, a response in faith which raises possibilities for one's own life as an individual or community and one which is foundational in mission formation.[28]

Conclusion

Theological reflection pursued in the service of God's Kingdom is a powerful tool in mission formation. It considerably enhances the insight and missional capacity of those prepared to develop competency in using it as a way of engaging with mission issues as they are experienced. To disregard its importance is to risk encouraging spiritual consumerism, and to sell short those who, in good faith, seek leadership wisdom and accompaniment in their formation for mission.

---

[28] A helpful article dealing with the kind of Biblical interpretation to which theological reflection invites the exploring Christian is to be found in Tad Dunne, 'Scholarship and the Bible': users.wowway.com/~tdunne5273

INTERFAITH LEARNING IN A
RELIGIOUSLY PLURAL WORLD

Edmund Kee-Fook Chia

My first exposure to the study of religions other than Christianity took place in a Roman Catholic religious novitiate, while undertaking theological studies in the seminary. This was in Malaysia and it was more than thirty years ago. Had I been trained in a Christian-majority country or if I had entered the novitiate thirty years earlier, in all likelihood that would not have been part of my experience. Having said that, it must also be hastily noted that the study was by no means formal nor was it required. It happened that the professor was himself thinking through some interfaith issues at that time and saw fit to introduce them to us, rather like an appendix to the systematic theology course that he was teaching. In a way, it was akin to my present assignment of writing this chapter which serves merely as a 'case study' in a book dedicated to theological education and mission! The paper, therefore, begins by exploring the dynamics surrounding the ambivalence of interfaith learning. It then goes on to discuss plausible methods for developing interfaith awareness amongst students of theology being prepared to minister in a world which is becoming increasingly multicultural and multi-religious.

The Context of Theological Education

It is not too far-fetched to suggest that interfaith dialogue and learning about religions other than one's own are tasks many Christians subscribe to but find difficult to practise. That practically all societies and nations on earth have become more multi-religious needs no further discussion. It makes intuitive sense therefore for Christians to learn more about the religious beliefs and practices of their neighbours. Not only will they understand and appreciate these religions, they will also discover how God is acting outside the Christian tradition. For those engaged in theological studies for purposes of ministry, this becomes all the more important since they will certainly have to be dealing with persons who adhere to faiths other than Christianity. A pastor might have an imam from the mosque across the street coming to enter into a covenantal relationship; a hospital chaplain might have to attend to a sick call from a Buddhist patient or assist in end-of-life care; a teacher in a Christian school might have Hindu students asking religious questions. Or, some members of the pastor's own congregation might be practising different forms of yoga disciplines or

Taoist ritual healings, or have children in interfaith marriages, or be assigned to work in a Muslim-majority nation. In cases like this, it helps if the pastor is knowledgeable enough to discuss interreligious issues and concerns appropriately.

These examples, of course, do not include the experience of theological students living in Christian-minority countries such as in Asia where Christians number no more than a few percent, or in some countries even less than one percent, of the entire population. In these contexts the tables are turned. Encounters with persons of religions other than Christianity become the rule rather than exception. When I was studying at a public teachers' college in Malaysia, there were fewer than 100 Christians in the student population of more than 3,000. Many pastors and Christian ministers in Asia also have members of their own family, including spouses, who adhere to faiths other than Christianity. Thus, the family dinner every evening is already an interfaith event or one might be sharing a bed with an interfaith partner! In such contexts, interfaith learning becomes even more essential, not only because graduates of Christian ministry have to attend to questions from their own congregations but also because they have a crucial role to play in their respective societies. As one dean of a seminary put it, 'Our graduates are not only pastors, religious functionaries or caretakers of congregations, but they are also leaders of the local community, embracing the whole community.'[1]

While the contextual realities seem to augur well for serious engagement with religions other than Christianity, the practical reality is that only a few Christian seminaries and schools of theology actually incorporate such engagement into their educational curriculum. Those which do often have to place interfaith learning as an appendix, relegated to an elective or optional course, attended to only after all the required courses have been fulfilled. This is partly because seminaries serve their sponsoring churches, whose immediate need is for trained personnel to take charge of parishes and related ministries. Specific needs in such contexts are urgent. In the global North, this often means arresting the decline in church membership or the strengthening of outreach, for the purpose of attracting the unchurched into their communities. In the global South, especially where Christians are a tiny minority, concerns with protecting their religious rights and very existence often supersede any form of outreach to the religious 'other' for the purpose of mutual learning. It is not too surprising then to find interfaith learning relegated to the back burner.

Hence, religious pluralism *de facto* (as a matter of fact) does not necessarily translate into interest in interfaith learning. Many challenges still need to be attended to before Christians are able to open their minds

---

[1] J. Paul Rajashekar, 'Theological Education for Interfaith Engagement: The Philadelphia Story', in *Changing the Way Seminaries Teach: Pedagogies for Interfaith Dialogue*, David A. Roozen and Heidi Hadsell (eds) (Hartford, CT: Hartford Seminary, 2009), 157-82, at 163.

and hearts to their neighbours of other faiths. For those in so-called 'Christian' countries such as the United States, the challenge has been expressed in statements such as this: 'Given Christianity's privileged status for most of US history, and certain evangelical historiographies concerning the origins of our nation as Christian through God's providential governance (Christendom versions of Manifest Destiny), it is very difficult for many within the evangelical community to move beyond seeking to safeguard and protect such privileged status.'[2] Unfortunately, the priorities are not too different in the global South either, especially in countries which were previously colonised, as 'generally speaking, the kinds of theological education brought to Asia were copies of theological schools from western countries. With their structures, disciplines and curricula'.[3] It is for these reasons and many more that interfaith learning has not made too much headway in Christian theological education either in the West or even in Asia.

Historical and Theoretical Bases for Interfaith Learning

What exactly do we mean by interfaith education or interreligious dialogue? A seemingly terse remark by the Jesuit priest Thomas Michel, who himself has been engaged in promoting relations across religions for about a half century, captures the activity well: 'What interreligious dialogue really means is how we relate to people who have no interest in becoming Christians.'[4] This clarification is relevant here as there are a number of seminaries which do offer courses on the study of religions other than Christianity but they do so for other motives, one of which is as follows: 'Understanding other religious traditions improves ability to effectively proselytise to members of other faith communities.'[5] That explains why these interfaith courses are usually offered through the faculty's World Mission departments.

Interfaith education has a totally different purpose. Its aim is to enlighten minds and open hearts to enable Christians (and others) to cultivate a more

---

[2] Sang-Ehil Han, Paul Louis Metzger and Terry C. Muck, 'Christian Hospitality and Pastoral Practices from an Evangelical Perspective', in *Theological Education*, 47/1 (2012), 11-31, at 11.
[3] Dietrich Werner, 'Memorandum on the Future of Theological Education in Asia: ETC Reference Document 2011', in *The Ecumenical Review*, 64/2 (July 2012), 209-22, at 214.
[4] Thomas Michel (*National Jesuit News*, November 1997, 7) as cited in James D. Reddington, '"Interreligious Dialogue" at the Jesuit School of Theology, in the Graduate Theological Union, at Berkeley', in *Changing the Way Seminaries Teach: Pedagogies for Interfaith Dialogue*, 31-56, at 34.
[5] Justus Baird, 'Multifaith Education in American Theological Schools: Looking Back, Looking Ahead', in *Teaching Theology and Religion*, 16/4 (October 2013), 309-21, at 312.

positive disposition and attitude towards their neighbours of other faiths. Their religious neighbours are then viewed not so much as competitors or targets of evangelism but as partners or co-pilgrims in the journey towards God and God's Kingdom. This is a very new ministry, with equally new theological presuppositions. Mutual learning and witnessing are the order of the day. Herein lies the challenge as not every Christian believes he/she needs to be witnessed to or have anything to learn from their religious neighbours. Suffice it to say that debates surrounding the need for interfaith education and dialogue continue amongst Christian theologians. Unlike mission and evangelism, the history of interfaith dialogue is brief, and the benefits and incentives for putting it into motion are often less than obvious.

For the Roman Catholic Church it was the 1960s renewal from the Second Vatican Council which set into motion a conscious acceptance of and openness towards religions other than Catholicism and Christianity. Appealing to God as the 'origin' and 'final goal' of all humanity while examining the church's 'relationship to non-Christian religions' (§1), the Vatican II document *Nostra Aetate* states unequivocally that 'the Catholic Church rejects nothing that is true and holy in these religions' (§2).[6] Of course, prior to this watershed event, many of the other Christian denominations were already coming together in what was to become the modern ecumenical movement. The 1910 World Missionary Conference in Edinburgh is often regarded as its starting point, and the formation of the World Council of Churches in 1948 as a major fruit of this ongoing effort. Even prior to these milestones was the hosting of the Parliament of the World's Religions in Chicago in 1893 that brought together a number of luminaries from both West and East to discuss interfaith issues. This event 'is generally recognised as the beginning of organised interreligious dialogue'.[7] Numerous other interfaith movements have since evolved – for example, the United Religions Initiative, Religions for Peace, the Global Interfaith Movement, etc. All these movements helped in generating a gradual movement towards the unity of humankind and their institutions, 'ushering in by the latter part of the twentieth century the Age of Global Dialogue'.[8]

---

[6] Second Vatican Council, *Declaration on the Relation of the Church to Non-Christian Religions: Nostra Aetate* (28th October 1965): www.vatican.va/archive/hist_councils/ii_vatican_council/documents/vat-ii_decl_19651028_nostra-aetate_en.html

[7] Sallie King, 'Interreligious Dialogue', in *The Oxford Handbook of Religious Diversity*, Chad Meister (ed) (New York: Oxford University Press, 2011), 101-14, at 102.

[8] Leonard Swidler, 'The History of Inter-Religious Dialogue', in *The Wiley-Blackwell Companion to Inter-Religious Dialogue*, Catherine Cornille (ed) (Hoboken, NJ: Wiley-Blackwell, 2013), 3-19, at 6.

While these centripetal forces in society are swirling about, the churches and especially the seminaries which they sponsor are basically in the game of playing catch-up as far as interfaith relations are concerned. To be sure, progress has been made, albeit at varying degrees and in different constituencies. In 2007, the Association for Theological Education in South East Asia (ATESEA) officially recommended that theological education should promote 'interfaith dialogue as well as intrafaith communion and communication, for the fullness of life and well-being of society'.[9] In 2008, the Congress of the World Conference of Associations of Theological Institutions (WOCATI) similarly advised its membership 'to explore innovative theological programmes to promote interfaith dialogue in theological education'.[10] In 2012, the Association of Theological Schools (ATS) of North America revised its accreditation standards to include the following: 'MDiv education shall engage students with the global character of the church as well as ministry in the multi-faith and multicultural context of contemporary society. This should include attention to the wide diversity of religious traditions present in potential ministry settings, as well as expressions of social justice and respect congruent with the institution's mission and purpose.'[11]

All these advances are signs that change is slowly but surely taking place. The following reflection on the situation in North America, even if sounding a bit too optimistic, is poignant: 'We may have arrived at the moment when teaching theology and religion in America – even within the hallowed walls of a seminary – can no longer be confined to the boundaries of a particular religious tradition.'[12]

Methodological and Practical Bases for Interfaith Learning

Let us at this juncture take another look at what interfaith education entails. A definition from a 1984 document (commonly known as *Dialogue and Mission*) of the Vatican's dicastery for relations with religions other than Christianity might prove helpful here. In positing the Catholic Church's stance towards other religions as one of 'dialogue', it defines dialogue as 'not only discussion, but also includes all positive and constructive interreligious relations with individuals and communities of other faiths

---

[9] 'Guidelines for Doing Theologies in Asia: Association for Theological Education in South East Asia', in *International Bulletin of Missionary Research*, 32/2 (April 2008), 77-80, at 80.
[10] 'WOCATI Congress Message', in *International Review of Mission*, 98/1 (2009), 155-60, at 158.
[11] Stephen Graham, 'Christian Hospitality and Pastoral Practices in a Multifaith Society: An ATS Project, 2010-2012', in *Theological Education*, 47/1 (2012), 1-10, at 9.
[12] Justus Baird, 'Multifaith Education in American Theological Schools', 311.

which are directed at mutual understanding and enrichment' (§3).[13] Effective interfaith learning in theological education, therefore, has to attend to the multifaceted dimensions of the relational experience of Christians with persons of other religions. It is not merely a cognitive (dialogue of the head) task of discussion but includes as much the affective (dialogue of the heart), volitional (dialogue of the will), and psychomotor (dialogue of the hands) dimensions of an individual's life.

The *Dialogue and Mission* document, in fact, spells out four types of interfaith learning or dialogue, and defines each as follows:

> (i) The Dialogue of Life – 'a manner of acting, an attitude; a spirit which guides one's conduct. It implies concern, respect, and hospitality towards the other' (§29).

> (ii) The Dialogue of Works – 'that of deeds and collaboration with others for goals of a humanitarian, social, economic, or political nature which are directed towards the liberation and advancement of mankind' (§31).

> (iii) The Dialogue of Experts – 'dialogue at the level of specialists, whether it be to confront, deepen, and enrich their respective religious heritages or to apply something of their expertise to the problems which must be faced by humanity in the course of its history' (§33).

> (iv) The Dialogue of Religious Experience – 'persons rooted in their own religious traditions can share their experiences of prayer, contemplation, faith, and duty, as well as their expressions and ways of searching for the Absolute' (§35).

These four types of interfaith learning or dialogue can similarly be expressed in common parlance in these five steps below:

(A) Attitude change vis-à-vis other religions;
(B) Be with persons of other religions;
(C) Collaborate with persons of other religions;
(D) Discuss religious issues with persons of other religions;
(E) Experience religion with persons of other religions.[14]

Thus, what we see today in seminaries which strive to provide interfaith learning are the various forms of educational opportunities which attend to some of the types and steps of dialogue enumerated above. Here are a few models. First, the most basic and perhaps the most common would be to have a singular course or subject on the world's religions (this is often entitled 'World Religions' which is a contested nomenclature, since the criteria for which are 'world' religions is at best ambiguous). Others might include a more focused study on one or two of the religions, especially

---

[13] Secretariat for Non-Christians, *The Attitude of the Church toward Followers of Other Religions: Reflections and Orientations on Dialogue and Mission* (10th May 1984): www.cimer.org.au/documents/DialogueandMission1984.pdf
[14] Edmund Kee-Fook Chia, 'Toward an Asian Theology of Dialogue', in *Edward Schillebeeckx and Interreligious Dialogue: Perspectives from Asian Theology* (Eugene, OR: Pickwick Publications, 2012), 127-50, at 144.

those which are dominant in the particular context of the seminary (e.g. Islam in Algeria or Hinduism in India or Buddhism in Thailand). These courses could include an assignment which requires students to visit a place of worship which was not Christian, and engage in dialogue and collaboration with the adherents of that religious tradition. Second, instead of offering courses to understand the beliefs and practices of the other religions, some theological institutions offer a course such as the *Christian Theology of Religions,* which essentially is an inward look into one's own Christian faith to examine its attitudes towards the religious 'other'. Other courses addressing Christian theological and doctrinal positions vis-à-vis other religions which have become common offerings have titles such as *Christian Theology of Dialogue* or *Christian Theology of Salvation* or *Christian Theology of Mission.*

Other seminaries may take a more integral approach in that, instead of creating additional courses, they integrate the study of the world's religions into existing courses or programmes. Obviously, the degree of integration varies. Some integrate into their core curriculum some aspect of interfaith learning such as requiring all students to begin the semester with a weekend or week-long interfaith immersion programme, or to participate in a weekly field ministry at an institution which belongs to a faith other than Christianity. Travel programmes where theological students go for extended visits to a culture and context which is predominantly Hindu or Muslim or Buddhist have also constituted forms of this integration process. It is worthwhile to note a comment on such programmes: 'Due to their experiential, holistic, and intense nature, travel seminars focused on the promotion of interfaith learning can shape a future religious leader's outlook on religious communities across the course of her entire career.'[15] There are also theological institutions which may decide that integration of interfaith learning is best done by encouraging individual lecturers to explore aspects of their subject-field from an interfaith perspective. The lecturer for the *Church History* course, for example, could dedicate a session or two to examining the church's positive interactions with the Muslim community during the time of the Crusades or in the colonial era; the *Liturgy* class could engage the students in comparing Christian initiation ceremonies with Hindu rites and practices; while the theology professor could discuss understandings of Christ as a Confucian sage or as a Boddhisattva, or the images of God from a cosmic or non-theistic perspectives.

Another way where interfaith learning is integrated into seminary formation is for the entire programme to have an interfaith focus. This takes integration a step further as the whole course would then be structured from

---

[15] Gordon S. Mikoski, 'Going Places: Travel Seminars as Opportunities for Interfaith Education', in *Teaching Theology and Religion* 16/4 (October 2013), 352-61, at 352.

an interfaith perspective. The course on *Revelation* or the course on *Scriptures*, for example, would discuss not only Christian revelation or Scriptures but also Islamic, Buddhist, Hindu perspectives of the same. The *Mysticism* course would look at Sufism and Kabbalah apart from Christian, Sikh, Jain and other forms of the mystical tradition. The *Ethics* course would in the main be comparative as it explores the various aspects of ethics from a truly interfaith perspective. A lot of these courses engage the new discipline of Comparative Theology.[16] Perhaps the most radical model for interfaith learning is where the seminary itself becomes interfaith. This is usually brought about by twinning arrangements or mergers between a Christian seminary and one or more formation institution of other religions, such as a Jewish theological seminary or an Islamic college or an institute for Buddhist studies. Where this happens, the Christian seminarian is then not only studying another religion from a lecturer who is of that tradition but also doing so while sitting alongside other seminarians who are members of that tradition as well. The following reflection from the director of such a programme says it all: 'The joint courses are valuable on multiple levels. Students benefit from learning and articulating their ideas in the presence of the religious "other". Faculty members explore areas of common academic interest from new vantage points. Relationships are built and deepened through the discovery of similarities and differences. There is a growing consensus that these courses are not only valuable but also essential to our respective missions.'[17]

Challenges and Conclusions

The models for interfaith education discussed above are not only possible options but are also what is already happening in theological institutions in different parts of the world today. While models exist for proactively facilitating interfaith learning and engagement with believers of other faith traditions, resistance to the same also abounds. Some of the fears and hesitancies are associated in part with the challenges which interfaith dialogue poses. Reaching out to learn about the 'other' is not a problem, but returning to examine one's own faith in light of this new learning is. As Raimon Panikkar (often regarded as a 'patriarch' of interreligious dialogue) opines, if I were engaged in interreligious dialogue, I usually follow that up with an intra-religious dialogue where I begin to reflectively ask questions about my own Christian beliefs in an attitude of 'accepting the challenge of

---

[16] See Francis X. Clooney, 'Comparative Theology and Inter-Religious Dialogue', in *The Wiley-Blackwell Companion to Inter-Religious Dialogue*, 51-63.

[17] Jennifer H. Peace, 'The Role of Theological Seminaries in Increasing Interfaith Co-operation in the United States: The CIRCLE Program of Andover Newton Theological School and Hebrew College', in *Journal of College & Character*, 12/1 (February 2011), 1-7, at 4.

change, a conversion, and the risk of upsetting my traditional patterns'.[18]
For many, this can be extremely challenging, not only emotionally and
psychologically but also religiously and theologically.

A document issued in 2000 by the Vatican's Congregation for the
Doctrine of the Faith expresses this challenge unequivocally. Entitled
Dominus Iesus, it has this to say: 'In the practice of dialogue between the
Christian faith and other religious traditions, as well as in seeking to
understand its theoretical basis more deeply, new questions arise that need to
be addressed' (§3).[19] It then spells out some of the theological issues which
could become problematic, especially if the praxis of dialogue leads to the
slippery slope of relativism:

> The Church's constant missionary proclamation is endangered today by
> relativistic theories which seek to justify religious pluralism, not only *de facto*
> but also *de iure* (or in principle). As a consequence, it is held that certain
> truths have been superseded; for example, the definitive and complete
> character of the revelation of Jesus Christ, the nature of Christian faith as
> compared with that of belief in other religions, the inspired nature of the
> books of Sacred Scripture, the personal unity between the Eternal Word and
> Jesus of Nazareth, the unity of the economy of the Incarnate Word and the
> Holy Spirit, the unicity and salvific universality of the mystery of Jesus
> Christ, the universal salvific mediation of the Church, the inseparability –
> while recognising the distinction – of the Kingdom of God, the Kingdom of
> Christ, and the Church, and the subsistence of the one Church of Christ in the
> Catholic Church (§4).

To be sure, similar misgivings and apprehensions are experienced by
many other Christians and Christian communities. That accounts for why
the agenda of interfaith learning and dialogue remains low on the priority
of many seminary curricula. At the same time, it is also an agenda
acknowledged as important, given that Christian ministers today have no
choice but to minister in a world where religious diversity has become the
norm. Discerning how to attend to interfaith learning is certainly no mean
task. Perhaps a recommendation from the joint commission of the three
main world Christian umbrella bodies (viz. mainline Protestants, Roman
Catholics, and Evangelicals) is instructive here. It recommends that the
membership of these bodies '*encourage* Christians to strengthen their own
religious identity and faith while deepening their knowledge and
understanding of different religions, and to do so, also taking into account

---

[18] Raimon Pannikar, *The Intrareligious Dialogue* (New York: Paulist Press, 1999),
75.
[19] Congregation for the Doctrine of the Faith, *Declaration 'Dominus Iesus' on the
Unicity and Salvific Universality of Jesus Christ and the Church* (6th August 2000):
www.vatican.va/roman_curia/congregations/cfaith/documents/rc_con_cfaith_doc_2
0000806_dominus-iesus_en.html

the perspectives of the adherents of those religions'.[20] Rootedness along with relatedness seems to be the way to go. As alluded to earlier in the article, seminaries are taking care of the former well enough, often at the expense of the latter. But the recommendation is for both to be operative at the same time. It is certainly sound advice and, hopefully, something that will be taken more seriously in theological formation throughout the world.

---

[20] World Council of Churches, Pontifical Council for Interreligious Dialogue, World Evangelical Alliance, *Christian Witness in a Multi-Religious World: Recommendations for Conduct* (28th January 2011): www.vatican.va/roman_curia/ pontifical_councils/interelg/documents/rc_pc_interelg_doc_20111110_testimonianz a-cristiana_en.html

MIGRATION AND THEOLOGICAL EDUCATION

Dawit Olika Teferssa

Introduction

As I was asked to write on 'Migration and Theological Education' from my context, it was natural to think of the migrant community I have been part of, and still belong to, in Norway and Sweden, combined with my experience and background as a theological student and teacher in Ethiopia; here lies the other dominant influence on my Christian life and theological perspectives. Based on reflections on my theological education and teaching experiences from these two contexts, I have chosen to focus on providing practical input and experience on how theological education is equipping and forming Christians and leaders for an authentic mission from a migrant church's perspective.

I hope that this approach can fulfil the desire of this volume to include a broad perspective and emerging models of theological education, especially from the global South. This is also in line with the theme of this volume 'Reflecting on and Equipping for Christian Mission' that is derived from *Theological Education and Formation*, which was an important study theme for Edinburgh 2010 and was highlighted in the *Edinburgh 2010 Common Call* in the following way:

> Recognizing the need to shape a new generation of leaders with authenticity for mission in a world of diversities in the twenty-first century, we are called to work together in new forms of theological education. Because we are all made in the image of God, these will draw on one another's unique charisms, challenge each other to grow in faith and understanding, share resources equitably worldwide, involve the entire human being and the whole family of God, and respect the wisdom of our elders, while also fostering the participation of children.[1]

The paradigm shifts in mission and theology during the last few decades, as well as the diverse and changing mission situation in Europe today, have created the need for a renewed model of theological education to provide a renewed vision of authentic Christian mission and evangelism.[2]

---

[1] World Council of Churches, Edinburgh 2010: Common Call: www.edinburgh2010.org/fileadmin/Edinburgh_2010_Common_Call_with_explanat ion.pdf, 2010 (accessed 22nd September 2014).
[2] 'To develop innovative models for theological education is a key mandate for mainline churches all over the world in the 21st century as migration is hugely and fast changing the global landscape of Christianity.' Dietrich Werner, 'Theological education with migrant Christians in the changing landscape of World Christianity':

Theological education has a central and key role in this process: to sustain the missional identity and passion of a church and equip committed leaders for this vision. But theological training in Europe, at least in its present shape, has not been successful or satisfactory in shaping, leading and equipping the church with authenticity for Christian mission due to several reasons – such as the challenges of pluralism, the continuous decline of passion and interest for evangelism in theological institutions in Europe, a bias towards academic study, and a common trend of shift from theology to religious studies.[3]

> The Danish theologian Mogens S. Mogensen claims that 'the missional church does not, however, simply need an academic theological education, but also a spiritual theological formation of its pastors and (other) leaders and co-workers'. The Danish-Norwegian theologian Knud Jørgensen gives expression to a similar line of thought when he says that missional leadership must especially 'emphasize the credibility that grows out of personal discipleship, a fully formed life of faith, and a personality that is whole'. This does not contradict the need for academic study, but raises questions around whether the current theological education at theological training institutions is satisfactory and meets the needs of pastors and the church.[4]

Migrants' theological education, and their new energies and commitments with regard to theological education and life, can challenge the monocultural denominations and academically oriented theological education in the West by providing lessons on different ways of being a church, introducing mission-oriented theological education, and sharing experiences of addressing cultural, theological and linguistic pluralism within Christian practice. This can contribute to the advancement of theological education in the West, in the migrants' diaspora situation as well as for their home churches. Whenever the issue of migration is raised in theological contexts, what is often discussed is the hardships and difficulties migrants face and the ethical response to be given to them. But much can be learned from the experience and background of migrant Christians' theological education with regard to equipping for authentic Christian mission. And this can contribute towards reshaping and equipping

---

www.oikoumene.org/en/resources/documents/wcc-programmes/education-and-ecumenical-formation/ete/wcc-programme-on-ecumenical-theological-education/theological-education-with-migrant-christians-in-the-changing-landscape-of-world-christianity, 1st December 2010 (accessed 6th December 2014).
[3] World Council of Churches, *Resource Book, WCC 10th Assembly, Busan* (Geneva: WCC, 2013), 113-23. W.A. Visser't Hooft, 'Evangelism among neo-pagans', in *International Review of Mission*, 66.264 (1977), 349-60.
[4] M. Dysjeland, 'Theological education for a missiological church: A perspective from a Theological Training Institutions in Brazil', in M. Lorke and D. Werner (eds), *Ecumenical Visions for the 21st Century: A reader for Theological Education* (Geneva: WCC, 2013), 33-34; Dietrich Werner, 'Oslo: The Future of Theology in the Changing Landscapes of Universities in Europe and Beyond', in *The Ecumenical Review*, 64.3 (October 2012), 395.

leaders for Christian mission in the West through a renewed model of theological education.[5] As part of his recommendations for developing a new theological theory in the West to re-imagine and renew theological education and mission, J.R. Steinke suggests the importance and role of mutual learning:

> Incarnational theological education also attends to the question: *With whom* do we best learn the ways of God in the world that will prepare both laity and diaconate and pastors to bear witness in the world? ... If we are serious about an incarnational theological education, we must be serious about ways to study alongside our brothers and sisters in the Global South.[6]

Therefore, there is a need for a positive theological dialogue and for multicultural networks that are built on the principles of interdependence, mutual recognition and learning to meet an emerging global crisis in theological education that has the potential to threaten the future of Christianity in the West.[7] It is within this framework of thought that I will present a brief overview of the characteristic features of the theological education of migrant Christians, their home churches and their theological institutions, with major emphasis on the experience of the Ethiopian Evangelical Church Mekane Yesus (EECMY). But, before that, I will give a brief background and status of the theological education of migrants.

Background and Status of Migrants' Theological Education

The number of migrants and the intensity of migration are increasing, and this has been expressed in different ways as 'people on the move', 'the irruptions of migrants' and 'the age of migration'. Among global migrants today, the largest group is Christian (49%) and its major destination is

---

[5] Drea Frötchling and Joseph Moloney, 'Theological Statement on Migration: The "Other" is my Neighbor, Developing an Ecumenical Response to Migration': https://www.oikoumene.org/en/folder/documents-pdf/Final_GEM_Report_2012.pdf, 2012, 97 (accessed 18th December 2014).
[6] Robin J. Steinke, 'Theological Education: A Theological Framework for Renewed Mission and Models', in *Dialogue: A Journal of Theology*, 50.4, Wiley Periodicals and Dialog (December 2011), 365. 'Imaged as a "reverse flow": the religion of immigrants attracts attention as a force that reshapes the religious landscapes of Europe and hides the impact of religion's decline in the Northern hemisphere'; Ogbu U. Kalu, 'Multicultural Theological Education in a Non-Western Context, 1975-2000', in David V. Esterline and Ogbu U. Kalu (eds), *Shaping Beloved Community: Multicultural Theological Education* (Louisville, KY and London, UK: Westminster John Knox Press, 2006), 238.
[7] World Council of Churches, *Resource Book*, 115. See also Knud Jørgensen, 'Mission in the Postmodern Society', in K.O. Sannes, E. Grandhagen, T. Hegertun, K. Jørgensen, K. Norseth and R. Olsen (eds), in *Med Kristus till Jordens ender: festskrift till Tormud Engelsviken* (Trondheim, Norway: Tapir akademisk forlag, 2008), 117-19.

Europe.[8] The number of migrant churches and fellowships in Europe is also increasing rapidly.[9]

> During the 16th to early 20th century, migration from Europe to countries of the South has brought models of theological education from the northern hemisphere to be planted (and later transformed) in contexts of the South... But in the last two decades of the 20th century and in the beginning of 21st century there are new realities emerging with regard to the presence of African and Asian Christian and non-Christian communities emigrating to Europe and the US due to trends in global reverse migration, and many are gradually forming their own churches, including new patterns of theological education.[10]

In most migrant-receiving countries, Christian worship is taking place in multicultural congregations. For example, in Sweden where I live and work, the number of migrant churches has grown from only 17 in the year 2000 to 67 in 2010.[11] The leaders and pastors of migrant churches obtain their theological education from different sources like online studies and distance education if they have not already been trained in the theological institutions back home prior to coming to the receiving country. It is common that many migrant congregations are led by lay people that have low or no background of theological education. A number of migrant church leaders have a negative attitude towards joining theological institutions in Europe for fear that they can be alienated from their theology and faith, and be victims of the influence of the academically oriented

---

[8] 'Of the total number of global migrants, an estimated 106 million (49%) are Christians, 60 million (27%) Muslims, Hindus (5%), Buddhists (3%), Jews (2%), other faiths (4%)... the major destination regions for Christian emigrants are Europe (38%), North America (34%) and Asia Pacific (11%)'; Melisande Lorke and Dietrich Werner, '"Other" is My Neighbor – Developing an Ecumenical Response to Migration, conference of the global Ecumenical Network on migration, Beirut/Geneva', in Melisande Lorke and Dietrich Werner (eds), *Ecumenical Visions for the 21st Century; A Reader for Theological Education* (Geneva: WCC, 2013), 272.

[9] Dietrich Werner, 'Theological education with migrant': www.oikoumene.org/en/resources/documents/wcc-programmes/education-and-ecumenical-formation/ete/wcc-programme-on-ecumenical-theological-education/theological-education-with-migrant-christians-in-the-changing-landscape-of-world-christianity

[10] Dietrich Werner, 'Challenges and major tasks for ecumenical theological education in the 21st century' (WCC/ETC): www.oikoumene.org/en/resources/documents/wcc-programmes/education-and-ecumenical-formation/ete, 2008, 10 (accessed 20th December 2014).

[11] Ø. Tholvsen, *Frikyrkan flyttar, En studie av frikyrkornas utveckling i Sverige 2000-2010 (Free churches move: the study of the development of free churches 2000-2010, author's translation)* (Örebro, Sweden: 2011), 27-28.

western style of education. The high academic requirements of western institutions are also difficult for many of them to fulfil.[12]

Despite the high percentage of migrant Christians in Europe and their big impact in changing our landscape, very often church thinking and theology in the West are still 'white', and migrant theology is given low and sometimes no representation at all in important theological conferences. There is segregation in worship and in diaconal and theological views that makes it hard to see migrants as equal contributors.[13]

> The concern here is that inadequate attention has been paid to the emergent model of theological education, namely 'ministerial formation by engagement' (MFE)... Western models of education erode the sense of the supernatural and eclipse the experiential dimension of the Christian faith. The MFE model counters with a spiritual model of education that advocates dependency on the Spirit.[14]

For example, representation of migrant churches and new models of theological education from migrant backgrounds were weak at the conference held in Oslo concerning the future of theology in Europe.[15] Often there is mistrust and prejudice against migrants' theology due to their conservative views on homosexuality, the emphasis on conversion, problems related to attempts of healing and prophecies, etc. 'The biographical and narrative theologies of many migrant Christians are by and large viewed as pre-Enlightenment and "like we believed in the fifties".'[16] In addition, migrants' theology is sometimes referred to '... as being "one mile wide, but only one inch deep"'.[17] Moreover, there is a lack of interaction and dialogue on the theological and ethical differences for better understanding between the western and migrant theologies.[18] But during the last few years, the necessity of creating networks and dialogue between migrant churches and local churches/theological institutions has started to receive attention, to design innovative models of theological

---

[12] Gerrit Noort, 'Emerging Migrant Churches in the Netherlands: Missiological Challenges and mission frontiers', in *International Review of Mission*, 100.1 (April 2011), 15.

[13] '... theology is white... the Western academic standards are leading, while there is very little emphasis on a practical ministerial formation and contextual learning by experience in the community'; Gerrit Noort, 'The Impact of Migration on the Churches and the Ecumenical Movement; Netherlands Mission Council', in *Final GEM Report*: https://www.oikoumene.org/en/folder/documents-pdf/Final_GEM_Report_2012.pdf, 2012, 85 (accessed 18th December 2014); G. Campese, 'The Irruption of Migrants: Theology of Migration in the 21st Century', in *Theological Studies*, 73.1 (February 2012), 6-8: http://tsj.sagepub.com/content/73/1/3 (accessed 25th November 2014).

[14] Kalu, 'Multicultural Theological Education', 238.

[15] Werner, 'Oslo: The Future of Theology in the Changing Landscapes', 394.

[16] Noort, 'Emerging Migrant Churches', 14.

[17] Werner, 'Oslo. The Future of Theology in the Changing Landscapes', 396.

[18] Noort, 'Emerging Migrant Churches', 7.

educations and bridge programmes[19] that can provide introductory courses that address theological, ministerial and cultural issues to empower these pastors for effective and contextualised mission in the West.[20]

Characteristic Features of Migrants' Theological Education

How theological education is conducted and formed is what shapes the life, ministry and mission of the church, church ministers and individual Christians. There is therefore a very close interrelatedness between Christian mission and theological education.[21] Below are some of the common characteristics of this interrelatedness in the context of migrants' theological education.

The divine call: basic requirements and criteria for migrants' theological education

In the context of migrants' theological education, both in the diaspora and in their home country, joining theological education is very closely connected with the vocation of an individual to be a minister, leader or pastor of a church. As far as my experience as a theological student and teacher in Ethiopia is concerned, even if there are a few cases where relatives and family members of senior church officials were offered the

---

[19] Dietrich Werner lists possible options for achieving this goal: 'a) self-organized, church-based courses on theological education for immigrant church leaders, supported by networks of immigrant churches or smaller Bible colleges; b) non-degree courses for theological education of immigrant church leaders provided by supporting mission agencies and ecumenical associations of churches in a given region; c) certificate degree courses of theological education by extension provided for immigrant churches in co-operation with existing institutions of missiological training and theological education (ATTIG model); d) the establishment of new graduate degree courses in established institutions of theological education within the Bologna system of theological degrees (BA in Mission and World Christianity, planned in Hermannsburg/Göttingen; and MA of Intercultural Theology in Hermannsburg/Göttingen) (see Frieder Ludwig in: epd. Dok 35, August 2010 on 'Theologische Ausbildung im Horizont der weltweiten Christenheit'); e) integration of immigrant church candidates into existing degree courses of non-university institutions of theological education of the protestant free churches (Elstal, BFP); f) integration of immigrant church candidates into external theological degree courses offered by non-European institutions within Europe (UNISA courses; Concordia and St Louis courses).' Dietrich Werner, 'Theological education with migrant Christians': www.oikoumene.org/en/resources/documents/wcc-programmes/education-and-ecumenical-formation/ete/wcc-programme-on-ecumenical-theological-education/theological-education-with-migrant-christians-in-the-changing-landscape-of-world-christianity
[20] Noort, 'Emerging Migrant Churches', 15.
[21] WCC, *Resource Book,* 121.

chance to join theological studies without receiving a personal call, in most cases internal and external calls are a basic requirement and precondition for joining theological seminaries. The internal call is the personal feeling and conviction of the individual, and this should be supplemented by an external call extended to him/her based on the fruits and witness of his/her life and ministry in the church at least during the last 3-5 years before joining theological training.

Spiritual formation: the goal and the nature of migrants' theological education

The common understanding and practice within theological education in the migrants' context is that the purpose and goal of it is to promote spiritual formation. Both the students and teachers of theological education are continuously transformed through personal and communal devotional life, meditation on and study of the biblical texts, lectures and reading of different materials in order to be equipped for authentic Christian mission. Migrants' theological education and institutions in most cases function primarily as a spiritual workshop that transforms the individuals, and not just as a professional education.

> The history of modern theological education has been a history that has increasingly diminished the power of the Spirit as an institution embodied in modernity and rationalism, any talk of non-rational, unpredictable, non-empirical being that guides and enlivens our beings has been less than acceptable within the curriculum... Theological education is a miss if it continues to adopt the rationalism of modernity over against the work of the Holy Spirit.[22]

Theological education should bring us closer to God through spiritual formation, prayer and openness to the Holy Spirit, developing a personal and intimate relationship with God. Theological education that marginalises prayer and contemplation will not succeed in proper spiritual and character formation. 'The best theological education will involve character formation as well as intellectual development. Our chief aspiration is to become more like Christ and to model that for others.'[23] As far as my experience of studying and teaching theology in the South and immigrant contexts shows,

---

[22] Kyle J.A. Small, 'Missional Theology for Schools of Theology: Re-engaging the Question "What is Theological about a Theological School?"' in Craig van Gelder (ed), *The Missional Church & Leadership Formation, Helping Congregations Develop Leadership Capacity* (Cambridge: Eerdmans, 2009), 46, 51, 61; Roar G. Fotland, 'The Southern face phase of Christianity': The contribution of the Global South to the church in the Global North', in T. Engelsviken, E. Barbakk, R. Olsen and T. Strandenaes (eds), *Mission in the world, communicating the Gospel in the 21st Century* (Oxford, Regnum, 2008), 215-29.
[23] Darren Cronshaw, 'Re-envisioning Theological Education: Mission and the Local Church', in *Mission Studies*, Vol. 28, No 1 (2011), 104.

I believe that it is only theologians that have become disciples of Christ and have gone through a life-transforming encounter, who through their life and witness are able to draw people to Christ and equip them to do the same thing with others.

The Bible: the unshaken ground for migrants' theological education

In general, the Bible has the highest authority and respect in the life of migrant Christians and their fellow Christians in their home country. Most theological students have a strong faith in the Bible and are familiar with many biblical texts prior to their joining theological institutions. The Bible is seen as a guide, foundation and source of their education, whatever field of theology they are studying. Students bring their Bible to classrooms and use it in all the courses, no matter whether it is church history, missiology, dogmatics, pastoral care or counselling. Such an attitude towards the Bible and the way it is used in migrants' theological education can bring inspiration to western theological education where historical critical methods put much focus on mastering the sacred text and critiquing it.

> ... Interpretation in the twenty-first century is as confusing as ever. Enlightenment assumptions have detached the reader from the text in a type of sterile analytical approach. Students in seminary still struggle with letting the text touch them and change them – and they are especially resistant to having the text get under their skin. The scientific approach the Enlightenment promotes has taught generations of scholars to stand above the text and critique it according to approved historical methods.[24]

From the perspective of migrants' theological education, unless the Scripture is given a central place to influence, touch, change and transform the life of theological students, it will be hard to equip them for authentic Christian mission.

Missiology: an integral and central part of migrants' theological education

In the context of migrants (both in the homeland and diaspora contexts), Christian mission is a red thread that runs through all courses given in theological institutions. Mission is seen as the central identity of a church and the prime goal of theological training; it is intrinsically interrelated with discipleship-making as an obligation of all Christians. Most migrant theological education has a high focus on the equipping of a Christian or a

---

[24] Scott W. Sunquist, *Understanding Christian Mission: Participation in Suffering and Glory* (Grand Rapids, MI: Baker Academic, 2013), 174: 'The protestant theological education is a creation of modernity, and it has been captured by modernity. It recognizes authority within the individual, not in external sources'; Small, 'Missional Theology for Schools of Theology', 63-64.

church for the central task of evangelism and disciple-making as the prime goal of theological training. Churches and theological institutions in Europe can learn from and be inspired by this interrelatedness between theological studies and mission/evangelism in a contextualised way.[25]

> As children of the Enlightenment, we distinguished between theory and practice. An encounter with theologies from the Global South will help us to understand that theology cannot and must not be separated from the concrete world... Theology must therefore be based on missional/missionary experience...[26]

The majority of migrant churches are devoted to *internal mission* (mission among people that speak the same language, belong to the same ethnic background, and come from the same country), and to *external and/or common mission*, that intentionally focuses on post-Christians beyond the limit of ethnic and geographical borders.[27] Such a commitment and conviction of missional identity and faithfulness are often the result of a theological education that is mission-oriented and mission-centred.[28]

Congregation-related and oriented theological education of migrants

In the Ethiopian context, theological institutions are mostly receiving students from congregations; they train and equip them academically and send them back to the congregations. Engagement and participation in the local congregation/practical placements and field training throughout the period of study are commonly used to give students the challenge and opportunity to apply their studies in their life and ministry in a practical way. Field education assignment to a nearby local congregation to participate in different ministries and outreach programmes, summer and Christmas holidays services, engagement in the local congregation, Theological Education by Extension (TEE),[29] and evening classes that

---

[25] For example; according to a study made by Jehu J. Hanciles among the pastors of African immigrant churches in the USA, 70 of the pastors believed in evangelism/mission as the principal area of ministry. Jehu J. Hanciles, *Beyond Christendom: Globalization, African Migration and the Transformation of the West* (Maryknoll, NY: Orbis Books, 2008), 364.

[26] Knud Jørgensen, 'Mission in the Postmodern Society', 118-19; Craig L. Nessan, 'Mission and Theological Education – Berlin, Athens, and Tranquebar: A North American Perspective', in *Mission Studies*, 27 (2010), 176-93.

[27] Noort, 'Emerging Migrant Churches', 12.

[28] '... the changing faces of global migration have huge implications for contextual theology and teachings on evangelism as the majority of migrant churches have a self-understanding which is positive on evangelism.' Dietrich Werner, '*Evangelism in Theological Education in Europe – 12 considerations from ETC/WCC*' (paper for Bossey consultation of WCC/CWME, Bossey, Switzerland, 2102), 8.

[29] For example, in Ethiopia and Tanzania, theological education by extension (TEE) has been one of the best models used to keep the necessary balance between theoretical and practical aspects of theological studies. See M. Dysjeland,

provide the opportunity for participation in the local ministry, are some of the common trends within theological education in Ethiopia. This is effective in bridging the gap between the academic aspects of theological education and involvement in congregational life and ministry, equipping the students with methods and skills that they can use for ministry, and empowering them to be multiculturally sensitive and engaged.[30] 'A re-envisioned theological education will engage with local churches as well as the academic requirements of college life.'[31] The importance of participation and engagement in the local congregation is not limited to students but applies also to the teaching staff.

> For faculty, part of their modelling and basis for teaching can draw on their local church involvement. Ideally, this will involve faculty dedicating time to serving in local church ministry or other mission appointments...[32]

Both from my own experience and that of others as a teacher in a theological seminary in Ethiopia, I can tell how busy the weekends and most of the evenings during the week used to be due to teaching and preparation for preaching at Sunday services, speaking at spiritual conferences, training lay ministers and conducting short courses related to the ministry of the church, preaching and teaching in home-to-home prayer gatherings, in addition to routine teaching in the seminary. Such a connection with the congregation's life and ministry is highly enriching to both students and teachers.

Conclusion

I do believe that characteristic features of theological education of migrants as mentioned above can challenge and inspire traditional models of western theological education by sharing experiences and lessons on how to address diaconal and missiological challenges in multi-religious, multicultural, ethnically and linguistically diverse contexts and situations. Multiculturalism is the major challenge for European contextual theologies.[33]

Gerrit Noort points out that the presence of migrant churches in the West demands the rethinking of missiological understanding and practice in our changed society in order to identify missiological challenges and mission frontiers.[34] To achieve this, the development of networks of theological education and dialogue in Europe where migrant Christians are given the

---

'Theological education for a missiological church', 33-48, concerning a similar experience in theological training in Brazil.
[30] Cronshaw, 'Re-envisioning Theological Education', 94-95.
[31] Cronshaw, 'Re-envisioning Theological Education', 109.
[32] Cronshaw, 'Re-envisioning Theological Education', 109.
[33] Noort, 'Emerging Migrant Churches', 13.
[34] Noort, 'Emerging Migrant Churches', 4, 11.

opportunity to share from their theology, experiences, and tradition, is important.[35] Therefore migrant Christians' full participation and fair representation in all types of European and global theological networks and consultations can be a valuable contribution to a renewed form of theological training that can help Christians and churches to rediscover the importance of evangelism and to equip the church and its members for authentic mission.[36]

> Learning how to theologize together, without reducing such practices as healing and exorcism to superstition, and without declaring western styles of believing as unbelief, requires an intercultural hermeneutic that does not equate an intercultural approach to theology with relativism, but that supports the student to identify and strengthen identity in the context of migration.[37]

We live through a time of transition and paradigm shifts that challenge western theology to positively but critically welcome fresh insights, experiences, initiatives and theologies. There are some churches and institutions that have begun such a process to welcome and listen to the theology from the South which is going to have a significant role in Christianity in the future. But more needs to be done to increase the level and scale of our engagement in such theological networking that may create new opportunities of mutual learning, to rediscover and reaffirm the importance and practice of authentic mission, to find new and fresh ways of sharing the Gospel in a multicultural and multi-religious Europe today.[38]

Promotion of experience-sharing through the exchange of students and guest lecturers, building networks of friendship and partnerships that are

---

[35] 'The changing nature of theology has further implications for theological education and leadership training. Centers of theological education need to be established and further developed in the South as there is a great need for non-Western exegetical studies which will help us understand the Bible better, and which will complement the work that is being done by Western writers.' Todd Johnson & Sandra S. Kim, *The Changing face of global Christianity*: www.bostontheological.org/assets/files/02tjohnson.pdf (accessed 20th May 2014), 28. '… We will see that today, although vestiges of missionary hardware remain, the experiment with tertiary education by African churches has created a new opportunity for the application of an indigenous model of theological education. In fact, in recent years, young educated Christians have designed a new strategy of "formation by engagement"'; Kalu, 'Multicultural Theological Education in a Non-Western Context', 226-27.

[36] Lemma Desta, 'God's Transforming Mission and Norwegian Churches and Mission Organizations: Some Observations from a Migrant Perspective', in B. Fagerli, K. Jørgensen, R. Olsen, K. Storstein Haug and K. Tveitereid (eds), *A learning missional Church: reflections from young missiologists* (Edinburgh 2010) (Oxford: Regnum, 2012), 13-14.

[37] Noort, 'Emerging Migrant Churches', 15.

[38] 'The task for providing accessible and contextually relevant forms of theological education for each part of the worldwide fellowships of Christian churches is far from being accomplished', WCC, *Resource Book,* 115.

based on mutual respect, and learning with institutions and fellowships that have fresh and active experience on evangelism and mission, increasing the presence and representation of international/migrant students/teaching staff in theological institutions in Europe, offering courses on different theologies from the South, and genuinely recognising and considering Christian scholarship from the South/East, and working on their translation into English and non-European languages, as well as encouraging more research, are among the many things that can be done.[39] The fact that there are always things that all cultures can learn from each other is not only calling for the integration of global perspectives into theological courses, but it also underlines that theological education will be richer as a non-Eurocentric exercise.[40]

---

[39] 'Re-envisioned theological education in the global context, and the multi-cultural context of the Western world, has to be cross-cultural... A culturally diverse student body helps develop intercultural skills', Cronshaw, 'Re-envisioning Theological Education', 102-103.

[40] Cronshaw. 'Re-envisioning Theological Education', 104.

ECUMENICAL FORMATION IN THEOLOGY (ECUFIT)

Werner Kahl

The History Behind the Programme
Ecumenical Formation in Theology

The programme *Ecumenical Formation in Theology* (EcuFiT) is a pilot project that was developed and which is organised by the *Missionsakademie* in Hamburg, Germany. It aims at serving the theological formation of people – both with and without migration experiences – who are interested in shaping the Protestant Church in Germany (EKD) in the light of a cross-cultural opening of the church.

At the *Missionsakademie*, the first course of EcuFit was due to begin in the second half of 2015. It has replaced the programme *African Theological Training in Germany* (ATTiG) at the *Missionsakademie*. ATTiG is a two-year programme which was inaugurated in 2001. It was designed for preparing theologically migrant pastors from West Africa for cross-cultural service in Germany, focusing especially on enhancing the cultural sensitivities of participants. ATTiG exclusively addressed the needs of pastors from West Africa. This restriction was due to two developments: first, the primate of the Aladura Church in Nigeria, on a visit to Hamburg in the second half of the 1990s took the initiative of encouraging the teaching staff of the *Missionakademie* to design a programme for preparing African migrant pastors for service in Germany. Second, from the 1990s onwards, African congregations have by far outnumbered other migrant churches in Germany. In Hamburg alone, more than eighty such congregations can be counted; all over Germany, about one thousand is a realistic informed guess.

In the past fourteen years, more than one hundred pastors, apostles, elders and prophets of African migrant churches in the northern regions of Germany have successfully passed through ATTiG. Through this programme, the competence of these church leaders for societal and ecclesial integration – in the sense of a cross-cultural inclusion involving all partners – has been boosted. At the same time, points of contact between churches of a charismatic-pentecostal orientation with an African origin and membership on the one hand, and of the Protestant Church in Germany on the other, have been created or enlarged. A good number of ATTiG alumni have participated in joint church projects in past years. And they have engaged contexts of traditional church life in Germany with their particular versions of the Christian faith and with their faith experiences. Examples are the active participation of former ATTiG students in the

Evangelische Kirchentag (bi-annual national church gathering) in 2013 in Hamburg, in the monthly *International Gospel Services* in the St Georg community in Hamburg, in the organisation of the very first intercultural confirmation class for children of both German and African descent, also in St Georg. In addition, ATTiG alumni have come up with new initiatives by means of which they have made a lasting impact on church life in Germany. Examples are the organisation of an international and inter-confessional women's conference in 2014, and the formation of para-church organisations for young people of mixed descent, like *GADED* ('God all day every day') in Hamburg. And the first batch of BA students of the recently established *Fachhochschule für interkulturelle Theologie* in Hermannsburg (FIT) is made up primarily of ATTiG alumni. ATTiG has prepared them sufficiently for successfully undergoing theological studies at this college of higher education, in conjunction with Göttingen University.

The majority of African migrant church leaders in the northern regions of Germany (Hamburg-Berlin-Lübeck-Kiel-Hannover-Osnabrück-Bremen) have passed through ATTiG. In the past few years a change in the composition of the student body became obvious: fewer and fewer pastors applied for ATTiG; instead more church members in limited leadership positions – Bible study teachers, elders, etc. – began to show an interest in ATTiG. Younger applicants began to apply. Increasingly, young adults of African descent – second generation – who have been educated or formally trained in a professional school in Germany have participated in ATTiG. This has generally led to an enhanced ability to reflect critically upon theological traditions – a majority of former ATTiG students had not passed through higher institutions of learning in their home countries, while some had only a rudimentary experience of formal education. The language of communication in ATTiG has shifted from English to German. The student body of ATTiG has become more international: participants from Anglophone West Africa – Ghana and Nigeria – are not in the majority any more. The student body has become diverse, with members coming originally from West, East and Central Africa, including Francophone countries. In addition, members of German free churches – Baptists and Pentecostals – have been admitted to ATTiG. While in the first years of ATTiG a strong apologetic tendency was dominant among the students, especially on the side of non-compromising Pentecostals, participants have become more self-critical and more balanced in their assessment of European church traditions and theologies. In addition, an increased interest and competence can be registered in actively shaping the *Evangelische Kirche* as the majority protestant church in Germany. All these transformations indicated the need for a replacement of ATTiG by another programme.

The Relevance of the Programme
Ecumenical Formation in Theology

The transformation experienced in ATTiG coincided with contemporary initiatives and projects of the EKD churches that aimed at an *intercultural opening* of the church. For example, at the end of 2014, the Council of the EKD published a position paper on future co-operation with 'migrant churches' ('Gemeinden anderer Spräche und Herkunft' – churches of a different language and origin): 'Gemeinsam evangelisch! Erfahrungen, Theologische Orientierungen und Perspektiven für die Arbeit mit Gemeinden anderer Sprache und Herkunft' (EKD Texte 119) – 'Being evangelical together! Experiences, theological orientations and perspectives for co-operation with churches of a different language and origin'. At various levels of church life, recommendations are given not only for integration and inclusion, but for joint programmes and projects aiming at a reshaping of the EKD churches – in the light of the changed, i.e. culturally and ethnically varied, make-up of the contemporary German population. Christians who – or whose parents – originated from a region outside Germany, are taken seriously as Christians who represent different versions of the Christian faith, who have different experiences with the faith, and who express the faith in ways different from those common in German church traditions. These Christians with their particular traditions are appreciated as a source of inspiration enriching the church in Germany. Representatives of the second and third generation come into special focus here. Some young adults with an African background have begun to create new parishes in Germany at the interface of the cultural and religious traditions of their parents and the traditions and values of their homeland Germany which they have internalised to a certain extent. These younger believers have a rich experience and ability in cross-cultural communication, and they represent a new, globally conversant generation, creating a 'third space'. As such, they have an important role to play in the re-formation of EKD churches.

EcuFiT reacts to this *kairos*. ATTiG served as a space for preparing representatives of African migrant churches for qualified encounters with EKD churches. EcuFiT has the task of enabling both Christians with and Christians without an immediate experience of migration, for *a joint effort at creating and shaping cross-cultural faith communities* within the EKD. In short, EcuFiT serves EKD programmes and projects of an intercultural opening of the church. Inasmuch as participants study and reflect together as diverse people, cross-culturality is being experienced and learned in this pilot project.

The *Missionsakademie* at the University of Hamburg is the appropriate location for such a project in Germany due to its manifold relationships with the EKD churches at all levels, to the faculty of theology at the University of Hamburg and to various migrant communities in Hamburg. All three partners have expressed a serious interest in the creation of

EcuFiT. It is expected that EcuFiT will – like its predecessor ATTiG – inspire similar projects in different parts of Germany.

Addressees and Structure of the Programme
Ecumenical Formation in Theology

A course of EcuFiT is designed for twenty participants who are able to communicate without difficulty in German. Participants will be invited from the following groups residing in the northern regions of Germany (Lübeck, Kiel, Hamburg, Bremen, Berlin, Hannover):

* Representatives in leadership positions from migrant churches (about ten participants)
* Representatives in leadership positions from EKD churches (about five participants)
* Students of theology (about five participants who will earn credit points for the course)

The duration of EcuFiT is one year in two semesters (two modules). Each semester consists of four weekend blocks of 12 hours each (one semester: 48 hours): October-January / April-July. In between these semesters, two weekend blocks (in February and March) will be offered which are obligatory for non-student participants and will involve exposure programmes in faith communities with subsequent reflections.

During the first semester, the relevance of cross-cultural faith communities will be explored from the perspective of various theological fields: biblical-exegetical, church history, systematic theology, and mission studies. In the second semester, cross-cultural ministry will be reflected in perspectives of practical theology: liturgy and homiletics, pastoral care, pedagogy of religion, and diaconical work. University lecturers and experts from churches will be invited to lead the various subjects. Particular attention will be given to the inclusion of lecturers with migration experience.

EcuFit is about getting used to learning, teaching and celebrating together the church in diversity – as an anticipation and preparation of a cross-cultural re-formation of the church which might become meaningful to a diversified population.

Example of an Alternative Liturgy

The members of the very last ATTiG course of 2014-15 proposed, after a consultation process with German theologians, the following alternative liturgy. This proposal might serve as an example of what EcuFiT is about.

Theological reflection

A service should be celebrated in a manner that allows for the experience of the Gospel, i.e. the good news about the dignifying acceptance of the individual by God. Forms of interaction should be implemented that are conducive to making this fundamental meaning of Gospel transparent. In this sense, a welcoming culture has to be practised: a friendly greeting of individual visitors which is motivated by a sincere interest in the visitor for his or her own sake, and an expression of appreciation of visitors for their presence, during the course of the service. The individual is treated as a special person with whom God has established a relationship. Forms of active participation that facilitate a productive inclusion of the individual perspectives in the service are explored. A successful service has an uplifting and life-affirming effect on participants.

The structure of the service is printed in a flyer with all texts (songs, Creed, Lord's Prayer) included for participants. The lyrics of songs can be projected onto a screen or wall. Participants are invited to stand up for the songs, the prayers and the concluding benediction.

The service has a duration of approximately 1½ hours. Not all proposed elements need to be included.

Structure of service

- *Introductory songs* (with organ/choir/band):
  meditative to lively   00:00
- *Trinitarian opening*   00:10
- *Free prayer* for the presence of God   00:11
- *Greeting* of participants with greeting ritual and song   00:14
- *Reading of sermon passage* by an elder   00:20
- *Bible study* on the passage in small groups with the
  subsequent possibility of sharing observations
  with the whole congregation   00:24
- An open and prepared (but not fixed in writing) *sermon*,
  with the pastor engaging the participants while he or she
  links it with the observations gained during the Bible study   00:34
- Invitation to recite the *Apostolic Creed*
  (with introduction for visitors)   00:44
- *Song* (with collection of *offerings*)   00:47
- Participants – after consultation with the pastor – are given
  the chance to share a significant *faith experience*
  in front of the congregation   00:51
- Open invitation for an *individual prayer request with laying
  on of hands* (by the pastor, with choir/organ in background)   01:01
- Open *intercessory prayer* with an invitation to participants
  to communicate aloud spontaneous prayer requests,

with the congregation responding with a refrain (organ)   01:12
- *The Lord's Prayer*   01:20
- *Benediction* (pastor)   01:23
- *Closing song*   01:24
- *Announcements and Farewell*   01:28

JOHN STOTT AND THE
LANGHAM SCHOLARSHIP PROGRAMME

Ian Shaw

On 20 September 1969, the Parish Church Council of All Souls Church, Langham Place, where John Stott (1921- 2011) had been Rector since 1950, met in Buckinghamshire for a day conference. It had become increasingly clear that the pivotal role Stott was playing in global evangelicalism was no longer compatible with maintaining full-time parish ministry in an increasingly international church in the heart of London. Out of that meeting came the decision that All Souls would bring in someone to take over the leadership of the church, and allow Stott to undertake a wider ministry, although he would retain the title of Rector, and continue to share the preaching. When Michael Baughen (1930-), was subsequently appointed Vicar of All Souls in 1970, Stott shared with the church his belief that this new arrangement would 'enable me to respond to the call to a wider ministry'.[1] In time it became clear that the focus of that 'wider ministry' was to be upon the Two-Thirds World.

In typical Stott fashion, the organisational restructuring at All Souls had been carefully thought through and prepared for. A key issue was how the wider ministry would be financed. This had led to the establishment in 1969 of the Langham Trust (named after the London street on which All Souls stands), encouraged by the Church Treasurer, Raymond Dawes, an investment banker. Dawes served as chair of the trust for more than twenty years. The Declaration of Trust set out a wide range of purposes for which the funds could be used, but at its heart was a desire to 'Promote and maintain the Evangelical Ministry', at home and overseas, and to support societies whose object was the 'advancement of the Christian faith'.[2] The doctrinal foundations of the Langham Trust rested on the Thirty-Nine Articles of Religion of the Church of England, considered a 'general exposition of the Reformed Faith', with particular emphasis laid on four doctrines: Scripture, 'the only rule of Christian faith and conduct, sufficient for salvation, and supreme in its authority'; Justification 'on the ground of the atoning death of Christ alone, through faith alone'; the Ministry and

---

[1] All Souls Newsletter, June 1970, cited in Timothy Dudley-Smith, *John Stott: A Global Ministry* (Downers Grove, Illinois: IVP, 2001), 141.
[2] Declaration of Deed of Trust Document for Langham Trust, 1969, John Stott Archives, Lambeth Palace Library, File STOTT / 3 / 15 / 1 – Langham Trust UK 1969-1989, Ff. 78-85.

Sacraments; and the Church, whose 'spiritual unity' already exists and has never been destroyed, and whose 'calling is to worship God and witness to Him in the world'. The Langham Trust was firmly anchored on the Bible, the classic doctrines of Protestant Evangelicalism, and an ecclesiological horizon that was global and missional.[3]

The Langham Trust became the main source for funding for Stott's ministry and the administration and travel associated with it, and existed separately from the All Souls Church accounts. Because Stott was widely known in North America, a significant amount of donation income quickly began to be received from there for Langham Trust. One early donor was Billy Graham. In the letter that accompanied the April 1970 donation he wrote 'I am absolutely thrilled that the possibility has arisen that you may be able to give more of your time to ministering to the world church. I am only a steward of the money that the Lord sends me through His people. You have as much right to use it as I do.' [4]

In March 1971, exploratory discussions were held into extending the trust's work into America, and in August of that year lawyers were instructed to incorporate the Langham Trust as a charity in the USA.[5] This US branch was to become the Langham Foundation, which held its first formal meeting in November 1974. Apart from its own running expenses, all income was to go to the Langham Trust in the UK. Thus was launched a global ministry which produced a series of programmes which have never in terms of size of staff or budget been large, but have had a strategic international impact that has consistently exceeded the sum of their parts.

John Stott a Global Figure

Although he already had an international profile, the creation of the Langham Trust assisted the transformation of Stott into a global evangelical leader. John Pollock described him as 'in effect the theological leader of world evangelicalism'.[6] He played a prominent role in 1974 as chair of the drafting committee for the Lausanne Covenant at the International Congress on World Evangelization. He was also chair of the drafting committee for the Manila Manifesto, a document produced by the second Lausanne International Congress in 1989. He was vice president of the International Fellowship of Evangelical Students from 1995 to 2003, and

---

[3] Doctrinal Foundations of Langham Trust in Declaration of Deed, Langham Trust, 1969.

[4] Letter from Billy Graham to John Stott in John Stott Papers, 30 April 1970, cited in Dudley-Smith, *Global Ministry*, 142.

[5] 'The First Twenty Years of the Langham Trust', Minutes of Langham Trust; F23-26, Lambeth Palace STOTT / 3 /15 / 1.

[6] Quotation from cover of *John Stott At Keswick: A Lifetime Of Teaching - A collection of John Stott's teaching from his years at Keswick* (Authentic Media: Carlisle, 2008).

President of Tear Fund from 1983 to 1997. Stott wrote over fifty books and hundreds of articles which had a global impact – *Basic Christianity* sold more than two million copies and was translated into more than 60 languages.[7] Billy Graham said of Stott, 'I can't think of anyone who has been more effective in introducing so many people to a biblical world view. He represents a touchstone of authentic biblical scholarship that, in my opinion, has scarcely been paralleled since the days of the 16th century European Reformers.'[8]

In the years after 1970, Stott increasingly devoted his considerable abilities to assisting the training of a generation of gifted Christian leaders from the global South. Between 1956 and 1959 Stott was already travelling overseas every year for one or more university missions, and his 1959 trip included ministry opportunities in Uganda, Kenya, Rwanda-Burundi, and South Africa.[9] He was moved by the growth of global Christianity, but came to believe that the theological institution was key for the future of the church,[10] as he later explained 'the health of a congregation depends largely on its pastor, the pastor on his seminary, and the seminary on its faculty.... Indeed, as Third World Christians continue to grow, there is an urgent need for more seminary teachers who combine evangelical faith, personal godliness and academic excellence.'[11]

Supporting Scholars

The decision to invest a significant amount of his time and resources in training leaders at postgraduate level, especially to gain PhD qualifications was highly significant. The use of the funds donated to the Langham Trust in the early years was fairly broad, but the primary focus on the global South became quickly clear. In 1970 the Langham Trust for the first time funded visits by John Stott to the global South to lead student missions, preach at international gatherings, and to lecture in seminaries and theological colleges. In early 1984, Stott spoke at seven theological colleges in Africa during a visit of one month.[12] On these and many subsequent visits he was often introduced to young evangelical leaders who had a need to study further at a higher level to enable them to be more effective teachers and leaders. However, resources to support evangelical Christian leaders from outside the West to undertake higher level study,

---

[7] Timothy Dudley-Smith, *John Stott: The Making of a Leader* (Leicester, U.K./Downers Grove, Ill.: Inter-Varsity Press, 1999), 89, 93-94; and Dudley-Smith, *Global Ministry*, 291.
[8] Quoted in Langham Partnership News, Australia, May 2007.
[9] Dudley-Smith, *Making of a Leader*, 398-419.
[10] John Stott - Letter to friends, March 1994, in John Stott's personal papers.
[11] John Stott, Personal Statement about the Langham Trust Scholarships with Advert for post of Administrator for Langham Trust, April 1989.
[12] Langham Trustees Meeting 30 April 1984, F. 66-67.

especially at doctoral level, were almost non-existent. A separate bursary account within the Langham Trust was formally opened in June 1974 to finance opportunities for postgraduate studies for students from the global South. In 1976 this formally became the Langham Trust 'Third World Scholarship Fund', and scholars began to be known as Research Bursars.[13]

The other major project to grow out of the Langham Trust was the London Institute for Contemporary Christianity (LICC), which grew out of the London Lectures in Contemporary Christianity started in 1974. LICC was founded in 1982, and Stott served as Director until 1986, running short courses of around 10 weeks, although it was not his full-time work. LICC sought to train lay people to 'think Christianly', enabling them to integrate Christian faith, life, and mission, True to his growing concern for the global South, it was designed to have an international student body, with 'strong input from the developing countries'.[14] LICC and the Langham Trust, which became Langham Partnership, were Stott's two dearly loved 'children',[15] with close connections between them remaining. In 1987, the Langham Third World Scholarship Fund was contributing £5000 per year into the LICC Third World Scholarship Fund.[16] The global South was to be where Stott focussed his remaining energies.

A strong connection between the investment by the Langham Trust in scholarships for global South students and another of Stott's projects, the Evangelical Fellowship in the Anglican Church (EFAC), should be noted. EFAC had been constituted in 1961 in order to provide a structured network for evangelicals throughout the global Anglican Communion, who often found themselves extremely isolated.[17] Stott was its first secretary, and he was largely responsible for an EFAC bursary fund to enable Anglican leaders from the global South to undertake further theological studies. The scheme combined 'study and experience' of a cross-cultural nature, enriching the students, the college in which they studied, and local churches to which they were linked.[18] By 1977, EFAC had taken around 60 evangelical clergy from Asia and Africa to study in the UK, mainly at Bachelors and Masters level.[19] However, EFAC had insufficient resources to extend this work, so in 1976 the Langham Trust agreed to take on some

---

[13] Minutes of Langham Trust, F23-26 – Typed document – the first 20 years of the Langham Trust, Lambeth Palace STOTT / 3 / 15 / 1.
[14] John Stott Memorandum, 14 August 1980, in Dudley-Smith, *Global Ministry*, 288.
[15] The phrase was used by Frances Whitehead in a Personal Interview with Dr Ian Shaw, 7 March 2015.
[16] John Stott Statement to Scholarship Committee about the Langham Trust Third World Scholarship Fund, on 9 January 1987.
[17] On EFAC, see Dudley-Smith, *Global Ministry*, 51-56.
[18] Notes for a talk by John Stott, on 14 October 1986 Celebrating the 100th person on the EFAC Bursary Scheme, cited in Dudley-Smith, *Global Ministry*, 55.
[19] Dudley-Smith, *Global Ministry*, 142.

of the postgraduates receiving funding, with assistance from the Langham Foundation in USA. After Stott stepped down as General Secretary of EFAC in 1981 it progressed less well. When in 1986, it was, in Stott's words, in need of 'resuscitation,' this was offered by the Langham Trust, and between 1986 and 1990, discretionary grants of between £1,000 and £5,000 were given from the Langham Scholars bursary fund or discretionary funds.[20] As good quality Bachelors and Masters programmes in theology developed in the global South, the need to fund scholars to study at that level in the West declined, and the EFAC scheme was eventually ended.

The First Langham Scholars

The first scholar formally supported by the Langham Trust was Vinay Samuel, from India, who studied at Cambridge between 1971 and 1975, and the second was John Ray, from Pakistan, who took a BA in Theology at Oxford in June 1976. Ray worked in Iran for a short time until Ayatollah Khomeini rose to power, and he later became IFES Regional Secretary for Islamic Lands.[21]

The limited resources of the Langham Trust were only able to cover Samuel's university fees of about £4500 pounds a year, and a small allowance of £12 per week. The ability to live very economically on limited resources was to be typical of other Langham scholars over the years. Stott invited Samuel to visit him at least twice a year and worship at All Souls. Each year they went to stay at Stott's retreat in Pembrokeshire, the Hookses. After graduating from Cambridge in 1975 with an M. Litt. degree, Samuel returned to India. In 1983 he helped Chris Sugden to found the Oxford Centre for Mission Studies as a centre where global Christian leaders could engage in postgraduate theological study with a view to transforming the contexts and the people they serve. Samuel also helped found the International Fellowship of Evangelical Mission Theologians (INFEMIT) in 1987.[22] When Stott was looking for someone to bring new

---

[20] Langham Trustees Meeting 21 October 1986; List of Langham Trust Grants to EFAC, compiled by Frances Whitehead, 26.3.1991 - Lambeth Palace STOTT / 3 / 15 / 1, Lf93

[21] Evangelical Fellowship in the Anglican Communion papers; 'Third World Research Bursars', information leaflet written by John Stott, December 1976, Lambeth Palace Library, STOTT 3 / 12 / 1 EFAC 1978-2003. Ray was listed in Stott's leaflet, but because he did not take a postgraduate degree he is not recorded in the Langham records as formally being a Langham Scholar.

[22] Dudley-Smith, *Global Ministry*, p. 299; C. Sugden, 'A History of the Oxford Centre for Mission Studies: A Personal Memoir', *Transformation*, 28 (4), 2011, 265-78. Details on his own period of study were kindly supplied by Vinay Samuel.

life to EFAC he turned to the first Langham Scholar and Samuel served as its International General Secretary from 1986-89.[23]

The first Langham Scholar supported who went on to complete a degree at doctoral level was Michael Nazir-Ali from Pakistan. In 1974 he completed a B. Litt. at Oxford University before undertaking postgraduate studies at Cambridge. Nazir-Ali was awarded an M. Litt. from Cambridge University in 1977, and then a ThD from Australian College of Theology in 1985. After Cambridge he returned to serve in Pakistan for ten years as a theological educator, priest and then Bishop of Raiwind in West Punjab (1984–86), at the time the youngest bishop in the Anglican Communion. He was later General Secretary of the Church Missionary Society 1989-1994, and Bishop of Rochester 1994-2009. He was one of the candidates for the role of Archbishop of Canterbury after the retirement of Robert Runcie.

Although he started his doctoral studies after Nazir-Ali, Noel Jason was the first Langham Scholar to graduate with a doctorate. Jason was from a well-known Hindu Brahmin family in South India, and was converted aged 24. He undertook research for a PhD in Christology at Sheffield University from 1975-1978, and returned to lecture in theology in India, before taking a senior role in the Church of South India.[24]

The fifth Langham Scholar to gain a doctorate was John Chew, who completed a PhD on the Patriarchal Narratives in Genesis at Sheffield University in 1982. Chew went on to become Principal of Trinity Theological College, Singapore, and then in 2006 was installed as the Archbishop of the Anglican Province of South-East Asia. Another noted scholar in the early years was Ki-Ban Lee, a Korean, who had trained to be a Buddhist monk, and who after conversion had become a noted Christian leader. [25] He completed a PhD at Birmingham University in 1989 and returned to seminary and university teaching in South Korea.

John Stott clearly had the ability to identify people not only with academic ability, but with significant leadership potential for Majority-World theological education, and global Anglicanism. They fulfilled the vision of the Scholarship Fund, set out in 1987 as to enable future leaders to become 'seminary teachers', or exercise 'theological leadership in the wider church'. Stott remained sure that 'the seminaries are the key to the

---

[23] Langham Trustees Meeting 21 October 1986; List of Langham Trust Grants to EFAC.
[24] John Stott, 'Third World Research Bursars', Information Leaflet, December 1976.
[25] Langham Trustees, 5 March 1985.

churches' health'.[26] The phrase 'seminary teachers' also included teaching in a 'University or research centre'.[27]

In 1992 the Langham Research Scholarship Fund (or Two-Thirds World Scholars Fund as it was now called) became independent in operation from the Langham Trust, although it remained in close 'partnership' with it. Although the terms 'Third-World', 'Two-Thirds World', and latterly 'Majority World' were never formally defined, it was decided in 1995 that applications from Korea, Singapore, Hong Kong, Japan and Taiwan should be afforded 'low priority', although some 'strategic grants' could still be made in special cases.[28]

The Langham 'Logic'

The 'logic' for what the Langham Scholarship Programme was intended to achieve was outlined by John Stott in 1978. He believed that little was of more importance 'for the future health and growth of God's worldwide church' than 'the equipment of gifted and godly pastors'. In particular 'developing countries' needed 'evangelical bishops and seminary teachers who can give strong theological leadership and resist the encroachments of liberalism and syncretism'.[29] The World Council of Churches Theological Education Fund programme was believed to have been highly influential, but Stott grew concerned that many Majority-World leaders had been sent to study under leading theologically-liberal scholars in Western universities and seminaries, and then transplanted such theological perspectives into their own countries.

Stott connected the work of the seminary with what happened in the pulpit. In 1989 Stott once again noted, 'Our main concern is to raise the standard of discipleship by raising the standard of preaching'. This became known as the 'Langham logic' –

1. God wants his church to grow into maturity in Christ.
2. Nothing leads people into this Christian maturity like the Word of God.
3. The Word of God reaches people mainly through faithful biblical preaching.
4. Biblical preaching and teaching are the primary God-appointed responsibility of pastors.
5. Pastors catch (or lose) their vision for preaching in the seminary (theological college).

---

[26] John Stott's Statement to the First Meeting of the Langham Trust Scholarship Committee, 9 January 1987.
[27] Minutes of Langham Trust Scholarship Committee (LSC) Meeting, 9 January 1987.
[28] LSC Minutes, 13 March 1995.
[29] 'Third World Research Bursars', Publicity leaflet, John Stott, December 1976.

6. The seminary exerts its influence on students primarily through its teaching staff.
7. Seminary teachers need to combine academic excellence with personal godliness.

Stott concluded, 'In sum, we long to see the world's seminaries staffed by godly evangelical scholars, so that the world's pulpits may be occupied by faithful preachers of the Word of God.' [30]

As a leader in global evangelicalism, Stott's focus was always serving students and seminaries from within the evangelical tradition. In 1999, the possibility of accepting candidates from Roman Catholic or Orthodox traditions was discussed, and while this was not ruled out, the need to concentrate resources on the large number of applicants from the evangelical tradition was emphasised.[31] The following year, the question of whether training scholars to work in liberal theological institutions, and thereby bringing an evangelical perspective into those institutions, was explored, and a few scholar selections were subsequently made with this end in mind.[32]

The selection of candidates was always done in partnership with Majority-World leaders. Those selected needed strong recommendation from 'trusted leaders' known personally to Stott and the Langham Trust's committee. [33]

The Development of the Langham Trust

The ability to raise the considerable funds needed for the Langham Scholars programme owed much to John Stott himself, widely respected as a man of integrity and reliability. Yet at times he commented on how hard it was to secure funds for the long-term investment of training scholars for key leadership positions, in comparison with other projects.[34] Stott took an early decision to direct the royalties from his writings to charity, but most of the funds went not to Langham Scholarships, but to the Evangelical Literature Trust. By 1996 over half a million pounds sterling had been donated. [35]

After the formation of the Langham Foundation in the USA in 1974, other 'Langhams' began to appear globally. In 1978 a Langham Trust in Canada was established, and one in Australia the following year. They all undertook to share the financial responsibilities of the original Langham Trust's work, including supporting Langham Scholars. The Langham

---

[30] 'John Stott explains the Langham Scholarship Strategy', in Langham Research Scholarships Newsletter, February 1998.
[31] LSC Minutes, 23 September 1999.
[32] LSC Minutes, 29 February 2000.
[33] Stott Statement, 9 January 1987
[34] Frances Whitehead, Interview with Dr Ian Shaw, 7 March 2015.
[35] Smith, *Global Ministry*, p. 357.

Foundation in Hong Kong was founded in 2002, and Langham New Zealand in 2007. Funding from outside the UK transformed the potential of the Langham Scholars programme from a very small scale project, helping a few individual scholars, into a movement for global leadership training of considerable potential. Between 1996 and 2012 the Langham Foundation in the USA was known as John Stott Ministries (JSM) - although Stott was never comfortable with the organisation bearing his name - before it was renamed Langham USA.

The question of the continuance, or not, of the Langham Trust after the death of their founder was already under discussion at Stott's instigation as early as 1999.[36] He wanted the programmes to continue and expand, only 'so long as they are perceived to be necessary and are still wanted by Third World Christian leaders'. [37] A group of key international leaders meeting at the Wycliffe Centre in Horsleys Green agreed that a successor to Stott should be identified.[38] This led to the appointment of Dr Chris Wright, then Principal of All Nations Christian College in Hertfordshire, as International Ministries Director. He started work in 2001 when Langham Partnership International was formed from the Langham organizations in the U.K., United States, Canada and Australia, which agreed to work together with a common statement of faith, vision and mission.[39] The Langhams in Hong Kong and New Zealand later joined after their formation. The newly formed Langham Partnership International also brought a merger of the two separate charities – the Langham Trust (with its scholars programme), and the Evangelical Literature Trust, which became Langham Literature under the leadership of Pieter Kwant. A third programme, Langham Preaching, was launched in 2002, led by Jonathan Lamb, seeking to equip pastors and lay leaders from the Majority World with biblical preaching skills.

After John Stott handed over the leadership of the Langham Trust he continued to provide support and encouragement to the new leadership, but executive responsibility was handed to them, although they did consult him frequently. He continued regularly to attend the Langham Scholarship Committee into his 80s. By the time of his death in 2011 his Langham legacy was firmly established.

Slow Growth in Scholar Numbers

In the twenty years after the first support given to Vinay Samuel by the Langham Trust in 1971, only 25 scholars had been supported with partial or total funding. Ten had completed doctorates and all had returned to their

---

[36] Smith, *Global Ministry*, pp. 389, 421.
[37] 'John Stott Ministries (USA) and the Langham Trust (UK). An Easter 1999 Memorandum from John Stott about the future: Five Third World Ministries,' in Smith, *Global Ministry*, p. 422.
[38] Dudley-Smith, *Global Ministry*, 422-23.
[39] LSC Minutes, 27 Feb 2001.

own countries; the rest achieved other postgraduate degrees, or were still in process. [40] Thereafter, the pace at which the programme grew increased noticeably. By 1997, 50 Langham Scholars had completed doctorates, four were principals of seminaries, and 12 were academic deans. [41]

The costs of supporting Langham Scholars steadily mounted from the £4,500 Samuel had received, and most scholars were themselves contributing between 30% and 75% of the cost of their studies. [42] The scholarship fund has been a remarkable story of funding meeting the commitments made to scholars, although usually with little margin or surplus. [43] In 2000, the 100th Langham Scholar was welcomed, by which time 75 scholars had completed either a Masters or Doctoral qualification with Langham Support. [44] The programme reached its largest size in 2007/2008, when there were 97 current scholars. [45]

In this growth, the role played by Langham in the USA was highly significant. The Langham Trust board encouraged the American organisation to consider supporting an 'outstanding Third World doctoral student' at an evangelical seminary or graduate school' in the USA. The first scholar recorded as being supported directly by Langham in the USA was Tewoldemedhin Habtu, of Eritrea, who studied at Trinity Evangelical Divinity School (TEDS), Deerfield, Illinois. He has gone on to a long and distinguished career teaching at the Nairobi Evangelical Graduate School of Theology, now Africa International University. [46] In 1990 a Scholarship Committee was established by the Langham Foundation Board, primarily to select students for study at TEDS, where all Langham Scholars in the USA studied until 1998. Scholars were subsequently supported at institutions including Westminster Theological Seminary, Fuller Seminary, Wheaton College, Calvin College, Asbury Seminary, Princeton Theological Seminary and Boston University. [47] The work of providing scholarships for scholars from the Majority World to study in the USA was further developed in 2001 as a result of the merger between JSM and the Foundation for Advanced Christian Training (FACT), headed by Merrit Sawyer, which was itself already supporting a number of doctoral scholars from the Majority World in American and Canadian seminaries. [48]

---

[40] *The Langham Trust: Serving the Church Worldwide*, brochure for 20th anniversary of the Langham Trust, 1989, in Lambeth Palace Stott Archive, F12-15.
[41] LSC Minutes 25 September 1997.
[42] Stott, Statement to LSC, 1987, 2.
[43] Stott, Statement to LSC, 1987, 2.
[44] LSC Minutes, 21 September 2000.
[45] Langham Partnership, UK and Ireland News, January 2008.
[46] Langham Trust, 18 July 1988.
[47] LSC Minutes, 22 September 2005, paper by Stephen Travis 'Criteria for Selection of Scholars'.
[48] Langham USA Website, 'Our History' www.langham.org

The other Langham organisations around the world followed the example of the USA in beginning to support scholars to study locally. In 1989 Pedro Garcia Zamora of Spain was accepted as a scholar to undertake a ThD at Wycliffe College, Toronto. His award came from Canadian Langham Trust funds.[49] In 2005, Ma'afu Palu from Tonga became the first Langham scholar to study for a doctorate in Australia, based at Moore College, Sydney. In the same year, the first scholar to study in Hong Kong was supported by funds from Langham Hong Kong. Langham New Zealand began to support its first two scholars for study in New Zealand in 2011. The possibility of a French Langham Scholarship programme was discussed in 1999 with Professor Henri Blocher, of Vaux-sur-Seine Seminary, and a small committee was formed the following year, but its work did not proceed further.[50]

The Pastoral Dimension

From the outset, the Langham Scholars programme emphasised the importance of offering pastoral care to scholars, as well as financial support. The period of doctoral research was to be a time of 'spiritual formation'. In 1987 this covered four areas – i) linking scholars to a 'host' evangelical church; ii) making introductions to Christian leaders who could help them; iii) 'accepting a measure of pastoral responsibility for them'; iv) alerting scholars to appropriate meetings and conferences they should attend.[51] In the provision of pastoral support, and leadership mentoring, John Stott personally invested considerable time. When numbers of scholars were small, small groups of 2 or 3 scholars and their families were invited to the Hookses, which was considered a highlight of their scholar-experience.[52] Central to his 'care' for the scholars was a commitment to regularly pray for them. He wrote personal letters, and when newsletters were sent out by Frances Whitehead, he would add personal notes to them. When there was specific need, he would telephone the scholar.[53]

In 1989, these burdens were considerably lessened by the appointment of Geoffrey Gardner as part-time Administrator. In addition to handling applications, grant payments, correspondence with scholars relating to their progress, Gardiner offered pastoral support to scholars through personal visits. [54] This allowed Frances Whitehead to step down from her administrative role with Langham Scholars to concentrate on other duties,

---

[49] LSC Minutes, 8 March 1989.
[50] LSC Minutes 23 Sept 1999; 29 February 2000.
[51] Stott, Statement to LSC, 9 January 1987.
[52] Frances Whitehead Interview, March 2015; John Stott Statement, 1987.
[53] Frances Whitehead Interview, March 2015.
[54] R.T. France's comments in *Langham Trust Third World Scholarship Fund Newsletter* 1991-92.

but she remained a valued committee member.[55] Geoffrey Gardiner served as Administrator from 1989-1997, and was succeeded by Paul Berg (1997-2006) after his retirement as Vicar of Christ Church, Clifton, in Bristol. Howard Peskett (2006-2008) held the post after his retirement from teaching at Trinity College, Bristol, before in 2008 Dr Ian Shaw was appointed as the first full-time Langham Scholar Director in the UK.

After Ian Shaw became Associate International Director of the Scholarship programme in 2011, the pastoral care of Langham Scholars, a number of whom were now studying in the Majority World, was gradually placed into the hands of part-time regional Scholar Care Co-ordinators, one each for those studying in the USA; UK and Europe; Asia; East and West Africa; and South Africa. In late 2012, Dr Riad Kassis from Lebanon became the programme's International Director, a part-time role he combined with being Director of the International Council for Evangelical Theological Education. It was a notable appointment, because he was truly a 'son' of the programme, being the 50th Scholar to complete a doctorate with Langham support.

John Stott continued to offer pastoral and mentoring support to the scholars, speaking at the annual orientation course for new Langham Scholars held each year. He often quoted Bishop Handley Moule's aphorism, 'Beware of an untheological devotion and of an undevotional theology.' In 1996, he spoke of the need for growth in 'academic excellence and personal godliness at the same time'. He warned of a scholar returning home 'an academic success but a spiritual failure, a "doctor" (qualified to teach) but no longer a "disciple," possessed by no new vision, power, or holiness'. He urged Langham Scholars to become not only competent teachers of theology, but also people who will 'truly know and worship the God they talk about'. [56]

In 1999 an annual Scholar consultation was started, held in Cambridge University, bringing together scholars currently studying in the UK with Langham staff for four days of fellowship, academic discussion, mutual sharing and worship. In the early years, John Stott himself often gave an address.

The Langham Scholarship Committee

At the start of the programme, the scholars were effectively hand-picked by John Stott, although he never did this without looking for strong personal recommendation from Majority-World leaders from their context. On his

---

[55] LSC Minutes, 28 September 1989; Job Description for Administrator, Langham Trust Third World Scholarship Fund, written by John Stott, April, 1989.
[56] 'An Admonition from John Stott', in *Fellowship of Langham Scholars Newsletter*, No. 2, April 1996. See also the author's personal notes of Langham Scholars Orientation course, Oxford Centre for Mission Studies, September 1993, which the author attended as a grantee of the Whitefield Institute.

travels, he kept an eye open for, in his inimitable phrase, 'blokes worth watching' – young men with leadership abilities and capacity for advanced learning, who would play a key role in helping evangelicalism grow to maturity in the Majority World.[57]

As the programme grew, unsolicited applications began to be received, and the need for a wider panel of reference was clear. A scholarship committee to assist the Langham Trust in selecting and supporting candidates began its work in 1987. Its membership has always included very senior figures within evangelicalism, together with representatives from the Majority World (the first committee included Vinay Samuel and John Sentamu), alongside Langham staff.

The committee carefully scrutinised, discussed, and prayed over each application. Stott's views in the end tended to be those followed, but this was often to do with the fact he had met many of the applicants personally, or knew their context and those recommending them.[58] In September 1989 the first discussion was held as to whether women should be accepted as Langham scholars, and this proposal was approved in February 1990.[59] The first woman to become a Langham Scholar studying for a doctorate was Eileen Poh, from Singapore, who was selected in 1993.[60] In 1996, Joseph N'goma of Congo was accepted as the first Langham scholar to study in France, at Vaux-sur-Seine Seminary, near Paris.[61]

The number of applications always exceeded the funds available - as Dick France, chair of the Scholarship Committee wrote in 1992, 'It was not a matter of picking out the good from the indifferent, but of making agonizing decisions about which of the highly commended applicants we must decline to help'.[62] By 2004, the 94 applications received by Langham UK were well above its capacity to assist.[63] In 2012 the process of dealing with all Langham Scholar applications was adapted, with the creation of two selection committees, one for students applying for study in the UK and Europe, and one for those studying in the USA and the Majority World.[64]

---

[57] Frances Whitehead Interview, March 2015.
[58] Frances Whitehead Interview, March 2015.
[59] LSC Minutes, 28 September 1989; 5 February 1990.
[60] Alice Mutua of Kenya was earlier supported to complete a Master's degree at TEDS, starting in 1991.
[61] LSC Minutes, 13 March 1996.
[62] R.T. France, in *Langham Trust Third World Scholarship Fund Newsletter*, 1991-92.
[63] LSC Minutes, 16 March 2004.
[64] LSC Minutes, 20 March 2012.

Working in Partnership

From the early partnership with EFAC onwards, the Langham Scholarship Programme worked closely with like-minded organisations. In 1988 discussions about a partnership with TEAR Fund's Overseas Evangelism and Christian Education Department started,[65] and two TEAR Fund nominees joined the scholarship committee. By September 1989 the TEAR Fund contribution to scholarship funds was £21,960.[66] This collaboration with TEAR Fund helped extend the purpose of the Langham Scholarship Programme beyond training seminary lecturers, to seeking to build the Church 'through the development of creative, indigenous, evangelical theology.'[67]

In 1984 the Christian International Scholars Foundation was established in the USA by three of John Stott's former study assistants, Tom Cooper, Steve Hayner and Mark Labberton. Although aspects of the remit of the two organisations were different, since 1987 CISF (now Scholar Leaders International) has often jointly supported Langham Scholars in their doctoral studies, and a partnership in selection and support of candidates has been developed.[68] Similar joint-funding arrangements have been arranged with Overseas Council in the USA, and Overseas Council in Australia and New Zealand.

As a significant provider of scholarship grants to assist faculty training in the Majority World, Langham has invested in efforts to ensure high standards of doctoral education globally. This resulted in two of Langham's leaders, Chris Wright and Ian Shaw, playing a significant role in the International Council for Evangelical Theological Education's Doctoral Initiative, which arranged meetings of international representatives from global evangelical theological-education institutions in Beirut (2010) and Bangalore (2011). From this process came the ICETE Beirut Benchmarks – a series of core statements on excellence in doctoral-level education for evangelical seminaries and universities, with a version for professional doctorate programmes, and a series of Best Practice Guidelines for doctoral studies.[69]

Partnership with Global-South Seminaries

The need to create a sense of 'partnership' with the church in the Majority World has been a significant theme in the Langham Scholars programme. By having Majority-World leaders on its selection committees, and only

---

[65] LSC Minutes, 19 February 1988.
[66] LSC Minutes, 28 September 1989.
[67] LSC Minutes. 9 March 1993.
[68] Stott, Statement to LSC, 1987, 2.
[69] LSC Minutes, 23 March 2010. For the Benchmarks see http://www.icete-edu.org/beirut/. These were published in printed form in 2015.

accepting candidates with strong endorsement from their home context a sense of 'ownership' has been sought. In 1990 the need for the programme to 'serve the needs of the Third World as they are perceived by Third World Christian leaders' was emphasised.[70] In 1985, surplus scholarship funds were sent to assist the Scholarship fund of the Nairobi Evangelical Graduate School of Theology, which Stott had recently visited.[71] 10% of the annual budget was in 1988 set aside for 'exceptional and deserving cases who do not precisely fit our criteria', allowing for the possibility of scholars to study in the Majority World, avoid 'excessive rigidity', and foster a 'family feeling' within the worldwide evangelical constituency.[72]

Another aspect of this Majority-World partnership has been the policy for scholars receiving sponsorship to sign a commitment to return to the Majority World for at least ten years after completing their doctorates. This grows from the conviction that key faculty members have been 'entrusted' to Langham for training, and should return back as soon as possible to enhance theological educational provision there. Sponsorship funds are considered a loan, and if a scholar fails to return, they are repayable over ten years.

The desire for partnership with institutions outside the West, and the steady increase in their capacity, led to a growing focus on enabling Langham Scholars to undertake doctoral studies in the Majority World. In 1987, the Langham Scholarship Committee agreed that although its first focus should be on doctoral students studying in Britain, its second was to be on those who 'wish to study in their own context.'[73] This was revisited in 1997 by the Langham Scholarship Committee. The policy that emerged was summed up by Howard Peskett - 'We will *gradually need to change* to meet the changing situation'.[74]

In 2004, a further paper on this issue was presented by Chris Wright, as a result of wide consultation among graduated Langham Scholars and partner institutions, addressing the issue of how standards of excellence could be ensured, and students maintain access to high-quality library and other resources. The split-site model, whereby scholars did their research partly in the West, and partly in the Majority-World, such as the one used by the Oxford Centre for Mission Studies, was positively encouraged.[75] As a result the Langham Partnership International Council made a commitment that 10% of scholarship income should be used for In-Majority-World study scholarships.

In 2010, with 22% of Langham Scholars then studying in the Majority World a development plan was introduced to increase the number to 50%

---

[70] LSC Minutes, 25 September 1991.
[71] Langham Trust, 25 March 1986.
[72] LSC Minutes, 19 February 1988.
[73] LSC Minutes, 9 January 1987.
[74] LSC Minutes, 22 January 1997.
[75] LSC Minutes 16 March 2004; LSC Minutes 23 September 2004.

within five to eight years, [76] a target reached in 2014. In 2012, Langham also made Francophone Africa a strategic priority for scholarship selections to tackle the issue of theological poverty in the region. [77] To support scholars on these In-Majority World doctoral programmes, funding to assist short-term study residency visits to the best Western seminaries and libraries was made available, such as at the Centre for World Christianity at Edinburgh University.[78]

Universities and Seminaries Where Most Langham Scholars Have Studied	Number of Scholars
United Kingdom	
Edinburgh University	26
Oxford Centre for Mission Studies	26
Aberdeen University	21
Cambridge University	17
Oxford University	10
United States	
Fuller Seminary	58
Trinity Evangelical Divinity School	34
Majority World	
International Baptist Theological Seminary, Prague	9
Stellenbosch University	6
Africa International University, Nairobi	6
Kwa-Zulu Natal University	6
Hong Kong Baptist University	3

Support for Langham Scholars Post-doctorate

The need to disseminate the research findings of Langham Scholars into both the global and local academic discourse and wider church contexts was increasingly recognised. Since 1999 scholars have been able to benefit from the Langham Writers programme, assisting them to write books to serve theological students and church leaders in their own contexts.[79] In 2011 Langham Literature began the publication of the doctoral theses of Langham Scholars, under the Langham Monograph imprint.

The lack of opportunities scholars teaching in seminaries and colleges in the Majority World had for study leave to write and advance their research field was addressed after 2010 by the creation of a series of postdoctoral fellowships. Lasting for up to four months they provided Langham graduates with opportunities for study, writing, and refreshing professional

---

[76] LSC Minutes, 14 September 2010.
[77] LSC Minutes, 20 March 2012.
[78] LSC Minutes, 18 September 2012.
[79] LSC Minutes, 23 September 1999.

skills. In 2009, for the first time, an award was made to allow Langham Scholar Abraham Kovacs, to undertake the further post-doctoral research and writing to gain habilitated status in Hungary, bringing formal professional acceptance within the wider academic community in Eastern Europe.[80]

Another project, the International Research and Training Seminar, to support the postdoctoral research and doctoral supervision skills of Langham Scholars was started in 2011, developed by Ian Shaw from an idea by Professor Markus Bockmuehl of Oxford University to create a supportive community of evangelical researchers and future doctoral supervisors for Majority-World seminaries. A group of twelve postdoctoral fellows met for 4 weeks each year between 2011-14, at a centre of academic excellence, each with a senior academic mentor to serve as a dialogue partner. Over the four years the postdoctoral fellows between them produced more than 60 books, articles, or chapters in books.[81]

Assessment of the Significance of John Stott and the Langham Scholars Programme

Overall assessments of John Stott's achievements have tended to emphasise his work in Anglicanism and within England.[82] In *The Global Diffusion of Evangelicalism*, Brian Stanley has helped to redress this focus, stressing that it was because of his global ministry that Stott became the 'dominant intellectual influence and role model for a whole generation or more of those who assumed positions of leadership in evangelical churches and para-church organisations in many parts of the world'. He goes on to highlight the Langham Scholars programme which has proved 'extraordinarily strategic' in providing high-level training for evangelical theological educators and church leaders from beyond the West'.[83] *Christianity Today* described Langham Partnership as 'preeminent among the organizations [John Stott] launched.'[84]

This view is echoed from those who have been leaders in theological education in the Majority World. For example, Tony Wilmot, first Principal of NEGST, believed Stott's Langham Scholars ministry had played a 'significant role in creating a theologically-qualified leadership for the Third World'.[85]

Yet, there have been criticisms, suggesting that Langham Partnership could be seen as 'yet one more expression of Western dominance in the

---

[80] LSC Minutes, 15 September 2009.
[81] LSC Minutes, 31 March 2015.
[82] D. Edwards, 'The Rev. John Stott', *The Times*. 29 July 2011.
[83] B. Stanley, *The Global Diffusion of Evangelicalism: The Age of Billy Graham and John Stott* (Downers Grove: IVP Academic, 2013), 114-15.
[84] Tim Stafford, 'John Stott Has Died', *Christianity Today* 27 July 2011.
[85] LSC Minutes, 25 Sept 1991.

worldwide church', especially because, in the early years at least, Majority-World students were supported to study in the West. There were also times when the Enlightenment-dominated theological approach Langham Scholars had been trained in did not always mesh well with the cultures and life categories of their home countries, and some cultural re-translation was needed.[86] However, Andrew Walls has highlighted how a 'second age of world Christianity has dawned, indeed an age of global Christianity.' The shift in global Christian geography to the southern hemisphere is being matched by a shift in the geography of theological education and theological discourse. Currently 'biblical and Christian interaction with the cultures of Africa and Asia has begun to open a whole range of new theological issues and the possibility of fuller and clearer thought on some old ones'. Walls believes this may help Christian theology escape from the Enlightenment worldview by which it has been dominated for the past 200 years. He presents a picture of a global 'theological workshop busier than ever... its workers are more varied in language, culture and outlook'.[87]

In this 'new reformation' currently underway, Langham's scholars programme has played its role. With some 400 doctoral theses produced, or being produced, by Majority-World scholars supported by Langham, many of them subsequently published, and Langham Scholars engaged in teaching in the Majority World, the contribution played, although modest, has been significant. A large number of these grapple with key contextual issues. Half of the theses being produced by Langham scholars in 2014 were being written in the Majority World itself. Many Langham Scholars have quickly assumed key leadership positions there. By 2005, 97 Langham Scholars had gained doctoral degrees. Of these, 8 had become seminary principals, 15 were academic deans, 36 were seminary lecturers, and 10 were university lecturers. Two held positions as 'international leaders', nineteen were 'national leaders.[88] In 2014 Langham graduates were serving in 64 countries. 145 Langham scholars had come from Asia, 136 from Africa, 51 from former-communist Eastern Europe, 17 from Latin America, 13 from the Middle East, and 2 from Pacifica.

While disentangling influences on a particular person's rise to strategic leadership is very difficult, and too much must not be claimed, there must be some correlation between the fact that a number of those holding very significant Christian leadership positions in the Majority World have been Langham Scholars – such as the late Douglas Carew (Vice-Chancellor of AIU), Tim Gener (President of Asia Theological Seminary, Manila), Stephen Lee (President of China Graduate School of Theology), and Riad Kassis (Director of ICETE). The programme nearly produced an

---

[86] Chapman, *Godly Ambition,* 151–152.
[87] Andrew F. Walls, 'The Rise of Global Theologies', in J.P. Greenman and G.L. Green (eds), *Global Theology in Evangelical Perspective* (Downers Grove: IVP Academic, 2012), 32-34.
[88] LSC Minutes, 22 Sept 2005.

Archbishop of Canterbury, as well as John Chew, Principal of Trinity Theological College, Singapore, before becoming Archbishop of South-East Asia. It is also worth noting how doctoral programmes have emerged in seminaries in the Majority World where a number of Langham Scholars work. John Stott's legacy has over the past forty years played a notable role in shaping the future of global evangelical theological education, which is increasingly found in the Global South, and rests more and more in the hands of Majority World Christian leaders like the hard-working men and women who have been supported by the Langham Scholars programme.

THEOLOGICAL EDUCATION AND CONTEMPORARY MISSION IN CHINA – WITH SPECIAL REFERENCE TO BISHOP K.H. TING'S DIALOGICAL THEOLOGY OF MISSION

WEN Ge

Introduction

The number of Christians in China has increased dramatically from 700,000 in 1949 to about 25 million in 2013. The Communist Party's attitude towards Christianity has shifted from hostility to the promotion of the positive role of Christianity in the building of a harmonious society. Both facts tell us that Christian mission in China still continues despite many challenges and hardship since the 1950s. Although most of the 22 Chinese Protestant seminaries and Bible colleges do not have special courses on missiology in their curricula, what kind of theology informs Chinese Christians of mission in a socialist country?

The late Bishop K.H. Ting (1915-2012) has guided theological education in China by serving as the principal of Nanjing Union Theological Seminary until 2010. This essay aims at describing the making of a Chinese mission theology with Bishop K.H. Ting's dialogical theology of mission as an example, in order to describe how the Chinese churches have understood and carried on mission in a dialogical spirit, which may also contribute to the shaping of the ecumenical mission theology.

Background

Since the 1950s, Christian mission in China has gone through ups and downs. What then are the particular challenges that confront the Chinese churches?

First of all, due to the inextricable relation between Christianity and colonialism over the last 100 years in modern Chinese history, the Chinese churches in the socialist country were under harsh nationalist criticism in the 1950s. Chinese Christians were accused of being on the side of foreign invaders due to their belief in the colonists' religion and their link with colonists' educational programmes in foreign languages which, to some extent, de-sinolised Chinese young people. Therefore, Chinese churches had to do away with the colonial version of Christianity first and make Christianity Chinese, but without losing the ecumenical dimension.

Secondly, the Chinese churches underwent an early moratorium on western mission when the East-West ideological and military conflict was intensified in 1950s. As a result of the lack of financial and personnel resources from the West, Chinese churches of various former denominational backgrounds inherited from the West had to merge and form a uniting post-denominational church. So did theological seminaries in China. Consequently, the former denominational structures were also removed and replaced by the National Committee of the Three-Self Patriotic Movement of the Protestant Churches in China, founded in 1954. After the Cultural Revolution (1966-1976), when churches and seminaries were reopened, the China Christian Council was established in 1980 to deal with intra-ecclesial affairs. But what is the particular ecclesial selfhood of the Chinese uniting churches?

Thirdly, Chinese society has been undergoing a radical reorganisation and reconstruction since the 1950s. At this moment, the radically revolutionary Christians warmly welcomed this new proletarian development as the sign of God's Kingdom on earth while conservative apolitical Christians remained indifferent to the great changes taking place and tended to isolate themselves from socialist society. What should then be the relationship between Christianity and socialism? How should Christians face the atheist Communist Party and respond to social change?

Last but not least, influenced by the dogmatic Marxist definition of religion as opiate, some radical party cadres and scholars in China heavily criticised the negative function of religion to 'euthanatise' people, preventing them from fighting against the oppressive ruling class in the feudal and capitalist society. In their eyes, religion must be removed or annihilated. But was Karl Marx's metaphor sufficient to define complex religious phenomena? Could Christianity also play a positive role in a socialist country?

In the light of these challenges, Chinese churches needed to work out a Chinese mission theology. With hindsight, the moratorium on western mission in China provided the opportunity for such reflection. Ting proposed that the dual task of Protestant mission theology in mainland China since 1949 was to seek the socio-political legitimacy of Christianity in a socialist country *extra ecclesia*, and to strive to build up the Chinese uniting indigenous churches in living interaction with the ecumenical churches *intra ecclesia*.[1] The former apologetic task involved dialogue with both government and secular academia through the lens of social sciences, while the latter constructive task took a post-colonial perspective to contextualise Christianity and to strengthen the unity of the post-denominational church. This essay tries to describe the dual task with

---

[1] K.H. Ting, 'An Update on the Church in China (1994)', in K.H. Ting, *Love Never Ends: Papers by K.H. Ting,* Janice Wickeri (ed) (Nanjing: Yilin, 2000), 458. (Cited hereafter as LNE.)

Bishop K.H. Ting's dialogical theology of mission as an example, and to show how his theological idea of the cosmic Christ offered an all-embracing framework to integrate the two tasks.

The Apologetic Function of
Chinese Mission Theology *Extra Ecclesia*

According to Ting, religion in socialist China, unlike the former Soviet Union, was not an ideological matter of life and death, but a matter of the united front.[2] This offered Ting the basis to seek the socio-political legitimacy of Christianity in China, not through confrontation, but through dialogue with the government.

First, the Chinese church needed a theological understanding of socialism. What should be the proper relationship between Christianity and socialism? Were these two compatible with each other? Ting argued that Christianity, above all, should not be understood as an ideology, at least not an ideology identified with capitalism and western socio-political systems, hence letting Chinese Christians to be caught up in an East-West conflict. What was needed was a scrutiny of both capitalism and socialism – to see which served humankind better.

But after comparing socialism with capitalism, Ting made his socialist decision: socialism as a large-scale love can be closer to justice than the acquisitive capitalism focusing on individualism and competition in the market. Drawing on the theory of John Maynard Keynes, Ting points out that capitalism only 'safeguards individual ownership of the means of production, safeguards oppression, places the fate of the broad working masses into the hands of the capitalists'.[3] In contrast, Ting believes that the 'universalization of love is the goal of socialism' which 'is love on a large scale, organized love, love which has taken shape as a social system.'[4] In fact, socialism has helped to solve the problem of hunger for China with such a large population. So it is based on the common values of love and justice and community which Christianity and socialism have in common that Ting finds out that Christianity is compatible with socialism with Chinese characteristics. As Ting says,

> We attach our hope to socialism, not so much because we know exactly in detail what the socialist way is, but because we are fed up by all the other choices open to us. What is common in these other choices is the large scale of private ownership of the means of production and the unfair distribution of

---

[2] Ting, 'On Religion as Opiate: A Talk with Friends Outside the Church (1985)', LNE, 223.
[3] Ting, 'Inspirations from Liberation Theology, Process Theology and Teilhard de Chardin (1985)', LNE, 219.
[4] Ting, 'Inspirations from Liberation Theology, Process Theology and Teilhard de Chardin (1985)', LNE, 219.

wealth, requiring the masses of the people to bear the cost by enduring endless suffering.[5]

However, Ting is not unaware of the danger of the distortion of both Christianity and socialism which can be inimical to both people and society.[6] It is for this reason that Ting refuses to identify theology with politics. At the same time, Ting also thinks it unrealistic to separate theology from politics. His mediating position to keep theology and politics in a living interaction allows him to engage Christianity and the socialist context in a mutually critical correlation.

Secondly, Ting tries to mediate between Christians and atheists based on the common values they share. Chinese Christians should not reduce Christianity to an ideology either. If the Chinese Constitution still ensures the freedom of religion, and if there is still room for dialogue between government and the churches concerning the civil aspect of religion, Ting believes that Chinese Christians should not, as the West usually advocates in a condescending manner, risk martyrdom.[7]

Ting divides atheists into three groups: immoral atheists, honest atheists with agnostic and nihilistic tendencies, and humanitarian atheists like the reformers and revolutionaries in society who have a strong temperament of protest atheism and argue against the false gods of the oppressors legitimise structural sin.[8] Ting believes that philanthropic atheists can be of great help to Christians not only to purge the dark side of religion and Christianity that enslaved people spiritually during colonialism, but also to co-operate with Christians to serve the common good of the nation, and the whole of humanity.[9] At this point, Ting is strongly influenced by the English Christian socialist movement led by F.D. Maurice who tries to mediate the 'unsocial Christians and the unchristian socialists'.[10] He quotes William Temple to say that 'the atheist who is moved by love is moved by the Spirit

---

[5] See Ting, 'One Chinese Christian's View of God (1993)', LNE, 431.
[6] Joe Slovo, 'Shared Values: Socialism and Religion', a talk at the Summer School of the Department of Extra-Mural Studies at the University of Cape Town, 25th January 1994. See Li Pingye, 'Xinyang butong, dan women shi pengyou (1994)' [We are friends although our faiths are different]. In *Tianfeng ganyu:zhongguo jidujiaolingxiu Ding Guangxun* [The Heavenly Wind and the Timely Rain: The Chinese Church Leader Ding Guangxun], Liu Huajun (ed) (Nanjing: Nanjing UP, 2001), 60.
[7] Ting, 'An Update on the Church in China (1994)', 455-56.
[8] Ting, 'A Chinese Christian's Appreciation of the Atheist (1979)', LNE, 35-6.
[9] Ting, 'A Chinese Christian's Appreciation of the Atheist (1979)', LNE, 37; see also Ting, 'One Chinese Christian's View of God (1993)', LNE, 432.
[10] *The Life and Letters of Frederick Denison Maurice Chiefly Told in His Own Letters*, two vols. (London: Macmillan, 1884), 1:458, quoted in Hans Schwarz, *Theology in a Global Context: The Last Two Hundred Years* (Grand Rapids, MI: Eerdmans, 2005), 150.

of God: an atheist who lives by love is saved by his faith in the God whose existence (under that name he denies)'.[11]

On the other hand, Ting also opposes the false communist revolutionaries, i.e. the political ultra-leftists who try to perpetuate class struggle and abolish religious freedom.[12] They did great harm not only to Chinese intellectuals and good government officials, but also to religious people, and not least to Christians. Therefore, Ting tried his best to fight against the ultra-leftists in order to reclaim the proper right of religions in China. For example, he was engaged in the revision of the 1978 Constitution with an article that allows for the freedom to propagate atheism.[13] Thus religious people could enjoy equal rights to propagate theism.

Finally, Ting also joins others to defend a scientific understanding of religion independent of ideological prejudice. In the 1980s, there appeared an interesting debate over the nature of religion in China between the northern and the southern group: the former holds to the Marxist dogmatist concept of religion as opiate, while the latter argues for a more comprehensive understanding of religion.[14] Ting joins the southern camp, pointing out that religion as opiate is but a metaphor, insufficient to explain the complexity of religious phenomena within human cultures; even wrong politics can have the same so-called narcotic effect of misleading people. Furthermore, religion can also play a positive role in social reconstruction and nation-building.[15] What the churches need is the legal and institutional permission to re-enter the public sphere to serve.

With Ting's proposals, the Chinese churches are now carrying on public mission in the following four aspects:

First of all, Christianity is conducive to promoting a holistic understanding of life. People who are aware of their own limits, such as inner emptiness and death, are longing for transcendence. This is the ultimate concern for all. At this point, Ting does not subordinate Christian faith to socialism although he fully acknowledges people's material need of life's necessities. For him, the task of Christianity is to tell people that

> if much of European theology helps believers live with the reality of world hunger, and liberation theology moves them to share in the struggle for overcoming hunger, we in new China are concerning ourselves with evangelistic task of showing our fellow-citizens, to whom hunger is no longer

---

[11] Ting, 'A Chinese Christian's Appreciation of the Atheist (1979)', LNE, 38.

[12] Ting, 'Theological Mass Movement in China (1984)', LNE, 147.

[13] Ting, 'Religious Liberty as a Chinese Christian Sees It (1987)', LNE, 278-79.

[14] See Duan Dezhi, 'Guanyu zongjiao yanpianlun de nanbei zhanzheng jiqi xueshu gongxian' ('On "the War of the Southern and the Northern" of "the Theory of Religion being opium" and Its Academic Contributions'): http://iwr.cass.cn/zjyzx/201107/t20110729_7501.htm (accessed 30th December 2014).

[15] Ting, 'On Religion as Opiate: A Talk with Friends Outside the Church' (1985), LNE, 223-33.

the number one problem, that we do not live by bread alone, but by the word of God's mouth.[16]

From his post-colonial and liberational perspectives, Ting underscores people's material life. But he moves beyond socialist materialism by maintaining the Christian sense of transcendence in a post-liberation context. The spiritual dimension is also decisive for a holistic human life. Ting's integrated view on human life enables him to call on people to balance physical and spiritual needs without falling prey to either materialism or idealism. This is still relevant when China starts to be influenced by consumerism and utilitarianism brought about by economic globalisation.

Secondly, Ting believes that Christianity as an advanced religion should play a very important role in the moral reconstruction of contemporary China. To manifest the ethical vitality of Christianity is in accordance with both traditional Chinese humanist culture and Christ's teachings.[17] For Ting, Christianity cannot become an amoral or even an immoral religion, but uphold 'social righteousness and social justice' with its strong voice to criticise corruption and the practice of using public resources for personal profits in China.[18] Ting holds that the kind of Christianity that is concerned solely with the individual's salvation is but a lame Christianity.[19] Furthermore, Ting argues that the restoration of the position of Christian ethics in church life should even be the starting point of Chinese contextual theology[20] so that Christianity can better fit in with socialist society.[21] Therefore, bearing an ethical witness to Christian faith in Chinese socialist society is an easy and effective way to do mission.

Thirdly, Ting holds that to run local churches in a democratic spirit can be conducive to Chinese social reconstruction. When the former denominational structures of churches in China were removed, Ting kept reminding church leaders to nurture a democratic spirit in church affairs. For Ting, democracy has a theological root in the Trinity: 'The Christian Church confesses God as the Creator of the whole human race. Christ's redemption is extended to all men and women. The Holy Spirit inspires wisdom in all people. One finds here the seed of the democratic idea.'[22]

It is very interesting to see here that Ting seems to take the intra-Trinitarian communication as the theological basis of democracy. The three persons interact with each other, and no person shall monopolise this personal communication. This democratic manner is shown already in the Trinity's creation of human beings. Thus this democratic spirit should also

---

[16] Ting, 'Theological Mass Movement in China (1984)', LNE, 147-48.
[17] Ting, 'An Interview with Bishop Ting (1997)', LNE, 530.
[18] Ting, 'Creation and Redemption (1995)', LNE, 481.
[19] Ting, 'Creation and Redemption (1995)', LNE, 481.
[20] Ting, 'What Can We Learn from Y.T. Wu Today? (1989)', LNE, 330.
[21] Ting, 'Remembering Kuang Yaming (1997)', LNE, 535.
[22] Ting, 'What Can We Learn from Y.T. Wu Today? (1989)', LNE, 336.

be reflected in human communities, not least in churches. According to Ting,

> the democratic spirit consists not only of majority rule in voting, but also of respect for other people's opinions and giving them due authority if they are given their office; as well, it consists of keeping in touch and keeping informed. On major issues, we must seek consensus in charity and in a spirit of fellowship, after full consultation and discussion, having taken into serious consideration the desires and aspirations of others.[23]

In the same manner Christians should deal with intra-ecclesial matters. To nurture the church's democratic spirit is conducive not only to the building of the faith community, but also to the democratic construction in the country. 'For it cannot be good for the country if all goes well in every other area except in the church.'[24] Therefore, one of the civil functions of the church is to be the school to train democracy at the grassroots level.[25] To run the church in a democratic way is already a contribution to the social transformation in China.

Finally, Ting points out that diakonia is one of the church's most important ministries in the world as the church is mandated to love God and one's neighbour as well. Yet one of the difficulties for Chinese Christians in carrying out this ministry, according to Ting, is the antithesis between 'being spiritual' and 'being societal', with the latter branded 'social gospel people'.[26] Ting tries to correct this unhealthy way of being spiritual by claiming that the world is still God's world despite the human fall. To be really spiritual is not to escape from the world, but enter the world to meet people's need. Christ himself set a good example for us to serve people. It is based on the Christlike love of all suffering people that Christians should seriously engage the socio-political context in a dialogue, and even join liberating enterprises to support those marginalised people. Again, Ting's emphasis on diakonia carries a strong ethical overtone in society. Today, when the Communist party and government affirm the diaconal ministry of Christianity in building up a harmonious society,[27] doors are open for the once privatised Christianity to re-enter the public sphere in order to serve people and the whole of humanity. For example, Ting calls on Christians in China and abroad to protect God's good creation

---

[23] Ting, 'What Can We Learn from Y.T. Wu Today? (1989)', LNE, 337.

[24] Ting, 'What Can We Learn from Y.T. Wu Today? (1989)', LNE, 337.

[25] Ting, 'Letter to Alumni/ae of Nanjing Seminary (1995)', LNE, 501.

[26] Ting, 'What Can We Learn from Y.T. Wu Today? (1989)', LNE, 333.

[27] For example, six national agencies of China's party and central government jointly issued a decree in February 2012 to encourage religious communities to be actively involved in social charity work. See Cai Xin, 'Religious Organizations Can Establish Foundations, Social Welfare Organizations, and Nonprofit Hospitals in Accordance with the Law': www.chinadevelopmentbrief.cn/?p=637 (accessed 26th April 2014).

against pollution in 1990.[28] In contemporary theological education, diakonia has become a very popular subject understood as an indispensible part of a holistic mission. The consciousness of social service is being raised not only in seminaries, but also in Christian training centres at various levels.

In short, Christianity can play a very positive role in the social reconstruction of China. Ting points out that the mission of the church in the world is to become the 'carrier of the Incarnation'.[29] Influenced by liberation theology, Ting holds that, to bear witness to God's love, Christians should intend not only to bring Christ to people, but also to bring Christ who is in the poor out of people through praxis in a concrete society.[30] By aiming at creating an integrated human life, lifting up the ethical principle, nurturing the democratic spirit and promoting the diaconal ministry, the Chinese church can gain its socio-political legitimacy, find its structural niche in socialist society, and become a sign of the Kingdom of God through its mission.

The Constructive Function of the
Chinese Mission Theology *Intra Ecclesia*

To contextualise Christianity in a particular socio-political milieu is one of the most important aspects of mission. In this section I will mainly summarise Ting's deliberations to construct a Chinese theology and to forge the ecclesial selfhood of the Chinese church through dialogues with Chinese culture, such western theological ethos as process theology, and the ecumenical churches; here is the basis for a holistic understanding of mission in China.

Ting's version of a contextual Chinese theology is centred on the concept of the all-embracing and revealing cosmic Christ. Influenced by Teilhard de Chardin, Ting started to talk about the 'cosmic Christ' in 1979, by which he basically means that Christ extends his providence to the whole universe, and the nature of his providence is love.[31] He proposes a high Christology based on the Gospel of John, and the books of Ephesians, Hebrews and Colossians in the New Testament – a Christology which 'sees all creation as embodying Christ from the very beginning'.[32] Christ as Logos is also compared by Ting with the Chinese philosophical concept of the supreme all-encompassing *Tao* that gives life to all things, and guides all things without lording over them.[33] The pre-existent Logos has a cosmic

---

[28] Ting, 'Caring for God's Creation (1990)', LNE, 399-401.
[29] Ting, 'Life Should Have a Mission (1984)', LNE, 185.
[30] Ting, 'Inspirations from Liberation Theology, Process Theology and Teilhard de Chardin (1985)', LNE, 196.
[31] Ting, 'The Cosmic Christ (1991)', LNE, 411.
[32] Ting, 'Chinese Christians' Approach to the Bible (1990)', LNE, 384.
[33] Ting, 'The Cosmic Christ (1991)', LNE, 418.

nature, which is more conspicuous in the Chinese expression. The Chinese translation of the cosmos is *yuzhou*, which has a richer philosophical meaning than cosmos or universe: *yu* means 'what comprises the four points of the compass together with what is above and below', while *zhou* refers to 'what comprises past, present, and future'; *yuzhou* is the 'Great One' in the Chinese philosophy 'which is defined as "that which has nothing beyond"'.[34] Such a Christ of *yuzhou* creates and redeems all things through his incarnation and redemption. His incarnation links God-humanity-nature, and affirms the continuity between the human and divine, between nature and grace, and between society and church despite the human fall.

The creative and redemptive ministry of such a cosmic Christ cannot be confined to the church, but is immanent in the whole of God's continuous creation to bring forward truth, goodness and beauty. Therefore, the cosmic Christ can also work through philanthropic atheists, and such a cosmic Christ becomes the dialogical and co-operative basis between Christians and atheists in China. In this light, Richard J. Mouw points out that Ting is proposing a 'larger faith' in a 'generous God', instead of a 'stingy God', who is open to both Christians and non-Christians, not least to atheists.[35] This ushers in Ting's understanding of a loving God who wills not power, but fellowship.[36]

Ting's cosmic Christ reveals God as the cosmic lover whose creation continues. As Ting claims, 'Our Christology is not one that lingers at the divinity and Godlikeness of Christ, but is one that tells of the Christlikeness of God.'[37] What is more, Ting points out that 'Christlike love is the way God intends for the running of the cosmos'.[38] Influenced by process theology, Ting is against such images of God as a ruling Caesar or a moralistic judge or the first mover, as in classical theism. On the contrary, he highlights love as the most important attribute of God. Ting holds that God's transcendence points to the inexhaustible love, while his immanence means the presence of God's love with the whole creation,[39] which is revealed by the cosmic Christ. Such a God continues his creation not to coerce, but to persuade all people to continue to grow. In the light of God's *creatio continua*, both Christians and non-Christians – and not least atheists – are all God's 'half-completed products'.[40] Furthermore, human beings are

---

[34] Fung Yu-Lan, *A Short History of Chinese Philosophy (1948)*, bilingual edition (Nanjing: Jiangsu wenyi chubanshe, 2012), 334.
[35] Richard J. Mouw, 'The Cosmic Mission of Christ', in *Seeking Truth in Love*, Wang Peng (ed) (Beijing: China Religious Culture, 2005), 301-302.
[36] Ting, 'One Chinese Christian's View of God (1993)', 436.
[37] Ting, 'Theological Mass Movement in China (1984)', LNE, 149.
[38] Ting, 'The Cosmic Christ (1991)', LNE, 417.
[39] Ting, 'Inspirations from Liberation Theology, Process Theology, and Teilhard de Chardin (1985)', LNE, 212.
[40] Ting, 'One Chinese Christian's View of God (1993)', LNE, 432.

not qualitatively, but quantitatively, different from the incarnate Logos just as the long and short arcs are compared with a full circle. [41] Both Christians and atheists have the seeds of logos (*logos spermatikos*), a phrase Ting often quotes from Justin Martyr, and will be educated by God through Christ to seek the transcendence of their life. God of Christlike love persuades both Christians and atheists to grow into the new Christlike humanity,[42] and to continue expanding God's Trinitarian communion of love in the world.

Concerning the task of shaping the ecclesial selfhood of the uniting post-denominational Church and strengthening its unity, Ting first wants to clarify the relationship between the local and the ecumenical churches from a post-colonial perspective. For Ting, it is quite natural and even legitimate for a local church to assume its national and cultural features so that the Gospel can become more appealing to people with their particular mindset.[43] Due to the confusion of the cross and colonialism in the past history of Christian churches in China, however, Ting tries to sort out the relationship by divesting Christianity of its colonial apparel so that the churches will be no longer be duplicates of western churches, but be Chinese churches.[44] The moratorium on western mission in the 1950s provided the opportunity so that western sending churches could no longer control the Chinese churches, and the implementation of the three-self principles, i.e. self-administration, self-support and self-government, enabled the Chinese churches to unite and to develop gradually their selfhood in the socialist context. So the 'three-self' in China, according to Ting, does not intend to be an 'anti-missionary movement',[45] cancelling mission, but allows the Chinese churches to have their own sovereignty and to stand on an equal footing with the traditional sending churches for mission in partnership in the Chinese context.

Yet this 'three-self' should not lead to self-isolation. Ting also realises that the 'national selfhood' of the Chinese churches is always relative to ecumenical faith in Jesus Christ and the Gospel, which the whole church universal shares in common.[46] But Ting also claims, 'The universality of the church only exists in all the particularities of the local church. The local church is the place where the meeting between Christianity universal and cultural particularities occurs to maximum advantage.'[47] With this understanding of the local-ecumenical relationship in mind, Ting is confident in developing the ecclesial selfhood of the Chinese churches. After the disastrous Great Cultural Revolution, the Chinese churches

---

[41] Ting, 'You Have the Words of Eternal Life (1985)', LNE, 190.
[42] Ting, 'Understanding the Heart of God (1993)', LNE, 442.
[43] Ting, 'Sermon in Sydney Cathedral (1984)', LNE, 159-60.
[44] Ting, 'Address at Worship (1983)', LNE, 118.
[45] Ting, 'An Update on the Church in China', LNE, 450.
[46] Ting, 'Sermon in Sydney Cathedral (1984)', LNE, 159-60.
[47] Ting, 'A Rationale for Three-Self', LNE, 131.

resume this task and have continued to explore a common confession of faith, liturgy and church polity in order to strengthen the unity of the uniting post-denominational churches, which is indispensable for a holistic understanding of mission in China. Chinese theological education shoulders this responsibility to continue developing a Chinese contextual theology and strengthening church unity through dialogue with western and ecumenical theological achievements, which in the Chinese context we should not copy without discrimination.

A Note on Contemporary Challenges

The situation of Chinese churches varies due to the size of the country and the difference of local cultures and traditions. So I can only summarise, as far as I can see, some important challenges in terms of theological education and mission. First of all, as the Chinese churches are still developing contextual theology, there is not a unifying doctrinal criterion to be taught in theological education. When facing heretical teachings and theological arguments, some Christians may easily pick up certain earlier denominational standards of orthodox faith with the current popularity of the reformed tradition as an example.[48] This may undermine post-denominational church unity, and make doctrinal diversity within the uniting church stretch and split.

Secondly, there has emerged a Sino-Christian theological movement *extra ecclesia* in China since the 1980s. Ting welcomed these 'culture Christians' who, unlike western cultured despisers of Christianity in 19th-century Europe, may not be confessing Christians, but are sympathetic and are doing academic theology in secular universities and research institutes. According to Ting, they are the important 'bridge' between the church and academia,[49] but their studies may pose serious challenges to ecclesial theologies due to their epistemological 'prejudice' on objectivity and rationality.[50] Therefore, Chinese theological education should also pay attention to the 'intellectual mission' and 'cultural mandate' in China.

Finally, with China's furthering of its policy of openness and reform, Chinese society is undergoing dramatic changes especially when its economy develops so fast but in an unbalanced way between the costal areas and inland. Confronted by various new challenges, scholars in China have started to explore the possible role of Christianity in shaping a civil

---

[48] For example, see Pei Lianshan's criticism of this phenomenon in Pei, 'qiantan jiaerwenzhuyi yu zhongguo jiaohui' (On Calvinism and Chinese Churches) *Tianfeng* 5 (2014): 32-3.
[49] Ting, 'An Update on the Church in China', LNE, 458.
[50] See my article, 'Engaging University Theologies with Church Theologies: A Postliberal Appraisal of the Emerging Sino-Christian Academic Theology', in *What Young Asian Theologians are Thinking*, Leow Theng Huat (ed) (Singapore: Trinity Theological College, 2014), 50-64.

society with Chinese characteristics.[51] In this connection, the Christian churches should deepen dialogue with the social sciences so that Christianity can bear a more effective witness to Christ in the public sphere.

Conclusion

Contemporary Chinese theological education is committed to equipping the uniting Chinese churches in a socialist country for mission by first laying out a Chinese framework to understand Christ's holistic mission. Consequently, a Chinese mission theology inspired by Ting will continue with its unfinished apologetic and constructive tasks via creative dialogue with the governments, the Chinese academia, Chinese culture, social sciences, and the ecumenical churches. I may as well conclude this essay with Bishop Ting's words, 'We are on a new path, untrodden before. Let the Holy Spirit guide us. Let us support each other. Let us develop a new way for the Chinese and ecumenical churches.'[52]

---

[51] For example, see Huang Haibo, 'Zouxiang jiangou zhong de gongmin shehui: 2010 nian zhongguojidujiaode zeren yu fansi' (Towards a Civil Society in Construction: The Responsibility of and Reflection on Christianity in China in 2010), in Zhongguo zongjiao baogao 2011 (Annual Report on Religions in China), Jin Ze et Qiu Yonghui (ed) (Beijing: Social Sciences Academic Press, 2011), 128-72.

[52] Ting, 'Taking a New Way', LNE, 310. The translation of the last sentence has been revised by me according to the Chinese version.

ESSENTIAL FUNCTIONS OF THE CHURCH AND ITS MISSION – A MODEL IN CONTEXTUAL THEOLOGICAL EDUCATION

Yalin Xin

Introduction

Several years ago when I researched and reflected on the Word of Life movement (WOL), its history, structure and missiological significance, one of the themes stood out among stories and experiences of the WOL community of believers: theological education.[1] It was regarded as an indispensable part of the church, or, 'one of the three supporting legs of the church' (in their own terms, established churches, theological education, and the Gospel Band). I highlighted this in my writings in diagrams and shared with colleagues and students about the importance of theological education in the development of the WOL community. Incidentally, this model of the church was affirmed by Patrick Johnstone in his recently published book, *The Future of the Global Church*,[2] in which he proposed 'A 21st Century Missional Church/Congregation' framework that includes the exact three components of the WOL community. Johnstone's emphasis seems to be on the balance of the three functions of the church. It is the purpose of this paper to demonstrate, through the case study of the WOL movement, how theological education was essential to the growth and dynamic of the WOL community as it is intimately and dynamically related to the other two functions or 'supporting legs' of the church, and as such, it should provide valuable insights to the global church.

It is also the observation of this paper that, when believers faithfully respond to the leading of the Holy Spirit in context, it often results in their finding God's heart and establishing structures that are more consistent with a biblical model. The case of the WOL movement seems to validate this observation. The movement grows and its dynamic impacts large

---

[1] This paper is limited to the study of theological education with the WOL movement or network, a house church community that started in the rural areas of central China in the 1970s. There has been no official relationship between theological education within the WOL movement and the seminaries under the Chinese Christian Council. Nor has there been significant amount of interaction between the WOL and the TSPM.
[2] Patrick Johnstone, *The Future of the Global Church: History, Trends and Possibilities* (Colorado Spring, CO: IVP, 2011).

sectors of China's rural population because of the work of the Spirit and the faithful responses of believers.

A Biblical/Missional Model of Church Structure

This paper assumes the validity of Johnstone's observation, that Jesus modelled in his earthly ministry the normative structure of the church, as it is shown in Figure 1 – that the three functions of local congregation, apostolic teams, and theological education demonstrate the essential structure of the church.[3]

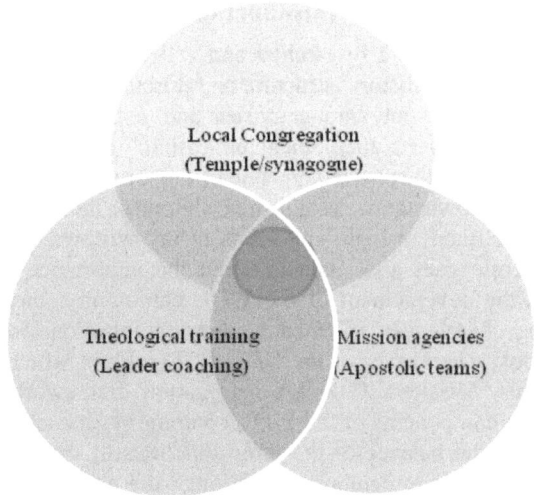

Figure 1: The Ministry of Jesus / The Early Church[4]

Johnstone points out the significance of the three functions of 'gathering, training and sending' in balance![5] Although this Jesus model was continued in the early church, the shift and imbalance caused by the institutionalisation of the church historically has obviously affected the effectiveness of Christian mission. Johnstone's call for 'A 21st Century

---

[3] This paper refers to data in the author's previous publications, primarily *Inside China's House Church Network* (Lexington, KY: Emeth Press, 2009) and 'Inner Dynamics of the Chinese House Church Movement: The Case of the Word of Life Community', *Mission Studies* 25, No.2 (2008): 157–84.

[4] This diagram is adapted from Fig 8.1 of Patrick Johnstone, *The Future of the Global Church: History, Trends and Possibilities* (Colorado Spring, CO: IVP, 2011), 225.

[5] Johnstone, *The Future of the Global Church*, 225.

Missional Church/Congregation' model is a heartfelt cry for the 'restoration for the original balance for the Church both globally and locally'.[6]

The WOL Structure

The God we believe in is a living God, so that when we respond to his calling in faith, his Spirit guides us in the choices we make in life. There is no lack of evidence scripturally, historically or cross-culturally. The WOL movement presents itself as such a witness. As a rural Christian movement, it finds its beginnings in the 1960s during the height of China's Cultural Revolution, when a small number of Christians started to connect with one another in worship and fellowship, and started small-scale evangelism in the neighbourhood. This eventually developed into something more phenomenal in central China: revival furnaces – the beginning of the later house church families in central China. The height of the development of the WOL movement was in the 1980s and 90s, with its network stretching out to various regions of the country.[7] Its structure was unique, but biblical, more of a product of theological 'doing' than 'thinking' (Figure 2).

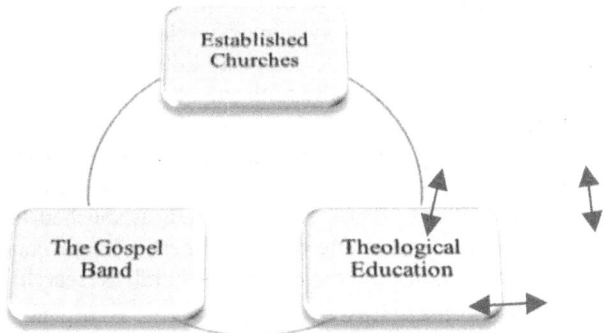

Figure 2: Dynamic WOL Structure

Structurally speaking, the WOL movement is supported by three constituent parts: 1) the Established (House) Churches, 2) Theological Education (seminaries or training schools), and 3) the Gospel Band. Key to the functionality of the structure is the dynamic motion of the structure as seen in the diagram. The interaction between the three supporting legs internally and externally set the whole WOL community in motion. How each part relates to and interacts with the other parts causes change and

---

[6] Johnstone, *The Future of the Global Church*, 225.
[7] The WOL movement, named as the 'Born Again Movement' in Johnstone's *Operation World* (2001), was numbered as one of the largest congregations in China, with 16 million members.

produces growth. First, the Established Churches support the ministry of the Gospel Band and Theological Education, through prayer and financial resources, and select and supply trainees for Theological Education. It also works with the Gospel Band to provide care, discipleship and training for their members, i.e. through Life/Truth meetings and short-term training. Second, some graduates from specialised training classes in Theological Education such as the Pillars' TE, would then go back to their own communities and become pastors of established house churches. Other graduates would join the Gospel Band and be assigned to frontier evangelism. Theological Education also works with house churches in co-ordinating trainee interns at the end of each level of training in the Theological Education system. Third, the Gospel Band enjoys a continuous supply of graduates from Theological Education, whom it sends for frontier evangelism. The three constituent parts of WOL work closely together to keep the wheel spinning outwards, thus enlarging the WOL network.

Theological Education –
a Contextual Model of Equipping for Ministry

As shown in the dynamic structure of the WOL movement, theological education is an integral part of the system of development. Each constituent part, i.e. Established Churches, Theological Education, and the Gospel Band, works closely and relationally with the other parts of the structure, with mission to the unreached at the heart of the movement. Mission spirituality is intentionally integrated in the various levels of training that undergirds the continuous dynamic spinning of the development cycle. A tremendous amount of new house churches were established through the ministry – 'a significant milestone of the Chinese Church construction', according to research done by the Chinese Church Research Center in Hong Kong (CCRC 1986, 13).

Curriculum for theological education

A key to theological education in any context, the experience of the WOL movement seems to suggest, is the development of a contextual curriculum that involves the participation of local believers. This seems to be a crucial step in Paul Hiebert's model of critical contextualisation.[8] Though not developed specifically for theological education, the model can be readily referenced in any forms of contextual ministry. The community of believers have to be actively involved in the process of their own contextual theological education!

---

[8] Paul Hiebert, 'Critical Contextualization', in *International Bulletin of Missionary Research*, 11/3 (July 1987), 104-12.

WOL believers might have to find this out the hard way, given all the limitations of the environment, including the lack of any Christian resources. Selected leaders of the movement dedicated themselves to the task of compiling their own training manual[9] as the curriculum for Theological Education. The work came out in handwritten form in 1984, titled, 'Salvation through the Cross'. It basically addressed seven areas of theology and ministry that the team judged as important and relevant: (1) salvation through the cross, (2) the way of the cross, (3) discerning the adulteress, (4) building the church, (5) providing for life, (6) interlink and fellowship, and (7) frontier evangelism. These seven principles are not just categorical numbers, these are closely related to who they are and what they do, i.e. reports and reflections from annual retreats consistently supply sources to supplement and update the manual.

The manual is also divided into two parts and later renamed *Truth Practice Curriculum* (I and II). *Curriculum I* deals with establishing the foundation of new life in Christ, which includes systematic study of relevant passages of the Scripture concerning Christ, sin, repentance, faith and salvation. *Curriculum II* deals with salvation history and theology, the life and ministry of Jesus, church history, mission history, and the theology of evangelisation.[10]

Training schedule

Unique to this Theological Education model is the nature of its intensive training in an enclosed location. This was simply the reality of the environment in which Christians found themselves. Its training schedule was particularly designed for the quick production of workers for the Kingdom of God, obviously designed in a way that may look very different from a conventional seminary (Figure 3). The timetable template included in the training manual is actually referred to as Workers' Training Classes. Almost two decades after the TEs were initiated in WOL, their timetables remained much the same, with significant attention given to spiritual formation of individual trainees as they fed on the Word of God. Many graduates go on to be itinerant evangelists and leaders of the church.

---

[9] A note has to be added here that the training manual was initially sketchy and more focused on the first part, Salvation through the Cross. The rest of the manual was supplemented and revised regularly, incorporating the collected wisdom of a much larger group of leaders. The 2003 edition is an approximately 300,000-word document.

[10] Refer to 'Seminaries of the Fields, Report 2', in *China and the Church*, 57 (1987), 14.

Timetable for Workers Training Classes

(translated and adapted by the author)

5:00 am	Rise (watchful, prompt, quiet)
5:15-7:15 am	Devotional time (content: worship, Bible reading, prayer; state of mind: watchful, spiritual warfare, intimate fellowship)
7:30–8:00 am	Breakfast (thankful, quiet and meditative, hygienic)
8:00–8:30 am	Worship (hymn-learning, meditation, spiritual fellowship)
8:30–10:00 am	First class (taking notes; concentrating and emphasising application; keeping quiet in class and avoiding procrastination)
10:20–11:50 am	Second class
12:00–12:30 pm	Lunch (thankful, quiet and meditative, hygienic)
12:30–2:00 pm	Afternoon break (keeping quiet and avoiding disturbing others)
2:00–2:30 pm	Worship (singing hymns and meditating with heart and mind)
2:30–4:00 pm	Third class (taking notes, concentrating and emphasising application; keeping quiet in class and avoiding procrastination)
4:30–6:00 pm	Fourth class
6:30–7:00 pm	Supper (thankful, quiet and meditative, hygienic)
7:00–8:30 pm	Review (quiet; review and homework)
8:30–9:30 pm	Evening prayer (retrospective of the day, thanksgiving and interceding)
10:00 pm	Bedtime (prompt)

Figure 3: Timetable Template for Theological Education

A schedule like this comes up to about 12 hours of work in a day. In three months, students would have completed approximately 18 semester hours of work. Speedy turnout of workers for ministry is one of the clear marks of the WOL training structure. Operating under the restraint of the context, believers responded in faith to the needs of theological education, establishing contextual structures and creating their own curriculum. There may be questions to ask about whether it was reasonable or healthy to design a schedule like this, or concerns about whether the curriculum was adequate. The result of this training, however, answers different sets of questions: 1) it took much less time to produce and send out a worker for ministry; 2) it met, to a certain extent, the pastoral needs of the local house churches; 3) it supplies workers for the Gospel Band; 4) it contributes to the dynamic motion of the WOL structure with its supply, training and sending out of Kingdom workers. Though not orthodox in its appearance, the WOL TE model is biblical, contextual and fruitful.

System of training and equipping for mission

WOL Christians were conscious of their calling and commission as ambassadors for Christ, sharing the good news of the Kingdom of God with fellow Chinese who were yet to come to a saving knowledge of Jesus as Lord. So mission was at the heart of their existence from the beginning. As the movement grew, it always had mission at the heart of its existence. In other words, everything they did revolved around mission! The initial structure of WOL seems to reflect the Jesus model outlined in Johnstone's book,[11] despite the fact that there was little contact between WOL and the global church, nor was any Christian literature available.

The system of training gradually took form in the WOL community in the 1980s, enabling and equipping believers for ministry. First, the church in various areas conducted evangelistic meetings, to which believers invited families and friends and in which the good news of Jesus Christ was shared with those attending the meeting. A typical evangelistic meeting usually lasted three to five days, in which the preacher would address questions concerning the meaning of life, i.e. (in their own words) 'Where do humans come from and where are they going after death? What circumstances do they find themselves in right now, and what can they do about it? Through the speaking of the Biblical truth, we helped the people realize the reality about themselves. When they realized their situation and how dangerous their positions were, they started to seek a way of salvation, and there was one available.'[12]

The first level of training, in this case, the evangelistic meeting, provided ground for following up at the next level of training. Recommendations were made from seekers in the evangelistic meetings for Level 2 training, which was the 'Life meeting', a form of week-long revival meeting that was organised in a closed up location. Intensive teaching and preaching on the following biblical and theological aspects, together with devotions and counselling, were integral parts of the training: God's creation, the fall, the judgement of sin, the consequences of judgement, the love of God, salvation through Christ (birth, ministry, death, burial, resurrection, ascension, the second coming of Jesus Christ, with a focus on the Cross), the work of the Holy Spirit, repentance, faith, rebirth, righteousness and salvation.

When seekers, under the illumination of the Holy Spirit, understood in their heart and mind the reality of human sin, the love of God in Jesus Christ, the salvation through Jesus Christ, they accepted Jesus Christ as their Lord and savior and received salvation, just as those Israelites who looked up to the bronze snake in faith and were healed. When they were clear about their salvation, their whole being was renewed and they were totally different! And

---

[11] Refer to Johnstone, *The Future of the Global Church*, 225.
[12] From an interview with movement leaders in 2005.

a desire for seeking God was developed in their hearts because the Spirit of God was in them pressing them forward.[13]

The next level of training was the 'Truth meeting' that normally lasted seven to fifteen days. In this session, participants were devoted to the study of the key content of the training manual and relevant scriptural teachings, engaged in personal and group devotions, and participating in other needed areas of the temporary communal life. Typically, these trainees were those who responded to God's calling in faith, preparing for Christian service.

At the end of the 'Truth meeting,' some with an affirmed conviction for service would be recommended, after sessions of counselling with the leaders of the training and regional/area elders, to the short-term training classes, which were later called pre-TE, in which, for about forty days, the theme of salvation through the cross was dealt with in a systematic manner. 'When these believers graduated, they knew how to share the gospel with others. And often they were able, with the support of experienced co-workers, to lead evangelistic meetings and "Life meetings". Some even participated in leading the "Truth meetings".'[14]

After about six months of ministry exercise, these new workers were called back from the fields to start TE-1 (three to four months in length), where the content of the training manual, i.e. the *Seven Principles*, were dealt with in a more systematic and detailed manner. On graduation from TE-1 they were sent out to the field to lead evangelistic meetings, 'Life meetings', 'Truth meetings' and short-term training classes. These ministerial practices (almost like internships) usually went on for about a year before the TE-1 graduates were once again called back to TE-2 for another six months, where they would study the whole Bible one book after another. Students, after completing TE-2, were able to grasp fairly well the content of the Bible, background, authors, themes and outlines of each of the books, Christology in each of the books, church history, and basic apologetics. Students graduating from TE-2 were also qualified as itinerant evangelists.[15]

Teachers involved in TE-2 attended biannual retreats organised by the WOL church, where, under the leadership of seniors and leaders, they studied the Scripture together, analysing the issues that appeared and might appear in teaching. So there were conscious communal efforts involved in the TE training – as teachers, they were bearers of the responsibility of equipping believers for ministry, by the power of the Spirit of God, through the support of the WOL community. It was a group project.

Towards the beginning of the 1990s, increased interaction with overseas missionaries alerted leaders of the WOL movement to the need to study western theological tradition in an effort to broaden their own theological

---

[13] From an interview with movement leaders in 2005.
[14] From an interview with movement leaders in 2005.
[15] From an interview with movement leaders in 2005.

reflection. As a measure to meet this need, TE-3 was established. 'TE-3 was based on our Chinese indigenous theological training, which was brought into being under the guidance of the Spirit of God, while absorbing and inheriting from the rich historical legacy and foundation of western traditional theology,' one of the leaders said. The WOL community was much enriched at this time, being able to dialogue with the parts of the same body vertically and horizontally. They were also able to send some students overseas to study in degree programmes in formal seminaries.[16] This was called special TE (hereafter called TE-Special). In this way, theological education among WOL was connected with international theological education for mutual enrichment.

The success of the system of training was obvious. According to the Chinese Church Research Center, the majority of students at various levels of training (which were conducted in a number of regions and provinces) came from the same region or province where training was operated. After a year's training, house churches in the regions and provinces experienced great revivals and the number of Christians and churches more than doubled. Through TE training, there were not only increased numbers of workers in the churches, but also the quality of the whole congregation increased. Therefore, TE training was the primary reason behind the revival of the house churches.[17]

This system gradually stabilised towards the beginning of 1990s and has played an integral part in the continual development of WOL. Devoted believers constantly joined the cycle of training, as the system continues its spinning, yielding workers for the Kingdom in hundreds, thousands, and tens of thousands.

Insight for the Global Church

The success of the WOL movement is obvious, with the extension of its network in various parts of the country and the establishment of great numbers of house churches. Its emphasis on interlink and fellowship has greatly facilitated the renewal of churches, often when renewal from one house church or area is channelled through to others within its network. Its unique theological educational model speaks volumes to the fundamental structure of what a biblical church is supposed to be. What can the global church glean from the WOL experience?

1. The Holy Spirit is the ultimate cause of all genuine church growth and vitality, but often co-operates with human beings in accomplishing his purposes. In other words, believers need to

---

[16] My respondents included several former itinerant evangelists as well as several who had recently completed their seminary studies overseas.

[17] Jonathan Chao, *Purified by Fire: The Secrets of House Church Revivals in Mainland China* (Taipei: CMI, 1993), 84-85.

identify the signs of God's Spirit and faithfully respond to his leading in context. In seeking God's will, believers often rediscover the heart of the Gospel and what is important for a specific time and context.

2. The WOL experience illuminates for us how we can follow a biblical model of church where we are. If Jesus, as the head of the church, has demonstrated the essential functions of the church, and the WOL movement has testified in its own success story of the Jesus model, there is no doubt that it should inform the global church.

3. The WOL theological education provides an alternative venue for the generally accepted model: its speedy production of workers has undoubtedly fuelled the explosive growth of the movement.

4. Theological education should not foster dependency, either on trainers or training materials. WOL believers have demonstrated how they relied on the Spirit of God and the accumulated wisdom of the community of believers in creating curricula for themselves. Referencing each other's resources is not the issue here, but local believers should actively participate in theologising and decide what is important in training and leadership formation.

A SEMINARY AT THE URBAN CROSSROADS: A CASE STUDY OF CITY SEMINARY OF NEW YORK[1]

Mark R. Gornik and Maria Liu Wong

The mission of City Seminary of New York is to seek the peace of the city through theological education. We fulfil our calling of forming persons for ministry through an intercultural learning community for the study of Scripture, mission, applied theology, and the church.

Flushing, Queens – the end of the Number 7 subway line in New York City – is the world in a city. It is a neighbourhood where the signs, smells of food, shops, churches and religious activities are not confined to immediate streets and blocks, but reach beyond local boundaries to include Asia and the world. Here even the physical steps announce a global city, as each is engraved with a different language found in the library's holdings.

On a Saturday morning, students and faculty from City Seminary of New York begin to meet on the stairs to the Queens Public Library in Flushing. We have gathered to pray and break bread, to learn about the history and contemporary dynamics of Flushing, to read Scripture, and then walk and pray in small groups, re-gathering to reflect on our experiences and then eat *dim sum* in a local restaurant.

Pray and break bread. NEW YORK CITY, an annual series of community prayer events held in every borough of New York City, is an introduction to our understanding of theological education, 'theology on the ground', at City Seminary. It is an experience of the body, the senses, and ultimately of God in relationship to the city. By seeing God at work in the city, we come to view the world, others and ourselves in new ways. As a way of accompanying church leaders learning to minister more fruitfully in a complex urban world, our approach to theological education is about community, grounded in urban life, and emphasises the practices of praying and eating together.

'Pray to the Lord for the city, for if it experiences peace, you too will experience peace,' we hear in Jeremiah. Responding to this Biblical calling, City Seminary nourishes a way of being in the city that helps draw people into new relational patterns and practices of ministry.[2] It is a space for

---

[1] This is a revised paper first given at Overseas Ministries Study Center (OMSC) on 28th April 2012. Copyright by the authors and City Seminary of New York.

[2] Theological education has experienced a paradigm shift in the area of Christian practices through the work of Craig Dykstra. See, most recently, D.C. Bass and C.

cultivating a new imagination to see and join in what God is doing in the city.

We offer this case study of City Seminary, not as a community that has arrived, but as an account of our pilgrimage into better understanding God, the city and learning together, articulating some of the ways we have sought to build a seminary amidst the adaptive challenges of our moment.[3]

A New Terrain

In the words of Rowan Williams, the former Archbishop of Canterbury, 'theology arises when the world looks different from what you thought it was.'[4] What is it about our world today that looks different? How should it impact not just theology but theological education?

Here we highlight two accelerating social and religious changes that are reshaping the terrain in which theological education takes place in New York and also around the world. Each new direction presents an adaptive challenge with enormous opportunities for the city, church and academy.

The first is urbanisation. In 1900, the world was approximately 9% urban. Today, more than 50% of the world's population lives in cities, and by most estimates, will reach 75% within a few decades.[5] As part of this urban world, nearly one billion people live in informal housing or settlements. An ever-moving assembly of people, institutions and networks, the city presses upon people of all walks of life questions of complexity, change, diversity, pluralism, sustainability, instabilities and social arrangements.

The second is world Christianity. In 1900, over 80% of Christians lived in Europe and North America. Today, the majority of Christians live in Africa, Asia and Latin America.[6] It is a time of the Spirit, a period of the church flourishing from the ground up. When the church of a great multitude worships God, forms disciples, faces spiritual realities and reads Scripture, it begins with a wide range of questions and works with a vast

---

Dykstra (eds), *For Life Abundant: Practical Theology, Theological Education, and Christian Ministry* (Grand Rapids, MI: Eerdmans, 2008).
[3] Ronald J. Heifetz, *Leadership Without Easy Answers* (Cambridge: Harvard University Press, 1994).
[4] Rowan Williams, 'CEFACS Lecture, Birmingham – Centre for Anglican Communion Studies', 3rd November 2004.
[5] The work of sociologist Saskia Sassen charts this urban shift, and not just in the area of the global city. A document that captures something of the profound scale and diversity of our global planet is R. Burdett and D. Sudjic, *The Endless City* (New York: Phàidon, 2008). Equally important is the pioneering work of Harvie M. Conn. See also Mark R. Gornik, 'The Legacy of Harvie M. Conn', in *International Bulletin of Missionary Research*, 35.4 (2011), 212-17.
[6] T.M. Johnson and K.R. Ross, *Atlas of Global Christianity: 1910-2010* (Edinburgh: Edinburgh University Press, 2009).

array of cultural materials. Every aspect of church life and theology is impacted.

With the ascension of Christianity in the global South and the recession of Christianity in the West, the demographics of faith have changed. However, this geography of Christianity is not inert. Through urban networks, migrations, media, revivals, preaching and healing, developments in Seoul, Lagos and Kingston have become woven into the fabric of New York, London and Amsterdam. Webs, not walls, describe this church.

As Andy Crouch and Richard Mouw have recently observed, North American seminaries exist within a changing institutional ecosystem of churches, leaders and partners.[7] In New York City, we see the replenishment of the ecclesial ecosystem in a global way. As a result of recent immigration, we estimate that African, Asian and Latin American leaders have started more than 2,000 new churches in New York City. The new ecosystem is largely Pentecostal/charismatic in practice, evangelical in conviction, and grounded in transnational networks. Notably, these churches were formed and operate independently of western leaders, histories, institutions, organisations and issues.

A certain type of opportunity now arises. As diverse cultural encounters with the Gospel meet in the city, we are able to share with one another, worship together, and grow together in service to Christ. Within the story of redemption, this is the gift of mutuality. Andrew Walls, who has walked with and been a central part of City Seminary from its inception, speaks here of an 'Ephesian moment'.[8] This moment in New York, one that focuses on the body of Christ and its connectedness, underlies the unique possibilities for theological learning that has shaped City Seminary. In this Ephesian moment of many tongues, we are able to come together around the practices of Christian ministry in the city.

A Brief History

Following more than a decade of ministry in Sandtown, Baltimore, in 1998, Mark Gornik moved to New York to help begin a new church and community development ministry in Harlem. After working for several years on this project, he began to see new patterns of urban life that had implications for church life. Working with Andrew Walls, then a visiting

---

[7] A. Crouch and R. Mouw, *The Seminary of the Future*, September 2011: http://future.fuller.edu

[8] See Andrew F. Walls, *The Cross-Cultural Process in Christian History: Studies in the Transmission and Appropriation of Faith* (Maryknoll, NY: Orbis Books, 2002). For additional background, see W.R. Burrows, M.R. Gornik and J.A. McLean (eds), *Understanding World Christianity: The Vision and Work of Andrew Walls* (Maryknoll, NY: Orbis Books, 2011).

Professor at Princeton Theological Seminary, he also began to document and worship with African churches in the city. This experience with African churches became formative, and began to redirect him to theological education as a way of serving the city, building community and rethinking urban ministry. In 2003, City Seminary was launched full-time, and as one part of its activities, began a co-operative relationship with the Urban Mission program of Westminster Theological Seminary in Philadelphia. Working with Manuel Ortiz and Susan Baker, who have provided leadership to City Seminary for more than a decade and modelled a heart for Christ and the urban church, a Westminster MA degree was fashioned that allowed students to take classes in New York City and Philadelphia, completing the degree in four years of part-time study.

Among the students was Maria Liu Wong, who joined the staff in 2006, and now is the Dean of City Seminary. Her subsequent doctoral work at Teachers College, Columbia University, in Adult Learning and Leadership, focused on African, Asian, Asian North American and West Indian/Caribbean women in theological leadership.[9]

Between 2003 and 2010, some forty students graduated from the Westminster MA program. Recognising that most urban programmes related to traditional seminaries at some point close or falter,[10] from its inception City Seminary committed to developing its own institutional capacity and graduate programme. Thus, in 2010, in a way that should be recognised for its success, City Seminary concluded its relationship with Westminster.

For our first few years, we moved around the city, the hallway of a church basement serving as our primary classroom. In 2005, we moved into a Harlem storefront. In the fall of 2010, a new campus across the street was added. Here we have the ability to serve more students in a space designed for collaborative learning and research. While we are a seminary for the whole city, we are also very committed to our immediate Harlem context.

In 2007, as a seminary community we travelled to Dakar, Senegal, and to Johannesburg and Cape Town, South Africa. Through dialogue with Emmanuel Katongole, who has been an important part of our community, we came to see this trip not as a class in another location, a cross-cultural immersion, global tourism or a mission trip, but as a pilgrimage. Pilgrimage, he observes, is 'a vision of the Christian life as a journey... grows out of the sense of being pilgrims together, pilgrims who feel the

---

[9] Maria Liu Wong, 'Dancing into the Spiral Labyrinth: Racial/Ethnic Minority Women Leaders in Global Christian Theological Education' (EdD thesis, Teachers College, Columbia University, 2015).

[10] This was a sub-text of the case studies found in E. Villafane, B.W. Jackson, R.A. Evans and A. Frazier Evans (eds), *Transforming the City: Reframing Education for Urban Ministry* (Grand Rapids, MI: Eerdmans, 2002).

dust under their feet and come to know the places where they sojourn'.[11] A pattern was established, and each year we go on an urban pilgrimage, either domestic or international.

With the generous support of the Lilly Endowment, in 2010 the Ministry Fellows Program was launched. Since then, almost 150 students have completed this nine-month certificate-level course of study based on a cohort model of small group learning and faculty teams. This initiative has also helped us further establish our capacity in a wide variety of areas.

The Ministry Fellows Program is organised around four modules:

- Understanding the City
- Seeing the Church in the City
- Living Ministry in the City
- Spiritual Formation for Leadership

The Program uses small group discussions, visits to churches, readings, guest lecturers and panels, experiential activities, research projects, and a pilgrimage to another city as ways of learning and growing into a deeper understanding of Christian faith in practice in an urban setting.

Within these four modules, spiritual formation is an overarching theme. This involves prayer and seeking to be attuned to the presence of the Holy Spirit and Christ in our lives. It is about listening and being on a journey together, collaboration, and sharing our stories and lives. To guide the work of formation, throughout the whole programme, we read and reflect together on the Gospel of John, with Jean Vanier's *Drawn into the Mystery of Jesus through the Gospel of John* as a companion.[12]

In North American theological education, there is an ongoing question regarding how to move from classroom learning to active engagement in ministry.[13] Because our typical student is already in ministry, the gap to implementation is narrowed. However, we continue to explore ways to better understand and support the multiple transitions that our students are taking. Through 'collaborative inquiry' and action learning, small groups of faculty and graduates engage each spring in a season of small group reflection on ministry praxis, transitions and reintegration.[14] This enables us

---

[11] Andy Crouch, 'From Tower-Dwellers to Travellers', in *Christianity Today*, 51.7 (July 2007), 36.
[12] Jean Vanier, *Drawn into the Mystery of Jesus Through the Gospel of John* (Mahway, NJ: Paulist Press, 2004).
[13] C.R. Foster, L. Dahill, L. Goleman and B. Wang Tolentino, *Educating Clergy: Teaching Practices and Pastoral Imagination* (San Francisco, CA: Jossey-Bass, 2006); and E.R. Campbell-Reed and C. Scharen, '"Holy Cow! This Stuff is Real!" From Imagining Ministry to Pastoral Imagination', in *Teaching Theology and Religion*, 14.4 (2011), 323-42.
[14] A collaborative inquiry is a tool for action learning and research that brings together a group of individuals who answer a compelling question of mutual interest through cycles of action reflection, creating a generative space for fostering transformative learning. For more information, see J. N. Bray, J. Lee, L.L. Smith

to enrich ways of supporting our students and graduates, and also engages us in a larger dialogue with the field of adult learning.[15]

As Andrew Walls has emphasised, a research climate is crucial for developing theological leadership.[16] 'Scholarship,' he notes, 'has its own part in the great drama that brings Christians into true mutuality, with research and scholarship in Christian history having a part in a reconciliation that enables the new temple of Ephesians to be built.'[17] Christian scholarship is therefore a vocational and spiritual calling.

Documentation is a key element of this calling,[18] and reinforces the importance of history as a lens for scholarship and ministry. Through the Global New York Church Project, we have designed a wiki to introduce the changing religious ecology in the city. It also provides a framework around which we are collecting source materials and ephemera such as bulletins, calendars, hymnals and videos from African, Asian and Latin American churches in our city.

Our approach is to combine traditional forms with innovative action research and programme design, all feeding into ongoing curriculum development. Integrated into the daily life of the seminary, it is how we train reflective scholar practitioners for the practice of faithful ministry.

An important new seminary-wide initiative is the Next Generation Project. Launched in 2012, its purpose is to explore the future of the 1.5, second and third generations in new immigrant churches through action research and ethnography.

One way we share our research is through the Walls-Ortiz Gallery and Center, named after Andrew Walls and Manuel Ortiz, individuals who were formative in shaping City Seminary. The Gallery is a street-level public space for the translation of our research and learning. Exhibits have included urban community photography by adults and youth, and works-in-progress by local artists, while others planned include Asian/American

---

and L. Yorks, *Collaborative Inquiry in Practice: Action, Reflection, and Making Meaning* (Thousand Oaks, CA: Sage, 2000).

[15] A paper, 'Collaborative Inquiry and Transitions in Urban Ministry: Creating Time and Space for Reflexive Praxis in Community', was presented at the 10th Annual International Transformative Learning Conference (San Francisco, November 2012), based on our learning from one season of inquiry.

[16] See Andrew F. Walls, 'Christian Scholarship and the Demographic Transformation of the Church', in R.L. Peterson and N.M. Rourke (eds), *Theological Literacy for the Twenty-First Century* (Grand Rapids, MI: Eerdmans, 2002), 166-83.

[17] Andrew F. Walls, 'World Christianity and the Early Church', in A.E. Akinade (ed), *A New Day: Essays on World Christianity in Honor of Lamin Sanneh* (New York: Peter Lang, 2010), 28.

[18] Again, this is an area encouraged by Andrew F. Walls. See Michael Poon, 'Andrew F. Walls and Documenting World Christianity in the Twenty-First Century', in W.R. Burrows, M.R. Gornik and J.A. McLean (eds), *Understanding World Christianity* (Maryknoll, NY: Orbis Books, 2011), 169-93.

artists re-imagining theologies, a travelling exhibition out of South Africa focused on reconciliation, and a Harlem-focused interactive community project in collaboration with local institutions.

The early years of City Seminary provided space to discover and confirm our *charism* – one of serving the city and its growing church life from Africa, Asia, the West Indies and Latin America. It is not as much our focus as *who we are*, and therefore maintaining accessibility is part of what it means to honour our calling.

As with any start-up, beginning a new seminary means operating with risk, of living with vulnerability. Our strategy has been to focus on doing a few things well, building slowly, and keeping costs low. Developing a strong relational network with diverse partners is also part of our story. However, our experience is not just one of vulnerability but of God's abundance, and we have encountered this through the profound commitment of our partners, the significant generosity of individuals willing to invest in something new, and the prayers, friendship and sacrifice of our community. We are continually learning to be dependent upon the Lord, our city and our community, and to be a seminary grounded in prayer and fasting.

While City Seminary is a community, it is also an institution.[19] This is important as we look to the difference we hope to make into the future as we develop our faculty, expand the student community, and advance institutional capacity.

In a world of decentralised global church networks, City Seminary acts as a node or connection point for networks, increasing the effects of its work in multiple ways.[20] As part of a learning community that works for the peace of the city within the systems and networks of a city, others will accomplish even 'greater things' (John 14:12).[21]

Who is City Seminary?

Our students range in affiliation from Pentecostal to Presbyterian, African Independent to Apostolic, Baptist to Episcopalian, living in every borough,

---

[19] More broadly, on the many issues facing theological education, see Daniel O. Aleshire, *Earthen Vessels: Hopeful Reflections on the Work and Future of Theological Schools* (Grand Rapids, MI: Eerdmans, 2008) and Dietrich Werner, 'Theological Education in the Changing Context of World Christianity – an Unfinished Agenda', in *International Bulletin of Missionary Research*, 35.2 (April, 2011), 92-100.

[20] A way of looking at this comes from Mark C. Taylor, *The Moment of Complexity: Emerging Network Culture* (Chicago, IL: University of Chicago, 2001).

[21] Based on his experience in Boston, this theory is developed in very important ways by Douglas Hall in *The Cat and the Toaster: Living System Ministry in a Technological Age* (Eugene, OR: Wipf & Stock, 2010).

and coming from around the world. They are pastors, church leaders, missionaries, church planters, community developers and Christians in various occupations who desire grounding in applied theology and mission. They are servant-leaders striving to be more effective in mediating faith as abundant and life-giving in the city.

Nearly all our students are bi-vocational church leaders – whether pastors or lay leaders and, to accommodate their busy schedules, all classes are held at evenings and weekends. Yet even within this framework, a major trend we see that has many implications for theological education is that in a setting of world Christianity, ministry is not something a few train to do, but is a lifestyle and calling embraced by many. Today, the whole people of God are exercising _charisms_ in every sphere of life. Therefore, binary western frameworks can be limiting in helping us understand emerging ecclesiastical structures and movements, church offices and titles, and ministry activities.

The best way to explain this and introduce the City Seminary community is through some of our students, graduates and faculty.

- Ola Jewoola – Ola came to the Ministry Fellows Program by way of a faculty member, Pastor Adebisi Oyesile. Part of Nigerian church networks in Brooklyn, he shared at his graduation about the ways he has come to appreciate the body of Christ in its unity and diversity at City Seminary, as he now worships with and embraces brothers and sisters from cultures and traditions, once unfamiliar to him, with new eyes and understanding.

- Adrienne Croskey – Adrienne is a community chaplain and also part of a new church in Harlem. She was born and raised in the neighbourhood, and served as a prison and hospital chaplain before her transition to pastoral work. A graduate of the Master's program at City Seminary, she is a living testimony of a New Yorker at heart who lives in, and loves, her community with her particular gifts and story.

- Jonathan Roque – A bi-vocational pastor, Jonathan is a graduate of the Master's program, faculty/administrator at City Seminary, and Bishop of his denomination, an international network of more than 200 Latino Pentecostal churches. His passion for Christ and the city, and enthusiasm for the space to reflect and grow at City Seminary, has led members of his church and family to become part of our learning community over the past several years. He now works at City Seminary as enrolment manager.

- Kari Jo Cates – Originally from Kansas but living in New York City now for almost twenty years, Kari Jo is a graduate and now faculty of the Ministry Fellows Program. Through this program, she was helped to reframe the way she thinks about and lives in the city. A regular attendee at our conferences and seminars, she applies her learning in the context of her family of six, community and church home, Redeemer Presbyterian Church: West Side.

• Biju George – A pastor from Kerala, India, Biju moved to New York City. At City Seminary, he fulfilled a lifelong dream to attend seminary, graduating from the Master's program. While he works in the New York City Department of Housing, he is also the pastor of a Church of God congregation. Biju and his family (his wife and older son have also been part of the Ministry Fellows and Youth Ministry Fellows Programs, respectively) have a heart for Christ and discipleship in the city.

When we consider our learning community, we see how the city itself has enabled the cultural diversity of the whole church to come into a closer relationship, giving us a richer glimpse of Christ. For, in a global age, many of the most significant developments in the spread of Christianity are taking place from the ground up and within multiple circuits of urban connection.

Developing Curriculum and Faculty

City Seminary is a response to the mission and ecclesial vibrancy that are occurring in our city. What our experience and research have come to show us is that pastors and ministry leaders in the growth areas of the church in New York City have frequently not had access to formal and sustained theological education, nor has there been reflective sensitivity in training contexts to a global urban setting. However, these urban mission workers remain at the forefront of mediating a vision of faith to their congregations and worlds of influence, and are engaged in pioneering theological and mission activity.

Recognising that we have been given a gift to begin something new, we have taken developing our curriculum as a matter for careful planning and prayerful discernment. Simply offering a course on world Christianity or urban ministry within a traditional curriculum, while this can be an important step for many, is not sufficient in our context. Nor is importing a curriculum or model of seminary education suited to another time and place. Instead, we have sought to develop a curriculum and approach to learning that arises out of the urban context and the whole church in the city. This has been a demanding and intense planning and theological process, involving multiple cycles of action learning and research, but has helped to give us a clarity and coherent purpose.

With support from Faith as a Way of Life (Yale Divinity School), a Lilly Endowment-supported project, a comprehensive approach to present and future programmes of City Seminary was developed over a one-year study in 2008. The concept of a continuum of learning came out of this period of institutional reflection, data collection, interviews and community evaluation. Rather than viewing 'seminary' as a discrete process of two or three years of learning, we propose that 'seminary' be re-framed as a lifelong community of learning and practice, with multiple ways of entering and staying engaged in the process. Ways to enter our continuum of learning include praying and breaking bread. NEW YORK CITY, the Ministry Fellows Program, Pilgrims' Progress, Alumni Praxis Groups, and a forthcoming MA Degree Program in Ministry in the Global City. Throughout the year, we also offer seminars, workshops, symposia, and contexts for dialogue that are open to our entire learning community of over 200 persons.

Our view is that education is for life; it should not end when a programme ends *and* it should meet ministry practitioners at their point of learning. It should be about theology for all of life, for as the Reformed tradition of Kuyper stresses, Christ is Lord over all, and as the churches of Africa, Asia and Latin America emphasise, salvation is holistic.

In our framework for theological education for Christian leadership, learning strives to be:

*   Transformational – Drawing on the life histories and ministry experiences of students, learning occurs through critical reflection, experiential learning, journal writing, collaborative inquiry and discourse.[22] Faculty and students engage in this intentional process for the purpose of individual and collective spiritual growth.

*   Communal – Rather than simply teach classes, we build community; instead of graduating students, we incorporate them into a lifelong community of learning and practice. By creating a safe space, or 'holding environment', for relationships to be built and critical reflection to occur, there is shared ownership of change and growth. Here we learn the practice of reading Scripture together.

*   Intercultural – Every culture, as it interacts with the Gospel, helps advance theological knowledge. Building on the Body of Christ from around the world in New York City, we emphasise the fruit of intercultural learning for ministry and theology.

*   Interdisciplinary – Because knowledge, theology and urban life are interrelated, the curriculum is developed thematically across disciplines. New discoveries and perspectives are being developed as the fields of learning expand.

*   Urbanised – With the city and its churches as our living classroom, every part of our curriculum assumes an urban focus, and we concentrate on the skills and practices of ministry for a complex world. In the specificities of New York, but also in comparative

---

[22] For additional information on the theoretical framework of transformative learning, see Jack Mezirow and Associates, *Learning as Transformation: Critical Perspectives on a Theory in Progress* (San Francisco, CA: Jossey-Bass, 2000), and Mary Hess and Stephen Brookfield (eds), *Teaching Reflectively in Theological Contexts: Promises and Contradictions* (Malabar, FL: Krieger, 2008).

ways, we learn how to pray in and for the city, to understand it, to worship, work creatively within an urban world, and to think theologically about everyday life.

- Missiological – Because theological energy comes out of mission and new questions, there is no curricular line between theology and mission. All learning is for the blessing of persons, communities and the city.[23]

A significant dimension of City Seminary is an emphasis on *faculty formation and development*.[24] In line with the unique challenges of urban church leadership development and scholarship that is grounded and interdisciplinary, faculty involved in this programme have primarily grown out of the existing learning community at City Seminary of New York. A process of continued professional development is critical to City Seminary's grassroots model of theological education, allowing faculty to continue to engage in critical and spiritual reflection on urban ministry.

For example, the faculty team engages in a collaborative inquiry process to reflect on and evaluate the teaching and learning process and specific programme activities. Prioritising thoughtful praxis, time has been set aside for faculty to engage in individual and team learning and reflection. Faculty meetings involve worship, prayer, reflection, debriefing, and planning. In many ways, our way of teaching and working together is our curriculum. We actively seek to understand and re-frame the assumptions and essential questions of our epistemological and pedagogical practice through a double-loop learning process.[25]

In summary, our approach to learning is not about identifying problems and giving simple solutions, but cultivating persons and a community that, living in the Spirit, are able to think theologically about the adaptive challenges and complex opportunities that they will come to face into the future.[26]

---

[23] For reflections on education and shalom for all areas of life, see Nicholas Wolterstorff, *Educating for Shalom: Essays on Christian Higher Education* (Grand Rapids, MI: Eerdmans, 2004), and David F. Ford, *Christian Wisdom: Desiring God and Learning in Love* (Cambridge: CUP, 2007).

[24] See also Maria Liu Wong, 'Transformative Faculty Development in Urban Theological Education' (EdD Qualifying Paper, Teachers College, Columbia University, 2012).

[25] For more information on 'double loop' and 'single loop' learning, see C. Argyris and D.A. Schon, *Theory in Practice: Increasing Professional Effectiveness* (San Francisco, CA: Jossey-Bass, 1974), and L. Yorks, 'Adult Learning and the Generation of New Knowledge and Meaning: Creating Liberating Spaces for Fostering Adult Learning through Practitioner-Based Collaboration Action Inquiry', in *Teachers College Record* 107.6 (2005), 1217-44.

[26] Kenneth E. Bailey sees something like this in *Paul Through Mediterranean Eyes: Cultural Studies in 1 Corinthians* (Downers Grove, IL: IVP, 2011). See also Kwame Bediako, *Christianity in Africa: The Renewal of a Non-Western Religion* (Maryknoll, NY: Orbis Books, 1995).

Metaphors of Learning

To summarise our approach to learning, we offer the following metaphors.

- Bridge – As a bridge for communities around the city and world, we cross boundaries by bringing together uncommon friends who might not otherwise find each other. We see a microcosm of the Kingdom of God come into our midst each time we gather together for class or fellowship.

- Shoes – We commit to walk alongside each other on our journeys in knowing self, Christ and others more deeply and intimately. Our posture of learning is one that values each other's experience and expression of Gospel truth in our lives, and we understand that it is in being together we may more fully become the body of Christ in our city.

- Kitchen Towel – Leadership may be seen, understood and articulated in a myriad of ways. As servants to Christ and each other, we offer ourselves to each other and our communities to be used for the most and least important needs. As protection when things are hot, or to clean up whatever mess has been made, we are as a community a part of each other's lives.

- Flower Pot – City Seminary exists to be a space, or a container for the growth, cultivation and flourishing of a Gospel community that loves God and loves the city. We provide opportunities for those in our midst to share and commit to praying, worshipping God, wrestling with Scripture, and discerning the Lord's will together.

- Glasses – We look through different lenses at the city, ministry and the world. In doing so, we invite self-reflection and re-framing of perspectives so that we can in turn better serve our own communities, having examined other urban ministries from historical, sociological, economic and pastoral views.

Conclusion: At the Crossroads

As with any new effort for the Kingdom, in building the seminary we have found at times the work is beyond our abilities and capacities. Among the elements we have developed here, there is discernment of the model, the work of dialogical pedagogy, community and faculty formation, resource development, and much more. But the Spirit creates and empowers, so we trust not in ourselves, but God. Joy comes from inviting God to lead, even though we don't always know where.

We believe that grassroots and contextual theological education can play a vital role in the life, growth and faith of the urban church, and therefore also in the city. For this reason, we are working to build a sustainable seminary that prepares church leaders to thrive in the global church and in the city. A networked world suggests new opportunities for theological education. Certainly, it calls for scholarship within and for an urban and world Christian context, moving across disciplines and adding new fields of study and approaches of inquiry.

But whatever the challenges, moving into a new educational moment is vital, because this is where the church and world have moved; we experience City Seminary as a gift we have been given by the Lord. It is possible and important to consider many outcomes, but new forms of belonging, friendships that can only be formed at the urban crossroads, may be the one that is most important.

As we learn together at City Seminary, individuals and, through them, the congregations and networks they represent, gain a framework for practice central to effective ministry in the city. Our students and faculty become part of a learning community of ministry peers that provides the context for constructing relevant and resonant urban theology, of learning to see the new things that God is doing in the city.

Practices, beliefs and experiences go together. So when we walk together, pray together, read Scripture together, and eat together, all in the name of Jesus, we are not only creating a curriculum, but seeing that God's new world is possible here and now. In this way, we are fulfilling our mission calling to seek the peace of the city.

PARTNERSHIP IN PREPARING THE LEADERSHIP FOR MISSION AND MINISTRY: A CONTINUED STORY OF THE FOUNDATION FOR THEOLOGICAL EDUCATION IN SOUTH EAST ASIA

H.S. Wilson

A Historical Note about FTESEA

In the early twentieth century there was an increased awareness among churches and mission bodies in the West that it was crucial that the Christian communities in Asia that have emerged as a result of mission outreach should have their own leaders trained locally to assist in ministries and ongoing mission. As Christian communities were divided into various Protestant denominations, forming interdenominational (ecumenical) seminaries was one of the avenues that was tried to accomplish that goal. To illustrate this, I am citing a brief account of what was tried and accomplished in China.

In 1911, Bible schools belonging to North American denominations of the Disciples of Christ, Methodist and Presbyterian mission boards merged to form an interdenominational seminary called the Nanking (present Nanjing) Bible Training School. The school was officially renamed Nanking Theological Seminary in 1917.[1] In 1918, the seminary began offering a Bachelor of Divinity degree programme.[2] According to the faculty report in 1919, the student body had grown to 146, 'representing 16 denominations, 11 provinces and Korea'.[3] Much of the financial and personal support for the seminary came from North American mission boards. In 1931 Rebecca Wendel Swope and her sister Ella Wendel, residents of New York City, bequeathed a large sum of money to be used for Nanking Seminary. This boosted its financial situation. In 1932, the Board of Managers of the seminary, when making changes in its constitution, facilitated the formation of an interdenominational Board of Founders of Nanking Theological Seminary in New York City to manage income from the Swope-Wendel bequest for theological education through

---

[1] Frank T. Cartwright, A River of Living Water. A Historical Sketch of Nanking Theological Seminary, Nanking, China and The Board of Founders (Singapore: The Board of Founders, 1963), 53.
[2] Cartwright, A River of Living Water, 6.
[3] Cartwright, A River of Living Water, 62.

Nanking Seminary and in China; this was the predecessor of the Foundation for Theological Education in South East Asia (FTESEA).[4]

Political developments in China that led to the establishment of the People's Republic on 1st October 1949 with its capital in Beijing escalated anti-imperial and anti-American feelings in the country. Educational institutions belonging to foreigners (especially churches and mission boards from the West) were nationalised. Following the Korean War in 1950, such attitudes were extended towards western missionaries and seminaries. Western missionaries were expelled from China which eventually led to an end to the engagement of the The Foundation for Theological Education in South East Asia in 1951. As a result, sending financial support and providing theological professors had to cease. Continued political developments in China called for the complete delinking of the involvement of churches in North America and the Board of Founders in China. 'Meanwhile, in China, the Nanking Theological Seminary was reorganised as Nanking Union Theological Seminary in 1952. Bishop K.H. Ting was named principal of the united seminary, which brought together 12 schools from around the country.'[5] The seminary was closed during the Cultural Revolution from 1966 and reopened again in 1981.

In 1951, in order to be more effective, the Board of Founders sponsored a survey of Protestant theological seminaries in South East Asia, including the theological training of Chinese diaspora communities. As a result of the survey, *The Anderson-Smith Report on Theological Education in Southeast Asia,*[6] the Board of Founders began supporting theological seminaries in South East Asia, giving attention to the training of Chinese leaders in diasporas in that region, so that when China opened up, there would be an adequate supply of theologically trained persons to provide the needed leadership.

In August 1954, taking advantage of Asian theological educators and western missionaries serving in Asia and attending the second Assembly of the World Council of Churches at Evanston, Illinois, the Board of Founders organised a consultation at Williams Bay, Wisconsin, on the theme 'Regarding Theological Education in Southeast Asia'. The Williams Bay

---

[4] As from 1952, the Board of Founders was not able to relate to Nanking Seminary or engage in China, so they began to use the income to support theological education in South East Asia with a focus on reaching out to diaspora Chinese. Eventually, in 1963, after getting legal opinion, the name was changed to the Foundation for Theological Education in South East Asia.

[5] A Brief History of the Foundation for Theological Education in South East Asia. 75th Anniversary Celebration, Pittsburgh Theological Seminary, September 29, 2012: www.ftesea.org/FTE75th.pdf

[6] *The Anderson-Smith Report on Theological Education in Southeast Asia: Especially as it Relates to the Training of Chinese for the Christian Ministry: the Report of a Survey Commission, 1951-1952* (Board of Founders, Nanking Theological Seminary, 1952).

consultation was followed by a major conference on theological education in Asia jointly organised by the World Council of Churches, International Missionary Council (East Asia), and the Board of Founders, in conjunction with the World Student Christian Federation who were also planning to hold a conference for theological students on the theme, 'Theology in the Service of Evangelism'. The conference was held in Bangkok in 1956 with broad representation of Asian and ecumenical leaders from the West. 'There were sixty-nine delegates and visitors for the Theological Conference and forty-one to the student conference, a total of one hundred and ten.'[7] The conference generated new impulses for theological education in the post-colonial situation in many Asian countries.

The conference was considered an opportunity for the meeting of minds of both East and West on the challenges for ministerial training.[8] It dealt at length with teaching methods and the production of theological textbooks in relation to curriculum. Some leaders at the conference like Dr Liston Pope, Dean of Yale Divinity School, made a plea for radical changes in theological education to serve the Asian realities. Pope 'warned against "slavish mimicry of the West"' in theological education and raised the question: 'You have answers from the West; but are they the answers to Eastern questions?' He suggested that, 'The traditional structure of the faculty may not be best for Asia. Why not have a chair of Christian freedom, of Christian social change, of Christian family life?'[9] One of the suggestions made at the conference was the creation of an Association of theological schools in South East Asia to set standards for theological education throughout the region.

With strong roots in the pattern of theological education received from western missionaries, the new visions generated at the conference were only partially implemented. One of the concrete outcomes of the conference was the formation of the Association of Theological Schools in South East Asia (ATESEA),[10] facilitated by the Board of Founders in 1959 with sixteen theological seminaries; this has grown to a hundred members in sixteen countries in South East Asia.

With the creation of the Theological Education Fund (TEF) by the International Missionary Council in 1957, the Board of Founders and TEF developed a close relationship in the service of theological education in Asia.[11] In 1977, the partnership between FTESEA (the successor to Board of Founders) and the Program on Theological Education (PTE – the

---

[7] *The Anderson-Smith Report*, 2.
[8] *Conference on Theological Education in Southeast Asia, Bangkok, Thailand, Feb. 21-Mar. 8, 1956; Record of Proceedings* (Malaya Publishing House, 1956), 3.
[9] *Conference on Theological Education in Southeast Asia*, 16.
[10] In 1981, the name was changed to The Association for Theological Education in South East Asia: www.atesea.net
[11] Cartwright, *A River of Living Water*, 20.

successor to TEF) of World Council of Churches was reaffirmed with FTESEA providing the support for the PTE/WCC Asia Executive and the programmes.[12]

The relationship with Protestant theological education in China was re-established in 1980. In addition to Nanjing Union Theological Seminary,[13] FTESEA was requested to extend support to another thirteen seminaries in China related to the China Christian Council. The number of seminaries has now increased to 21. A number of training programmes especially for laity is also carried out by the Three-Self Patriotic Movement and the China Christian Council (TSPM/CCC), and by some large congregations. In the 1990s, FTESEA began providing scholarships for graduate candidates from China to study at the WCC Ecumenical Institute at Bossey in Switzerland, and two Chinese candidates are trained there annually.

Since the history of FTESEA and its contribution to leadership training has been researched and is now available as a book published in 2010,[14] I shall briefly narrate a few new involvements of FTESEA since that time. In 2012, FTESEA celebrated its 75th anniversary at the Pittsburgh Theological Seminary and used the occasion for a seminar with partner representatives to hear from them the assessment of the partnership relationship in recent decades and their expectation from FTESEA for the future. The seminar also provided an occasion to consider expanding the ministry of FTESEA to the Mekong region, and especially to Vietnam, Cambodia and Laos. The presence of two graduate theological students from Vietnam then studying in the USA at the seminar and their input contributed to this decision. The seminar was followed by a revisioning session of Board members in 2013 for FTESEA to adapt to the changed situation in partnership relationship with Christian communities in China and South East Asia. The revisioning provided space for self-criticism and a venture into a new partnership termed 'Towards new Patterns of Partnership' (TNPP). Specifically, what emerged was identifying three areas of engagement within the overall mandate of FTESEA for faculty and library development. The Board appointed three working groups on those concerns:

1. Faculty and Theological Development to monitor the impact of FTESEA's support of the Church and society in China and South East Asia;[15]

---

[12] Samuel Pearson (ed), *Supporting Asian Christianity's transition from Mission to Church. A History of the Foundation for Theological Education in South East Asia* (Grand Rapids, MI: Eerdmans, 2010), 266.

[13] www.njuts.cn

[14] Person, *Supporting Asian Christianity's transition from Mission to Church.*

[15] In order to have a firsthand knowledge of faculty and library development, and to provide needed partnership support in consultation with partners, Board members – along with the Senators of ATESEA Theological Union – visited twelve ATU seminaries in July 2014. A similar type of joint team visit of FTESEA and

2. Women in Leadership: to affirm and invest in female leadership with priority given to female theological educators, and also women leaders in general;[16]
3. Exchange – Enrichment of Asian/North American Asian theological educators through exchange visits and teaching opportunities. [17]

The search for developing new avenues of resources led FTESEA to facilitate the formation of a fellowship of Asian North American theological educators (slightly over one hundred), teaching in seminaries and divinity schools in the USA and Canada, willing to engage in the support of graduate-level theological education in South East Asia and China in their personal capacity, and also engaging their respective seminaries in North America. A formal association has emerged out of this, called the Association of Asian/North American Theological Educators (AANATE).[18] This is an attempt to reverse the phenomenon of 'brain drain to brain gain'.[19] Asian American theological educators, like other immigrants, have been serving as unofficial ambassadors in promoting Asian theologies in North America, and assisting their Asian colleagues in accessing graduate-level research facilities in North America. These migrant Asian theologians, like other migrant communities, have also been helping to change the monoculture into multicultural theologies in North America, and as such, they are a good channel for introducing Asian theologies to North American churches and theological communities.

The Mission Context of Asian Christians

The conspicuous realities of Asian communities have been identified as mass poverty (with various programmes to address it), and the multi-religious, multicultural and multi-lingual lives of its peoples.[20] Asian countries are also experiencing rapid urbanisation, industrialisation,

---

theological professors of seminaries in China was planned for November 2015, to include ten China Christian Council-related seminaries.

[16] FTESEA, in consultation with ATESEA, has planned for an all-Asia consultation of women theological educators in Manila in June 2015, to plan for programmes to empower female leadership, especially in theological education.

[17] Peter Notebom. Report on 'Revisioning the Ministry and Mission of FTESEA, October 7-8, 2013, Berkeley, California', 6.

[18] www.aanate.org

[19] H.S. Wilson, 'Brain drain to brain gain. Asian North American theologians as resource for theological education in Asia: a few initiatives of FTESEA', in Atola Longkumer, Po Ho Huang, Uta Andree (eds), *Theological Education and Theology of Life: Transformative Christian Leadership in the 21st Century. A Festschrift for Dietrich Werner* (Oxford: Regnum, 2015).

[20] These continued Asian realities have called for 'Triple dialogue' with the poor, with people belonging to multicultural and multi-religious communities for Asian Christianity to root itself in Asia – Thomas Fox, *Pentecost in Asia. A new way of being church* (Maryknoll, NY: Orbis Books, 2002).

escalating migration and experimentation with a variety of political models to address the Asian ethos and other challenges. These realities have a strong bearing on Christian communities. Consequently, the tensions that exist among larger communities as a result of these realities are also experienced to varying degrees in Christian communities. Christian mission and ministry constantly seek to address these realities as best they can.

In spite of centuries of mission work, Christians are still a minority in most Asian countries. Peter Phan notes that 'one of the bitter ironies of Asian Christianity is that, though born in (South West) Asia, it returned to its birthplace as a foreign religion, or worse, the religion of its colonisers, and is still being widely regarded as such by many Asians'. [21] Felix Wilfred notes that 'Asia, though the cradle of Christianity, has always proved to be an "obstacle" for its expansion because of its established cultural and religious traditions and societal structures'.[22] Therefore, the impact Christians can make depends on their collaboration with the like-minded people of other living faiths and cultures. Ministries and theological education try to incorporate these concerns in multiple ways, e.g. by analysing the social, political and religio-cultural situations that perpetuate these realities, and offering alternatives by their own effort and in partnership with the governmental and non-governmental organisations, engaging with local political parties, and international NGOs and movements. But engaging with the larger community for needed transformation is often not welcomed by large sections of the Christian community as their faith formation has been too narrowly focused on a religiosity to the exclusion of the larger community except when there is threat to their communities and institutions. This is a constant challenge to theological and religious education and formation in Asia. Therefore the study of Christian theologies, mission and ministries, unless they are done from the perspective of multicultural, multi-religious and multi-lingual perspectives, will not be satisfactory. In Asia, Christianity itself is not an issue. The issue is that it is over-burdened with philosophical and cultural baggage that seldom provides a natural link with local religious and cultural worldviews. For decades there has been a plea for the 'decolonisation of theologies' but there is a long way to go to accomplish that vision in Asia.

When catechetical and Bible training institutions were set up in Asia by western missionaries in the nineteenth century, it was primarily to prepare leaders to assist in the type of ministerial and mission work that was initiated by these missionaries themselves. The pattern of ministry and theological education that was introduced in Asia was a copy of western Christianity. Such patterns of ministry and mission have been deeply engraved in the psyche of Asian Christians. In many Asian situations, it

---

[21] Peter Phan (ed), *Christianities in Asia* (Malden, MA: Wiley-Blackwell, 2011), 2.
[22] Felix Wilfred (ed), *The Oxford Handbook of Christianity in Asia* (New York: OUP, 2014), 2.

continues to be the case, with some local adaptation, including a few new courses and theological emphases. Theological education therefore remains highly structured with a traditional fourfold faculty: Bible, theology, church history and ministry. Teaching and assessing methods remain as they were originally introduced, often with more rigidity, unlike the changes that have taken place elsewhere, especially in North America.

However, the explicit nature of curriculum with its academic focus is often complemented by the implicit nature of curriculum,[23] with missional formation in theological education in Asia due to the existential reality of Christians in Asia. No serious theological student can close their eyes to the mission challenges dictated by the Asian context. The overall ethos of theological education in Asia did not, and still does not, have the option and luxury of setting aside the missionary thrust and focusing narrowly on ministry-management of the Christian community. Christianity still functions as a missionary community in spite of the absorption of church structures and polity from its missionary forebears. Especially in the post-western mission era in Asia with its minority status as a religion, and the survival nature of a number of Christian communities, Christianity has to engage with its neighbouring faith and cultural communities one way or another – and in a missionary sense as a witness to the richness that the faith can offer. Even Christian social organisations cannot shy away from faith and witness. Whether Christians like it or not, those of other faiths see Christians as mission-minded persons. Christians cannot get rid of that trademark. As I was writing this article, a section of Indian political leaders opened up the polemics that even Mother Theresa's charitable work is not neutral; it was motivated towards converting people to Christianity. The people who are enrolled in theological seminaries are primarily motivated by their zeal for mission as they understand it, largely from western missionaries and early converts. That zeal and expectation continue even today.

To tell theologically trained Asian Christian clergy or lay people that you are expected to be a missionary in addition to being a skilled theologian is in fact to insult that person. In the Asian context, for any Christian who takes her/his faith seriously, there is only one way to be Christian, to be a witnessing and missionary Christian in line with one's talents and motivation. The bulk of Asian Christians may not engage in missionary methods like open-air and street preaching, trying to distribute gospel tracts at religious festivals and gatherings of people of other faiths. But they will use every occasion to witness to their faith as circumstances allow. In a minority situation they are aware that they still remain Christian

---

[23] Les Bell, *Transforming Theology: Student Experience and Transformative Learning in Undergraduate Theological Education* (Eugene, OR: Wipf & Stock, 2013), 20.

because there is something valuable in their faith that others can benefit from. They are prepared to share it as circumstances demand and allow.

Mission Challenges and Responses

Instead of relying only on possible implicit missional formation in theological seminaries, theological educators are also aware of the challenges for Christian witness in Asia that should be reflected in any structured theological education. Some of these challenges are:

Awareness of the pre-Constantinian ethos of Asian Christianity

Even though Protestant churches emerged as a result of the mission outreach of western Christianity that was nurtured in a Constantinian ethos and shaped by a Christendom mindset, the reality of Christianity in Asia since the end of colonial rule is that of a pre-Constantinian ethos. Asian Christians do not have the same political and cultural status as in the western colonial era. Christian communities in most of Asia are on the margins and despised. In some Asian countries, Christians are persecuted on the pretext of being western agents. Therefore their mission calling has been to constantly challenge this false image of themselves and to defend their continuing existence as a useful faith community.

Christianity is a minority in Asia except in the Philippines and East Timor, and does not have a privileged position. Christians as communities enjoy a certain recognition due to inherited educational and health institutions, and as owners of huge properties in key sections of certain towns and cities. In wider society, they are often respected – not because of their faith but for their personal and professional leadership.

Responding appropriately to the resurgence of Asian religions, such as Buddhism, Hinduism, Islam, Sikhism and Jainism that claim superiority and rootedness in Asia

Christianity cannot deal with them with a western Christian mentality, making a counter-claim for its superiority. In each context it has to find an amicable way of co-existing with openness to constant interfaith dialogue, engagement and relationships focusing on the well-being of all the members of a given community. In Asia, religious affiliation is a public matter. Religious affiliations are closely related to social and often political affiliation. When religious conversions take place, the whole community has to adjust – something which is increasingly perceived as socially and politically disruptive.

Many Asian theologians and others interested in Asian religions have worked on comparing and seeing commonality between the vision and mission of Jesus, and that of Asian religious teachers like Buddha, Krishna, and ethical teachers like Confucius, Tao, or the social reformer Mahatma Gandhi, and highlighting the relevance of the message of Jesus for the liberation of marginal communities, aborigines, Dalits, tribals and *minjung*, in order to build bridges to Asian realities.

The resurgence of Asian religions has the social and political component of asserting themselves as legitimate powers in society. The criticism is that their legitimate power was reined in during the western colonial era as Christianity was given precedence over Asian religions and cultures. For example, the Indian External Minister Sushma Swaraj recently proposed that the *Bhagavad Gita* should be given national scriptural status.[24] This was countered even by some Hindus arguing that the Constitution is the 'Holy Book' of India. But that could easily be denied since the Indian constitution has strong roots in western tradition which in turn is rooted in western Christian values. Some Islamic communities do not shy away from claiming the imposition of Sharia law against secular constitutions. Asian Christians have been promoting the cause of interfaith dialogue, engagement and relationships, and that has to be continued with much vigour. Their cause will be strengthened if Christians worldwide, especially where they are a majority, engage in interfaith relations with migrant communities in their neighbourhoods so that such relations and engagement are seen as a core concern of Christianity.

Greater attentiveness to socio-economic needs of the people

Asians became Christians not necessarily because they understood the doctrinal richness of western Christianity. They embraced Christianity also for the sake of new means of being persons and community rather than being marginalised and oppressed. They could be freed from century old shackles of bondages with the possibilities offered by the new faith Christianity, in spite of several sacrifices they had to make culturally and socially. The social values that Christianity still upholds, like liberation, equality, justice, and peace are still welcome by Asians. Therefore, Asians continue to embrace Christianity because of the possibility of a new humanity it offers in the context of several centuries of old socio-cultural bondages.

Culturally rooting Christian faith

With the critical distancing from western Christianity through indigenisation, enculturation and promotion of contextual theologies, Asians have generated examples of new possibilities of being Christians in Asia. These attempts are still a work in progress. The bulk of Christian

---

[24] www.rediff.com/news/report/sushma-wants-gita-as-national-book-do-you/20141208.htm

communities in Asia continue to be marked by the pietistic mindset and other worldly foci in their exercise of faith. In some senses, they share that view with other faiths in Asia. But too much piety and other-worldliness rob Christianity of its role in public engagement. Today, televangelists, especially from North America and their followers in Asia, offer a type of Christianity which glaringly imitates contemporary pop culture more than the western missionary Christianity of the previous century. Such Christianity is seen as part of a harmful influence from the West. How to prepare Asian Christians not to fall victim to that type of Christianity, and how to avoid it being perceived by people of other faiths as an distorted expression of contemporary Christianity are huge challenges.

Responding appropriately to the Asian segment of global concerns, like appropriate discernment to work creatively within different political systems, such as communist, socialist, or a military dictatorship, and a variety of democratic systems, often controlled by the majority religious or ethnic communities; being hospitable towards migrant communities; engaging in ecology and environment protection; providing proper assessment of the causes of escalating terrorist activities undergirded by religious and ideological claims. In a global situation of human existence, major issues that affect humanity are no longer isolated but interlinked, perpetuating the problems of finding solutions.

From the above, one could easily discern, as Jingyi Ji says about Christianity in China,[25] that Christianity in most countries of Asia exists as a marginal religion with multiple characteristics. The Asian ethos makes it necessary for Christians to live with multiple affiliations and differentiated identities. Christian identity in an exclusive sense may evolve as circumstances demand. There are ample opportunities to relate to others and work towards common causes in Asia, including holistic living for all.

Theological educators have always tried to address concerns in church and society. Among the FTESEA partners, the China Christian Council and ATESEA in South East Asia have been trying to address these challenges. The theological educators of seminaries of the China Christian Council have been working on a new perspective of a 'Theology of Reconstruction'. It is a self-theologising effort. The Protestant church in China with its commitment to three-self principles, and as a post-denominational form of Christianity, is committed to reassess inherited biblical teachings, historical theologies and pastoral ministries, and reformulate them in China's context to help its members to be patriotic citizens of their socialistic society, and to contribute to the vision of the People's Republic of China in building a harmonious society. Thus,

---

[25] Jingyi Ji, *Encounters Between Chinese Culture and Christianity: A Hermeneutical Perspective* (New Brunswick, NJ: Transaction Publisher, 2007), 14.

theological reconstruction is envisioned as a means of reintegrating theology into socialist society.[26]

ATESEA has formulated new 'Guidelines for Doing Theological Education in Asia',[27] adopted in 2007, a successor to the 'Critical Asian Principle' (CAP) formulated in 1972 as a guide for doing theological education. Since ATESEA serves in sixteen South East Asian countries, the guidelines cover a wide range of concerns like multi-religious reality, plurality of cultures, indigenous and others, economic concerns of poverty and marginalisation, gender equality, and migration and ecological concerns.

Conclusion

In the continent of Asia – from Afghanistan to Japan and Mongolia to East Timor – the two dominant and most populous countries, India and China, are competing to exercise power in the region, China with its 'One Belt, One Road' initiative,[28] and India with 'Project Mausam'.[29] China wants to revive the historic silk trade route stretching from the north-west of China through Central Asia and the Middle East to Europe. In addition, it wants to revive the maritime spice route stretching through South China to South East Asia. India wants to revive the trade routes that connected the countries linked to the Indian Ocean, and the trade carried out for centuries following the pattern of the monsoon in the Indian Ocean region. In this nostalgic revival of past accomplishments, Christianity does not feature at all. In both these and in their immediate neighbours, Christianity is a minority faith. As China and India aim to be political and economic powers in the region, such moves will certainly have hegemonic implications and imperial ambitions. For example, 21 Asian countries and five European ones (the UK, Germany, France, Italy and Switzerland) have already expressed their willingness to join the Chinese initiative of starting the Asian Investment Bank (AIIB), to be formally established by the end of 2015. The plea of the United Sates to European leaders not to join AIIB has fallen on deaf ears.

---

[26] Janice and Philip L Wickeri (eds), *A Chinese contribution to Ecumenical Theology. Selected Writings of Bishop K.H. Ting* (Geneva: WCC, 2002); Philip L Wickeri, *Reconstructing Christianity in China: K.H. Ting and the Chinese Church* (Maryknoll, NY: Orbis Books, 2007); H.S. Wilson, 'Theological Reconstruction in China: Ecumenical Accompaniment in the Self-Theologizing Effort in Theological Education', in *International Review of Mission* (Vol. 98, Issue 1, April 2009), 77-93.
[27] www.atesea.net
[28] www.fmprc.gov.cn/mfa_eng/zxxx_662805/t1163558.shtml
[29] The word *mausam* means 'weather' or 'season'. It refers to a distinct wind system of the Indian Ocean region when ships can safely travel: http://thediplomat.com/2014/09/project-mausam-indias-answer-to-chinas-maritime-silk-road

In these developments, in spite of their minority status, Christians in Asia – as members of the world Christian family – have a calling to be prophetic and missional in the public affairs of Asia, along with other faiths and movements striving for life with dignity and integrity for all. Therefore, mission in Asia has to be broad-based to include engaging with individuals, communities, religions, social networks and political parties that resonate with Gospel values for the well-being of humans and the whole of creation. To assist this, theological education has to continually reshape it ministerial and missional formation to equip its candidates for dialogical engagement at all levels of human interaction from Christian perspectives that are locally reformulated. The common challenge to Christians is to discern the kind of multicultural and multi-religious society that they need to nurture for themselves and for generations to come, and do the needed preparation by shedding all inherited prejudices. Christians should do a better job in focusing on factors of interconnectivity that exist between Christians[30] as well as with the larger Asian community.

---

[30] H.S. Wilson, 'Contextual theologies to theologies of connectivity' in Wati Longchar (ed), *Doing Contextual Theologies in Asia. Essay in honour of Huang Po Ho* (Kway, Taiwan: Program for Theology and Cultures in Asia, 2014), 64-82.

SECTION FOUR

CONCLUDING CHAPTER

DIVINE SUPERINTENDENCE

J. Nelson Jennings

The dizzying array of topics in this volume indicates the complexity of instructing and otherwise equipping mission servant-leaders. To attempt to do justice to the breadth and variety inherent to this volume's theme, we editors structured the essays within the three sections of historical and missiological perspectives, crucial issues, and case studies. We are grateful to the contributing authors for extending their experienced expertise to what we trust will be a wide readership of this important volume.

In this concluding chapter, I wish to focus on one thread interwoven throughout any tapestry depicting constructive preparation for Christian mission. This volume's presentations concentrate on contemporary issues and contemporary examples of theological education and formation for mission. Such a contemporary emphasis is appropriate in the light of the dramatic adjustments to mission training required by the epochal mid-twentieth-century directional shift in Christian mission from a modern European base to a worldwide plurality of sending stations of those who have been announcing the glad tidings of the Christian gospel. Even so, the thread I wish to highlight here runs throughout world history, not just history's most recent generations.

That thread is divine superintendence over the training of mission servant-leaders. That divine involvement includes the massive variety of methods used for equipping missionaries, some of which have been presented elsewhere in this strategic volume. As an earlier essay put the matter, 'Instructors and trainers prepare potential missionaries using institutions, resources and methods. Even so, if God is not somehow involved in shaping mission servants, the most polished and carefully refined methods of preparation ultimately will prove inadequate.'[1] To borrow an oft-cited biblical image, 'Unless the Lord builds the house, those who build it labour in vain' (Ps. 127:1).

This concluding chapter will trace chronologically the thread of divine superintendence over the training of mission servant-leaders. The essay will move through successive sections of Creation-Primeval, Old Covenant/Israel's Nationhood, and New Covenant eras. Some closing remarks will summarise what is covered, both in this chapter and in the entire volume.

---

[1] See in this volume J. Nelson Jennings, 'Broader Implications of the *Missio Dei*'.

Creation-Primeval Settings

God has equipped his emissaries since the dawn of world history and throughout the Old Covenant. Genesis 1:14-18 gives the divine origin of the first witnesses or missionaries, namely the sun, moon and stars:

[14] And God said, 'Let there be lights in the expanse of the heavens to separate the day from the night. And let them be for signs and for seasons, and for days and years, [15] and let them be lights in the expanse of the heavens to give light upon the earth.' And it was so. [16] And God made the two great lights – the greater light to rule the day and the lesser light to rule the night – and the stars. [17] And God set them in the expanse of the heavens to give light on the earth, [18] to rule over the day and over the night, and to separate the light from the darkness. And God saw that it was good. [19] And there was evening and there was morning, the fourth day.

Especially, given the heaven-to-earth or 'cross-cultural' nature of the witness, or signs, that the sun, moon and stars were to give, understanding these heavenly bodies as missionaries not only is not far-fetched, but it is appropriate.

The divine initiative or superintendence of these celestial witnesses' or mission servant-leaders' preparation – creation – goes without saying.

Old Covenant/Israel's Nationhood

The creation of Israel for the sake of redeeming all peoples and the whole cosmos begins with Abram, of Ur of the Chaldeans.

The patriarchal period

As the biblical narrative moves into the Abrahamic era, specifically into Genesis 12:1-3, a pivotal passage for God's world mission bursts forth:

[1] Now the Lord said to Abram, 'Go forth from your country and your kindred and your father's house to the land that I will show you. [2] And I will make of you a great nation, and I will bless you and make your name great, so that you will be a blessing. [3] I will bless those who bless you, and him who dishonours you I will curse you, and in you all the families of the earth shall be blessed'.

The phrase 'all the families of the earth' has inspired many mission speakers and practitioners towards cross-cultural mission service.

God prepared Abram – renamed 'Abraham' at the instigation of the covenant of circumcision – for this calling to leave Haran and enter the promised land of Canaan. A sketch of that preparation is given in the preceding verses, Genesis 11:27-32:

- Abram was one of three sons born to Terah.
- One of Abram's brothers, Haran, died in the family homeland of Ur of the Chaldeans. Surely losing a brother was a painful experience for Abram?

- Abram married Sarai, who painfully, frustratingly and shamefully 'was barren; she had no child' (Gen. 11:30).

- Abram, Sarai and their nephew Lot (as part of a large caravan and entourage) were taken from Ur in south-eastern Mesopotamia towards Canaan, but settled in the north-western Mesopotamian city of Haran, the politically stable and flourishing caravan city, where Abram's father Terah died.

God shaped Abram in the crucible comprised of close relatives' deaths, uprooting from the family homeland, the agony of life as a childless (i.e. seen to be cursed, unfruitful and useless) couple, and adjusting to a new and different life-context in Haran.

Through Abraham and Sarah's child of promise Isaac and his scheming younger son Jacob-renamed-Israel, the twelve tribes of Israel were born in Canaan. God specially used Abraham's great-grandson Joseph in transporting the budding twelve tribes to Egypt for the ensuing 400-year period so vital within God's overall mission.

How God prepared Joseph for his mission calling in Egypt is what particularly concerns us here. As a proud dreamer, the teenaged Joseph was sold as a slave, and then rose to bear extensive political responsibility in Egypt. Trumped up charges by Potiphar's wife landed Joseph in jail, where he languished despite again being given responsibility and aiding fellow prisoners to leave jail through interpreting their dreams. Through interpreting Pharaoh's dream Joseph not only left prison but was given responsibility for administering all of Egypt. He was given an Egyptian name (*Zaphenath-paneah*) and wife – who bore him Manasseh and Ephraim – becoming an Egyptian, culturally and linguistically.

Joseph then facilitated Jacob's entire household to be resettled in Goshen, 'in the land of Egypt, in the best of the land, in the land of Rameses' (Genesis 37–47).

God's instruction and preparation of Joseph for his mission of resettling the people of Israel in Egypt included 'hardship' and 'affliction' (41:51-52) as well as cultural and linguistic reconfiguration. In so doing, God deepened and reconfigured Joseph's/*Zaphenath-paneah's* faith such that, unlike earlier instances, he attributed the interpretation and fulfilment of Pharaoh's dreams to God (41:25-32), as well as recognising God's hand in his brothers having sold him away: 'God sent me before you to preserve life... to preserve for you a remnant on earth, and to keep alive for you many survivors. So it was not you who sent me here, but God' (45:5-8).

Israel's kingdom formation

Generations later 'there arose a new king over Egypt, who did not know Joseph... They set taskmasters over [the people of Israel] to afflict them with heavy burdens... In all their work they ruthlessly made them work as slaves'. Moreover, the king of Egypt ordered the Hebrew midwives to kill all male Hebrew newborns; Pharaoh then commanded all Egyptians to throw all newborn Hebrew sons into the River Nile (Ex. 1:8-22). God again used pain and suffering to prepare his people for mission service, in this instance for Israel's exodus from Egypt.

'During those many days the king of Egypt died, and the people of Israel groaned because of their slavery and cried out for help. Their cry for rescue from slavery came up to God. And God heard their groaning, and God remembered his covenant with Abraham, with Isaac, and with Jacob. God saw the people of Israel – and God knew' (2:23-25). God was preparing a mission servant-leader to deliver them.

Born to a Levite couple, a three-month-old baby boy was found by Pharaoh's daughter, who adopted him and named him Moses (2:1-10). The boy 'was instructed in all the wisdom of the Egyptians, and he was mighty in words and deeds' (Acts 7:22). For all practical purposes, the Israelite-Levite-born Moses had become an Egyptian at forty years old, as the daughters of Midian reported to their father (Ex. 2:16-19). Another forty years in yet another cultural setting, in which Moses was given a Midianite wife, Zipporah, who bore him a son Gershom ('sojourner'), further prepared Moses for God's mission calling in the burning bush (2:21-4:14).

Following the conquest of Canaan and the lengthy 400-year period of the Judges, David son of Jesse replaced the handsome, immensely talented, yet heartbreakingly disappointing, first king of Israel, Saul, son of Kish. God's preparation of David to lead Israel into full nationhood is well known, especially David's skilful musical abilities by which he soothed the tormented soul of King Saul (1 Sam. 16:14-23) and later composed psalms for Israel's cultic worship, his faithfulness as a sheep herder in protecting his father's animals against wild animals (1 Sam. 16:34-37), and the young boy's bravery and dexterity in slaying the boastful Philistine warrior champion Goliath (1 Sam. 17:1-58). Surely David's upbringing in the godly household of his father Jesse was central to the young shepherd's preparation for servant-leadership within God's overall mission to make the world right again?

But God specifically sought out David as 'a man after his own heart' (1 Sam. 13:14), hence divine superintendence over David's spiritual growth was ongoing. David had to flee from the explosive, quick-tempered King Saul. The prophet Nathan's rebuke of King David's treacherous adultery with Bathsheba and subsequent cover-up murder of her stellar husband Uriah exposed the depths of David's pride, lust, greed and deceitfulness. Later, the successful coup by David's conniving, vengeful and jealous son Absalom led to King David's humiliating flight from Jerusalem. The deaths of David's first child by Bathsheba, then David's grown sons Admon and then Absalom, each led to varying degrees of grief for David. Finally, God's pestilence inflicted on Israel as judgement for David's prideful census-taking brought further humbling and a sense of justice to David.

God's use of suffering in shaping his mission servants is no more evident than throughout the life of one of the Bible's central figures, David. A few generations after David's reign, the Syrian general Naaman had led successful military campaigns into Israel. One of those raids resulted in a little Israeli girl being taken as booty and working in Naaman's household, under his wife's supervision. Upon learning that the great military general over her household had leprosy, the Israeli slave girl exclaimed to her mistress, 'Would that my lord were with the prophet [Elisha] who is in Samaria! He would cure him of his leprosy'. This witness inspired Naaman to ask the king of Syria for permission to go to Israel in search of a cure for his debilitating illness (2 Kgs 5:1-5).

How did that little girl have the faith to give such a witness? How could she care about such a monster who had effectively yanked her away from her home, family and friends, thus traumatising her through untold sufferings, having to perform menial tasks, and living in a totally new and strange setting?

The Scriptures do not reveal the girl's age, except to say that she was 'little'. Surely God had used her family and community in Samaria to instil in her a simple, real faith in the God of Israel, thus preparing her for this crucial time of witness within God's worldwide mission.

A few generations later, God prepared the Ninevites for the Gospel of his impending judgement, mercy, and compassion. During the early eighth century BCE, Assyria had been weakened through external conflicts while Israel experienced a period of resurgence. It was during this period that 'the word of the Lord came to Jonah the son of Amittai, saying, "Arise, go to Nineveh, that great city, and call out against it, for their evil has come up before me"' (Jon. 1:1-2).[2]

How God had prepared Jonah during his upbringing in the small northern town of Gath-hepher (2 Kgs 14:25) is unclear. What is clear is God's equipping and shaping of the reluctant prophet through a merciful rescue when Jonah initially fled from God's call to preach to the Ninevites (Jon. 1:7-2:10). After God's second call to Jonah and the Ninevites had actually received Jonah's message, God continued to instruct Jonah through object lessons about divine compassion for all of creation (Jon. 3–4).

The exilic period

Divine superintendence over the equipping of Jeremiah – made explicit to the young prophet in a way that surely indicates God's preparation of all mission servant-leaders – was explained to him when God called him to prophetic ministry: 'Now the word of the Lord came to me, saying, "Before I formed you in the womb I knew you, and before you were born I consecrated you; I appointed you a prophet to the nations"' (Jer. 1:4-5).

---

[2] *ESV Study Bible* (Wheaton, IL: Crossway Bibles, 2008), 1683-84.

While such explicit revelation about a pre-conception call might be unusual for mission servant-leaders, other references to divine shaping of human beings within our mothers' wombs (Ps. 139:13) and to the triune God's choosing of the church in Christ 'before the foundation of the world' (Eph. 1:4) indicate that all mission servant-leaders, and indeed all of God's people in Christ, can rest assured of the divine superintendence of our calling from all eternity.

God's equipping of Jeremiah continued across his forty-year prophetic ministry, which ran across three kings of Judah and into the beginning of the Babylonian Captivity (Jer. 1:2-3). How Jeremiah's preparation progressed during his upbringing in the town of Anathoth, just north-east of Jerusalem, can be inferred in part from his father Hilkiah's priestly status (1:1, 29:27, 32:7-9). Jeremiah's proximity to the capital city informed him of realities there that required prophetic addresses. That Jeremiah's prophetic ministry was rejected by his home-town kinsmen was painful (11:21-23) and instructive (12:1-13). Even so, God taught Jeremiah about longsuffering faithfulness, instructing him to buy a field in Anathoth during the Babylonian siege of Jerusalem in anticipation of a future return (32:6-15).

God shaped Jeremiah through suffering and even persecution (20:1-6, 37:11-38:13, 43:1-7). God instructed him never to marry (16:1-4), and only two people – Baruch, his scribe, and Ebed-melech, an Ethiopian eunuch in the king's service – are listed as having responded favourably to Jeremiah's message. Jeremiah most likely died in exile, perhaps in Egypt (43:1-7).[3] God's common use of pain and suffering in shaping his mission servants was clearly evident in the life and ministry of Jeremiah.

Echoes of Joseph's, Moses' and others' multicultural experiences reverberate when considering the divine superintendence of the mission preparation of Daniel and his three friends Hananiah, Mishael and Azariah. Having been taken back to Babylon under King Nebuchadnezzar's orders and conscripted to be trainees for service in the Babylonian court, for three years the four young men were to be taught 'the literature and language of the Chaldeans' and were given Babylonian names: Belteshazzar, Shadrach, Meshach and Abednego (Dan. 1:1-7).

Unlike Joseph, Daniel and his friends had already been well honed for their exile experience, standing out among their peers by resisting defilement by the standard royal diet and instead remaining devoted to proper food and drink (1:8-16). Similarly to Joseph, Daniel 'had understanding in all visions and dreams'. Also, as happened with Joseph in Egypt, God gave Daniel and his three friends favour within the royal household, such that King Nebuchadnezzar 'found them ten times better than all the magicians and enchanters there were in all his kingdom' (1:9-21). Subsequently, in answer to the fours' urgent prayer, God revealed to

---

[3] *ESV Study Bible*, 1364.

Daniel in a night vision both the content and interpretation of a troubling dream that the capricious King Nebuchadnezzar had had, but that none of his normal advisors had been able to discern, resulting in Daniel (and his three friends) being promoted to the most responsible positions in Babylon (2:1-49). Early and consistent training had dovetailed with God's gracious provision of needed gifts to enable Daniel and his friends to witness boldly, resist temptations firmly, and prophesy imaginatively and confidently throughout three successive reigns of Nebuchadnezzar, Belshazzar and Darius (the Mede; 3-9).

The Medes and Persians supplanted Assyria as the reigning empire in Mesopotamia, or the vast region 'from India to Ethiopia' (Est. 1:1). During the reign of the Persian king Ahasuerus (Xerxes I), the Jewish girl Hadassah, better known as Esther, remarkably rose to be queen. The Jewish festival Purim has ever since commemorated how Esther boldly saved Jews throughout the massive empire from a plot to massacre them. As the message conveyed from her uncle Mordecai encouraging her to act put it, 'Who knows whether you have not come to the kingdom for such a time as this?' (4:14).

God prepared the orphaned Hadassah/Esther for her mission service through the tender upbringing and ongoing coaching of her uncle Mordecai. The events leading to her ascension as queen, including how 'the king loved Esther more than all the women... so that he set the royal crown on her head and made her queen instead of Vashti' – surely were all providentially governed (1:10-2:18)?

As represented by the examples cited here, Old Covenant Israel as a people was shaped through suffering; cross-cultural movements, encounters and experience; faithful witness to God's goodness and glory from a position of weakness in the midst of such powerful kingdoms as Egypt, Syria, Assyria, Babylon and Persia; special gifting of seeing and interpreting dreams and visions; and, the consistent upbringing of children. These factors repeatedly proved vital for equipping Old Covenant Israel as a people for their mission among other nations, as well as for Israel's individual mission servant-leaders. God's superintendence over all of these means was foundational for all the equipping and shaping that occurred.

New Covenant Settings

Old Covenant Israel's mission role as a light to the nations culminated in producing the Messiah. Just as divine superintendence equipped the people of Israel and Israel's individual mission servant-leaders, so has God continued to equip his emissaries throughout the period of the New Covenant.

New covenant biblical settings

Just as divinely created heavenly bodies inaugurated God's witness to the world about divine faithfulness, so did heavenly beings, namely an eastern star and numerous angels, first announce the coming of the Messiah and the New Covenant. A special God-placed 'star' of the 'king of the Jews' rose and led 'wise men from the east' – likely Persian astrologers or magicians of some sort – first to Jerusalem, then to Jesus' birthplace in Bethlehem (Matt. 2:1-12); it is worth nothing that a warning in a dream steered the wise men clear of the pathologically murderous King Herod on their return home.

Similarly, divinely created and commissioned angels had been equipped for issuing the announcement of the Messiah's appearance through innumerable previous assignments, including the small sample guarding the Garden following Adam and Eve's expulsion (Gen. 3:24), disputing with the devil about Moses' body (Jude 9), and protecting the prophet Elisha against a mighty Syrian army (2 Kgs 6:8-23). The angel Gabriel thus announced the birth of Jesus' forerunner John to his father Zechariah (Luke 1:11-20), then the birth of Jesus to his mother Mary (1:26-38). Subsequently, 'an angel of the Lord appeared to Joseph in a dream', encouraging him to follow through with his betrothal to Mary and marry her, even though she had already become pregnant (Matt. 1:18-25). Around Bethlehem when Jesus was born, a divinely commissioned 'angel of the Lord' appeared to nearby shepherds, with 'the glory of the Lord shining around them'. After the angel announced Jesus' birth to the shepherds, 'suddenly there was with the angel a multitude of the heavenly host praising God and saying, "Glory to God in the highest, and on earth peace among those with whom he is pleased!"' (Luke 2:8-14).

As God's heavenly messengers had announced, Emmanuel, 'God with us', had come!

Vast studies have been made of how Jesus himself equipped the disciples – including the apostle Paul, the one 'untimely born' (1 Cor. 15:8). After watching and learning from Jesus, then walking with the resurrected Jesus prior to his ascension, the apostles were baptised by the Holy Spirit at Pentecost and were empowered to be Christ's witnesses to the end of the earth in all directions, just as Jesus predicted (Acts 1:8, 2:1ff).

Overlooked by some Christian traditions is Mary Magdalene (and the other women who followed Jesus), who was actually the first to see the risen Lord Jesus and thus became 'the apostle to the apostles' (John 20:1-18; cf. Luke 24:1-12, Mark 16:1-11, Matt. 28:1-10). Jesus had specially prepared Mary for this unique mission role, having rescued her from oppressive demon possession and prostitution, as well as patiently instructing her during his earthly ministry.[4]

How God equipped Philip the evangelist, one of the first seven deacons (Acts 6:5), who at the direction of an angel went and gave witness from Isaiah to the Ethiopian eunuch (8:26-40), and who had a house in Caesarea (21:8), is unclear. Perhaps he had the same intercultural instincts as those Christians from Cyprus and Cyrene who, finding themselves scattered by persecution in Antioch, 'spoke to the Hellenists also, preaching the Lord [*Kurios*] Jesus' (Acts 11:20), thus paving the way for the risen Jesus to shoulder his way into the Greco-Roman religio-philosophical world, beyond the Hebraic confines of Judaism.

Subsequent new covenant settings

Through being prepared for Christian witness as a stoic philosopher to be a mission theologian and apologist, Pantaenus (d. 200 CE) of Sicily headed the Alexandrian catechetical school and taught, among others, Clement. Pantaenus was well equipped as a mission witness to serve-lead Christians in Ethiopia, who claimed to have received St Matthew's gospel in Hebrew from St Bartholomew.[5]

During the late third to fifth centuries CE, the so-called Desert Mothers (*ammas*) and Fathers (*abbas*) moved into demon-filled, barren areas in Syria, Palestine and Egypt. Fleeing the 'Great Persecution' of Emperor Diocletian, which began in 303 CE, motivated some to move to safer desert areas; after Christianity was recognised by Rome, fleeing a Christian lifestyle that was taking on the trappings of Roman imperial society motivated others to seek the fullest expression of loving God by battling the demons and temptations of the desert, after Jesus' own example.

Just as Antony is the best known of the many *abbas* whose teachings are accessible, writings of four *ammas* – Matrona, Sarah, Syncletica and Theodora – have been preserved for study and reflection. Both the Mothers and Fathers who battle evil forces, as well as countering societal pressures that take God's people away from God and from living well as a part of God's creation, are mission servant-leaders to all who will hear their witness.[6]

---

[4] James E. Kiefer, 'Mary Magdalene, First Witness of the Resurrection', in *Biographical Sketches of Memorable Christians of the Past*: http://justus.anglican.org/resources/bio/206.html
[5] 'St Pantaenus', in *Catholic Online*: www.catholic.org/saints/saint.php?saint_id=808
[6] Mary C. Earle, *The Desert Mothers: Spiritual Practices from the Women of the Wilderness* (New York: Morehouse Publishing, 2007); Editors, 'St Anthony and the Desert Fathers: Extreme Faith', in *Christian History Institute*, Issue 64: https://www.christianhistoryinstitute.org/magazine/issue/anthony-and-the-desert-fathers-extreme-faith

Two young brothers who seemingly were unprepared for their mission service in Axum were Frumentius and Aedesius. Sailing with their merchant uncle Meropius, their ship stopped at the port of Adulis – and all aboard were massacred, except the two young boys. They found favour with the royal court, serving the king as steward and cupbearer while no doubt becoming Axumites culturally and linguistically. Frumentius in particular bore great governmental responsibility and built churches for Roman merchants in the country. When they became young men, Aedesius returned to Tyre while Frumentius travelled to Alexandria to seek a bishop for the church in Axum (Ethiopia). Athanasius consecrated Frumentius himself, traditionally in 333 CE.[7] Themes common to earlier young believers in foreign empires – Moses, Joseph, Daniel and Esther – emerged once again.

Patrick is much beloved as Ireland's patron saint. God's preparation of this mission servant-leader included the common theme of suffering through being taken as a slave, in Patrick's case being taken to Ireland at the age of fourteen by a raiding party into Scotland. Patrick learned the language and customs of his Irish hosts, thus being shaped into a well-adapted missionary to Ireland.

God deepened Patrick's Christian faith during his enslavement, until at the age of twenty Patrick obeyed a dream to go to the coast where he was taken by sailors to Britain, to be reunited with his family. A subsequent dream showed him the people of Ireland calling out to him, 'We beg you, holy youth, to come and walk among us once more.' Studies and ordination to the priesthood ensued, then the missionary Patrick returned to Ireland in his mid-forties and served for forty fruitful years.[8]

Pope Gregory the Great (590-604 CE) is best known for dispatching the Gregorian mission, led by Augustine of Canterbury, to evangelise the pagan Anglo-Saxons of England. One biographer asserts that, having admired some blonde-haired English slaves in the Roman Forum, Gregory never forgot them and thus wanted to Christianise them.[9] That example demonstrates how God often equips mission servants through seemingly random, innocuous experiences that later connect with their divine mission calling.

The Syriac-speaking Persian bishop Alopen was the first recorded Christian missionary to reach China. He arrived via the Silk Road in the T'ang Dynasty's capital city of Changan (Xian), in 635 CE. Syrian missionaries no doubt would have arrived earlier, had not the overland route between Persia and China been barred by Turkestan (and likely there were Syrian Christians in China who had arrived among traders before the

---

[7] A.K. Irvine, 'Frumentius, fl. 4th Century, Orthodox, Ethiopia', in *Dictionary of African Christian Biography*: www.dacb.org/stories/ethiopia/frumentius_.html
[8] 'St Patrick', in *Catholic Online*: www.catholic.org/saints/saint.php?saint_id=89
[9] F. Homes Dudden, *Gregory the Great: His Place in History and Thought* (London: Longmans, Green, 1905), 99.

Turks had shut off the trade route). By 630 CE, T'ang forces had providentially reopened the Old Silk Road. Divine superintendence over mission service includes governing wider realities.

Alopen's initial work in China focused on translating Syrian Christian sutras. Working together with Chinese associates, by 638 Alopen et al had produced the first Christian work in Chinese, *Xuting mishisuo jing* (*The Sutra of Jesus the Messiah*).[10] It can be inferred that Alopen had been prepared for this task through linguistic gifts, training, and a personality type able to focus on the daily grind of translation work.

Two of seven brothers, Michael (later Methodius) and the youngest, Constantine (later Cyril), were born in the ninth century in Thessalonica to a Greek naval officer father and perhaps to a Slavic mother. Living in Thessalonica, plus possibly having a Slavic mother, meant that the brothers would have learned Slavic. When their father died, one of the Byzantine Empire's chief ministers, Theoktistos, became their protector. Theoktistos' leadership in establishing a wide-ranging educational programme led to Constantine teaching in the newly established University of Magnaura. Not long afterwards, he was ordained a priest.

Constantine had also learned Arabic and Hebrew, so he was dispatched to the Abbasid Caliph al-Mutawakkil to discuss theology and to improve political relations. Constantine's second mission was to the Khazar Khaganate (north-east of the Black Sea), enabling him to add the Khazar language to his linguistic repertoire. After teaching philosophy in Constantinople while his brother Michael was both active in Byzantine political and administrative affairs as well as a monastery abbot, in 862 CE Constantine and Michael were sent by the Byzantine Emperor to minister among the Slavic subjects of Prince Rastislav of Great Moravia – who wanted more political independence from the Latin West. It was among the Slavic peoples of Moravia that Constantine (Cyril), and later Michael (Methodius), earned their lasting legacy through their translation and ecclesiastical leadership.[11]

---

[10] Jingyi Ji, *Encounters Between Chinese Culture and Christianity: A Hermeneutical Perspective Contact Zone*. Explorations in Intercultural Theology Series, Book 3. LIT Verlag, 2007, 37; 'Nestorian Christianity in the Tang Dynasty' Chapter One: www.orthodox.cn/localchurch/jingjiao/nest1.htm; Samuel Hugh Moffett, 'Alopen – 7th Century' Biographical Dictionary of Chinese Christianity, 2003-2012.

[11] 'Sts Cyril and Methodius', in *Catholic Online*: www.catholic.org/saints/saint.php?saint_id=39]; Ladislas Abraham, 'Sts Cyril and Methodius', in *The Catholic Encyclopedia*, Vol. 4 (New York: Robert Appleton Company, 1908). 21 May 2015: www.newadvent.org/cathen/04592a.htm; 'Saints Cyril and Methodius: Christian Theologians', in *Encyclopædia Britannica*: www.britannica.com/EBchecked/topic/1345803/Saints-Cyril-and-Methodius

Divine superintendence over the brothers' linguistic, intellectual and socio-political upbringings, in tandem with providential oversight of wider political developments, are obvious themes in their preparation.

St Francis of Assisi's life (1181-1226) and conversion from wealth and debauchery to complete devotion to God, the church and a life of poverty are widely known. Francis's life and monastic 'order' have been deeply influential throughout subsequent western Christian history, including worldwide ventures of Franciscan missionaries. Like many other figures discussed here, Francis experienced enslavement (although that one year left him unchanged) as well as dreams and visions.[12]

Less well known is Francis's 1219 cross-cultural missionary venture, during the Fifth Crusade, to the court of Al-Malik al-Kāmil, Muslim sultan in Egypt. Divine preparation of these two exemplary figures is evident in 'Francis's attitudes to war and peace, which were shaped by his own traumatic experience as a soldier, and... al-Kamil's extensive dealings with Christians in Egypt, where the Copts regarded him as the most tolerant of Egypt's sultans'.[13] What resulted was, according to one analysis, 'an example of non-violence as a way of life that reverses and reconciles opposites and disseminated through shared dialogue across religious traditions'.[14]

Just as Marco Polo (1254-1324) chronicled his travels from Italy to Central Asia and China, so did Rabban bar Sauma (1220-1294) record his vast travels, first from Zhongdu (now Beijing), China, to Baghdad. Later, after spending time in Armenian monasteries, he was sent by the catholicos in Baghdad as head of a mission to Abagha, the Mongol Il-khan ('regional khan') of Iran; then he was sent on a diplomatic mission by Abagha's son Arghūn, a religious eclectic and Christian sympathiser, to Constantinople, Genoa, Paris, Bordeaux and Rome in the hope of establishing a Persian-European alliance to drive Muslims from the Holy Land. Later he was appointed chaplain to the Il-khan's court and still later retired to Marāgheh in Azerbaijan to found a church.[15]

---

[12] 'St Francis of Assisi', in *Catholic Online*: www.catholic.org/saints/saint.php?saint_id=50

[13] Paul Moses, *The Saint and the Sultan* 2009: www.saintandthesultan.com/about.html

[14] Cathy Hampton, 'St Francis of Assisi's Meeting with Sultan Malik al-Kamil and Interreligious Dialogue in the 21st Century', in *academia.edu* (submitted 3rd May 2013): www.academia.edu/3450232/St._Francis_of_Assisis_Meeting_With_Sultan_Malik_al-Kamil_and_Interreligious_Dialogue_in_the_21st_Century

[15] 'Rabban bar Sauma', in *Encyclopædia Britannica*: www.britannica.com/EBchecked/topic/52503/Rabban-bar-Sauma

Rabban bar Sauma had been prepared well through his multilingual capacities (Syriac, Turkic, and possibly Chinese)[16] and Christian upbringing in his wealthy Christian family's household in Zhongdu.

Francis Xavier (1506-1552) was born Francisco de Jasso y Azpilicueta in the Basque Xavier Kingdom of Navarre (now part of Spain). Four years after Francis had commenced studies at the Collège Sainte-Barbe in Paris in 1525, a new student fifteen years Francis' senior, Ignatius of Loyola, became one of his room-mates. Eventually, after much resistance, Francis joined Ignatius as one of the first seven Jesuits who took vows of poverty and chastity. Francis later led an extensive mission into Asia, mainly in the Portuguese Empire of the time, and was influential in evangelisation work, most notably in India.

God's preparation of Francis for mission service included his wealthy, politically active, and Basque-speaking, family heritage. Francis lost his father when he was only nine, and throughout Francis's childhood and adolescence Navarre was militarily suppressed by the Spanish Castilian kingdom.[17] It was against this backdrop that Francis became the zealous Jesuit servant-leader in India and other parts of Asia.

Divine preparation of Bartholomäus Ziegenbalg (1682-1719), the pioneer German missionary in South India, included the early loss of his parents and a high-school conversion experience. Ziegenbalg suffered repeated illness and inner conflicts while studying in Berlin and Halle. Even so, the able guidance of pietist leaders Joachim Lange and A.H. Francke enabled Ziegenbalg to persevere through a demanding programme of studies, including Greek and Hebrew, which served him and others well during his missionary days in India.[18]

There was no more pivotal missionary figure whose life spanned the nineteenth century than Samuel Ajayi Crowther. Crowther was born around 1807 in Osogun, in the Egba part of the Yoruba people, in today's western Nigeria. When Ajayi was about thirteen, he was taken as a slave by Fulani and Yoruba Muslim raiders, then sold several times before finally being bought by Portuguese traders for the transatlantic market. Ajayi's ship was intercepted by the British navy's anti-slave trade patrol, and he and the other slaves were liberated in Sierra Leone.[19] Echoes of Joseph reverberate once again.

---

[16] 'Bar Sauma', in *nestorian.org*: www.nestorian.org/bar_sauma.html
[17] 'St Francis Xavier', in *Catholic Online*: www.catholic.org/saints/saint.php?saint_id=423
[18] 'Ziegenbalg, Bartholomäus (1682-1719): Pioneer German Missionary in South India': www.bu.edu/missiology/missionary-biography/w-x-y-z/ziegenbalg-bartholomaus-1682-1719
[19] Andrew F. Walls, 'Crowther, Samuel Adjai (or Ajayi), c. 1807 to 1891, Anglican Church, Nigeria', in *Dictionary of African Christian Biography*: www.dacb.org/stories/nigeria/crowther5_samuel.html

Ayaji became a Christian in Sierra Leone and was given the baptismal name of Samuel Crowther. Coming under an English clergyman's tutelage, Crowther excelled in Hebrew, Greek, Latin and other studies. He became an instructor at Fourah Bay College and eventually participated in, then led, missionary expeditions back to the Niger region. In turn, Crowther established a new mission in Yorubaland, centred in Abeokuta, by now the homeland of Crowther's Egba people. He also co-ordinated the Yoruba Bible translation project. Having been ordained to the Anglican priesthood in 1843, in 1864 Crowther was appointed as 'Bishop of the countries of Western Africa beyond the Queen's dominions', thus becoming the first black African Anglican bishop.

God's equipping of Samuel Ajayi Crowther through his multilingual upbringing and painful experience of enslavement bore lasting Gospel fruit.

A younger contemporary of Crowther was the Scottish missionary to Calabar, Nigeria, Mary Slessor (1848-1915). Mary was the second of seven children. She credited her godly character to her 'sainted mother'. Mary's alcoholic father produced a family life of poverty and infighting. Mary started working at the age of eleven, and soon became the main family breadwinner.[20] Such struggle, pain and determination – carried out in dependence on God – served Mary Slessor well in her tireless missionary service in Nigeria despite illnesses, dangers and deterrents from mission superiors wanting to keep a single woman missionary safe.[21]

Archbishop Nicholas of Japan was born Ivan Dmitrievich Kasatkin in 1836 into a Christian home, in a village in extreme western Russia. His childhood was not easy, losing his mother when he was only five years old (with two young siblings). Ivan's father served diligently in the church, and family poverty and deprivation served to develop in Ivan the kind of determination to keep him first in his school class. Later, Ivan enrolled in Smolensk Theological Seminary, after which he entered St Petersburg Theological Academy. It was there that he offered himself to go to Japan as a single monk. He left in 1860 for the arduous trip across Siberia, during which he spent almost one year with an experienced missionary churchman. Nicholas finally arrived in Japan in 1861 and began his long, difficult, yet fruitful, ministry there.[22]

Archbishop Nicholas' long service in Japan included overseeing the construction of the magnificent Tokyo Cathedral of Christ's Resurrection. He also was involved in translation projects from the time of his arrival,

---

[20] 'Mary Slessor', in *History Makers: The Fuel of Missions Flame*: www.historymakers.info/inspirational-christians/ mary-slessor.html
[21] 'Mary Slessor Centenary: Building a Better Future': maryslessor.org/mary-slessor
[22] Archpriest Serafim Gan, comp., 'Nicholas (Kasatkin), Archbishop of Japan (In Memory of the 100th Anniversary of His Blessed Repose)', trans. by Priest Sergio Silva, 'The Russian Orthodox Church Outside of Russia', 2002: *www.synod.com/ synod/engdocuments/enart_stnicholasofjapan.html*

including a Russian-Japanese dictionary. As far-reaching in its effect as any period was during the 1904-1905 Russo-Japanese war, throughout which Nicholas remained in Japan to carry out his pastoral and missionary duties.

> The Glebo prophet William Wadé Harris, who had left Cape Palmas, Liberia, on July 27, 1913... headed east across the Cavally River, which separated Liberia and the Ivory Coast, in obedience – as he maintained – to Christ's commission in Matthew 28:19. Accompanied by two women disciples – excellent singers playing calabash rattles – he visited village after village, calling the coastal people to abandon and destroy their 'fetishes', to turn to the one true and living God, to be baptized and forgiven by the Savior; he then taught them to follow the commandments of God, to live in peace, and organized them for prayer and worship of God in their own languages, music, and dance, to await the 'white man with the Book' and the new times that were to come.[23]

How had God prepared this prophet, through whom over 100,000 baptisms took place?

Wadé grew up in a traditional Glebo village on the Liberian coast with a religiously mixed world headed by a 'heathen father' and 'Methodist mother'. As an adolescent, he came under the tutelage of his maternal uncle, the Rev. John C. Lowrie, who baptised Wadé and taught him to become literate in both Glebo and English. Harris was converted at age 21, immediately began preaching, and later married the daughter of an Episcopalian catechist. He built their 'civilised' house himself. Harris also became a regularly paid agent of the Episcopalian structures from 1893 to 1908, and in 1899 he became official government interpreter and go-between for local Liberian officials and the indigenous Glebo populations. Harris resented the Liberian government and campaigned for change to a British protectorate, even using occult practices to manipulate local Glebo chiefs in favour of the British and against the Liberian republic. His political actions put him in jail.

Then in June 1910,

> A trance-visitation of the angel Gabriel in a wave of light was to William Wadé Harris like a second conversion. During three appearances, he was told that he was to be prophet of the last times; he was to abandon his civilized clothing, including his patent leather shoes, and don a white robe: he was to destroy fetishes, beginning with his own; he was to preach Christian baptism. His wife would die after giving him six shillings to provide for his travel anywhere; though he was not thereafter to have a church marriage, he believed God would give him others to help him in his mission. He then received in a great wave of light an anointing from God where the Spirit

---

[23] David A. Shank, 'Wadé Harris, William, c. 1860 to 1929, Harrist Church (Église Harriste), Liberia/Ghana/Côte d'Ivoire', in *Dictionary of African Christian Biography*: www.dacb.org/stories/liberia/legacy_harris.html

came down like water on his head – three times. 'It was like ice on my head and all my skin,' he later reported.[24]

The angel Gabriel's missionary record now included calling William Wadé Harris – providentially raised in a traditional Glebo village and hence loyal to Glebo integrity but also tutored in English-language Methodism-Episcopalianism – into evangelistic ministry along the West African coastline.

This panoply of divinely superintended preparations of New Covenant mission servant-leaders represents how the totality of God's people in Christ have been assembled and prepared for our collective missional witness to unseen powers. As recorded in Ephesians 3:9-10, the preaching of the Gospel to all peoples is 'to bring to light for everyone what is the plan of the mystery hidden for ages in God who created all things, so that through the church the manifold wisdom of God might now be made known to the rulers and authorities in the heavenly places'. That *manifold* wisdom of God is displayed through the many different peoples brought together in Christ in the church. God has prepared us in our various settings not only to participate as mission servant-leaders, but to display together in the unseen realms the magnificent tapestry of divine grace in Christ. Even as we worship together with the heavenly hosts and other creatures as representatives of the tribes of the peoples of the earth (Rev. 4–5, 7:9ff), we bear witness as God's multi-textured tapestry 'to the rulers and authorities in the heavenly places' of the Good News of the triune God.

'Behold, I am making all things new' (Revelation 21:5)

Throughout all of history, God has called, prepared and sent witnesses throughout the cosmos to testify of his goodness, justness, mercy and grace. God made the sun, moon and stars to give light as testimony of divine light and goodness. God has created, redeemed and prepared sinful human beings to give witness – in some cases in the literal sense of dying as martyrs – to divine justice, mercy and grace. Collectively, God called together Old Covenant Israel and the New Covenant church to give witness to the surrounding peoples and heavenly beings. God's specially created and commissioned mighty angels have announced divine acts of judgement and redemption, pre-eminently in the coming of the Jewish Messiah and the world's Saviour and King. In the future, 'The Lord himself will descend from heaven with a cry of command, with the voice of an archangel, and with the sound of the trumpet of God' (1Thess. 4:16).

In the meantime, Christ's Spirit-empowered human witnesses continue to be called, prepared and sent throughout the earth (Acts 1:8). Specifically how we as witnesses are prepared and prepare others will vary according to

---

[24] David A. Shank, 'Wadé Harris, William, c. 1860 to 1929, Harrist Church (Église Harriste), Liberia/Ghana/Côte d'Ivoire'.

era and setting. This volume largely focuses on methods of preparation that fit with contemporary, modern and post-modern methodologies, programmes, institutions and planning. This concluding chapter has surveyed the wider historical tapestry of God's typical use of suffering, dreams, varied childhood upbringings (wealthy or poor, politically powerful or not, multicultural or not), and wider socio-political realities in shaping his servants. May God give wisdom to equippers of mission servant-leaders to recognise the divine superintendence involved in the bringing of individuals for further training, instruction and empowering for their mission callings.

SELECT BIBLIOGRAPHY

Aleshire, Daniel O., *Earthen Vessels: Hopeful Reflections on the Work and Future of Theological Schools*. Grand Rapids,, MI: Eerdmans, 2008.

Arbuckle, Gerald, *From Chaos to Mission: Refounding Religious Life Formation*. London: Geoffrey Chapman, 1996.

Arbuckle, Gerald, *Catholic Identity or Identities? Refounding Ministries in Chaotic Times*. Collegeville, MN: The Liturgical Press, 2013.

Baker, Jonny, 'Doing Mission for the Church's Theology', in Sexton, Jason and Noble (eds), *Doing Theology for the Church's Mission*. Oxford: Tyndale, 2015.

Baker, J. and C. Ross, *The Pioneer Gift*. Canterbury, UK: Canterbury Press, 2014.

Balia, Daryl and Kirsteen Kim (eds), *Edinburgh 2010: Witnessing to Christ Today*. Oxford: Regnum, 2010.

Banks, Robert, *Re-envisioning Theological Education: Exploring a Missional Alternative to Current Models*. Grand Rapids, MI: Eerdmans, 1999.

Bass, Dorothy C. and Craig Dykstra (eds), *For Life Abundant: Practical Theology, Theological Education and Christian Ministry*. Grand Rapids, MI: Eerdmans, 2008.

Battle, Agustin and Rosario, *Theological Education by Extension – A guide for workers in Developing Countries*. Nairobi: Uzima Press, 1983.

Bediako, Kwame, *Christianity in Africa: The Renewal of a Non-Western Religion*. Edinburgh: Edinburgh University Press and Maryknoll NY: Orbis, 1995.

Bellavin, Tikhon, *Exhortation to a new Priest by His Grace Tikhon, Bishop of Aleutian Islands and North America (future saint and Patriarch of Russia) as given at Holy Trinity Cathedral on April 9, 1900 to Fr Vladimir Alexandrov's ordination to be the first priest in Wilkinson, Washington* (translated by Victor Sokolov), in *Life* 1, No. 8 (April 1994).

_____, 'My People and My Beloved', in *The American Orthodox Herald*, No. 2 (1899), 50-51.

Bevans, Stephen, 'Revisiting Mission at Vatican II: Theology and Practice for Today's Missionary Church', in *Theological Studies*, 74, 2 (June 2013), 274-77.

_____, 'Wisdom from the Margins: Systematic Theology and the Missiological Imagination', in *Australian e-Journal of Theology* 5 (August 2005).

Biehl, Michael, 'Response to the "Global Survey on Theological Education"'. Paper presented during the first session of the Ecumenical Conversation No. 6: *Ecumenical Theological Education at the 10th Assembly of WCC in Busan*, October 2013.

Bosch, David J., *Transforming Mission: Paradigm Shifts in Theology of Mission*. Maryknoll, NY: Orbis Books, 1991.

Bowers, Paul, 'Theological Education in Africa: Why Does It Matter?' Unpublished paper presented at AIM-SIM Theological Education Consultation, Honeydew, South Africa, 19th-23rd March 2007.

Bray, J.N., J. Lee, L.L. Smith and L. Yorks, *Collaborative Inquiry in Practice: Action, Reflection, and Making Meaning*. Thousand Oaks, CA: Sage Publications, 2000.

Breck, John, John Meyendorff and Elena Silk (eds), *The Legacy of Saint Vladimir*. Crestwood, NY: St Vladimir's Seminary Press, 1990.

Brewster, Tom and Elizabeth S., *Language Acquisition Made Practical (LAMP): Field methods for language learners.* Colorado Springs, CO: Lingua House, 1976.

Bria, Ion, *The Liturgy After the Liturgy: Mission and Witness from an Orthodox Perspective.* Geneva: WCC Publications, 1996.

_____, 'The Church's Role in Evangelism: Icon or Platform?' in *International Review of Mission,* 64, No. 255 (July 1975), 243-50.

Brown, Stephen, 'The Global Digital Library on Theology and Ecumenism', in Odile Dupont (ed). *Libraries Serving Dialogue.* IFLA Publications Series 163: Berlin/Munich: De Gruyter Saur, 2014, 112-25.

Brueggemann, Walter. *The Prophetic Imagination.* Augsburg: Fortress Press, 1978.

_____, *The Creative Word.* Minneapolis, MN: Augsburg Fortress Press, 1982.

Brynjolfson, Robert and Jonathan Lewis (eds). *Integral Ministry Training: Design & Evaluation.* Pasadena, CA: William Carey Library, 2006.

Cai Xin, 'Religious Organizations Can Establish Foundations, Social Welfare Organizations, and Nonprofit Hospitals in Accordance with the Law': www.chinadevelopmentbrief.cn/?p=637 (accessed 26th April 2014).

Cameron, Julia, *John Stott's Right Hand.* Carlisle: Piquant, 2014.

Campbell-Reed, Eileen R. and Christian Scharen, '"Holy Cow! This Stuff is Real!" From Imagining Ministry to Pastoral Imagination', in *Teaching Theology and Religion,* 14:4 (2011), 323-42.

Chan, Leslie, Eve Gray and Rebecca Kahn, *Open Access and Development: Journals and beyond.* Brighton, UK: Institute of Development Studies, 2012.

Chao, Jonathan, *Purified by Fire: The Secrets of House Church Revivals in Mainland China.* Taipei: CMI, 1993.

Chapman, A., *Godly Ambition: John Stott and the Evangelical Movement.* Oxford: OUP, 2011.

Chinese Church Study Center, 'Seminaries of the Fields, Report I', in *China and the Church,* 6 (1986).

Chopp, Rebecca S., *Saving Work: Feminist Practices of Theological Education.* Louisville, KY: Westminster John Knox Press, 1995.

Conn, Harvie M., *Eternal Word & Changing Worlds: Theology, Anthropology, and Mission in Trialogue.* Grand Rapids, MI: Academic, 1984.

Cornille, Catherine (ed), *The Wiley-Blackwell Companion to Inter-Religious Dialogue.* Hoboken, NJ: Wiley-Blackwell, 2013.

Costas, Orlando E., 'Theological Education and Mission', in C. René Padilla (ed), *New Alternatives in Theological Education.* Oxford: Regnum, 1988.

Cronshaw, Darren, 'Re-envisioning Theological Education, Mission and the Local Church', in *Mission Studies,* 2011, No. 28. Leiden, Netherlands: Koninklijke Brill NV.

Cunningham, Loren, *Is that Really You, God?* (2nd edition). Seattle, WA: YWAM Publishing, 2001.

D'Orsa, Jim and Therese, *Explorers, Guides and Meaning-makers: Mission Theology for Catholic Educators.* Mulgrave, VIC: Garratt Publishing, 2010.

_____, 'Securing Mission at the Heart of the Australian Church' in N. Ormerod, O. Rush, D. Pascoe, C. Johnson and J. Hodge (eds), *Vatican II: Reception and Implementation in the Australian Church.* Mulgrave, VIC: Garratt Publishing, 2012.

_____, *Catholic Curriculum: A Mission to the Heart of Young People.* Mulgrave, VIC: Garratt Publishing, 2012.

_____, *Leading for Mission: Integrating Life, Culture and Faith in Catholic Education*. Mulgrave, VIC: Garratt Publishing, 2013.

_____, (eds), *New Ways of Living the Gospel: Spiritual Traditions in Catholic Education*. Mulgrave, VIC: Garratt Publishing, 2015.

Duan Dezhi, 'Guanyu zongjiao yanpianlun de nanbei zhanzheng jiqi xueshu gongxian' ('On "the War of the Southern and the Northern" of "The Theory of Religion Being Opium" and Its Academic Contributions'): http://iwr.cass.cn/zjyzx/201107/t20110729_7501.htm (accessed December 30, 2014).

Dudley-Smith, T., *John Stott: The Making of a Leader*. Leicester, UK/Downers Grove, IL: IVP, 1999.

_____, *John Stott: A Global Ministry*. Downers Grove, IL: IVP, 2001

Duqu, José, 'The Forest of Theological Education', in *Ecumenical Congress: Mission and Evangelism in Latin America*, IX Assembly of the World Council of Churches: https://www.oikoumene.org/en/folder/documents-pdf/WOCATI_2008_-_The_Forest_of_Theological_Education_-_Dr._Jose_Duque.pdf.

Dysjeland, M., 'Theological education for a missiological church: A perspective from a Theological Training Institutions in Brazil', in M. Lorke and D. Werner (eds), *Ecumenical Visions for the 21st Century. A reader for Theological Education*. Geneva: WCC Publications, 2013.

Earle, Mary C., *The Desert Mothers: Spiritual Practices from the Women of the Wilderness*. New York: Morehouse Publishing, 2007; 'St Anthony & the Desert Fathers: Extreme Faith', in *Christian History Institute*, Issue 64: https://www.christianhistoryinstitute.org/magazine/issue/anthony-and-the-desert-fathers-extreme-faith

Engelsviken, Tormod, Ernst Harbakk, Rolv Olsen and Thor Strandenæs (eds), *Mission to the World. Communicating the Gospel in the 21st Century*. Oxford: Regnum, 2007.

Esterline, David, Namsoon Kang and Joshva Raja (eds), *Handbook of Theological Education in World Christianity: Theological Perspectives, Regional Surveys, Ecumenical Trends*. Eugene, OR: Wipf & Stock, 2010.

Evangelische Kirche in Deutschland (EKD), *Gemeinsam Evangelisch! Erfahrungen, theologische Orientierungen und Perspektiven für die Arbeit mit Gemeinden anderer Sprache und Herkunft* (EKD Texte 119). Hannover: EKD, 2014.

Evangelisches Missionswerk in Deutschland (EMW), *Zusammen Wachsen. Weltweite Ökumene in Deutschland gestalten*. Hamburg, EMW, 2011.

Farley, Edward, *Theologia: The Fragmentation and Unity of Theological Education*. Philadelphia, PA: Fortress Press, 1983.

Ferris, Robert W. (ed), *Establishing Ministry Training Manual for Program Developers*. Pasadena, CA: William Carey Library, 1995.

Fiorenza, Elizabeth Schüssler, *Rhetoric and Ethic: The Politics of Biblical Studies*. Minneapolis, MN: Fortress Press, 1999.

Florovsky, Georges, *Bible, Church, Tradition: An Eastern Orthodox View*. Belmont, MA: Nordland Publishing, 1972.

Foley, Edward, *Theological Reflection across Religious Traditions: The Turn to Reflective Believing*. Lanham, MD / Plymouth, UK: Rowan & Littlefield, 2015.

Freire, Paulo, *Pedagogy of the Oppressed. 30th Anniversary Edition*. New York: Continuum, 2009.

Fung Yu-Lan, *A Short History of Chinese Philosophy* (1948), bilingual edition. Nanjing: Jiangsu wenyi chubanshe, 2012.

Fyfe, C. and A.F. Walls (eds), *Christianity in Africa in the 1990s*. Edinburgh: Centre of African Studies, 1996.

Gairdner, W.H.T., *Edinburgh 1910: An Account and Interpretation of the World Missionary Conference*. Edinburgh and London: Oliphant, Anderson & Ferrier; New York, Chicago and Toronto: Fleming H. Revell, 1910.

Gan, Archpriest Serafim, comp., 'Nicholas (Kasatkin), Archbishop of Japan (In Memory of the 100th Anniversary of His Blessed Repose)', trans. Priest Sergio Silva, in *The Russian Orthodox Church Outside of Russia*, 2002: www.synod.com/synod/engdocuments/enart_stnicholasofjapan.html

Gelder, Craig Van, *The Essence of the Church*. Grand Rapids, MI: Baker Books, 2000.

Gibaut, John and Knud Jørgensen (eds), *Called to Unity – For the Sake of Mission*. Oxford: Regnum, 2014.

Gibbs, Eddie, *Church Next. Quantum Changes in Christian Ministry*. Leicester: IVP, 2001.

_____, *Leadership Next. Changing Leaders in a Changing Culture*. Downers Grove, IL: IVP, 2005.

Glissmann, Volker, 'What is Theological Education by Extension?' in *The Theological Educator* (2014): http://thetheologicaleducator.net/2014/11/28/what-is-theological-education-by-extension

_____, 'The role of community in Theological Education by Extension (TEE)', in *The Theological Educator* (2015): http://thetheologicaleducator.net/2015/04/10/the-role-of-community-in-theological-education-by-extension-tee

Global Survey on Theological Education: Summary of Main Findings for WCC 10th Assembly, Busan, 30th Oct-8th Nov 2013. A joint research project by The Institute for Cross-Cultural Theological Education, McCormick Theological Seminary, Chicago; Ecumenical Theological Education Program (ETE), World Council of Churches, Geneva; and The Center for the Study of Global Christianity (GSGC), Gordon-Conwell Theological Seminary, Boston: http://www.oikoumene.org/en/resources/documents/wcc-programmes/education-and-ecumenical-formation/ete/global-survey-on-theological-education

Goodall, Norman (ed), *Missions Under the Cross: Addresses Delivered at the Enlarged Meeting of the Committee of the International Missionary Council at Willingen, Germany, 1952*; with Statements Issued by the Meeting. London: Edinburgh House Press, 1953.

Gornik, Mark R., 'The Legacy of Harvie M. Conn', in *International Bulletin of Missionary Research*, 35:4 (2011), 212-17.

Graham, Elaine, Heather Walton and Frances Ward, *Theological Reflection: Methods*. London: SCM Press, 2007.

Guder, Darrell L. (ed), *Missional Church: A Vision for the Sending of the Church in North America*. Grand Rapids, MI: Eerdmans, 1998.

Guder, Darrell L., *The Continuing Conversion of the Church*. Grand Rapids, MI: Eerdmans, 2000.

Gwayaweng, Kiki and Ed Parker, 'Is there a Better Way to Teach Theology to Non-Western Persons? Research from Papua New Guinea that Could Benefit the Wider Pacific', in *Australian eJournal of Theology* 21.2 (August 2014).

Haanes, Vidar L., 'The first Professor of Missiology in Norway: Professor O.G. Myklebust (1905-2001)', in *Norwegian Journal of Missiology*, 59:4 (2005).

Hampton, Cathy, 'St Francis of Assisi's Meeting with Sultan Malik al-Kamil and Interreligious Dialogue in the 21st Century', in *academia.edu*, submitted May 3, 2013:
www.academia.edu/3450232/St._Francis_of_Assisis_Meeting_With_Sultan_Ma lik_al-Kamil_and_Interreligious_Dialogue_in_the_21st_Century

Hanciles, Jehu J., *Beyond Christendom: Globalization, African Migration and the Transformation of the West*. Maryknoll, NY: Orbis Books, 2008.

Harley, David, *Preparing to Serve: Training for Cross-cultural Mission*. Pasadena, CA: William Carey Library, 1995.

_____, *Equipping for ministry and mission* (Edinburgh: 2010):
www.oikoumene.org

Harrison, Patricia J., 'Forty Years On: The Evolution of Theological Education by Extension', in *Evangelical Review of Theology*, 28.4 (2004), 315-28.

Haven, Max and Alex Khasnabish, *Radical Imagination*. Halifax and Winnipeg: Fernwood Publishing, 2014.

Hay, Rob et al, *Worth Keeping: Global Perspectives on Best Practice in Missionary Retention*. Globalization of Mission Series. Pasadena, CA: William Carey Library, 2007.

Hayward, Victor E.W., 'The End of a Missionary Era in China: Reflections on Lessons to Be Learned', in *Yale Divinity School Library Special Collections*, I. M. C. Committees: Willingen, July 5-21, 1952', 264.009, Fiche 10.

Heimans, Jeremy and Henry Timms, 'Old and New Power', in *Harvard Business Review*, 5th December 2014.

Hess, Mary and Stephen Brookfield (eds), *Teaching Reflectively in Theological Contexts: Promises and Contradictions*. Malabar, FL: Krieger, 2008.

Hiebert, Paul G. 'Critical Contextualization', in *International Bulletin of Missionary Research*, 11/3 (July 1987), 104–12.

Hope, Antone, Wati Longchar, Hyunju Bae, Huang Po Ho and Dietrich Werner (eds), *Asian Handbook for Theological Education and Ecumenism*. Regnum Studies in Global Christianity. Oxford: Regnum, 2013.

Hopko, Thomas, *Speaking the Truth in Love: Education, Mission, Witness in Contemporary Orthodoxy*. Crestwood, NY: St Vladimir's Seminary Press, 2004.

Huang Haibo. 'Zouxiang jiangou zhong de gongmin shehui: 2010 nian zhongguojidujiaode zeren yu fansi' ('Towards a Civil Society in Construction: The Responsibility of and Reflection on Christianity in China in 2010'), in Jin Ze and Qiu Yonghui (eds), *Zhongguo zongjiao baogao 2011* (Annual Report on Religions in China), 128-72. Beijing: Social Sciences Academic Press, 2011.

Illeris, Knud (ed), *Contemporary Theories of Learning*. London and New York: Routledge, 2009.

Illeris, Knud, *Transformative Learning and Identity*. Abingdon, UK: Routledge, 2014.

Jennings, J. Nelson, *God the Real Superpower: Rethinking Our Role in Missions*. Phillipsburg, NJ: P&R Publishing, 2007.

Ji, Jingyi, 'Encounters Between Chinese Culture and Christianity: A Hermeneutical Perspective ContactZone', in *Explorations in Intercultural Theology Series*, Book 3. LIT Verlag, 2007, 37.

Johnstone, Patrick, *The Future of the Global Church: History, Trends and Possibilities*. Colorado Springs, CO: IVP, 2011.

Johnstone, Patrick, Robyn J. Johnstone and Jason Mandryk, *Operation World, 21st Century Edition*. Carlisle, UK: Paternoster Lifestyle, 2001.

Joseph, M.P., 'Missionary Education: An Ambiguous Legacy', in David A. Kerr and Kenneth R. Ross (eds), *Edinburgh 2010: Mission Then and Now*. Oxford: Regnum, 2009, 105-18.

Jørgensen, Knud, 'Mission in the Postmodern Society', in K.O. Sannes, E. Grandhagen, T. Hegertun, K. Jørgensen, K. Norseth and R. Olsen (eds), *Med Kristus til Jordens ender: festskrift til Tormod Engelsviken*. Trondheim: Tapir akademisk forlag, 2008.

_____, *Equipping for Service. Christian Leadership in Church and Society*. Oxford: Regnum Books International, 2012.

Kalu, Ogbu U., 'Multicultural Theological Education in a Non-Western Context, 1975-2000', in David V. Esterline and Ogbu U. Kalu (eds), *Shaping Beloved Community: Multicultural Theological Education*. Louisville, KY and London, UK: Westminster John Knox Press, 2006.

_____, 'To Hang a Ladder in the Air: An African Assessment', in David A. Kerr and Kenneth R. Ross (eds), *Edinburgh 2010: Mission Then and Now*. Oxford: Regnum, 2009, 91-104.

Kee-Fook Chia, Edmund, *Edward Schillebeeckx and Interreligious Dialogue: Perspectives from Asian Theology*. Eugene, OR: Pickwick Publications, 2012.

Kerr, David A. and Kenneth R. Ross (eds), *Edinburgh 2010: Mission Then and Now*. Oxford: Regnum, 2009.

Keum, Jooseop (ed), *Together Towards Life: Mission and Evangelism in Changing Landscapes*. Geneva: WCC Publications, 2013.

Kiefer, James E., 'Mary Magdalene, First Witness of the Resurrection', in *Biographical Sketches of Memorable Christians of the Past*: http://justus.anglican.org/resources/bio/206.html

Kim, Kirsteen, 'Mission Studies in Britain and Ireland: Introduction to a World-Wide Web', in *British Journal of Theological Education* Vol. 11.1, 2000.

Kim, Kirsteen and Andrew Anderson (eds), *Edinburgh 2010. Mission Today and Tomorrow*. Oxford: Regnum, 2011.

Kinsler, Ross F., *The Extension Movement in Theological Education* (revised edition). Pasadena, CA: William Carey Library, 1981.

_____, (ed), *Ministry by the People, Theological Education by Extension*. Pasadena, CA: William Carey Library, 1983.

_____, *Diversified Theological Education: Equipping All God's People*. Pasadena, CA: William Carey International University Press Press, 2008.

Kirk, J. Andrew, *The Mission of Theology and Theology as Mission*. Valley Forge, PA: Trinity Press International, 1997.

Kool, Anne-Marie, 'Changing Images in the Formation for Mission: Commission Five in Light of Current Challenges – A World Perspective', in David A. Kerr and Kenneth R. Ross (eds). *Edinburgh 2010: Mission Then and Now*. Oxford: Regnum, 2009, 158-77.

Kraft, C.H., *Christianity in Culture: A Study in Biblical Theologizing in Cross-Cultural Perspective* (revised 25th anniversary ed). Maryknoll, NY: Orbis, 2005.

The Lausanne Movement, *The Cape Town Commitment*. Peabody, MA: Hendrickson Publishers Market, 2011.

Lienemann-Perrin, Christine, Atola Longkumer and Afrie Joye Songco (eds), *Putting Names with Faces: Women's Impact in Mission History*. Nashville, TN: Abingdon Press, 2012.

Livermore, David A., *Cultural Intelligence: Improving your CQ to Engage our Multicultural World*. Edited by Chap Clark. Grand Rapids, MI: Baker Academic, 2009.

Lonergan, Bernard, *Method in Theology*. London: Darton, Longman & Todd, 1972.

Lovejoy, G. and D. Claydon. 'Making Disciples of Oral Learners: Lausanne Occasional Paper 54', in *2004* Lausanne *Forum Occasional Papers*, 2005.

Ma, Wonsuk and Kenneth R. Ross (eds), *Mission Spirituality and Authentic Discipleship*. Oxford: Regnum, 2013.

Mabuluki, Kangwa, 'Diversified Theological Education: Genesis, Development and Ecumenical Potential of Theological Education by Extension', in Werner, Dietrich, David Esterline, Namsoon Kang, and Joshva Raja (eds), *Handbook of Theological Education in World Christianity: Theological Perspectives, Regional Survey, Ecumenical Trends*. Oxford: Regnum, 2010.

Madinger, Charles, 'A Literate Guide to the Oral Galaxy', in *Orality Journal* 2, No. 2 (2013), 13-40.

Maina Singh Chawla, *Gender, Religions and 'Heathen Lands': American Missionary Women in South Asia (1860s-1940s)*. New York: Garland Publishing, 2000.

Mbiti, John, *African Religions and Philosophy*. London: Heinemann, 1969.

Meyendorff, John, 'The Orthodox Concept of Church', in *St Vladimir's Seminary Quarterly*, 6 (1962), 59-72.

_____, *Witness to the World*. Crestwood, NY: St Vladimir's Seminary Press, 1987.

Mezirow J. and E. Taylor (eds), *Transformative learning in practice*. San Francisco, CA: Jossey-Bass 2009.

Moon, W. Jay, *African Proverbs Reveal Christianity in Culture: A Narrative Portrayal of Builsa Proverbs Contextualizing Christianity in Culture*. Vol. 5. American Society of Missiology Monograph Series. Eugene, OR: Pickwick Publications, 2009.

_____, 'I Love to Learn But I Don't Like to Read: The Rise of Secondary Oral Learning', in *Orality Journal*, 2, No. 2 (2013), 55-65.

_____, 'Understanding Oral Learners', in *Teaching Theology and Religion*, 15, No. 1 (January 2012), 29-39.

Mouw, Richard J., 'The Cosmic Mission of Christ', in Wang Peng (ed), *Seeking Truth in Love*. Beijing: China Religious Culture, 2005, 299-316.

Noort, Gerrit, 'Emerging Migrant Churches in the Netherlands: Missiological Challenges and mission frontiers', in *International Review of Mission (2011)*, World Council of Churches, 100.1.

Nouwen, Henri, *In the Name of Jesus. Reflections on Christian Leadership*. New York: The Crossroad Publishing Company, 1989.

O'Connell Killen, Patricia and John De Beer, *The Art of Theological Reflection*. New York: Crossroad Publishing Company, 1994.

Ong, W.J., *Orality and Literacy*. London: Routledge, 1982.

Osmer, Richard, *Practical Theology: An Introduction*. Grand Rapids: Eerdmans, 2008.

Ott, Bernhard, *Beyond Fragmentation: Integrating Mission and Theological Education. A Critical Assessment of some Recent Developments in Evangelical Theological Education*. Oxford: Regnum, 2002.

Pannikar, Raimon, *The Intrareligious Dialogue*. New York: Paulist Press, 1999.

Parker Palmer, J., *To Know As We Are Known*. San Francisco, CA: Harper & Row, 1983.

Pearson, Samuel (ed), *Supporting Asian Christianity's transition from Mission to Church. A History of the Foundation for Theological Education in South East Asia*. Grand Rapids, MI: Eerdmans, 2010.

Pei Lianshan, 'qiantan jiaerwenzhuyi yu zhongguo jiaohui' (On Calvinism and Chinese Churches), in *Tianfeng* 5 (2014), 32-3.

Perris, Robert W., *Renewal in Theological Education: Strategies for Change*. Wheaton, IL: Billy Graham Center, 1990.

Phan, Peter (ed), *Christianities in Asia. The Global Christianity series*. Malden, MA: Wiley-Blackwell, 2011.

Phiri, Isabel and D. Werner (eds), *Handbook for Theological Education in Africa*. Oxford: Regnum, 2013.

Pui-lan, Kwok, 'Teaching Theology in a Global and Transnational World': https://www.aarweb.org/publications/spotlight-on-theological-education-march-2014-teaching-theology-in-a-global-and-transnational-world

'Rabban bar Sauma', *Encyclopædia Britannica*: www.britannica.com/EBchecked/topic/52503/Rabban-bar-Sauma

Raiser, Konrad, 'The Future of Theological Education in Central and Eastern Europe: Challenges for Ecumenical Learning in the 21st Century', in *International Review of Mission*, 98, No. 1 (2009), 49-63.

Rajkumar, Peniel (ed), *Asian Theology on the Way: Christianity, Culture and Context*. London: SPCK, 2012.

Regier, Fremont and Sarah, *African Non-formal Theological Education Research Project*. Newton, KS: Commission on Overseas Mission General Conference Mennonite Church, 1994.

Roozen, David A. and Heidi Hadsell (eds), *Changing the Way Seminaries Teach: Pedagogies for Interfaith Dialogue*. Hartford, CT: Hartford Seminary, 2009.

Roxburgh, Alan, *The Missionary Congregation. Leadership and Limininality*. Valley Forge, PA: Trinity Press International, 1996.

Sachs, Jonah, *Winning the Story Wars: Why Those Who Tell (and Live) the Best Stories Will Rule the Future*. Boston, MA: Harvard Business Review Press, 2012.

Sanneh, Lamin, *Translating the Message – the Missionary Impact on Culture*. New York: Orbis Books, 1989.

Schmemann, Alexander, *Church, World, Mission*. Crestwood, NY: St Vladimir's Seminary Press, 1973.

Sendegeya, Fareth and Leon Spencer (eds), *Understanding TEE: A Course Outline and Handbook for Students and Tutors in Residential Theological Institutions in Africa*. Dar es Salaam, Tanzania: Anitepam, 2001.

Shank, David A. 'Wadé Harris, William, c. 1860 to 1929, Harrist Church (Eglise Harriste), Liberia/Ghana/Côte d'Ivoire', in *Dictionary of African Christian Biography*: www.dacb.org/stories/liberia/legacy_harris.html

Shaw, Perry, *Transforming Theological Education: A Practical Handbook for Integrative Learning*. Carlisle: Langham Global Library, 2014.

Shivute, Tomas, *The Theology of Mission and Evangelism in the International Missionary Council from Edinburgh to New Delhi*. Helsinki: Missiologian ja Ekumeniikan Seura RY; Suomen Lähetysseura, 1980.

Skreslet, Stanley, *Comprehending Mission*. New York: Orbis Books, 2012.

Snook, Stewart, *Developing Leaders through Theological Education by Extension: Case Studies from Africa*. Wheaton, IL: Billy Graham Center, 1992.

Snyder, Howard A., *Signs of the Spirit: How God Reshapes the Church*. Eugene, OR: Wipf & Stock, 1997.

Stanley, Brian, *The World Missionary Conference, Edinburgh 1910*. Grand Rapids, MI: Eerdmans, 2009.

_____, *The Global Diffusion of Evangelicalism: The Age of Billy Graham and John Stott*. Downers Grove, IL: IVP Academic, 2013.

Steinke, Robin J., 'Theological Education: A Theological Framework for Renewed Mission and Models', in *Dialogue: A Journal of Theology*, 50. 4 (2011). Wiley Periodicals and Dialog.

Stückelberger, Christoph and Amelie Vallotton, 'The Future Role of Online Libraries: Globalethics.net's Innovative Model', in Dietrich Werner, David Esterline, Namsoon Kang and Joshva Raja (eds), *Handbook of Theological Education in World Christianity*. Oxford: Regnum, 2010, 307-11.

Sunquist, Scott W., *Understanding Christian Mission: Participation in Suffering and Glory*. Grand Rapids, MI: Baker Academic, 2013.

Taylor, Mark C., *The Moment of Complexity: Emerging Network Culture*. Chicago, IL: University of Chicago Press, 2001.

Taylor, William D. (ed), *Internationalizing Missionary Training*. Grand Rapids, MI: Baker Books, 1991.

_____, (ed), *Too Valuable to Lose*. Pasadena, CA: William Carey Library, 1997.

Thornton, Margaret (ed), *Training TEE Leaders: A Course Guide*. Nairobi: Evangel Publishing House, 1990.

Turner, V., *The Ritual Process: Structure and Anti-Structure*. New York: Aldine De Gruyter, 1995.

University of the Nations catalogue 2014-2016. University of the Nations, 2013.

Veiling, Terry, *Practical Theology 'On Earth as it is in Heaven'*. Maryknoll, NY: Orbis, 2005.

Vella, Jane, *Learning to Listen, Learning to Teach: The Power of Dialogue in Educating Adults*. San Francisco, CA: Jossey-Bass, 2002.

_____, *On Teaching and Learning: Putting the Principles and Practices of Dialogue*. San Francisco, CA: Jossey-Bass, 2008.

Visser't Hooft, W.A., 'Evangelism among neo-pagans', in *International Review of Mission* (1977), 349-60.

Vyssotskaia, Anneta, 'Theological Education in the context of persecution and economic hardship', in *International Journal for Religious Freedom*, 5.2 (2012), 111-22.

Wall, Ruth, *Preparing adults for crossing cultures. A study of a transformative approach to Christian mission training*. PhD thesis, UCL–Institute of Education, London, 2015

Walls, Andrew F., *The Cross-Cultural Process in Christian History: Studies in the Transmission and Appropriation of Faith*. Maryknoll, NY: Orbis Books, 2002.

_____, *The Missionary Movement in Christian History: Studies in the Transmission of Faith*. New York: Orbis Books, 1996.

_____, 'Christian Scholarship in Africa in the Twenty-first Century', in *Journal of African Christian Thought*, 4, No. 2 (2001).

_____, 'Crowther, Samuel Adjai (or Ajayi), c. 1807 to 1891, Anglican Church, Nigeria', *Dictionary of African Christian Biography*: www.dacb.org/stories/nigeria/crowther5_samuel.html

Wen Ge, 'Engaging University Theologies with Church Theologies: A Postliberal Appraisal of the Emerging Sino-Christian Academic Theology', in *What Young*

Asian Theologians are Thinking, Leow Theng Huat (ed). Singapore: Trinity Theological College, 2014, 50-64.

Werner, Dietrich, 'Magna Charta on Ecumenical Formation in Theological Education in the 21st Century – 10 Key Convictions', in *International Review of Mission*, 98, No. 1 (2009), 161-70.

_____, *Theological Education in World Christianity: Ecumenical Perspectives and Future Priorities*. Tainan: Programme for Theology and Cultures in Asia, 2011.

_____, 'Theological Education in the Changing Context of World Christianity – an Unfinished Agenda', in *International Bulletin of Missionary Research*, 35, No. 2 (2011), 92-100.

Werner, Dietrich, David Esterline, Namsoon Kang and Joshva Raja (eds), *Handbook of Theological Education in World Christianity: Theological Perspectives, Regional Survey, Ecumenical Trends*. Oxford: Regnum, 2010.

West, Charles C., 'China and the World Mission of the Church: The Lessons of a Failure', in *Yale Divinity School Library Special Collections*, IMC Committees: Willingen, July 5-21, 1952, 264.011, Fiche 5.

Whitehead, James and Evelyn, *Method in Ministry* (revised edition). Washington, OR: Rowman & Littlefield, 1995.

Wickeri, Philip L., *Reconstructing Christianity in China: K.H. Ting and the Chinese Church*. Maryknoll, NY: Orbis, 2007.

Wilfred, Felix (ed), *The Oxford Handbook of Christianity in Asia*. New York: Oxford University Press, 2014.

Windsor, Raymond (ed), *World Directory of Missionary Training*. Pasadena, CA: William Carey Library, 1995.

Wilson, Henry and Werner Kahl, 'Race, Power, and Migration in Theological Education', in Werner, Dietrich, David Esterline, Namsoon Kang and Joshva Raja (eds), *Handbook of Theological Education in World Christianity: Theological Perspectives, Regional Survey, Ecumenical Trends*. Oxford: Regnum, 2010., 76-84.

Wolterstorff, Nicholas, *Educating for Shalom: Essays on Christian Higher Education*. Grand Rapids, MI: Eerdmans, 2004.

Woodberry, Dudley, Charles van Engen and Edgar J. Elliston (eds), *Missiological Education for the 21st Century: The Book, the Circle and the Sandals*. Maryknoll, NY: Orbis Books, 1996.

World Missionary Conference, 1910. *Report of Commission III: Education in Relation to the Christianisation of National Life*. Edinburgh and London: Oliphant, Anderson & Ferrier; New York, Chicago and Toronto: Fleming H. Revell, 1910.

World Missionary Conference, 1910. *Report of Commission IV: The Missionary Message in Relation to Non-Christian Religions*. Edinburgh and London: Oliphant, Anderson & Ferrier; New York, Chicago and Toronto: Fleming H. Revell, 1910.

World Missionary Conference, 1910. *Report of Commission V: The Preparation of Missionaries*. Edinburgh and London: Oliphant, Anderson & Ferrier; New York, Chicago and Toronto: Fleming H. Revell, 1910.

Wright, Chris (ed), *John Stott: A Portrait by his Friends*. Nottingham: IVP, 2011.

Yannoulatos, Anastasios, *Mission in Christ's Way: An Orthodox Understanding of Mission*. Brookline, MA: Holy Cross Press, 2010.

Youngblood, Robert L. (ed), *Cyprus: TEE Come of Age*. Exeter, UK: Paternoster, 1986.

YWAM Foundational Values. 2014: www.ywam.org (accessed 20th November, 2014)

Xin, Yalin, *Inside China's House Church Network: The Word of Life Movement and Its Renewing Dynamic.* Lexington, KY: Emeth Press, 2009.

_____, 'Inner Dynamics of the Chinese House Church Movement: The Case of the Word of Life Community', in *Mission Studies,* 25, No. 2 (2008), 157-84.

Zahniser, A.H.M., *Symbol and Ceremony: Making Disciples Across Cultures.* Monrovia, CA: MARC, 1997.

LIST OF CONTRIBUTORS

The Editors

Stephen Bevans, b. 1944, is a priest in the Roman Catholic mission congregation, the Society of the Divine Word (SVD) and Louis J. Luzbetak, SVD Professor of Mission and Culture (Emeritus) at Catholic Theological Union, Chicago. Has taught in North America, Asia, Europe and Africa, and spent nine years as missionary to the Philippines. Among his publications are *Models of Contextual Theology* (2002) and *An Introduction to Theology in Global Perspective* (2009). Editor of *A Century of Catholic Mission* (2013) in the Regnum Edinburgh Centenary Series, and member of Commission on World Mission and Evangelization.

Teresa Chai (PhD, Fuller Seminary) is faculty member at Asia Pacific Theological Seminary, filling the John Bueno Chair of Intercultural Studies, June 2013-March 2015; Global Mission Center Director, Administrative Committee member and Book Review Editor for APTS journal AJPS. Formerly president of Alpha Omega International College, Malaysia, serving there for nine years. For eight years, served as missionary in Bangladesh with the United Bible Societies and a Danish mission. An ordained minister with Assemblies of God, Malaysia. Teaches in Bible schools and seminaries in China, India, Malaysia, Romania, Samoa, Singapore and Thailand. Her most recent publication is a chapter entitled 'Pentecostal Theological Education and Ministerial Formation' in the Regnum Edinburgh Centenary Series *Mission Spirituality and Authentic Discipleship* (2013). Was editor for a festschrift honouring Wonsuk and Julie Ma in 2014.

J. Nelson Jennings, b. 1957. Executive director, Overseas Ministries Study Center and editor, International Bulletin of Missionary Research, New Haven, Connecticut, USA, 2011-2015. Professor of world mission, Covenant Theological Seminary, St Louis, Missouri, USA, 1999-2011. He and wife Kathy were Presbyterian missionaries in Japan, 1986-1999, in church planting; was then assistant professor of International Christian Studies, Tokyo Christian University. MDiv from Covenant Theological Seminary 1985, PhD from University of Edinburgh 1995. Author of *God the Real Superpower: Rethinking Our Role in Missions* (2007) and *Theology in Japan: Takakura Tokutaro, 1885-1934* (2005), and co-author with Hisakazu Inagaki of *Philosophical Theology and East-West-Dialogue* (2000).

Knud Jørgensen, b. 1942. MTh from University of Copenhagen, PhD in Missiology, Fuller Theological Seminary. Journalist and theologian, served with Radio Voice of the Gospel, Addis Ababa, Ethiopia, the Lutheran World Federation, Geneva, the International Mass Media Institute, Kristiansand, Go out Centre, Hurdal, Norway, Norwegian Church Aid, the Mekane Yesus Seminary, Addis Ababa, and the mission foundation Areopagos. Dean of Tao Fong Shan, Hong Kong, until 2010. Adjunct professor at the MF Norwegian School of Theology and the Lutheran Theological Seminary, Hong Kong. Has published several books and articles on journalism, communication, leadership and mission. One of the editors of the Regnum Edinburgh Centenary Series.

Dietrich Werner, b. 1956, ordained pastor of Lutheran Church in North Elbia, Germany, served as director of studies at missions academy at University of Hamburg; lecturer in missiology, ecumenism and world Christianity at University of Bochum, and at United Theological College, Bangalore, India; director of Ecumenical Theological Education Program in WCC. Currently serving as senior theological advisor to Bread for the World/Church Development Services, Berlin, and as honorary professor for missiology, ecumenism and development studies at University of Applied Science for Intercultural Theology, Hermannsburg, Germany.

Contributors

Graham Aylett, b. 1959. MA from University of Cambridge; PhD in Physiological Plant Ecology, University of Cambridge; BA from University of Durham; Advanced Diploma in Mission Studies from All Nations Christian College, UK. Ordained minister in the Church of England; partner with Interserve in Mongolia from 1998; with Mongolia TEE 1999-2013; member of the Increase Committee since 2010, with special interest in training; member of the Asia Theological Association Commission on Accreditation and Educational Development since 2013. Based in Malaysia since October 2014.

Jonny Baker is Director for Mission Education for Church Mission Society (CMS). Founded and leads CMS Pioneer Mission Leadership Training which began in 2010. Has authored and contributed to several books, most recently *The Pioneer Gift*. His focus in mission practice and training has been in western contexts.

Marina Ngursangzeli Behera, from the Presbyterian Church of India, Mizoram Synod, has served as an Associate Professor in the Department of History of Christianity, and also as Chairperson of the Department at United Theological College, Bangalore, 2005-2012. Currently teaching Ecumenical Missiology at the Ecumenical Institute at the Chateau de

Bossey, part of the World Council of Churches and attached to University of Geneva.

Stephen Brown, b. 1958. BA (Hons) in Development Studies from University of East Anglia, UK; MA in Theology from University of Cambridge; postgraduate studies at Humboldt University, Berlin; PhD in East German Studies at University of Reading, UK. Journalist and theologian; member of East/West Relations Advisory Committee of British Council of Churches, editor at Ecumenical News International, programme executive and programme director, Globethics.net; guest editor of several issues of The Ecumenical Review (The Barmen Declaration 1934-2009; Global Perspectives, 2009; Peace on Earth, Peace with the Earth, The Ecumenical Review, 2011); published many articles on contemporary church history, ecumenical studies and communication. Member of board of directors, and president, Europe region, World Association for Christian Communication.

Emmanuel Chemengich is currently Executive Director of the Association for Christian Theological Education in Africa (ACTEA), an organisation offering accrediting and support services to theological institutions in Africa; also an ordained minister with the Anglican Church of Kenya; graduate of St Paul's University, Kenya, of Westminster Theological Seminary, and of Lutheran Theological Seminary, Philadelphia, USA.

Edmund Kee-Fook Chia, b. 1962. MA in Human Development from University of Maryland; MA in Religion from Catholic University of America; PhD in Intercultural Theology from University of Nijmegen. Is a Malaysian who served 1996-2004 as executive secretary of interreligious dialogue for Federation of Asian Bishops' Conferences. Then joined Catholic Theological Union, Chicago, where latterly served as Associate Professor and Chair of Doctrinal Studies Department. Since 2011 has been on faculty of Australian Catholic University, Melbourne, where also serves as co-ordinator for interreligious dialogue. Author of *Edward Schillebeeckx and Interreligious Dialogue* (2012).

Steve Cochrane, b. 1959. Missionary with Youth With a Mission for the past 36 years, 30 of them in South Asia. PhD in 2014 in the History of Christian-Muslim relations from University of Middlesex via Oxford Centre for Mission Studies. Published several chapters and articles on missions, Christian-Muslim relations, and the monasteries of the Church of the East in Asia.

Therese D'Orsa has exercised senior leadership in Catholic educational systems, including roles as Diocesan Direction of Catholic Education and Director of Religious Education. Has taught in several tertiary institutions and is currently Conjoint Professor of University of Newcastle and Broken Bay Institute Sydney, Australia. Also research associate of Melbourne University of Divinity, and an honorary fellow of Australian Catholic University. Has published widely across her career and, with her husband Jim, has co-authored several books focused at the interface of missiology and education.

WEN Ge, b. 1975. STM from Christian Theological Seminary, Indianapolis, USA; PhD from Aarhus University, Denmark. Also studied at Bossey Ecumenical Institute, Geneva. Ordained pastor in the Chinese post-denominational churches, and lecturer of Systematic Theology and Sociology of Religion at Nanjing Union Theological Seminary, China. Has contributed article to the Regnum Edinburgh Centenary Series, 'Building up the Missional Fellowship of Love: A Review of T.C. Chao's Mission Theology', in *A Learning Missional Church: Reflections from Young Missiologists*, 2012.

Mark R. Gornik, b. 1961. MDiv from Westminster Theological Seminary; PhD from University of Edinburgh; Director, City Seminary of New York; pastor in Baltimore and New York City.

Tim Green, b. 1960. MA from University of Cambridge in Natural Sciences; MA from University of London in Islamic Societies and Cultures; PhD from University of London in Issues of Identity for Christians of Muslim background; Diploma in Religious Studies from University of Cambridge. Ordained minister in the Church of Pakistan. Mission partner with Interserve since 1988, serving with TEE in Pakistan 1988-2003, in Jordan 2003-2005, with Increase since 2008, and based in Malaysia since 2014. Trustee of SEAN International. Author of several TEE courses using print and electronic media, and papers on discipleship and identity for Christians of Muslim background.

Vidar L. Haanes, b. 1961. Professor of Church History and President of MF Norwegian School of Theology, Oslo. Chair of National Council for Theology and Religious Studies, and board member, Norwegian Association of Higher Education Institutions. Chair of Norwegian Network for Private Universities and Colleges; member of General Board of OECD's Institutional Management of Higher Education (IMHE), and Council of Europe Expert Group on Higher Education; Member of General Synod and Theological Commission in Church of Norway. Published several books and articles on history of theological education and Reformation studies.

Richard Kenneth Hart, b. 1947. PhD in Intercultural Studies from Trinity International University; MDiv from Denver Seminary; MA in Teaching,

Oakland University; BA, Houghton College. Served with Conservative Baptist Home Mission Society as Principal of Peace Baptist Primary School, Bermudian Landing, Belize; WorldVenture in Amman, Jordan; Executive Director of Program for Theological Education by Extension in the Arab world; Associate Secretary of Theological Education by Extension, International Council of Accrediting Agencies; Co-ordinator of TEE Services for International Council for Evangelical Theological Education; Accreditation Chair of Middle East Association for Theological Education; member of Commission for Accreditation and Educational Development of the Asia Theological Association; Director of Development at Roy and Dora Whitman Academy, Amman, Jordan. Has published articles, reference work entries and book chapters on theological education by extension, devotional reading of the Bible, ethnographic research, persecution, and Christian education.

Werner Kahl, b. 1962 in Essen, Germany. In 1992, PhD in New Testament Studies from Emory University. Taught New Testament studies at University of Ghana, 1992-2002. In 2004, completed post-doctoral habilitation at University of Frankfurt. Currently Associate Professor in New Testament at University of Frankfurt and Head of Studies at Academy of Mission at University of Hamburg. Primary areas of research are synoptic Gospels, New Testament miracle stories, intercultural biblical hermeneutics, and West African exegesis.

Tim Hyunmo Lee, b. 1957. BS from Seoul National University; MDiv from Korea Baptist Theological Seminary; PhD in Missions from Southwestern Baptist Theological Seminary. Founder and, until 2003, director of World Missionary Training Center of Korea Baptist Church. Professor of missions at Korea Baptist Theological University and Seminary (KBTUS). Dean of Graduate School of Mission and Dean of Graduate School of Pastoral Ministries of KBTUS. Published several books and articles on missions.

Atola Longkumer, from Nagaland, India, is a Baptist. Taught in Leonard Theological College, Jabalpur, India; currently in Bangalore as freelance theological researcher. Gained her theological education from India and the USA.

Kangwa Mabuluki is an ordained minister in the United Church of Zambia (UCZ), and is currently General Secretary of All Africa Theological Education by Extension Association. Has also served as Executive Director of Theological Education by Extension in Zambia, 2001-2014. Previously served World Student Christian Federation, first as Africa Region Secretary based in Nairobi, then as Co-Secretary General, based in Geneva. Holds certificate in Theology from UCZ Theological

College; Diploma in Theology from Makerere University, Uganda; Master in Theology from University of Oxford; is also a final year PhD student with University of KwaZulu Natal.

W. Jay Moon, b. 1961. PhD in Intercultural Studies from Asbury Theological Seminary, Kentucky. Missiologist and Professional Civil Engineer, served with SIM in Ghana, West Africa, ministering through church planting, theological education, and water development. Previously served as Professor of Intercultural Studies at Sioux Falls Seminary, South Dakota. Currently serving at Asbury Theological Seminary as Associate Professor of Church Planting and Evangelism, as well as Director of the Office of Faith, Work, and Economics. Currently also serving as Secretary of the American Society of Missiology, and Associate Editor of _Missiology_. Published several articles and books on orality, contextual theology, discipleship, and community development.

Benhardt Yemo Quarshie, b. 1954. BA from University of Ghana; ThM and PhD in New Testament Studies from Princeton Theological Seminary. Student of the New Testament and Minister of the Gospel since 1976; taught for over twenty years at University of Ghana, twice heading its Department for the Study of Religions; served as Chaplain to Methodist and Presbyterian students and chaired University's Chaplaincy Board. Continues to serve on executive bodies of ecumenical bodies such as Christian Council of Ghana and Bible Society of Ghana; also as Chairman of the Ga Presbytery of the Presbyterian Church of Ghana; chaired church's Constitution Review Committee. Published in areas of New Testament and mother-tongue theologising as well as of the engagement between gospel and culture. Currently serves as Rector of Akrofi-Christaller Institute of Theology, Mission and Culture, Akropong-Akuapem, Ghana; also as General Secretary of the African Theological Fellowship; also member of Global Networking Team of the International Fellowship for Mission as Transformation (INFEMIT).

Kenneth R. Ross, b. 1958, is a Presbyterian pastor and theologian with extensive experience in Scotland and Malawi. While teaching at University of Malawi in the 1980s and 1990s, was responsible for introduction of Bachelor's, Master's and PhD degrees in theology. Now based in Scotland, retains close links with Malawi where he was given the clan name 'Ngozo' by Chief Champwiti in 2011. Chaired the Scottish Towards 2010 Council which helped to pave the way for the Edinburgh 2010 study process and conference. Recent publications include _Edinburgh 2010: Mission Then and Now_ (Regnum) and _the Atlas of Global Christianity_ (Edinburgh University Press).

Ian J. Shaw, b. 1961. BA, University of Nottingham; PhD in Church History, University of Manchester. Church historian, lecturer, and cross-cultural mission organisation leader. Minister of Walkden Evangelical Church, 1986-1994. Lecturer in History of Christianity and Dean of Postgraduate Studies, International Christian College, Glasgow, 1996-2008; Honorary Lecturer, University of Glasgow, 2004-2008; Honorary Lecturer, University of Aberdeen, 1997-2012. Currently Associate International Director, Langham Scholarship Programme, since 2008; Honorary Research Fellow, Faculty of Divinity, University of Edinburgh since 2011; Research Fellow, University of Free State, South Africa since 2015. Published four monographs, one co-authored book, and numerous chapters in books and journal articles on missiology and the history of Christianity.

Dawit Olika Teferssa, b. 1975. BTh from Mekane Yesus Theological Seminary (MYTS), and Master of Philosophy in Theology from MF Norwegian School of Theology. Has served as administrator and evangelist at a congregation level; instructor, dean of study, co-ordinator for Theological Education by Extension (TEE); principal at Nekemte Christian Education College (NCEC) within the Ethiopian Evangelical Church Mekane Yesus (EECMY); was co-ordinator of the congregation's international work within Church of Sweden and an employment officer at the Swedish employment office. Currently a doctoral student at the MF Norwegian School of Theology, Oslo.

Eric G. Tosi, archpriest, is the Secretary of the Orthodox Church in America and former chairman of the Department of Evangelization. BA and MA from Fordham University; MDiv from St Vladimir's Orthodox Seminary; DMin from University of Toronto (Trinity). Has led parishes in Montana, Nevada and New Jersey; also teaches in mentorship programme at St Vladimir's Seminary and lectures on evangelism and mission. Has a number of articles and presentations on mission and evangelism in the Orthodox Church at such organisations as the World Council of Churches Joint Ecumenical Committee on Evangelism, the Lausanne Orthodox Initiative, the American Society of Missiology, and the Overseas Ministry Study Center.

Ruth M. Wall, b.1960. BSc and PGCE from Bristol University, UK; MA in Education management from Warwick University, UK; PhD in Education from University College, London (UCL) Institute of Education. Adult educator and experienced curriculum designer and transformative learning practitioner in South Sudan, Kenya and the UK. Tutor and mission trainer at All Nations Christian College, UK, since 2006. Chair of International Mission Training Network (IMTN) since 2011. IMTN supports a global conversation of mission trainers as part of the WEA Missions Commission.

H.S. Wilson has been Executive Director of the Foundation for Theological Education in South East Asia since 2007. Previously served as H. George Anderson Professor of Mission and Cultures at Lutheran Theological Seminary, Philadelphia. Has also taught at Wartburg Theological Seminary, Dubuque, Iowa; United Theological College, Bangalore; and Karnataka Theological College, Mangalore, India. Is a Presbyter of Church of South India and Presbyterian Church (USA).

Maria Liu Wong, b. 1976. MA in Urban Mission from Westminster Theological Seminary and in International Educational Development from Teachers College, Columbia University; EdD in Adult Learning and Leadership from Teachers College, Columbia University. Is a music teacher with New York City Department of Education; Volunteer Instructor at Gambela Teacher and Health Education College, Ethiopia; Adjunct Education Professor at Mercy College and Pace University, New York City; Dean, City Seminary of New York. Co-published article on world Christianity in the city, and book chapter on collaborative inquiry and diversity. Dissertation work on women, leadership and theological education, and upcoming publications on Pacific Asian North American women and wisdom leadership; also informal mentor amongst women leaders in theological education.

Chris Wright, b. 1947, from Belfast, Northern Ireland. MA and PhD in Old Testament economic ethics from University of Cambridge. Ordained Anglican minister in 1977, and served in pastoral ministry in Tonbridge, UK. Associate Professor of Old Testament at Union Biblical Seminary, Pune, India, 1983-1988, teaching at BA and MTh level. Served on the faculty of All Nations Christian College, UK, 1988-2001, first as Director of Studies and then as Principal. In 2001, took on leadership of Langham Partnership at invitation of John Stott as its International Ministries Director, and continues in that post. Author of several books, including *The Mission of God, The Mission of God's People, Old Testament Ethics for the People of God*, and commentaries on Deuteronomy, Jeremiah, Lamentations and Ezekiel. Chaired Lausanne Theology Working Group, 2005-2011, and chief architect and editor of the Cape Town Commitment, the statement of the Third Lausanne Congress, 2010.

Yalin Xin, PhD in Intercultural Studies from E. Stanley Jones School of World Mission and Evangelism, Asbury Theological Seminary, Kentucky, specialising in behaviour sciences and mission history, theology and practice, with a special interest in Christian renewal and revitalisation movements. Became research fellow with Center for the Study of World

Christian Revitalization Movements, Wilmore, Kentucky. Currently associate professor at William Carey International University, Pasadena, California; Senior Editor for the William Carey International Development Journal. Published a chapter in one of the earlier books in the Regnum Edinburgh Centenary Series.

INDEX

Regnum Studies in Global Christianity

In the latter part of the twentieth century the world witnessed significant changes in global Christian dynamics. The Regnum Studies in Global Christianity series explores the issues with which the global church struggles, focusing in particular on ministry rooted in Africa, Asia, Latin America and Eastern Europe.

Not only does the series make available studies that will help the global church learn from past and present, it provides a platform for provocative and prophetic voices to speak to the future of Christianity. The editors and the publisher pray particularly that the series will grow as a public space, where the voices of church leaders from the majority world will contribute out of wisdom drawn from experience and reflection, thus shaping a healthy future for the global church. To this end, the editors invite theological seminaries and universities from around the world to submit relevant scholarly dissertations for possible publication in the series. Through this, it is hoped that the series will provide a forum for South-to-South as well as South-to-North dialogues.

Volumes in this series are printed in paperback, unless otherwise stated.

Jesus and the Resurrection

David Emmanuel Singh (Ed)
2014 / 978-1-870345-58-4 / 205pp
Our aim here is to build a bridge between Muslims and Christians with Jesus in the centre of the discourse. As an idea, 'resurrection' is shared by and is central to the eschatologies of Christianity, Islam and Judaism. In Islam, the belief in life after death, resurrection and the day of judgement are so central that they are considered to be one of its 'Five Pillars'. Life has meaning because in resurrection, humanity will meet its maker on the Day of Judgement.

Seeing New Facets of the Diamond

Gillian Mary Bediako, Benhardt Y Quarshie, Kwabena Asamoah-Gyadu (Eds)
2014 / 978-1-908355-59-1/ 378pp
In the five years since Kwame Bediako passed away there has been a growing desire among colleagues and friends to put together a book that would honour his memory. The title has been chosen to reflect the range of interests and concerns that motivated Bediako's scholarly work, including his founding and nurturing of ACI.

Bernhard Reitsma
The God of My Enemy:
The Middle East and the Nature of God
2014 / 978-1-908355-50-8 / 206pp
Bernhard Reitsma lived and worked among Christians in the Middle East for several years. He has shared their struggles and was challenged to reconsider different kinds of Israel theology. In this the core questions is whether the God of my enemy can also be my God. How can the God of the present State of Israel also be the God of the Palestinians?

Following Jesus: Journeys in Radical Disciple-
ship – Essays in Honor of Ronald J Sider
Paul Alexander and Al Tizon (Eds)
2013 / 978-1-908355-27-0 / 235pp
Ronald J. Sider and the organization that he founded, Evangelicals for Social Action, are most respected for their pioneering work in evangelical social concern. However, Sider's great contribution to social justice is part of a larger vision – biblical discipleship. This book brings together a group of scholar-activists, old and young, to reflect upon theradical implications for the 21st century.

Relectuant or Radical Revolutionaries?
Cawley Bolt
2013 / 978-1-908355-18-8 / 287pp
This study is based on extensive research that challenges traditional ways of understanding some evangelical missionaries of nineteenth century Jamaica and calls for revision of those views. It highlights the strength and character of persons facing various challenges of life in their effort to be faithful to the guiding principles of their existence.

Contemporary Pentecostal Christianity:
Interpretations from an African Context
2013 / 978-1-908355-07-2 / 194pp
J Kwabena Asamoah-Gyada
Pentecostalism is the fastest growing stream of Christianity in the world. The real evidence for the significance of Pentecostalism lies in the actual churches they have built and the numbers they attract. This work interprets key theological and missiological themes in African Pentecostalism by using material from the live experiences of the movement itself.

For the full listing, visit www.ocms.ac.uk/regnum